TESTIMONY

TESTIMONY

A Philosophical Study

C. A. J. COADY

OXFORD · CLARENDON PRESS
1992

Oxford University Press, Walton Street, Oxford OX2 6DP
Oxford New York Toronto
Delhi Bombay Calcutta Madras Karachi
Petaling Jaya Singapore Hong Kong Tokyo
Nairobi Dar es Salaam Cape Town
Melbourne Auckland
and associated companies in
Berlin Ibadan

Oxford is a trade mark of Oxford University Press

Published in the United States
by Oxford University Press, New York

British Library Cataloguing in Publication Data
Data available

Library of Congress Cataloging in Publication Data
Coady, C. A. J.
Testimony : a philosophical study / C. A. J. Coady
p. cm.
Includes bibliographical references and index.
1. Knowledge, Theory of. 2. Witnesses. 3. Other minds (Theory of
knowledge). 4. Belief and doubt. I. Title.
BD181.C59 1992 121—dc20 91-26438
ISBN 0-19-824786-9

Typeset by Best-set Typesetter Ltd., Hong Kong.
Printed in Great Britain by
Bookcraft (Bath) Ltd, Midsomer Norton, Avon

For Margaret,
the ideal speaker-hearer

It seems, rather, that believing in other persons, in authority and testimony, is an essential part of the act of communicating, an act which we all constantly perform. It is as much an irreducible part of our experience as, say, giving promises, or playing competitive games, or even sensing coloured patches.

(J. L. Austin, 'Other Minds')

Preface

I FIRST began thinking about the epistemological status of testimony in the 1960s; when writing a thesis at Oxford on issues in the theory of perception. I doubt that my testimony about these origins is worth much now, though I recall being intrigued by some remarks of Elizabeth Anscombe on the topic during her lectures on the empiricists, and my supervisor, William Kneale, drew my attention early on to Archbishop Whately's brilliant spoof of Hume in *Historic Doubts Relative to Napoleon Bonaparte*. I had certainly read J. L. Austin's 'Other Minds', as a student, but it was only when I came to check a reference in the final stages of preparation for the book that I realized (or was caused to remember?) that he had written perceptively, if very briefly, about testimony. This led to a few alterations, including the use of one of Austin's comments as an epigraph for the book. It also made me think it likely that there are other forgotten influences that I will never be in a position to acknowledge. Let this admission stand proxy for the acknowledgments that cannot be given.

With regard to what I am told, my temperament inclines towards scepticism rather than gullibility. This inclination was reinforced by several years spent as a young man in the world of popular journalism. I was therefore initially reluctant to go down the path charted in this book, since its basic thrust is that our trust in the word of others is fundamental to the very idea of serious cognitive activity. However uncongenial, this outlook came to seem the only honest one to adopt, though the question remained how it could be integrated into a wider epistemological framework and so 'justified'.

When I began reading papers on the subject, my audiences mostly reacted with incomprehension, or the sort of disbelief evoked by denials of the merest common sense. Gradually, the climate of thought has changed and there is now more sympathy for the view that testimony is a prominent and underexplored epistemological landscape, although what sort of feature it is and how largely it looms are still naturally matters for disagreement. I will be pleased if this book produces more and better disagreement, even if it is with me. I will, of course, also be delighted if discussion and debate leads to some measure of agreement.

The book's format and development need some preliminary explanation. It is divided into four sections. The first, 'The Problematic', consists of three chapters of an expository and definitional character. Chapter 1 aims to show the extent to which our normal cognitive practices are underpinned by our reliance upon what others tell us, and to suggest the depth and apparent inevitability of this reliance. Chapter 2 provides an analytical clarification of what is involved in talk of testimony and defines a concept of testimony suited to our purposes in this investigation. Chapter 3 examines some consequences of this definition and defends it against misgivings arising from intuition and theory.

The second section, 'The Tradition', explores the work of those few philosophers who have written extensively upon the epistemology of testimony. Most attention is paid to the work of Hume, Price, Russell, and Reid, though the views of W. K. Clifford, F. H. Bradley, and others are also scrutinized. This analysis of the tradition helps expose the individualist emphases, already sketched in Chapter 1, and their influence upon the course of subsequent understanding. To this point much of the epistemological discussion has been critical, but the third section, 'The Solution', proposes a more positive account, in Chapter 8, of the status of testimony and a theoretical vindication, in Chapter 9, of that trust in the word of others which is implicit in our actual cognitive procedures.

The focus thus far has been on the standing and reliability of testimony at large (or, as we might put it, testimony as an institutional fact) but it shifts, for the second part of the book, towards issues of a more specifically methodological and 'applied' kind. The division is by no means watertight but it does represent a difference in attention, and the discussion in these final two sections relies, to some extent, on the outlook earlier developed. At the same time, it provides a certain testing of the adequacy of the outlook itself.

In Section IV, 'The Puzzles', three chapters deal with philosophical claims which either embody surprising theses about the acceptability of testimonial evidence in certain contexts, or can be shown to give rise to perplexing views about the treatment or standing of particular types of belief based upon testimony. Chapter 11, for example, provides a critique of the compelling but paradoxical thought that testimonial transmission must lead to a progressive diminution in the credibility of the transmitted message, and hence to the eventual 'disappearance of history'. Section V, 'The Applications', looks at four areas of thought and life in which propositions about the role of testimony have been put forward that are either at odds with the approach adopted here, or that call for the application or development of the theorizing so far presented. Chapter 13, for instance, treats of R. G. Collingwood's influential denial of any role for testimony in serious historical research or understanding, and Chapter 15 casts a critical and somewhat jaundiced eye upon persistent claims by psychological researchers that testimony is 'unreliable'.

My intellectual debts are as complex and numerous as accrue to most authors, and it is not possible to list them all. I would, however, like to acknowledge particularly the encouragement of my early mentors at Oxford, Elizabeth Anscombe, Paul Grice, William Kneale, and Gilbert Ryle. It was Ryle who said to me after a discussion of my ideas for this book, 'Philosophers have spent too much time asking what and how do *I* know, when they should have been asking what and how do *we* know.' Others who were helpful have mostly been acknowledged in the text, but I profited from discussions with Simon Blackburn, Myles Burnyeat, David Braine, Edward Craig, Gareth Evans, Benjamin Gibbs, Allen Hazen, Jennifer Hornsby, Mark Johnston, Bruce Langtry, David Lewis, David Luban, Len O'Neill, Joseph Raz, Dennis Robinson, Julie Rose, Barry Taylor, and Ralph Walker.

I am grateful to Richard Wyatt and Russell Grigg for research assistance, and I owe a particular debt to Andrew Alexandra who read the whole manuscript and gave me many valuable criticisms. He also compiled the Bibliography and helped extensively with editing and verifying references. Will Barrett worked valiantly on the index. My thanks also to Josie Winther, who word-processed beyond the call of duty.

While in grateful mood, I should also thank the University of Melbourne's Faculty of Arts for providing a period of teaching relief to work on this project and Corpus Christi College, Oxford, for making me a Visiting Fellow in 1982–3, part of which time I also devoted to the project. Various philosophy departments heard me out on aspects of this topic and helped me to understand better what I was trying to do—they include those at Princeton, Leeds, Illinois (in Chicago), Adelaide (of Adelaide), Sydney (of Sydney), Melbourne (of Melbourne), and Canberra (ANU). My thanks also to the publishers of the following philosophy journals, who gave me permission to use here material I originally published with them. Chapter 4 is a thoroughly rewritten version of my 'Testimony and Observation', *American Philosophical Quarterly* (1973); Chapter 13 is a revision of 'Collingwood and Historical Testimony', *Philosophy* (1975), and Chapter 14 revisits 'Mathematical Knowledge and Reliable Authority', *Mind* (1981). Further thanks to Kluwer Academic Publishers for permission to use, at various places in the book, parts of my 'Reid on Testimony' from *The Philosophy of Thomas Reid* (eds.) M. Dalgarno and E. Matthews (1989).

Finally, I should say that, although the book is primarily a philosophical work, it is not aimed exclusively at fellow professionals. A goodly proportion of current philosophical work is highly technical, and its results accessible only to sibling practitioners or to some who operate in closely related areas (as results in logic are available to mathematicians.) To some degree this is inevitable; philosophy as a discipline involves a commitment to theorizing and this commitment necessitates some involvement in technical terminology and internal debates. Values like precision and rigour are well served by this tendency. None the less, precision and rigour are instrumental values, and when they develop a life of their own, they can become detached from truth, importance, and wisdom. I have some sympathy with those who think that contemporary analytical philosophy has become too scholastic (though I think the point applies even more to much contemporary French and German philosophy.) If philosophical concerns are not, at certain points, turned outwards to the broader community and its intellectual condition, they lose focus and nourishment, and if the community has no access to the reflections of philosophers, it is deprived of valuable insights and self-understanding. In any case, I have tried here to keep philosophical technicalities to a minimum, and to write in a way that I hope will engage the attention and interests of philosophers and non-philosophers alike.

C. A. J. COADY

Melbourne, Australia
August, 1991

Contents

I

The Problematic

1

The Domain of Testimony

The statement of an authority makes me aware of something, enables
me to know something, which I shouldn't otherwise have known. It is
a source of knowledge.

(J. L. Austin, 'Other Minds'.)

It will be useful to begin by distinguishing between negative and positive
epistemology. Negative epistemology is concerned with theoretical problems posed by the challenge of radical or philosophical scepticism in
its various forms; positive epistemology takes it that the challenge of
scepticism is somehow overcome, or sidetracked, and proceeds to investigate the structure (or absence of structure) to be found in human knowledge or in that body of belief which can, scepticism aside, lay reasonable
claim to that title. Much of Moore's work in defence of common sense
would fall naturally into the category of negative epistemology while much
of Russell's work in the theory of knowledge would exemplify positive
epistemology (for instance, in *Human Knowledge*). More generally, the
difference in philosophical concern can be illustrated by considering that
style of philosophical argument called 'transcendental'. This aims to show,
amongst other things, that some performances or concepts or capacities or
whatever are deeply dependent upon others commonly considered to be
not so related. So, it is claimed, we cannot identify states of mind in
ourselves unless we can identify such states in others. When arguments of
this kind are used in epistemological settings they may have either a
positive or negative deployment. Notoriously, since Kant, they have been
used to combat various sorts of scepticism, but it is equally possible that
they could be used to give an account of the interrelatedness of our modes
of knowledge or belief whether or not this constitutes a challenge to
scepticism. I do not deny that most writings on the theory of knowledge
embody both approaches in differing degrees nor that the distinction itself
has a tendency to blur, but these considerations do not affect the use I
shall make of the distinction.

Positive epistemology is often foundational in character but need not be.
Standard empiricist epistemologies explain our developed 'system' of
knowledge or rational belief as ultimately based upon indubitable ideas or
sense-impressions plus certain fundamental insights into relations of ideas
and, as in Hume, certain habits of association. Since, even granting this
starting-point, there seems to be much more to our normal understanding of

what we know than this, there arise classical problems about how to 'justify' our incumbent system of knowledge in terms of this base. Hence we confront such celebrated problems as those of induction and other minds. On the other hand, certain forms of reaction against the empiricist tradition can still qualify for the title of positive epistemology even where they reject utterly the foundationist project. Karl Popper's critical falsificationism, for instance, rejects the search for foundations and sources of knowledge but it includes a positive account of what rational inquiry involves, an account to which Popper gives the name 'evolutionary epistemology'.[1]

Another enterprise dear to the hearts of positive epistemologists is that of defining knowledge. It is an enterprise of ancient lineage (tracing back at least to Plato) but it has become a 'growth industry' in twentieth-century philosophy, particularly in so far as it concerns the attempt to provide a definition that both incorporates the ideas of truth and belief and distinguishes mere true belief from knowledge proper. Plato, who was much exercised in both the *Theaetetus* and *Meno* by the need to distinguish true belief or true opinion from knowledge, thought that an additional factor involving the person's possession of a 'logos' or reason was required. Of course Plato was ultimately dissatisfied with his definition and his problem situation was different in certain respects from that of contemporary philosophers, none the less it is hard not to see his discussion as the forerunner of the modern debate and as providing (what a Plato might well provide) the form and exemplar of the definitions most debated amongst contemporary theorists. In one simple version such a definition would run as follows:

A knows $p = df$.
  (1) A believes p.
  (2) p is true.
  (3) A has legitimate reason r for believing p.

There are notorious difficulties for this definition or any of its relatives: belief and knowledge have been declared exclusive; the addition of a confidence or 'feeling sure' condition has been urged; the status and proper formulation of (3) have been criticized both with regard to potential circularity in the reliance upon the concept of knowledge for the understanding of what it is to have legitimate reason (a criticism anticipated by Plato) and with regard to the link between (3) and (1) (a criticism made particularly vivid in modern literature by the puzzle cases of Gettier). There are also problems posed for (3) by the claims of direct or intuitive knowledge. I propose no stand upon the validity of such definitions or the objections to them but I do hope to use the contentious clause (3) to help in the introduction and location of my own concerns about testimony.

---

[1] Sir Karl Popper, *Objective Knowledge* (Oxford, 1972).

Consider the way in which, in the *Theaetetus*, Plato tries to exhibit the difference between true belief and knowledge. Socrates uses the example of proceedings in a law case and points out that a jury may be convinced of certain facts about a robbery merely by the persuasive powers and rhetorical skills of a lawyer and yet they can hardly be said to know these facts even though their beliefs are true. Plato could perhaps have rested his case on the distinction between beliefs produced by rhetorical trickery or non-rational persuasion on the one hand and beliefs supported by relevant evidence on the other, but he seems to want to go further and insist that beliefs about the robbery could *never* amount to knowledge for the jury since these are facts 'which can be known only by an eye-witness'.[2] If we are to take seriously what Plato says here then he must be seen as placing a strong restriction upon what sorts of account or reason can be used to fill in clause (3) of the knowledge definition, a restriction which would relegate to the realm of mere true opinion all beliefs based upon report, even the report of eyewitnesses who may themselves know what is the case.

Plato offers no argument for this restriction (the remarks about orators and lawyers lend no support to it) but the spirit of his epistemology is notoriously puritan and the exclusion of testimony as a 'logos' for knowledge is consistent with that spirit. Indeed the passage we have been discussing is noteworthy amongst Plato scholars not for its dismissal of testimony as a source of knowledge but for its granting of that status to ordinary perception, an accolade which elsewhere Plato denies it. We shall not enter into the scholarly debate here except to observe that it may be possible to defend Plato's backsliding on perception by insisting that he is anxious in this passage to illustrate the difference between knowledge and true belief by appeal on an obvious and non-contentious example of mere true belief (a belief based on testimony) and, at the level of illustration, he is prepared to contrast it with sense-perception even to the point of treating the latter as providing knowledge.[3] This line of defence is interesting, from the point of view of our present inquiry, precisely because it has Plato relying upon some sort of 'obviousness' about testimony's not being

---

[2] *Theaetetus*, 201. The clause cited is from the Jowett trans. The trans. by Gwynneth Mathews in *Plato's Epistemology* (London, 1972) seems to suggest, however, that Plato's objection is not to testimony as such but only to hearsay. In her version, the Socratic example is one in which there were no witnesses to the robbery but the lawyers weave a story out of hearsay that is favourable to their clients and, as it happens, true. The relevant passages of the text are both interesting and complex, philosophically and linguistically, but Mathew's version especially in its use of the term 'hearsay' is surely misleading. For an excellent discussion of Plato's position in this passage see M. F. Burnyeat, 'Socrates and the Jury: Paradoxes in Plato's Distinction between Knowledge and True Belief', *Proc. of the Aristotelian Society*, supp. vol. 54 (1980), 173–91.

[3] Even so the defence would look healthier if Plato had not explicitly argued earlier in the dialogue that perception does *not* yield knowledge. Admittedly, this argument is primarily aimed at a Protagorean version of the view that knowledge is to be defined as perception.

a source of knowledge and about its inferiority, in this respect, to perception. Subsequent thinking about knowledge, at both the casual and the philosophical level, has been for the most part remarkably consistent with this intuition; either it has ignored testimony altogether or it has been cursory and dismissive.[4] Modern epistemologists tirelessly pursue the nature and role of memory, perception, inductive and deductive reasoning but devote no analysis and argument to testimony although prima facie it belongs on this list.[5] After all when we inquire into the basis of some claim by asking: 'Why do you believe that?' or 'How do you know that?' the answer 'Jones told me' can be just as appropriate as 'I saw it' or 'I remember it', 'It follows from this' or 'It usually happens like that'.

I shall argue that this tradition of neglect is a bad one and that our reliance upon testimony is too important and too fundamental to merit such casual treatment. I shall also propose some tentative explanations of the existence of this blind spot in positive epistemology. In modern times, there have been the influences of individualism and of the change in intellectual outlook which Ian Hacking has called 'the emergence of probability'.[6] Amongst the ancients and medievals, the view of knowledge as a kind of thoroughgoing rational understanding militated against treating beliefs based upon testimony as part of knowledge and may help to explain why there is generally so little discussion of the issues raised by our trust in the word of others.

First, however, we must confront the suggestion that the neglect of testimony is warranted by the fact that it really plays an insignificant, or not very significant, role in the formation of reasonable belief. I shall deal with this suggestion by parable; the parable will be narrated in the first person but is meant to reflect our common plight.

I am visiting a foreign city that is new to me—Amsterdam will do. When I arrive at my hotel I am asked to fill in a form giving my name, age,

[4] A notable non-neglector is Professor H. H. Price who has discussed the issue in his book, *Belief* (London, 1969). His chapter on this ('The Evidence of Testimony') has a quite different orientation to my discussion although he shows himself to be well aware of some of those defects in the traditional approach to which I shall be directing attention. Sydney Shoemaker also touches upon some of the issues discussed here in ch. 6 of *Self-Knowledge and Self-Identity* (Ithaca, NY, 1963). Although Shoemaker is not primarily concerned with testimony he does, as I do, reject the idea that the validity of testimony could be established by observation. His arguments, however, are very different from mine and reflect his basic concern with certain problems of self-knowledge and memory, as well as certain Wittgensteinian assumptions about memory, language, and philosophy which I do not wish to discuss or employ in what follows.

[5] A novelist may be thought more authoritative on the prima facie than a philosopher so I shall invoke the support of Thomas Hardy who writes in *Far from the Madding Crowd*: 'To find themselves utterly alone at night where company is desirable and expected makes some people fearful; but a case more trying by far to the nerves is to discover some mysterious companionship when intuition, sensation, memory, analogy, testimony, probability, induction—every kind of evidence in the logician's list—have united to persuade consciousness that it is quite in isolation' (ch. 2).

[6] I. Hacking, *The Emergence of Probability* (Cambridge, 1975).

date of birth, citizenship, passport number, and so on, all of which is accepted by the hotel clerk as true because I say it is and will be accepted by others as true because he says that I say it. (I use 'say' throughout in the sense that includes writing and perhaps other forms of communication as well as speaking). More interestingly still, a good deal of the information that I give so confidently and authoritatively is accepted as true *by me* on the word of others. That I am so many years old; that I was born on such and such a date; that number H11200 does indeed correspond to the number the Australian passport authorities have in their files—none of these are facts of my individual observation or memory or inference from them. They are based, sometimes in a complex way, on the word of others.

My first morning in Amsterdam I wake uncertain of the time and ring the hotel clerk to discover the hour, accepting the testimony of the voice just as I would accept the institutional testimony of a clock or watch; being early for breakfast I read a paperback history book I have brought with me which contains all manner of factual claims that neither I nor the writer can support by personal observation or memory or by deduction from either: the deeds of a man called Napoleon Bonaparte who is supposed to have done all manner of astonishing things more than 150 years ago, many of his exploits being performed in places neither I, nor even perhaps the author, has ever visited and the reality of which is accepted on the word of others. Indeed, spurred to geographical thoughts, I reflect that on arriving at a strange airport a day or so earlier I had only the aircrew's word that this was Amsterdam, although since then there has been much else in the way of testimony to support their claim. Venturing forth from my hotel I consult a map and commit myself once more to a trust in my fellow human beings, just as I do moments later when I buy a copy of *The Times* and read about a military coup in Spain, an election campaign in Britain, an assassination in France, and a new development in medical science. The fable could be extended but I suspect that enough has been said to deal, at least in a preliminary way, with the suggestion that the neglect of testimony is justified by its insignificance in the formation of reasonable belief.[7] No wonder that David Hume, who is one of the few philosophers to discuss the topic seriously, says of testimony, 'there is no species of reasoning more common, more useful, and even necessary to human life, than that which is derived from the testimony of men and the reports of eye-witnesses and spectators'.[8]

It seems then that testimony is very important in the formation of much that we normally regard as reasonable belief and that our reliance upon it

---

[7] I use 'reasonable belief' to cover precisely those beliefs specified in the parable which would certainly seem to the plain man to merit that title. Some philosophers may doubt whether reasonable belief amounts to knowledge or whether it is *really* reasonable but the relevance of such doubts will be examined later.

[8] David Hume, *An Enquiry Concerning Human Understanding* (Oxford, 1957), s. 88.

is extensive. Furthermore, this reliance is not limited to the everday or the merely practical, as my parable may have suggested, since highly developed theoretical activities are also marked by a reliance upon testimony. This is particularly noticeable in the social sciences and in such studies as history but it is also a feature of the physical sciences. History was touched upon in the parable and indeed the study of history seems so dependent upon testimony from the past that Collingwood has called the view that it is, 'The Common Sense Theory of History'. (I think that the common-sense theory is largely correct but I shall explain why and also deal with Collingwood's objections to it in Chapter 13.) Inasmuch as a social science has a strong historical element, like anthropology, then it will have a similar reliance upon testimony, but even such a discipline as psychology is very dependent upon testimony for its data, as is evident from the perusal of texts on social psychology or even perception. The following references from Professor R. L. Gregory's excellent book, *Eye and Brain*,[9] may serve as illustrations; it will be noticed that the reliance upon testimony is of two kinds, that concerning the testimony of an individual subject or group of subjects and that concerning the testimony of some other investigator. Gregory describes a case of recovery from early blindness which he personally investigated with another psychologist, the object being to throw light upon such questions as how much we have to learn to see and the relationship between touch and sight.[10] Throughout his account of this case Gregory often shows his reliance upon the reports his patient gives about how the environment appears to him, summing up this aspect of his method by the sentence: 'We tried to discover what his visual world was like by asking him questions and giving him simple visual tests'. Similarly, if a psychologist is investigating perceptual illusions he will need to know that he is not atypical in seeing a stick in water as bent, the Muller–Lyer arrows as unequal, and so on.

Perhaps even more significant, however, is the psychologist's dependence upon the testimony of his fellow scientists and other observers. Gregory, for instance, devotes a section of his book to exploring the hypothesis that various visual illusions can be explained in terms of constancy scaling in response to perspective cues; in the course of this discussion he tries to support the hypothesis by reference to the visual experience of peoples who live in a world with much less in the way of perspective than our own. Zulus, for example, live in what has been called a 'circular culture' of round huts, round doors, curved furrows, etc., and they either fail to 'get' illusions such as the Muller–Lyer arrow or get them to a reduced degree.

---

[9] R. L. Gregory, *Eye and Brain* (London, 1966).
[10] A fuller account of the investigation is given in the original monograph: R. L. Gregory and J. G. Wallace, 'Recovery from Early Blindness: A Case Study', *Experimental Psychology Society Monograph No. 2* (Cambridge, 1963). For the account in *Eye and Brain* see esp. 194–8.

Whatever the merit of Gregory's argument, it plainly depends not only on the testimony of the Zulus but on the testimony of various investigators that the Zulus do or do not say certain things and respond in certain ways. Gregory does not claim to have questioned and observed the Zulus and other non-Western communities himself, he is relying upon the published reports of his colleagues. Indeed, the only reference he gives is to a study by three psychologists whose own data is very much second-hand.[11] This sort of thing is not of course restricted to psychological theorizing but can be found in more 'objective' disciplines such as physics. Any given scientist, even the most authoritative, will argue from, presuppose, and take for granted numerous observations and experiments that he has not performed for himself. That this is so is obscured by the elements of individualist ideology built into our image of science, the scientist being pictured as utterly self-reliant and self-sufficient, and by the way in which writers tend to refer to 'established' observational and experimental facts as though they themselves had done the observing or experimenting. There need be nothing pernicious in this but it can contribute to a misleading image of science. A good example of the sort of tendency just mentioned can be found in Gregory's book. After introducing the case of S. B. (the initials refer to the man whose recovery from early blindness, as a result of a corneal graft, was studied by Gregory and Wallace) and explicitly saying that it was one which he 'had the good fortune to investigate at first hand' Gregory gets down to details as follows:

When the bandages were first removed from his eyes, so that he was no longer blind, he heard the voice of the surgeon. He turned to the voice and saw nothing but a blur. He realised that this must be a face, because of the voice, but he could not see it. He did not suddenly see the world of objects as we do when we open our eyes.

But within a few days he could use his eyes to good effect. He could walk along the hospital corridors without recourse to touch; he could even tell the time from a large wall clock, having all his life carried a pocket watch having no glass so that he could feel the time from its hands. He would get up at dawn, and watch from his window the cars and lorries pass by. He was delighted with his progress, which was extremely rapid.

When he left the hospital we took him to London and showed him many things he never knew from touch . . .[12]

A natural implication of this passage is that Gregory himself was present to observe the patient's reports and responses immediately after the operation and in the days following hard upon it, but recourse to the original Gregory–Wallace monograph reveals that the psychologists did not arrive

[11] M. H. Segall, T. D. Campbell, and M. J. Herskovits, 'Cultural Differences in the Perception of Geometric Illusions', *Science*, 139 (1963), 769–71.

[12] *Eye and Brain*, 194.

on the scene until nearly seven weeks after the first operation had been performed, and that they relied for the crucial information quoted above upon the reports of the surgeon, nurses, and the patient himself. I do not mean in any way to question Gregory's integrity or the reliability of the facts he cites; on the contrary, I am relying upon both to make my point.

Even the more abstract sciences, such as astronomy and theoretical physics, are dependent in different ways upon testimony. A great deal of research work in physics, for instance, is collaborative in character (considered synchronically) and dependent upon a tradition of investigation (considered diachronically). As to the first, more than two-thirds of physicists surveyed in the United States in the 1960s said that most of their work was collaborative either with co-workers within their discipline or with workers in other disciplines.[13] Much of this collaboration presumably involves the acceptance of observations and calculations of colleagues, and even where the scientist works, as it were, by himself, he relies upon such accumulated funds of information as are contained in reputable tabulations or stored in computers or even embodied in the standard treatment of issues that he is not directly concerned with but needs to know about for the progress of his own work. Reliance upon previous experimental work in science can, of course, go seriously astray but it seems also to be a condition of progress since even where results are theoretically 'replicable' it would be a practical absurdity for any given worker to replicate all the experimental and observational work upon which his own investigations depend. Indeed, it would often be literally impossible to do so, either because of an inevitable lack of time or lack of competence.[14]

I heard recently of a case which illustrates both the importance and the pitfalls of scientific reliance upon the observations of colleagues. It concerned that humble insect the European earwig (*Forficula auricularia*), some populations of which have the distinction of being polymorphic for the number of sex chromosomes. Investigations early this century apparently established that the distributions in the two male groups were $(22 + X_1Y)$ and $(22 + X_1X_2Y)$ and this thesis was thought to be confirmed by early experiments on females which apparently showed that they had the chromosome distributions that could be predicted from the male

[13] Howard M. Vollmer, *Work Activities and Attitudes of Scientists and Research Managers: Data from a National Survey* (Stanford, Calif., 1965).

[14] Hardwig cites an experiment with the fetching title, 'Charm Photoproduction Cross Section at 20 GeV', which had 99 authors from a variety of countries who contributed a range of different skills and informational inputs. It is also of interest that these scientists were all experimentalists in the area of particle physics and would not be competent to produce the theoretical revisions which might flow from the experiment and the prospect of which provided some part of the rationale for doing it in the first place. In addition, those theoreticians who could take advantage of these experimental results would almost certainly be incapable of having done the experiment. See John Hardwig, 'Epistemic Dependence', *The Journal of Philosophy*, 82/7 (1985), 346–8.

count, namely, 24 (22 + X_1X_1), 25 (22 + $X_1X_1X_2$), and 26 (22 + $X_1X_1X_2X_2$). On the basis of this early work, the earwig thesis passed into the literature as the standard view and many interesting speculations and theories were developed stressing the uniqueness of the *Forficula auricularia* as a species with sex chromosome polymorphism in both sexes. Recent work, however, has shown that the picture is quite different and that the reports early in the century were unreliable. More interestingly still, they were not, in the first instance, presented as particularly reliable, the evidence being admittedly scanty and unclear. One of the original researchers said that he could 'lay no weight on this evidence' and another made a similar disclaimer. It was not until 1970 that detailed examination of a large sample of male and female earwigs showed that 24 was the only correct diploid number for females (22 + XX) and that the males were XY and XYY polymorphic. The case not only illustrates the power of tradition and reliance upon testimony within a scientific community but also the way in which quite tentative claims can be distorted by that power and become enshrined in the literature with a status far beyond that their authors intended.[15] Where the author actually intends to deceive the results can of course be catastrophic.

On a happier note we might be cheered by the positive results obtained from Edmund Halley's reliance upon earlier testimony in identifying his famous comet and predicting its return at seventy-five-year intervals. It was while Halley was studying the comet of 1682 that he noticed the similarities between it and two other bright comets reported by earlier astronomers in 1531 and 1607. Noting the intervals of approximately seventy-five years he predicted the return of the comet in 1758—which proved correct although he did not survive to see it. Reports of the comet have now been traced back to 240 BC and it is known to have been in the heavens in 1066 during the Norman Conquest of Britain. This is a good illustration of the way in which astronomy uses testimony from the past; another would be Halley's use of ancient star maps to discover what is now called the proper motion of the stars.

In this connection it is worth remarking on another type of dependency upon the word of others to which intellectual work is prone. It is perhaps particularly worth remarking because it so often goes unremarked. Most, if not all, of the examples so far considered concern the ways in which a thinker relies upon the experiments, calculations, observations, and even theories of others in conducting his own research and coming to his own conclusions; so Gregory relied upon the observations of the medical and

---

[15] My information about this case comes mainly from a private communication from one of the authors of the report which was publ. in *Experientia*, 26 (1970), 1387–9: G. C. Webb and M. J. D. White, 'A New Interpretation of the Sex Determining Mechanism of the European Earwig, *Forficula auricularia*'. I am indebted to Richard Wyatt for drawing it to my attention.

nursing staff for some of his data in the analysis of S. B.'s predicament and upon other researchers for some of the confirmatory evidence for his theory of the causes of visual illusions. Sometimes, however, what others tell us is important as *corroboration* of what we have already found out (or think we have found out) for ourselves. The Scottish philosopher Thomas Reid makes this point in connection with mathematical research in the belief that, if it applies to the science 'in which, of all sciences, authority is acknowledged to have least weight',[16] it will be even more significant in other areas of thought and practice. Reid is worth quoting in full:

Suppose a mathematician has made a discovery in that science, which he thinks important; that he has put his demonstration in just order; and, after examining it with an attentive eye, has found no flaw in it; I would ask, Will there not be still in his breast some diffidence, some jealousy lest the ardour of invention may have made him overlook some false step? This must be granted.

He commits his demonstration to the examination of a mathematical friend, whom he esteems a competent judge, and waits with impatience the issue of his judgement. Here I would ask again, Whether the verdict of his friend, according as it has been favourable or unfavourable, will not greatly increase or diminish his confidence in his own judgement? Most certain it will and it ought.

If the judgement of his friend agrees with his own, especially if it be confirmed by two or three able judges, he rests secure of his discovery without further examination; but if it be unfavourable, he is brought back into a kind of suspense, until the part that is suspected undergoes a new and a more rigorous examination.[17]

This respect for the opinions of fellow professionals or experts runs very deep. It is connected with the very idea of objectivity via the concept of what is public. In quite non-theoretical contexts it is common, though not invariable, for an individual to accept corrections to firmly held perceptual and memory beliefs from others who were in a position to observe or remember the relevant state of affairs or happening. The judgements of others constitute an important, indeed perhaps *the* most important, test of whether my own judgements reflect a reality independent of my subjectivity. If I am hallucinated then standardly the testimony of others will establish that fact despite my firm convictions to the contrary. Russell, as

---

[16] Thomas Reid, *Essays on the Intellectual Powers of Man*, essay vi, ch. v, in *Philosophical Works*, with notes etc. by Sir William Hamilton (Hildesheim, 1967), 440.

[17] Ibid. It is interesting to contrast Reid's attitude with Descartes's. In the *Discourse on the Method*, Descartes says in discussing the influence of custom and example upon belief, 'And yet a majority vote is worthless as a proof of truths that are at all difficult to discover; for a single man is much more likely to hit upon them than a group of people'. *The Philosophical Writings of Descartes*, ed. J. Cottingham, R. Stoothoff, and D. Murdoch, i (Cambridge, 1985), 119. The confident individualism of this passage will be relevant to my discussion of the influences of individualist ideology upon the neglect of testimony. Descartes's thought here is not only at odds with the (surely genuine) phenomenon to which Reid draws attention but also with the facts of scientific co-operation and mutual dependency in the uncovering of truths that are (often extremely) difficult to discover.

we shall see in a later chapter, considered this aspect of our reliance upon testimony essential to the understanding of what it is to be a physical thing and he criticized logical positivism for its failure to appreciate the implications of this point.[18] In the *Analysis of Matter* he says explicitly, 'I mean here by "objective" not anything metaphysical but merely "agreeing with the testimony of others".'[19]

By now it will, I hope, have become clear that we are greatly indebted to testimony at the level of both common sense and theory for much of what we usually regard as knowledge. The neglect of the topic cannot be because of its actual unimportance but it may have been because of a supposed unimportance. In the post-Renaissance Western world the dominance of an individualist ideology has had a lot to do with the feeling that testimony has little or no epistemic importance. It is a commonplace that the political, social, and economic thought and practice of the West have been profoundly influenced in recent centuries by certain ideas and ideals stressing the powers, rights, dignities, and autonomy of the individual person. It is not my concern to explore this *Weltanschauung* here in any detail but if we admit its effects upon such notions as freedom, right, and society we should not be surprised to find similarly notable consequences for such concepts as knowledge, truth, rationality, and evidence. It may be no accident that the rise of an individualist ideology coincided with the emergence of the theory of knowledge as a central philosophical concern but, accident or not, the coincidence was likely to cast into shadow the importance of our intellectual reliance upon one another and hence obstruct a serious examination of the issues this reliance raises. Descartes's epistemology is strikingly individualistic not only in the way his 'project of pure inquiry' is actually set up but in the biases his explicit pronouncements about rational methodology reveal. In the *Discourse on the Method*, for instance, he disparages the effects of education upon our intellect and couples it with appetite as directing influences that our immaturity makes necessary but regrettable:

So, too, I reflected that we were all children before being men and had to be governed for some time by our appetites and our teachers, which were often opposed to each other and neither of which, perhaps, always gave us the best advice; hence I thought it virtually impossible that our judgements should be as unclouded and firm as they would have been if we had had the full use of our reason from the moment of our birth, and if we had always been guided by it alone.[20]

Individualist rhetoric is also prominent in the following remarks upon knowledge by John Locke, who was of course an influential proponent of individualist ideas in political and social theory:

[18] Cf. Bertrand Russell, *Logic and Knowledge*, ed. R. C. Marsh (London, 1956), 375.
[19] Id., *The Analysis of Matter* (London, 1927), 150.
[20] *The Philosophical Writings of Descartes*, i (Cambridge, 1985), 117.

I hope it will not be thought arrogance to say, that perhaps we should make greater progress in the discovery of rational and contemplative knowledge if we sought it in the fountain, in the consideration of things themselves, and made use rather of our own thoughts than other men's to find it: for, I think, we may as rationally hope to see with other men's eyes as to know by other men's understanding... The floating of other men's opinions in our brains makes us not one jot the more knowing, though they happen to be true. What in them was science is in us but opiniatrety.[21]

There is another matter which may have contributed to the neglect of testimony in modern philosophy and that is the rise of the mathematical theory of probability in the seventeenth century, or rather the change in mode of thought which accompanied and to some extent made possible probability theory. Ian Hacking[22] has presented a case in favour of the view that probability theory as initiated by thinkers like Pascal in the mid-seventeenth century was only possible because of a certain sort of breakdown in the medieval distinction between science and opinion. Hacking, following Byrne,[23] claims that the medievals gave the title 'science' to knowledge which was demonstrable from first principles of an intuitively evident kind. (To us they seem to have been amazingly optimistic about just what could be so classified but this is partly because we do not find their distinction between science and opinion really tenable.) They gave the title 'opinion' to beliefs or doctrine not so demonstrable and they used the term 'probable' in connection only with opinion. According to Hacking, however, 'probable' made no reference to reason or evidence: 'Probability pertains to opinion, where there was no clear concept of evidence.... It indicated approval or acceptability by intelligent people.'[24] Opinion and its probability or acceptability was then very much a matter of approvability by authorities; hence reliable testimony loomed large when one was concerned with questions of opinion. Hacking argues that through the work of empirics, alchemists, physicians, and other practitioners of 'the low sciences' the idea gradually arose that there could be natural, non-testimonial support of what the medievals would have classified as matters of opinion. The mediating notion here was that of 'sign'; it was through this that the move was made from people providing support for belief to Nature providing such support. Nature tells us through her signs what to believe, just as people testify to us in language. There is much talk in the transitional period of 'the book of Nature' or 'the book of the Universe' and of God as 'the author of Nature'. At last, the notion of natural probability becomes, in the work of men like Pascal and Jacques Bernouilli,

[21] John Locke, *An Essay Concerning Human Understanding*, ed. John W. Yolton (London, 1961), bk. 1, p. 58.
[22] Hacking, *Emergence*.
[23] Edmund F. Byrne, *Probability and Opinion* (The Hague, 1968).
[24] Hacking, *Emergence*, 22.

independent of authorities and testimony of any kind. The same movement of ideas led to the elevation and transformation of the domain of opinion so that, not only did the importance of contingent truths for theoretical inquiry become more acknowledged, but the sharp division between matters of ('eternal') scientific knowledge and matters of opinion began to dissolve, and incidentally made possible Hume's profound sceptical puzzles about empirical knowledge.

This then, in somewhat simplified outline, is Hacking's thesis. I lack the historical scholarship to assess fully its merits but there are a number of elements in his case that I find deeply puzzling. The idea, for instance, that probability once meant only approvability by authorities and hence made no reference to independent evidence surely raises the question of how the authorities arrived at their own authoritative opinions and in what light they viewed them. It also strains belief to suggest that ordinary people were once incapable of making certain elementary inferences and calling upon the 'evidences' in public justification of their conclusions. A medieval farmer, for instance, whose chicken pen was damaged and his chickens slaughtered, in an area inhabited by foxes and wolves, upon finding paw marks abounding in the soft earth in and around the pen, would surely opine, without benefit of authorities, that either wolves or foxes had killed the poultry. To determine which, he might consult a more authoritative local who could better distinguish the paw marks from his own experience. Are we to believe that none of this sort of thing occurred or was even possible before the developments of which Hacking writes? But such puzzles are not my concern here. I shall merely observe that, if Hacking is right, then it would not be surprising if the changed intellectual climate accompanying the 'emergence of probability' was inimical to an interest in testimony as a source of knowledge or reliable belief and produced a context in which any reference to dependence upon testimony could be viewed as a return to an unenlightened past.[25] Moreover, the same consequence would follow from the truth of a much weaker version of Hacking's thesis to the effect that medieval thought, lacking the modern concept of probability or perhaps lacking only some of the insights of the modern theory of probability, relied much more in the area of opinion upon reputable testimony and authoritative beliefs.

It is interesting in the light of this consideration that probability theorists themselves continued to be haunted, or at least teased, by the ghost of what they had supposedly killed. There are few major contributors to the development of probability theory from the seventeenth century to the early twentieth century who do not devote time to applying the calculus of chances to the assessment of some aspects of the reliability of witnesses.

---

[25] The passage from Locke, quoted earlier, may be an embodiment of this spirit, although, in terms of Hacking's thesis, it is rather a curiosity since it also appears to contain a commitment to something like the medieval distinction of science and opinion.

For the most part their efforts are not at all impressive but I shall have
more to say about this in Chapters 10 and 11.

So much then for speculation about how the importance of testimony
may have come, in modern times, to be ignored or minimized. Modern
and contemporary issues will principally concern us in the following
chapters since the theory of knowledge has been such a dominant concern in philosophy since Descartes. It may none the less be appropriate
at this point to add a few words about certain strands in pre-modern
philosophical thinking about testimony which do not fit neatly into the
pattern described by Byrne and Hacking. Certainly, in proportion as one
thinks of knowledge proper as the contemplation of self-evident first
principles, deductions from them, and the like, so will one's interest, as a
theorist, in what is learnt on the basis of testimony tend to be lower. This
tendency is clearly at work in Greek and medieval philosophy and the
associated model of knowledge persists even in Locke, as we can see in the
useful quotation from him already cited. Yet it is not only fair but also
instructive to note that some pre-modern philosophers who deny testimony the title of knowledge do concede it a significant role in the
formation of true and sometimes highly advantageous belief. One such
philosopher is Aquinas and indeed an adherent to an historically oriented
religion like Christianity must be disposed to see at least some testimony-
based beliefs as advantageous, namely those which constitute part of the
content of his or her faith. Aquinas certainly sees this, and more, though
he declines to call testimony a source of *knowledge* since, under the
influence of the Greeks, he sees knowledge as a product of an individual's
systematic reasoning from first principles. Much of what he and others of
a like cast of mind say about this issue reflects the concern to link genuine
knowledge with science, understood as a wide theoretical perspective
which conveys through and through understanding. In his commentary on
Boethius's *De Trinitate*, Aquinas treats our dependency upon others as a
species of faith—we might call it natural faith—and he sees it as necessary
for human society. Interestingly (in view of Hacking's and Byrne's theory)
he treats it as neither knowledge nor opinion but as lying half-way between the two. So he says:

> . . . faith has something in common with opinion, and something in common with
> knowledge and understanding, by reason of which it holds a position midway
> between opinion and understanding or science . . . In common with understanding
> and knowledge, it possesses certain and fixed assent; and in this it differs from
> opinion, which accepts one of two opposites, though with fear that the other may
> be true, and on account of this doubt it fluctuates between two contraries. But,
> in common with opinion, faith is concerned with things that are not naturally
> possible to our understanding, and in this respect it differs from science and
> intellection.[26]

---

[26] *Commentary on Boethius's De Trinitate*, qu. iii, art. i. 3. Cf. also *ST*, II-II, qu. 4, art. 1
and qu. 2, art. 1.

Expanding this last point, Aquinas claims that things may 'not be apparent to human understanding' for two very different reasons: either because of a defect in the things themselves or because of a defect in our understanding. Included under the second heading are certain truths of religious faith and under the first 'singular and contingent things which are remote from our senses' and which can be ascertained only by reliance upon the word of others.[27] As Aquinas puts it:

And since among men dwelling together one man should deal with another as with himself in what he is not self-sufficient, therefore it is needful that he be able to stand with as much certainty on what another knows but of which he himself is ignorant, as upon the truths which he himself knows. Hence it is that in human society faith is necessary in order that one man give credence to the words of another, and this is the foundation of justice... Hence also it is that no lie is without sin, since every lie derogates from that faith which is so necessary.[28]

I do not intend to explore here Aquinas's interesting and subtle theory of faith, but it is instructive to see the way he insists on the importance of our trust in the word of others while refraining from according its outcome, in the acceptance of various truths, the name of knowledge. There is, I think, a latent tension here between the idea of knowledge as justified or legitimate or secure grasp of the truth and the idea of knowledge (derived from Plato and Aristotle) as synoptic or scientific understanding. In modern epistemology a similar tension arises, in a somewhat different context, between internal and external definitions or analyses of knowledge. The internalist tradition insists on the knower having an insight into the justification of his or her belief which is such as to show him or her the connection between that belief and reality. The externalist is dismissive of such hopes and views the crucial element making for knowledge as the obtaining of a special relation between the subject's true belief and the state of affairs making it true. This relation, variously understood as reliability, causal connection from the state of affairs to the belief, or counterfactual tracking, makes for knowledge whether the subject has some insight into its nature and existence or not. The present fashion for externalist over internalist thinking in epistemology represents a triumph of pragmatist over intellectualist outlooks on man and his cognitive relationship with reality. Much of twentieth-century analytical philosophy (developing tendencies that go back to the seventeenth century) has consisted of a many-sided critique of the pretensions of the pure intellect and the associated ideals of reason and scientific knowledge to which, for instance, Aquinas seems to give expression in the quoted passage. Wittgenstein's discussion of understanding and rule-following in the *Philosophical Investigations* forms a major part of that critique.

The Greek—medieval attitude to these matters (and I do not suggest that it is the only epistemological stance taken amongst Greek or medieval

[27] Ibid.   [28] Ibid.

philosophers, though it is certainly a dominant one) may be seen as a very strong version of the internalist outlook, but the latent tension I referred to earlier was never far away. Plato's backsliding on the status of perception in the *Theaetetus* (and in the *Meno* where the man who has actually walked to Larissa *does* know the way)[29] may be a case of such tension surfacing, although there is, as we saw, a tactical explanation at least on offer. Certainly, Aquinas in the second passage quoted seems to treat perception as giving knowledge to those who exercise it and there seems to be a problem about how perception is accounted for in a model of knowledge dominated by the requirements of reason. The trouble is that if one relaxes one's theoretical guard for just a moment the sheer centrality and reliability of clear instances of perceptual belief can be overpowering. But then once one gets a proper perspective on the place of testimony in our lives, as Aquinas is at least beginning to, the same will be true of testimonial beliefs. Hence the tension.

A very good example of a great thinker in the tradition being subject to this tension is St Augustine. In his dialogue, *De Magistro*, Augustine argues for the paradoxical conclusion that it is impossible for any man to teach another what he knows—including, of course, the proposition that it is impossible for any man to teach another what he knows. It turns out that Augustine has rather special views about teaching and about knowing. In particular, he wants to hold that, no matter how useful it is to believe propositions on the basis of reliable authority, one cannot be said *strictly speaking* to know them in this way. In *De Magistro*, Augustine, like Plato in the *Meno* and the *Theaetetus*, allows that we may know not only by the light of reason in a sort of intellectual perception but also by ordinary sense perception.[30] Elsewhere (as in *De Utilitate Credendi*) he has it that sense perception provides only belief, though very useful belief.[31] In his *Retractationes*, which provide comments on and amendments to his earlier works, he endorses this view when discussing *De Utilitate Credendi*, but he allows for the strong temptation to speak of knowledge in the case of both perception and of testimony. He comes very close to holding a two-senses thesis about the term 'know': a strict sense which excludes perception and testimony and a loose sense which includes them. It could be argued, however, that he is insisting on the one strict sense and merely admitting that the widespread misuse in the cases of perception and testimony is, for common purposes, harmless and intelligible.[32] To judge

---

[29] *Meno*, 97 A–B.

[30] *De Magistro*, 39.

[31] *De Utilitate Credendi*, 25.

[32] The possibility of this interpretation was drawn to my attention by Myles Burnyeat who discusses aspects of Augustine's epistemology in an unpubl. paper on the *De Magistro*. I am much indebted to this paper though I diverge from it on a number of points. Burnyeat has incorporated parts of this paper into 'Wittgenstein and Augustine *De Magistro*', *Proc. of the Aristotelian Soc.*, supp. vol. 61 (1987), 1–24.

the merits of these two positions either as interpretations of Augustine's intentions or as internally consistent in their own right is beyond our concerns here. My own view is that Augustine wants to hold to the benign misuse position but that, in the light of what he says about its benignity, the position is dubiously coherent. In any case what is important here is the way his manœuvrings exhibit the tension I have been discussing. Here is the quotation from the *Retractationes*:

And when I said . . . 'What we know, therefore, we owe to reason, what we believe, to authority', this is not to be taken in such a way as to make us frightened in more ordinary conversation of saying that we know that we believe on adequate testimony. It is true that when we keep to the proper acceptation of the term we say we know only that which we grasp by firm reasoning of the mind. But when we speak in language more suited to common use, as even the Holy Scripture speaks, we should not hesitate to say we know both what we perceive by our bodily senses and what we believe on the authority of trustworthy witnesses, while nevertheless understanding the distance between these and that.[33]

A tolerant and pragmatic concept of knowledge is at least strongly tempting Augustine, but if he fails fully to give way to it here he surely succumbs elsewhere. Consider, for instance, a passage from *De Trinitate*, a book complete when Augustine was in his 60s, some twenty-four years after *De Utilitate Credendi*, which was itself three years later than *De Magistro*. In this work, Augustine presents once more his famous objections to scepticism, objections which find an echo in Descartes's philosophy twelve centuries later. Having, he hopes, established against the sceptics the utter indubitability of 'I know that I am alive', Augustine takes it that he has destroyed their basic programme and hastens to assure the reader that he does not share their doubts about perceptual knowledge. His position seems to be that, even on the sceptics' own premises, their universal doubt is untenable because of the survival of the key proposition about the existence of the doubting subject (and of an infinity of connected propositions such as 'I know that I know that I am alive', 'I will not to be mistaken', 'I know that I will not to be mistaken', and so on) and although this survival may teach us something about the understanding and reason it should not lead us to accept the sceptics' position about other items of putative knowledge:

But far be it from us to doubt the truth of what we have learned by the bodily senses; since by them we have learned to know the heaven and the earth, and those things in them which are known to us, so far as He who created both us and them has willed them to be within our knowledge. Far be it from us too, to deny that we know what we have learned by the testimony of others: otherwise we know not that there is an ocean; we know not that the lands and cities exist which most

---

[33] *Retractationes*, I. xiii. 3. My trans. is that supplied by Burnyeat in the unpubl. paper mentioned in n. 32. It reappears at 'Wittgenstein and Augustine' (cit. n. 32), 6.

copious report commends to us; we know not that those men were, and their works, which we have learned by reading history; we know not the news that is daily brought us from this quarter or that, and confirmed by consistent and conspiring evidence; lastly, we know not at what place or from whom we have been born: since in all these things we have believed the testimony of others. And if it is not absurd to say this, then we must confess, that not only our own senses, but those of other persons also, have added very much indeed to our knowledge.[34]

In such a mood Augustine is as confident a supporter of testimony as a source of knowledge as one could find but it is not clear how this support can be integrated into his overall epistemology. So far as I know, he makes only one attempt to do so and this occurs in a long letter to an obscure correspondent about an abstruse theological issue. In an extended and interesting epistemological prologue to the main business of the letter, Augustine accepts that it is reasonable to describe some of the things we believe on testimony as knowledge. Having distinguished two uses of the verb 'to see'—one to do with the inner "gaze of the mind" and the other that of the bodily senses, especially but not exclusively, the sense of sight—Augustine asserts that knowing is pre-eminently a matter of seeing in one or other of these ways. Perception and (with a little more argument) memory is thus included within the purview of knowledge but testimony seems excluded since it is not a matter of seeing but of believing. None the less, Augustine insists that 'our knowledge . . . consists of things seen and things believed'[35] and he goes on to say: 'Not without reason do we say that we know not only what we have seen or see, but also what we believe, when we yield assent to some fact under the influence of suitable evidence or witnesses.'[36] Yet how can this be? Augustine's answer is rather surprising. He seems to say that the right to speak of knowledge here comes from the fact that what we believe on testimony is open to the 'gaze of the mind'. As he puts it: 'if it is not inappropriate to say that we also know what we firmly believe, this arises from the fact that we are correctly said to see mentally what we believe, even though it is not present to our senses'.[37] The most natural interpretation of this passage is that the status of knowledge is conferred on our testimony-based beliefs by the fact that we know ('see') that we have these beliefs. But it is hard to credit Augustine with such a silly view since it is clear that one can perfectly well see and know that one has some belief without that belief being knowledge—most strikingly in the case where it is false. A usually reliable witness may tell me something false which I firmly believe yet no amount

---

[34] *De Trinitate*, xv. xii. 21. My trans. here is that of Dodds from *The Works of Aurelius Augustinus*, ed. Marcus Dodds (Edinburgh, 1871–6).

[35] *Letters*, letter 147 to Paulinus, in *The Fathers of the Church*, xx, ed. and trans. by Sr. M. I. Bogan (Washington, DC, 1953), 176.

[36] Ibid. 176–7.

[37] Ibid. 177.

of awareness that I believe it can turn the belief into knowledge. Perhaps Augustine has fallen into this absurdity (we should be wary of any 'principle of charity' preventing us from concluding that a great mind has been guilty of intellectual folly; too much speaks against such piety, not least the fact that great minds accuse each other of such lapses) but there is, I think, at least the beginnings of a rather better idea in what he says.

Although Augustine places the notion of sight at the centre of his epistemology, it would be unwise to understand the idea crudely. He does not, for instance, think that all exercises of the sense of (bodily) sight are veridical nor does he seem to think that we are always right about what we take ourselves to be mentally seeing. His position is not fully worked out, but I suspect that it should go as follows. When you are really seeing (either with the mind or the body) then you know; this is compatible with exercising the mind or the senses carelessly or in less than optimal conditions and so falling into error. (If this seems too much like Descartes it is worth recalling that, like Descartes, Augustine explicitly endorses a volitional theory of error.)[38] My suggestion about the accommodation of testimony into Augustine's framework then is that when the mind 'sees' its testimony-acquired beliefs it does not just know that it has those beliefs, rather, it somehow 'sees' that some of them are true. This suggestion acquits Augustine of the silliness inherent in the first interpretation, though at the cost of considerable obscurity since it is very hard to understand how the mind could 'see' anything of the sort. I doubt that Augustine's notion of seeing can really do the work required of it in this connection but I shall return to the question in a later chapter and try to construct an argument which has at least some affinities with Augustine's manœuvres at this point. We need only note here that Augustine's commitment to testimony as a source of knowledge and his, admittedly awkward, attempt to show how it could be fitted into his epistemological outlook, do not seem to have been followed up by his medieval successors.

In some of the chapters which follow I shall discuss what various modern philosophers have argued in detail concerning the epistemological status of testimony. I want to conclude this chapter by suggesting in a general way some possible lines of theoretical response to a realization of the extent of our intellectual and practical dependence upon what we are told.

1. The puritan response

In the spirit of Plato's remarks in the *Theaetetus* we might accept that human beings are reliant in various ways upon testimony for an enormous

---

[38] *De Trinitate*, IX, xi. 16.

amount of what they think they know but insist that because of this we must conclude that knowledge is much rarer than is usually believed. Just how rare will depend upon what conclusions we accept about the connections between testimony and whatever sources of real knowledge we allow. If, for instance, the existence of genuine memory is dependent in some way upon the reliability of a great deal of contemporary testimony then there will be difficulties in rejecting testimony as a source of knowledge (or as a candidate for entry in the third condition of the definition of knowledge) while continuing to accept memory. There are subtle and difficult issues here, to be examined later, but the nature of the problem is clear enough. Plato and Collingwood are examples of philosophers who adopt the puritan response, although interestingly they both think that, while the vulgar may have less knowledge than they believe, specialists have certain techniques which enable them to gain quite extensive knowledge. For Plato, epistemic salvation lies in philosophical reflection and the contemplation of the Forms; for Collingwood it is to be found in the exercise of the power of imaginative reconstruction. Collingwood's 'Puritan response' is concerned primarily with historical knowledge which none the less he thought a central and specially significant form of knowledge. Of the role of testimony in more mundane areas he is less emphatically sceptical but still far from enthusiastic. 'In the practical life of every day,' he says,

we constantly and rightly accept the information that other people offer us, believing them to be both well informed and truthful, and having, sometimes, grounds for this belief. I do not even deny, though I do not assert it, that there may be cases in which, as perhaps in some cases of memory, our acceptance of such testimony may go beyond mere belief and deserve the name of knowledge. What I assert is that it can never be historical knowledge, because it can never be scientific knowledge.[39]

Collingwood's final comment has affinities with some of the Greek and medieval views on knowledge discussed above, though there are differences in their underlying ideas of science.

2. The reductive response[40]

Here it is accepted that we may know in cases where we rely upon testimony but our dependence upon testimony is itself justified in terms of other supposedly more fundamental forms of evidence, namely, the individual's own observations and his inferences from them. J. L. Mackie[41] has very plausibly claimed that what I am calling 'the reductive response'

---

[39] R. G. Collingwood, *The Idea of History* (Oxford, 1970), 256–7.

[40] The word 'reductive' as used throughout this paragraph is intended as no more than a convenient label for the response in question and is not used in any strict technical sense.

[41] J. L. Mackie, 'The Possibility of Innate Knowledge', *Proc. of the Aristotelian Soc.* 70 (1970), 254.

is part and parcel of an ideal of 'autonomous knowledge', which he sees as central to the empiricist tradition. The autonomous knower can accept both the epistemic priority of individual observations and the reliability of testimony, only if it can be shown that reliance upon testimony gives rational support to our beliefs because each of us can somehow check observationally upon the fact that testimony is usually truth-preserving. A parallel with our attitudes to novel or unusual species of evidence such as telepathy might be suggested. If we came to accept the general reliability of telepathy it would only be in consequence of our having thoroughly checked some sample of telepathic claims against the reports of those whose thoughts were supposedly revealed by the new method; having established a sufficiently high correlation we would be entitled to trust telepathy in future as a reliable (though not infallible) source of knowledge. The analogy limps somewhat but it is useful as an illustration of what is attempted by the reductive response to testimony. David Hume is the archetype of the reductive responder and Bertrand Russell's discussion of the problem seems to fall into this category also. W. K. Clifford, that *enfant terrible* of nineteenth-century British philosophy whose 'Ethics of Belief' provoked William James to write 'The Will to Believe', is another who has such a response.[42] We shall examine these reactions more closely in later chapters.

3. The fundamentalist response

Agreeing with the proponents of the reductive response that testimony gives us knowledge, the fundamentalists refuse to accept that our reliance on testimony can be 'justified' in terms of some other supposedly more fundamental sources of knowledge as suggested in (2). Our reliance upon testimony should be regarded as fundamental to the justification of belief in the same sort of way as perception, memory, and inference are. In so far as it is useful to think of knowledge as a building with foundations then testimony is part of the foundations. Thomas Reid is the only philosopher, so far as I know, who has explicitly adopted a position like this. In some respects it is the approach closest to my own although there are, as we shall see, certain very important differences.

4. The end-of-epistemology response

This response has some affinity with (3) since it acknowledges the irreducibility of our reliance upon testimony but concludes from this, and other considerations, that positive epistemology, certainly in its foundationist

---

[42] W. K. Clifford, 'Ethics of Belief' in *Lectures and Essays*, ii (London, 1879).

form and perhaps in any guise, is a radically mistaken enterprise. There is an end-of-epistemology mood about in contemporary philosophy, a mood generated by considerations and attitudes that have little to do directly with worries about testimony. Quine, for instance, has argued[43] that the failure of such justificationist programmes as those of the Viennese logical positivists (he has in mind particularly Carnap's *Der logische Aufbau der Welt*) shows the need to conceive of epistemology as a branch of one part of natural science, namely empirical psychology, rather than as an independent study of the foundations of all science. There are many obscurities in Quine's position, not the least of which concerns how epistemological psychology can be in any sense normative, as its ancestor, philosophical epistemology, plainly aspired to be. One can hardly settle questions about what it is rational to believe, and why, by adopting a reverential tone of voice in uttering the word 'science' or 'physics' (with or without an initial capital letter). If we insist that epistemology consists in 'studying how the human subject of our study posits bodies and projects his physics from his data'[44] then we must also be ready with some answer to the question of whether that human subject's procedures satisfy criteria of rationality which have in the past, at any rate, seemed to be independently appealing. Quine would no doubt insist that the appeal is delusive, that the intuitive certainty attaching to, say, our understanding of mathematical and logical connections and truths, is no model for what it is rational to believe about empirical realities, but there seems at least to be a problem about providing a non-circular alternative and Quinean pragmatism suffers many of the flaws of Moorean dogmatism on this issue.[45] Similarly, Popper's 'evolutionary epistemology' sometimes seems, perversely, to be aimed at shoring up fundamental beliefs by an appeal to more speculative beliefs, such as parts of evolutionary theory, the survival of the fittest, and so on, which are themselves dependent on the reliability of the fundamental beliefs. Popper would not, of course, put the matter thus himself but it seems to me a fair description of the way the enterprise is sometimes presented and it highlights a difficulty that projects of this nature must face. Interestingly, Popper does, in one place, instance our reliance upon testimony as an objection to foundationist epistemology.[46]

[43] 'Epistemology Naturalised', in W. V. Quine, *Ontological Relativity and Other Essays* (New York, 1969). There is a distinct echo of Hume's naturalism in Quine's position.

[44] Ibid. 83.

[45] For a fuller exploration of these sorts of defects in Quine's position see Barry Stroud, 'The Significance of Naturalized Epistemology', *Midwest Studies in Philosophy*, 6 (1981), ed. P. A. French *et al.*, 455–71.

[46] Sir Karl Popper, *Conjectures and Refutations* (London, 1963), 21–4.

2

What is Testimony?

We have been operating so far with a rather loose notion of testimony and it is now time to be more precise. My aim in Chapter 1 was to indicate the extent and significance of our reliance upon the word of others, to note the surprising philosophical neglect of the topic, and to suggest the difficult and important epistemological problems that arise in the area; such an aim requires no more than a rough idea of what is meant by the term 'testimony', but further analysis or treatment of the philosophical problems needs more discrimination and definition.

To this end I shall in this chapter attempt to be more precise about the concept of testimony, although in speaking thus I do not mean to imply that there is obviously only one such concept. I shall define a concept of testimony which can then be used as an object of comparison and contrast with other common ways of talking about testimony or other uses of such terms as 'testimony' or indeed other types of discourse and judgement which seem to fall within the problem area. The concept of testimony that I will thus define and use is that of a certain speech act or, in J. L. Austin's terminology, an illocutionary act, which may be and standardly is performed under certain conditions and with certain intentions such that we might naturally think of the definition as giving us conventions governing the existence of the act of testifying.[1] For those with a textual bent it is perhaps worth noting that Austin recognized the existence of such an act in *How to Do Things with Words*,[2] where he classifies it as an 'expositive' in the company of reporting, swearing, conjecturing, and, more dubiously (at least his manuscript has queries at this point), doubting, knowing, and believing. A further advantage of the Austinian model is that Austin's distinction between primary and explicit forms of illocution, whatever its ultimate validity, brings into perspective the fact that we may testify by

---

[1] The place of conventions in the definition of speech acts is, of course, controversial. Some, such as Austin and Searle, see them as essential to such definitions where others, notably Strawson, deny this (J. L. Austin, *How to Do Things with Words* (Oxford, 1962); J. R. Searle, *Speech Acts* (Cambridge, 1969); P. F. Strawson, 'Intention and Convention in Speech Acts', *Philosophical Review*, 72 (1964)|). The nature of the dispute is not altogether clear but I need not take sides on the matter here, since a non-conventional account of the speech act of testifying will, I think, have to specify conditions under which a speaker may rightly be said to have testified and this is all that I need be seen as doing in this chapter. It seems to me natural (and defensible) to characterize these conditions as conventions that the speaker abides by in testifying, as long as the notion of convention is understood broadly enough, but this is a further issue.

[2] p. 161.

using some performative formula (e.g. 'I testify that . . .' or 'I give witness that . . .') or in less explicit ways such as simply saying what we have seen.

I shall begin the investigation with the legal context of testimony both because it is likely to provide a relatively firm footing for our initial steps and because certain features of legal testimony have influenced philosophical discussions of the topic as diverse as those of Locke, Bradley, and Marcel. It is, in any case, a natural starting-point since courts, inquiries, commissions, and the like spend a great deal of their time summoning witnesses and hearing their testimony, and it is probable that the elusive plain man so invoked by theorists most readily associates the word with legal and quasi-legal settings. It does not follow, however, that such legal situations are the only ones in which testimony can exist; it seems rather that the legal framework adapts and solemnizes an everyday phenomenon to which it may not be common to apply such a technical-sounding word. It is indeed uncommon to say, 'His testimony was such and such', in nonformal contexts; instead we frequently speak simply of 'His report . . .' or 'His version . . .' or simply 'He says . . .'. When I accept some report and in reply to questioning I stand firm on, 'His word is good enough for me', or 'Well, it's in *The Times*', then it would seem perverse to hold that merely because there is no legal context this cannot be a case of someone's accepting testimony. Indeed, legal testimony, like some other legal concepts (such as guilt and slander), seems plainly derived from a more mundane concept. It is this more fundamental idea that Thomas Reid classified as amongst the 'social operations of mind' and which he castigated philosophers for neglecting. He defined these operations as those which 'necessarily suppose an intercourse with some other intelligent being'[3] and instanced commanding, questioning, and promising as falling into this category, along with testifying.

It is possible of course to insist on reserving the word 'testimony' for the legal notion whilst admitting the existence and importance of the related lay notion and conceding the dependence, in some sense, of the one notion upon the other. This merely verbal issue seems to me to be of no great moment but there are advantages in conforming to the traditional philosophical terminology in which our problem area has been discussed and in keeping the word 'testimony' to acknowledge the relatedness of what is done in both legal and non-legal settings. None the less, to mark the differences that do exist, I shall call legal and quasi-legal testimony 'formal testimony' and the wider notion 'natural testimony'. Another advantage in beginning our inquiry with an analysis of formal testimony is

---

[3] Thomas Reid, *Essays on the Intellectual Powers of Man*, essay I, ch. viii, in *Philosophical Works*, 244. Reid's suggestive discussion of these social operations of the mind is an interesting, if brief, anticipation of some of the concerns which Austin and Searle were later to develop in their theories of illocutionary acts and speech acts respectively. I discuss Reid's interesting comments on 'the social operations' and testimony's place amongst them in Ch. 3.

that many legal systems, most notably English law and codes influenced by it, have exclusionary rules and admissibility requirements which determine what can be presented as evidence before their tribunals. Consequently these rules and requirements, shaping the particular notion of formal testimony employed in the relevant jurisdiction, are of value in defining a concept of formal testimony which can in its turn, by highlighting similarities and differences, help reveal the shape of natural testimony even when such strict legal notions as admissibility no longer have direct application.

Formal Testimony

Clearly testimony in a court of law or before a commission of inquiry or something of the sort is a kind of evidence: it is, specifically, the evidence provided by persons. This, at any rate, will serve in an introductory fashion although, as we shall see later, there are further complications. The persons in question are referred to as 'witnesses' but a visual analogy is not essential (obviously a blind man can be a perfectly good witness for some purposes and indeed, in some circumstances, e.g. the dark, he may be an even better witness than someone who is sighted). Nor are observers of some episode the only kind of witnesses likely to be called since expert testimony and character witnesses introduce complications. The kind of evidence in question here seems to be 'say-so' evidence: we are, that is, invited to accept something or other as true because someone says it is, where the someone in question is supposed to be in a position to speak authoritatively on the matter. But of course more remains to be said.

In a court case the jury is confronted with Constable Jones's statement that the defendant, Brown, broke down the door of Mrs Smith's house. Constable Jones was not on the scene at the time and is merely, let us say, inferring that it was Brown from the fact that the defendant had, in his presence, made threats against Mrs Smith, was known to be of a violent temper, and had been seen by Constable Jones in the vicinity of Mrs Smith's house at roughly the time of the offence. This is revealed to the jury during cross-examination and the judge directs them to ignore what the constable had said on the matter. It was not in fact testimony but opinion. However, the constable can legitimately testify to having seen the defendant in the vicinity at the time. Similarly, a ballistics expert might testify that a bullet shown to him in court did indeed come from a rifle shown to him in court (and testify further to the trials he had made of the matter in the laboratory) but he cannot on this basis testify that the defendant fired the bullet into the deceased nor can he testify to the defendant's fingerprints being those on the gun in question unless he is a fingerprint expert who has discovered as much. Nor can someone testify to another's character unless he is in a position to do so, by being, for instance, a more than casual acquaintance of the person.[4]

In general we may say in review of these cases that one who testifies must have a certain sort of competence or certain sorts of credentials. In English law this condition is usually taken to involve the requirement that testimony be firsthand and hence the famous, or notorious, rule against 'hearsay' evidence but it must be remembered that there are many quite formal inquiries in which there is no rule against hearsay and indeed many non-English legal systems have no such restriction. Furthermore, within English law the hearsay rule has numerous categories of exception, to which we shall turn later, and it is clear that a witness can have competence to testify even when the evidence is in no way firsthand, as indeed seems plainly the case with character evidence when it is testimony to reputation. With regard to hearsay it is also worth remarking that the normal operation of the exclusionary rule is not designed to prevent a witness testifying to what some third party has said or stated; it is designed to prevent the introduction of the third party's statement as evidence to the truth of what is stated. So Tom's evidence that he had frequently heard Arthur claim to be the Archangel Gabriel would be perfectly admissible as what lawyers call 'original' evidence where the question at issue is Arthur's sanity but quite inadmissible where what is to be determined is something to do with Arthur's true identity and the claim is made as evidence for the truth of the proposition that Arthur is the Archangel Gabriel. Hence we find hearsay defined by one legal authority as 'a third person's assertion narrated to the court by a witness for the purpose of establishing the truth of that which was asserted'.[5]

Yet although this orientation to the truth of what is said is important for understanding hearsay, the idea of hearsay is in need of further clarification. The definition given, for instance, is multiply ambiguous in a revealing way, an ambiguity which it shares with several other definitions in the legal literature. The different readings of the definition have significant philosophical implications. The plainest reading covers situations in which

---

[4] Actually in English law the term 'character' is ambiguous between what is called 'disposition' and 'reputation'. If one testifies directly to disposition one offers one's own assessment of the person's virtues and vices whereas if one testifies to reputation one reports on the assessment that others, the community at large, make of the man's disposition. The admissibility of any sort of character evidence is stringently controlled but it is a curious fact that English law frowns more heavily upon direct testimony to disposition than upon testimony to reputation, even though this has the consequence, noted by Stephen, that a witness 'may with perfect truth swear that a man, who to his knowledge has been a receiver of stolen goods for years, has an excellent character for honesty if he has the good luck to conceal his crimes from his neighbours'. (Quoted in R. Cross, *Evidence*, 3rd ed. (London, 1967), 329.) My remarks in the text about acquaintance apply more naturally to direct testimony to disposition although the point about credentials will also be relevant, in a different way, to testimony to reputation.

[5] Ibid. 4.

the witness explicitly tells the court that a 'third person' has asserted that something or other is the case, and in which the witness aims to persuade the court that the facts are as asserted by the third person. But there are cases, commonly, and understandably, regarded by the law as hearsay, in which one or even both of these elements are missing, yet which could be regarded as readings of the definition. So, the following four options, with the 'plainest reading' first, divide the logical space of 'hearsay':

1. The witness explicitly tells the court that the third party has asserted that p, and she aims to persuade the court that p.

2. The witness explicitly tells the court that the third party has asserted that p but she does not aim to persuade the court that p. Perhaps she is just answering the counsel's question and does not herself believe p to be so.

3. The witness merely asserts that p, on the authority of the third party and her assertion that p, but makes no explicit reference in court to the third party's assertion. She does so believing that p and aiming to persuade the court that p.

4. As in (3) except that the witness does not aim to persuade the court that p, either because she is indifferent to the truth of p, or to the court's proceedings, or, more strangely, because she doesn't believe that p.

In all of the above circumstances, with the possible exception of (4), the witness may be lying, or otherwise seeking to deceive the court. We shall see, in our discussion of the proposed definition of formal testimony, that there are reasons for treating the defect of insincerity as insufficient grounds for saying that no testimony at all has been given. Whilst adhering to this, we may none the less conclude that the false testimony which consists in inventing an informant who never existed or concocting a message which was never given does not count as any form of *hearsay*. There is, however, an interesting type of deception which should count as hearsay, and which constitutes a variation on categories (1) and (3). This is where the witness truthfully reports what another has said, either explicitly or by an endorsing assertion of her own, and aims to persuade the court, but doesn't in fact believe that p is true. I think that this form of deceptive testimony should count as hearsay since there is a third party's message which is intended by the witness to be reliably conveyed to the court. The witness thinks it unreliable, and intends to turn this to her advantage, but a chain of communication has at least been begun or continued, and it may well prove reliable in spite of the present witness's assessment. This point has some relevance to our proceedings in Chapter 11.

As for categories (2) and (4), the fact that the witness has no interest in establishing the truth of p does not disqualify them from being readings of the definition if we allow the purpose in question to be that of the court or of the examining lawyers. It is not entirely clear whether the definition envisages this, but it should, since (2) at least is a pretty common phenomenon. Case (4), however, is bound to be less common since the witness who says 'I was born in 1945' or 'My grandmother came to this country from England' or even 'Arthur kept a gun in his flat', when she has this information from others (as is inevitable in the first utterance), must be understood as endorsing the truth of such propositions in a way that need not be involved when she makes it explicit that the 'information' comes from another. This element of commitment makes (4) queer, if not impossible, unless we construe 'persuade the court' in a stronger sense than I here intend. I mean only that the witness should have the degree of interest involved in presenting herself as believing that p, not that she should have some great stake in being believed.

The philosophical significance of this disambiguation exercise lies in the analysis of transmission chains and the importance they have for everyday knowledge, history, and the law. Further discussion of some aspects of this will be deferred until Chapter 11, but the fact that hearsay can mean the explicit presentation of a proposition as the word of another (which may be in a 'take it or leave it' spirit), or can involve the endorsement of the proposition and its presentation as what the speaker knows or believes, should be remembered in the discussions of hearsay later in this chapter.

Since formal testimony is a kind of evidence it must be addressed to some issue which is at least technically in dispute and, by way of corollary, one's audience (or at least the relevant part of it) must not themselves already be in a position of equal or superior authority on the matter. If a witness says, inconsequentially, that his mother-in-law frequently makes bad puns, then, true and interesting as this might be, it is not testimony unless it is relevant to the case being tried. Nor would he be testifying if he were to say 'I am wearing a blue suit' before a jury of sighted people although they may be pleased to hear him testify that it is the same blue suit that he was wearing on the day of the robbery. It may of course happen that the audience is not as much in need of evidence as is standardly presumed. One of the judges or jurors may happen to know some or all of the facts, indeed he may be the culprit, but this would be an unfortunate accident and the legal system is obviously constructed on the assumption that such a situation does not obtain. The general point is neatly made by Hobbes: 'For no man is a witness to him that already believeth, and therefore needs no witness; but to them that deny or doubt, or have not heard it.'[6]

There is, however, a serious difficulty for the stipulation if it is put in terms of inferior audience authority. This is created by the possibility, and in general desirability, of corroborated testimony. If four witnesses to some event, which is important to the determination of the ultimate issue,

---

[6] Thomas Hobbes, *Leviathan*, ed. M. Oakeshott (New York, 1962), ch. 42, p. 366.

are called by the court and all give similar testimony then the jury ('the audience') may be in as good, or better, an evidentiary position as the fourth witness by the time he comes to testify. Let us suppose that there is no reason to doubt the reliability or honesty of any of the witnesses. It is hard to see how the stipulation can be defended once we admit, as we must, that corroboration can increase the credibility of what is reported.[7]

One response to the difficulty might be to drive a wedge between degree of confidence or certainty and authority. It might be said that the jury can be rightly confident that *p* to a high degree after hearing the first three witnesses but that, even where the fourth witness is less confident than they, he has an authority to assert that *p* which the jury lacks because he is a witness and they are not. I think that this line of reply has too many costs. It would mean that the witness (or, as I would prefer, the primary witness) is unable to pass on to others the epistemic authority he has to speak to and stand by the reported facts. This would seem to make nonsense of the realities of transmission of information to which we referred in Chapter 1 and which will concern us in later chapters, especially Chapter 11. It may indeed be argued that later informants in a single chain of testimony can never be as authoritative as the primary witness; I argue in Chapter 11 that this natural view is mistaken but, even were it true, there can be no plausibility to the idea that the legitimate increase in confidence that *p* which the recipient of transmitted testimony gains brings with it no authority at all to assert that *p*. In ordinary (non-formal) contexts anyone who learns that *p* from a reliable witness is thereby equipped with the credentials to carry forward the process of witnessing to the truth of *p*. Moreover, if someone learns that *p* from several reliable and independent primary witnesses he surely can become even more authoritative on the proposition than any one of them. Of course, in the context of formal proceedings, we can hardly call upon the jury to *give* evidence but this is not because they lack epistemic authority; it is because of their role. They are there to assess the evidence, not to give it. Nevertheless they exercise the epistemic authority they have gained when they come to give their verdict.

The problem is a vexing one but a solution should begin by noticing that, for formal testimony, we may legitimately allow for a certain amount of epistemic 'overkill' in the interests of both justice and the requirements of general procedure. It may well be that some given jury has all the evidence it requires on some matter, so that further corroboration is indeed idle to the point of not really being testimony for that audience, but we are loath to assume that all juries will have the same saturation level and reluctant to restrict the rights of the parties to call evidence. We therefore have reason to avoid rules like, 'The defence may call no more

---

[7] I am grateful to Andrew Alexandra for pointing out this difficulty.

than three witnesses to corroborate a point at issue', though it may be clear, in context, that further depositions to the same fact are unnecessary. Furthermore, the equal authority stipulation was introduced as a corollary to the idea that testimony must be relevant to an issue in dispute but we can now see that the issue may still be in dispute or somehow open even where the audience is in as good or better position to know than the witness. There is at least the possibility of a separation in some circumstances between two elements run together in the quotation from Hobbes; being in real doubt or ignorance can be seen as the most common, but not the only, circumstance in which a witness is necessary or useful. A report may be epistemically valuable to the resolution of a dispute where, taken in conjunction with other reports, it increases the level of confidence an audience has in the reported proposition, even if the audience is already legitimately more confident about the matter (on the basis of the prior reports) than the individual witness. Clearly, this sort of consideration will be particularly important when an audience is required to reach a high level of confidence, such as in the criminal law's standard of 'beyond reasonable doubt'.

There is also the fact that no matter how convinced an audience is that p there remains a general epistemic possibility that counter-evidence may arise to shake this conviction. If we think that our conviction amounts to knowledge this will have an air of paradox about it; if A knows that p then this seems to imply that no such genuine counter-evidence can exist and even, perhaps, that this is something he knows.[8] Its relevance here is simply that an audience may take it that a dispute no longer exists, a question is no longer open, and that they have legitimate certainty that p, yet be alive to the possibility that a further witness may cause the question to be re-opened and their certainty to diminish or disappear. It may be appropriate to allow procedural space for such a possibility, especially when we do not always know in advance that a witness will corroborate rather than disconfirm. In view of these considerations it is better not to insist on the equal authority stipulation. We shall say, instead, that the audience must be in need of evidence on the question; this will often mean lesser authority but not always.

A further requirement of formal testimony is that a witness be properly called and sworn in or in some other way be given status in the inquiry. If someone from the back of the court shouts that he saw the defendant fire the fatal bullet this could hardly be reported in the newspapers as a piece of testimony in the case, however true it might be.

So far we have the following marks of formal testimony:

(*a*) It is a form of evidence.

---

[8] For some discussion of this interesting issue see G. Harman, *Thought* (Princeton, NJ. 1973), 148–9.

(b) It is constituted by persons *A* offering their remarks *as* evidence so that we are invited to accept *p* because *A* says that *p*.

(c) The person offering the remarks is in a position to do so, i.e. he has the relevant authority, competence, or credentials.

(d) The testifier has been given a certain status in the inquiry by being formally acknowledged as a witness and by giving his evidence with due ceremony.

(e) As a specification of (c) within English law and proceedings influenced by it, the testimony is normally required to be firsthand (i.e. not hearsay).

(f) As a corollary of (a) the testifier's remarks should be relevant to a disputed or unresolved question and should be directed to those who are in need of evidence on the matter.

There are two ways in which this list might be extended but I shall argue that neither has sufficient claim for inclusion. Let us consider (g) the question of credit. Obviously someone can bear false witness against another, where this does not mean that he can merely be mistaken but that he can lie or be otherwise insincere (for example, by not telling the whole truth). In Austin's terminology such situations are *abuses* of testimony rather than *misfires*, for we are not inclined to say that the perjurer has not testified at all.[9] And in general this seems to be true no matter how much a person's credit may be destroyed.[10] Of course there may be cases of overlap, particularly with credit and competence, since a witness's lack of credit may involve lack of competence, as when his deceitful testimony involves laying claim to credentials he doesn't possess. There will also be borderline cases between lack of credit and lack of competence, for

---

[9] Cf. Austin, *Words*, 14–18.

[10] Yet there may be some pressure to say that no testimony has been given. Cross (*Evidence*, 221) quotes Justice Scrutton as follows: 'If by cross-examination as to credit you prove that a man's oath cannot be relied on, and he has sworn he did not go to Rome on May 1st, you do not, therefore, prove that he did go to Rome on May 1st; there is simply no evidence on the subject.' Here Scrutton seems to be saying that where credit is shown to be lacking then the testimony in question simply does not exist. Scrutton is of course concerned with the intricacies of the distinction between cross-examination as to credit and cross-examination as to fact, but where proof that 'a man's oath cannot be relied on' means showing that he is lying or probably lying then Scrutton's position seems unduly paradoxical. To see this we need to realize that the term 'evidence' is often subject to ambiguity between what really supports a conclusion and what is before an inquiry or an inquirer as supportive of a conclusion or contributive to the resolution of some issue. In the second sense we can speak of a man's evidence as worthless not only because it is known (or believed) to be insincere but also because it is known (or believed) to be mistaken, and in the latter case it would surely be perverse to deny that it is evidence at all. Indeed, if it is at least part of the definition of perjury that it is 'the deliberate giving of false evidence', Scrutton's position would guarantee that, if cross-examination had shown a witness to be lying, then he could not have committed perjury. It is probable that Scrutton was merely concerned with the possibility that a jury would make the wrong inference from having decided that an admitted piece of testimony was bad evidence. Having decided to ignore *A*'s evidence that he did not go to Rome on 1 May we would be wrong to conclude *merely from that* that he did go to Rome on 1 May.

instance, with witnesses who are engaged in self-deception (for example, Jones is very confident that he saw Smith, a black man, running away from the scene of the crime, *but* Jones is proved to have been much further away from the scene than he believes and the light to have been dimmer than he believes and he is known to be anxious to appear as a key witness in a court case and to be anti-black...).

Yet it seems as if, in general, condition (*g*) should be listed separately from the marks of formal testimony given above. The complications it creates have parallels in a great many other speech acts and concern what Searle has called 'the sincerity condition' in the definition of speech acts. The point is that the elucidation of most speech acts requires reference to a certain assumption of utterer sincerity even though it is perfectly possible to encounter instances of the speech acts in which the condition goes unfulfilled, for example, a statement which the utterer does not believe or a promise that he does not intend to keep. None the less, for many speech acts such as promising and stating it is an important part of understanding what they are to realize that sincerity is the norm. Whether this sort of sincerity requirement is best elaborated in the long run as a fact about specified speech acts or as some general maxim of conversation (in the way suggested by Grice) is a matter of some importance which cannot be our concern here. An answer along Gricean lines would make it clearer that there is no need to include a reference to credit in our definition of testimony, either formal or natural, but if we think of the sincerity condition in a Searlean way as attaching specifically to speech acts then we must at least see it as a different sort of condition from the others given in list (*a*) to (*f*).

The other way in which it might be thought desirable to extend the list concerns (*h*), the matter of corroboration. Corroboration has an important role in the assessment of testimony but in modern English law uncorroborated testimony is perfectly acceptable as evidence, except for some categories of witness (such as unsworn children). This was not always so in English law nor is it so today in Scottish law and canon law where the tradition of Roman law is strong and the maxim *testis unis, testis nullus* is the rule. I am not sure how the situation in Continental law should be described since I understand that the notion of admissibility of evidence is so different as hardly to bear comparison but certainly some Continental philosophers who make reference to the law when discussing testimony do think in terms of the Latin maxim.[11] Since my notion of formal testimony is taking its cue from the English law I shall take this as sufficient reason to exclude corroboration from my definitional list. Lest this be thought

[11] It is interesting that at least one such philosopher, Alphonse de Waelhens in an article entitled 'Ambiguïté de la notion de temoignage: La testimonianza', *Archivio di filosofia* (Padua, 1972), 467–77, has tried to develop two senses of testimony, one of which is defined largely by reference to the Latin maxim.

excessively (and perhaps characteristically) parochial of an 'English' philosopher I shall invoke at this point a further reason which seems to me intrinsically persuasive and in addition has the authoritative backing of Napoleon. The restriction of a corroboration requirement, Napoleon is said to have observed, would lead to a situation where, 'The testimony of one honourable man could not prove a single rascal guilty although the testimony of two rascals could prove an honourable man guilty'.[12]

We may take it, then, that our list (*a*) to (*f*) is complete but some points of clarification are still needed. To begin with, there is an ambiguity in (*f*) with regard to the way in which testimony can be directed to an issue and this gives rise to another way in which testimony may be disregarded.

A's testimony that he saw *B* raise a revolver and fire three shots through *C*'s window is addressed in the first place to the issue of what *B* was doing at such and such a time and place—it is first and foremost evidence that *B* did raise a revolver, etc. It is also addressed, more importantly perhaps, to the issue whether *B* murdered *C* and as such *A*'s testimony may fail or be inconclusive (for example, if it were shown that *C* had died three hours before the time of the shooting); and this is so even if what *A* says is good testimony and true. Consequently, formal testimony can be, and indeed usually is, addressed to a remote as well as an immediate issue but the connection between what the witness says and this remote issue will not always be what the witness intends it to be. Even if a man's testimony does not fail or is not inconclusive it may decide the remote issue in unexpected ways. It is also possible for the immediate and remote issues to coincide, as when the defendant testifies that he did not do what he is accused of.

With regard to (*c*), the question of competence or authority to speak is obviously important, though very complex. Credentials for testimony appear to include at some point some kind of direct acquaintance or observation, though this requirement will look very different in different circumstances; for example, someone's testimony that they saw *A* doing something will contrast with expert testimony that the odds against someone's dying from a certain disease are such and such, where the latter is based upon acquaintance or, rather, thoroughgoing familiarity with some area of medicine and, perhaps, statistics. With this must go certain skills, abilities, or expertise which are required for or involved in the relevant acquaintance. Most of us most of the time have the relevant abilities for the majority of situations in which anyone is likely to require our testimony, but it is obvious enough how testimony can be destroyed by the demonstration of the witness's poor eyesight or deafness or by proof that the object reported on was too far away for someone with only normal eyesight to see clearly. Some testimony, however, requires technical knowledge and expertise. Furthermore, even the normal competence can be

---

[12] Cross, *Evidence*, 163.

lacking and this is why madmen and very young children are regarded by the law as poor or even incapable witnesses. It is doubtful whether the insane can be relied on to distinguish fantasy and delusion from reality, and as regards credit we may have difficulty raising the question of sincerity with those of whom it can be said that in some degree they frequently do not know what they are doing. For this reason an inquiry into allegations of malpractice in a mental hospital faces great difficulty. I once attended such an inquiry where the presiding judge was even at a loss to know what to make of the testimony of ex-patients. Most behaved so strangely on the stand that their credit and competence were entirely ruined.

The case with young children is different again. It is partly that we may be unsure of their ability to distinguish fantasy and reality or to be even normally good at reidentifying faces, but partly that they may not understand the whole context of the testimony situation and may not realize the importance of telling the truth. They are also very likely to be even more intimidated by the formal, interrogatory context of court proceedings than adults. There is a connection here with our previous discussion of sincerity. I argued against the inclusion of a credit condition in our definition of formal testimony but the cases of the insane and the very immature suggest that *a capacity for sincerity* might very well be part of the credentials we require under condition (*c*). Such doubts about the normal presumptions of competence are expressed in English law by the requirement that children and the insane cannot give evidence unless the judge is satisfied that they understand the nature of the oath, although in criminal law a child 'of tender years' may give unsworn evidence if the judge is satisfied that the child understands his duty to tell the truth. There can, however, be no conviction on a child's unsworn evidence unless it has been corroborated and with a child's sworn evidence the judge is required by law to warn the jury of the danger of non-corroboration. Curiously, there is no such strict obligation with the testimony of the insane.[13]

I do not mean to suggest that there are no difficulties with the way the English criminal law treats the evidence of such categories of witness. In particular, interesting questions have been raised in recent years about the treatment of the evidence of young children, largely because of community alarm at the incidence of incest and other forms of child abuse. One need not be persuaded that child abuse is as universal as often claimed to sympathize with the idea that a child's evidence should be treated more generously and flexibly than the law at present allows. Some of the pro-

---

[13] Cf. R. Cross and P. A. Jones, *An Introduction to Criminal Law*, 4th ed. (London, 1959), 411–17. It is a further curiosity in this area that a child's otherwise dubious evidence may be acceptable because it has been corroborated by another child whose own testimony stands in need of corroboration. Cf. House of Lords decision in *DPP* v. *Kilbourne*, reported in *The Times Law Report*, 2 Feb. 1973.

posals for using specially trained interviewers, videotapes, and out-of-court settings for the eliciting of a child's testimony have considerable merit, as long as they do not eliminate altogether the defendant's right to (non-bullying) cross-examination. Yet common sense and the best psychological evidence seem to indicate that young children are, on the whole, less reliable witnesses than adults, and their testimony needs to be treated with some caution.[14] The traditional rules reflect this, though it may well be argued that they go too far, especially in the very strong requirements for corroboration.

I have been discussing competence to testify as this is embodied in English law and I think it is plain enough what I mean by the term 'competence', and that, so understood, it enters into the definition of formal testimony. None the less, 'competence' is itself a technical term in the law of evidence and in textbooks on evidence would not concern such matters as normal sensory capacities or special technical skills and would encompass other matters that hardly seem germane to my discussion above. There would be a considerable overlap with my treatment in, for instance, the discussion of restrictions on the evidence of children and the mentally defective, but the areas of difference need some attention.

In the first place, the lack of textbook analysis, under the heading of 'competence', of such obvious disqualifications from competence as sensory defect or inexpertise (where relevant) does not mean that such factors are not defects in competence to testify. In a textbook discussion of the circumstances under which expert evidence is admissible, for instance, one naturally finds reference to the way in which lack of relevant expertise disqualifies evidence from admission,[15] and where what is at issue is a non-technical question such as what a witness *saw* then it is surely clear that he would need to be sighted in order to be allowed to testify—although as a matter of practice such a question would hardly ever arise since such incompetence is obvious.

Secondly, questions that I have not discussed under the title of competence and which do get discussed under that heading in the law of evidence concern such things as the incompetence of an accused's spouse to testify against him or her and the incompetence of the accused to testify for the prosecution—subject in both cases of course, to complication, modification, and exception. The rationale of such disqualifications is far from clear but it appears to have little to do with such clear grounds of incompetence as, for instance, inability to understand the requirement to tell the truth. It is tempting to see here a connection with the past for English law long ruled as incompetent non-Christians, 'infamous' convicts,

---

[14] The best discussion I know of this issue is Donald Thomson's 'A Matter of Justice: Protecting the Rights of the Victim and the Accused in Child Sexual Abuse Cases', Seminar on 'Children as Witnesses', 19 Aug. 1988, Leo Cussen Institute, Melbourne.

[15] Cf. Cross, *Evidence*, 364–6.

persons with a pecuniary or proprietary interest in the outcome of proceedings, and parties to the proceedings. Indeed, under this last heading an
accused could not even testify on his own behalf. It is easy to see 'reasons'
why we might want to treat the evidence of such categories of person with
caution but harder to see why it should have been excluded altogether
from consideration. Perhaps some link with the idea of incompetence as I
have been using it may be available via the idea that non-Christians and
those convicted of infamous crimes had beliefs or a style of life which
made it impossible even to begin to take them seriously as acting from a
desire or duty to tell the truth or to credit their taking of the oath; parties,
their spouses, and persons with an interest may well have been thought to
have so powerful a self-interest as to be somewhat similarly beyond the
pale. Perhaps it would be possible to view the surviving restrictions on
spouses and defendants in a similar light, with the consequence, for good
or ill, that they should be treated as anachronisms. Of course, reasons
quite external to the formal conditions of valid testimony are adduced in
support of retaining these survivors (such as the need to preserve marital
peace). These need not concern us here, although it is perhaps worth
remarking that they seem to bear more relevance to questions of com-
pellability than competence.

Natural Testimony

Although the discussion of formal testimony has had, I hope, some intrinsic interest, in the context of our investigation its point is primarily to
prepare the way for an account of natural testimony. This latter phenomenon is to be encountered in such everyday circumstances as exhibit the
'social operations of mind': giving someone directions to the post office,
reporting what happened in an accident, saying that, yes, you have seen a
child answering to that description, telling someone the result of the last
race or the latest cricket score. In all such situations we have a speaker
engaged in the speech act of testifying to the truth of some proposition
which is either in dispute or in some way in need of determination and his
attestation is evidence towards the settling of the matter. Here we seem to
have a clear parallel with conditions (*a*), (*b*), and (*f*) of formal testimony.
The position is not, however, so clear with conditions (*c*), (*d*), and (*e*).
Certainly requirement (*c*) seems to carry over in some form to natural
testimony but the hearsay specification (*e*) does not. That is to say, in
ordinary life as in the lawcourts we will not treat just anybody at all as a
witness but we do not require natural testimony to be firsthand. Most of
the reports we unhesitatingly and rightly accept about race results, football
results and attendances, parliamentary happenings, and many geographical
facts are far from firsthand, and if this is thought suprising or in some way

discreditable it may help dispel the surprise or scepticism to look again at the role of the hearsay restriction in English law. The fact of the matter is that the hearsay prohibition is by no means absolute even within English law, not to mention its absence from other codes, such as Scottish law and much of Continental law. Since the passing of the Civil Evidence Act of 1968, hearsay evidence is now admissible (with some marginal restrictions) in the English civil law. Moreover, the exceptions to the rule, in the English criminal law, are numerous and wide-ranging, although the principles (if any) underlying them are quite unclear.[16] The major categories of exception in common law concern: (1) certain types of statements of persons now deceased such as, in certain circumstances, dying declarations against interest; (2) statements in public documents such as birth certificates; (3) admissions and confessions of the parties in a case; (4) a miscellaneous group including testimony to age (which is of course always hearsay) and evidence of reputation; (5) the rule of *res gestae* whereby a third person's statement may be received because it either accompanied and explained a relevant act or was contemporaneous with and directly concerned an event in issue or concerned the utterer's contemporaneous state of mind or emotion or physical sensation.[17] It is perhaps worth pausing to note some curious aspects of these exceptions.

As regards dying declarations the rationale seems to involve the idea that no one would want to die with a lie on his lips and this was no doubt strongly reinforced by the belief in an afterlife involving judgement and possible severe punishment. It has, for instance, been held that the exception has no application to the natives of Papua and New Guinea where the afterlife is believed to be spent in comfort on a neighbouring island and there is no sanction against lying when at the point of death. (I do not claim that this is true of Papuans and New Guineans, only that English judges thought it true.)[18]

The famous Bedingfield case is especially interesting for the *res gestae* category. Henry Bedingfield was accused of murder by cutting a woman's throat in the city of Ipswich in 1879 and his defence was that she had committed suicide after attempting to kill him. The woman, her throat badly gashed, came out of a room in which the accused was subsequently found and called out to two other women, 'See what Harry has done'.

She died shortly afterwards but the judge would not allow the report of her statement in evidence because it was not contemporaneous with the act and so not covered by *res gestae* (although if she had called out 'Don't Harry!' at the time and had been overheard it would have been admissible). The statement was also inadmissible as a dying declaration on

[16] The hearsay rule and its exceptions will be discussed more fully in Ch. 11.
[17] See Cross, *Evidence*, and R. Eggleston, *Evidence, Proof and Probability* (London, 1983), 45–54.
[18] Cf. Cross, *Evidence*, 419.

the grounds that she did not have 'a settled, hopeless expectation of death'.[19] Ironically, Bedingfield was convicted and hanged partly because, as Chief Justice Cockburn pointed out in summing up to the jury, the fact that it was the woman and not Bedingfield who ran out 'as though to make outcry or complaint' counted against his story that she had first cut his throat and then her own. It is surely bizarre that her saying something or other should carry such weight when what she said was inadmissible. What if she had said, 'I've done for both of us!'? In all fairness it should be added that there were other powerful circumstantial evidences against Bedingfield (as, for example, that the woman's throat wound was too severe to have been self-inflicted), and that Cockburn's exclusion of the statement was condemned at the time by a number of eminent lawyers.

The hearsay rule, then, is a somewhat curious restriction within English law and there have been serious and respectable voices raised in favour of its reform and even abolition. We should not be surprised to find that our definition of natural testimony need make no reference to it. Of course, it may be that in the *assessment* of natural testimony we should treat first-hand testimony with more respect than hearsay, whilst not excluding hearsay altogether. As a rule of assessment this has some plausibility but even here we should proceed with caution. There is a certain parallel with the matter of corroboration, discussed earlier. It is nice to have corroboration and it is nice to have firsthand testimony but their importance cannot be such as to rule out the possibility of uncorroborated testimony being preferred in particular circumstances to the contrary corroborated testimony and hearsay being preferred in particular circumstances to the firsthand testimony.[20] Both possibilities are primarily geared to situations in which the corroborated or firsthand testimonies are (or are believed to be) deceitful, but they may arise where the corroborated or firsthand testimonies are (or are believed to be) merely mistaken.

It may be that *if* there is some general superiority of firsthand over hearsay testimony it resides in the methodological claim made by John Locke[21] that testimony becomes progressively weaker in evidential value as it passes from one hand to another. This view of Locke's is very interesting and will be fully discussed later but it is perhaps worth noting at this point that such a consideration as Locke's does not seem to lie

---

[19] This phrase is actually Cross's version of what the law regards as a condition for the acceptance of a dying declaration (cf. 419). The judge in *R. v. Bedingfield*, Chief Justice Cockburn, was content to record his conviction that 'it did not appear that the woman was aware that she was dying'. For this and other details of the case see (1879) 14 Cox CC, pp. 341–5.

[20] As Thomas Reid puts it, 'In a matter of testimony, it is self-evident that the testimony of two is better than that of one, supposing them equal in character, and in their means of knowledge; yet the single testimony may be true, and that which is preferred to it may be false': *Intellectual Powers*, in *Phil. Works*, essay VI, ch. iv, p. 435.

[21] John Locke, *Essay Concerning Human Understanding*, ed. J. W. Yolton (London, 1961), bk. IV, ch. xvi, ss. 10 and 11. For a full discussion of this see Ch. 11.

behind the hearsay restriction in English law which seems rather to be based on the desire to have all admissible evidence properly sworn and subject to direct cross-examination.[22]

But if the hearsay specification of competence or authority to testify must be abandoned can we not insist that condition (c) requires, at any rate, that someone has had firsthand acquaintance with the fact reported and that the present reporter is connected to that someone by a sort of chain of reports. This seems plausible but the notion of acquaintance to be employed here will have to be very flexible; simple observation will not do since there seem to be many cases of testimony to facts which are not prima facie observational at all. For instance, a person's avowals of his psychological states have a reasonable claim to the title of testimony but it is doubtful that what he reports is something that he observes. There also seems to be a case for speaking of testimony in such areas as mathematics, for example, when a teacher tells a learner the fact that between any number and its double there exists at least one prime.[23] And again, we rightly believe many general empirical propositions on the evidence of testimony, although it is arguable that general facts are not observed at all.

A second kind of problem concerns reports of particular facts of the sort which appear to favour the present suggestion: there are many cases in which the attested fact, said to be ultimately 'a matter of observation for somebody', seems to be no such thing. Two examples may make this clearer. A tells B that there were 70,284 people at a certain football match. B asks for the source of this testimony and A produces a newspaper report. Unsatisfied, B goes to see the reporter who wrote the story who refers him to the club secretary, who refers him to the written report of the head gatekeeper. When confronted, the head gatekeeper admits that he did not watch the match or the crowd, although he was at the ground, nor did he have any deputy who either observed the whole crowd or counted it. It turns out that more than one hundred different gatekeepers observed different segments of the crowd enter the ground and observed different machines registering their numbers. Their separate tallies were added up by the head gatekeeper. Surely the fact of 70,284 people attending the game is no matter of simple observation for him, or for anyone else, although he can rightly testify to it. Or to take a different case, uncontaminated by numbers, A tells B that Russian sailors marched through Melbourne in a parade just a few hours before. He says he was

---

[22] This conclusion is reached both by Cross (*Evidence*) and by Glanville Williams in *The Proof of Guilt*, 3rd edn. (London, 1963), cf. 195–213.

[23] Bernard Williams, however, claims that one would only know in such circumstances that the proposition in question was a mathematical truth and that this would not amount to knowing that the proposition was true. A. J. Ayer agrees with him. See B. A. O. Williams, 'Knowledge and Reasons', and Ayer's 'Comments', in G. H. von Wright (ed.), *Problems in the Theory of Knowledge* (The Hague, 1972). I shall discuss this issue in Ch. 14.

told by C who, when asked, says that he saw the parade. This case seems tailor-made for the present suggestion but it must be stressed that C's observation *that the marchers were Russian sailors* is grounded on testimony and inference in a way that (or to a degree that) his observation that they wore clothes of a certain colour is not. Or again, A tells B truly that C is D's natural brother. Is this a fact that could be traced back through a chain of testimony to some individual's original observation that C is D's natural brother?

So much then for (c) and (e) but a word is now needed about (d) because natural testimony does not require the paraphernalia of oaths, witness-boxes, and so on. The point of condition (d) in legal and quasi-legal settings is such that one would expect this condition to be absent or less prominent in daily life. We insist upon condition (d) in lawsuits because, in the highly artificial setting of a court, we require a good deal of formality in order to be in a position to determine competence and credit. In more familiar surroundings and often with less weighty issues at stake these do not need to be tested, for either they are already well-enough determined or there can be no harm in assuming them. We will, of course, sometimes seek solemn assurances in order to determine the credentials and/or credit of witnesses in everyday life.

So we may take it that the conventions governing the speech act of testifying ('natural testimony') are specifiable as follows:

A speaker S testifies by making some statement p if and only if:

(1) His stating that p is evidence that p and is offered as evidence that p.
(2) S has the relevant competence, authority, or credentials to state truly that p.
(3) S's statement that p is relevant to some disputed or unresolved question (which may, or may not be, p?) and is directed to those who are in need of evidence on the matter.

But if this, or something like this, gives us a definition of natural testimony, considered as a speech act, there is still more to be said about the idea of testimony. To begin with, we must clarify the notion of evidence employed in the definition of natural (and earlier, formal) testimony, and address some questions that thereby arise about the relations between clauses (1), (2), and (3).

The idea that the speaker is not just offering some statement as evidence but that it *is* evidence (as (1) claims) is carried over from the definition of formal testimony, but this transition requires clarification, if not justification, since in legal or quasi-legal contexts the classification of utterances into different sorts of categories is a formal matter dictated by court protocol. Testimony is classified as evidence by contrast with the defence counsel's final address to the jury or the judge's summing up. This explicit procedural background is lacking in the case of natural testimony, but, none the less, the formal dignity attributed in the more ceremonial context arises from certain facts about the status of natural testimony, including contrasts between speech acts of different types.

Natural testimony falls into a category of evidence in something like the way promising, for instance, falls into the category of commitment. One who testifies must be seen as providing evidence for the truth of the relevant proposition p, just as one who promises must be seen as making a commitment to bring the relevant p state of affairs about. We might say that both are cases in which a speaker vouches for p but in different ways. By testifying that p one vouches for an ascertained connection between how one says things are and how they are actually. By promising that p one vouches for bringing about such a connection by changing how things are. (I do not mean this sort of phraseology to commit me to any strong version of a correspondence theory of truth. It could be rephrased more simply in terms of the truth of p.) People are entitled to base their beliefs on the reliability of the former and their actions on the reliability of the latter—though this is to put it too tersely since both reliabilities will sustain actions and beliefs. Condoling, by contrast, is a speech act which falls neither within the evidentiary category nor that of commitment. Its point is expressive and sympathetic. In saying these sorts of things about the speech act of natural testifying, I am contributing towards the elucidation of what Searle has called the 'illocutionary point' of such an act, and also towards a characterization of its 'mode of achievement' of that point.[24] Asserting, testifying, objecting, and arguing all have the same or similar illocutionary points—roughly, to inform an audience that something is the case—but they differ in other illocutionary respects. In the case of testifying, of either the formal or informal variety, the way of achieving the point is through the speaker's status as one having a particular kind of authority to speak to the matter in question, a matter where evidence is required. By contrast, the arguer that p must be seen as presenting the information that p for acceptance on the basis of its following from certain other propositions presented, quite independently of any status he or she may have as a witness. Assertion is, I think, different again, in that it is a more generic speech act. One who argues or testifies or objects thereby asserts, but the specific form of assertion is different in each case.[25] Searlian theory is useful for making these points, but, here as elsewhere, I

---

[24] These and other related distinctions are outlined most fully in J. R. Searle and Daniel Vanderveken, *Foundations of Illocutionary Logic* (Cambridge, 1985). See esp. 12–20 for an informal presentation of some of these distinctions. Searle has discussed these matters in other writings most notably in *Expression and Meaning* (Cambridge, 1979).

[25] There is some temptation to treat assertion as a specific speech act on a level with the others when we use the term to indicate the very emphatic presentation of a piece of information. Here its illocutionary *differentia* involve matters to do with degree of commitment to the proposition vouched for—rather like what Searlian theory calls 'degree of strength' of illocutionary point.

want to remain agnostic on the question of how fundamental speech-act categories are; it will not affect what I have to say if a more basic analysis of the illocutionary is available in terms of, say, complex speakers' intentions and associated conceptual paraphernalia.

None of this is to suggest that the concept of evidence employed in our definition is wholly unproblematic. Problems arise from several different directions. First, there is the obvious fact that particular pieces of testimony do not establish the truth of p when p is actually false. Should such claims not deserve the title of testimony or does this show that testimony is not evidence? Surely it is better to say that they are testimony and evidence, but this commits us to a concept of evidence such that e can be evidence for h even where h is, as it happens, false. That we do commonly use the term evidence in this way can hardly be denied. Suppose someone in Chicago is asked what the time is and, not having his own watch handy, he consults his wife's and says 3 p.m., not realizing that she has not yet reset it after a trip to New York. When the recipient of the misinformation complains of missing an important appointment, the informant is in a different position from someone who simply made an irresponsible guess. Unlike the guesser, he had and can provide evidence for what he said. We might try to drive a wedge between p's being someone's evidence that q and p's actually being evidence that q but I do not think that this is an attractive option. The temptation to do so arises from the fact that we sometimes operate with the idea of evidence in such a way that e cannot be evidence for h unless h is true. Achinstein, in an interesting discussion of evidence, calls this sense 'veridical evidence' and distinguishes it from 'potential evidence'. His account of the latter is nearer to the way in which I wish to use the term 'evidence'. So, to adapt one of his examples, Jones's yellow skin is (potential) evidence that he has jaundice, even if, in fact, he has some other rare disease instead which also produces just such a skin colouration.[26]

It is an interesting question just what sort of conditions a philosophical analysis of potential evidence should specify. Achinstein provides a complex analysis in terms of both probability and explanatory conditions but, since a thoroughgoing account of the nature of evidence at large is beyond the scope of this inquiry, I shall not discuss its adequacy.[27] Something along the lines of his account seems plausible and the fundamental idea that may be adapted to our purposes here, shorn of technicalities and applied to testimony, is that speakers who offer their remarks as evidence for some proposition are rightly regarded as having provided such evidence, even in cases where the proposition is false, given that certain

---

[26] See P. Achinstein, 'Concepts of Evidence', *Mind*, 87 (1978), esp. 22–45.
[27] See Achinstein, 'Concepts', esp. 35, for the analysis of potential evidence. Achinstein further discusses such matters in *The Nature of Explanation* (Oxford, 1983).

conditions are fulfilled which in general make the offering of such remarks conform to probability and explanatory conditions such as those spelt out by Achinstein. (Or if these are unsatisfactory, whatever better ones 'save the phenomena'.)

Of course, the definition cannot show that such conditions are indeed widely satisfied by the utterances we regard as testimony. The definition incorporates the view that the appropriate probabilistic and perhaps explanatory conditions are widely satisfied and this view is clearly part of the thinking that we as a community embody in such a term as testimony. But we should not imagine that there are no problems about what under-pins this view; indeed, a good deal of the present work will be devoted to examining just such problems.

There is, however, a question that needs to be settled at once about the relations between clause (1) and clauses (2) and (3) of the definition. Given that clause (1) claims that the speaker's stating that p is not only offered as evidence but is evidence that p, then we might suspect that clauses (2) and (3) are not *additional* conditions that an utterance has to satisfy but are merely amplifications of what it means for a speaker's utterance that p to provide evidence for p. There is some justice in this suspicion in the case of (3) but I think that (2) is importantly different. Condition (3) is conjunc-tive and the first part may well be no more than an elucidation of what is involved in anything's being evidence at all. The second part, however, may not seem to be a condition on evidence in general since some state of affairs e may be evidence that s even where no one 'needs' evidence that s. Take, for instance, the case where e is certain muddy footprints being on the carpet, and s is John's having failed to wipe his boots before coming into the house. Even where John has confessed and no one needs evidence, we might still think that e is evidence that s. I doubt that this intuition is sound, but we do not need to settle the matter. Let us suppose that (3) is, strictly speaking, redundant. I propose to make light of this possibility because it is still useful to have explicit reference made to this requirement, in the context of testimony, whether it be a requirement on all evidence or not. Condition (2) is, however, quite another matter, amplifying what it is for the utterance to be evidence of the kind that testimony is, not merely what it is for a speaker's statement that p to be evidence for p (even where it is offered as such). Consider the case of Jones whom we know to have been hypnotized by a master criminal. The criminal has programmed the unsuspecting Jones to state that the criminal's arch-rival is hiding out at a certain address and to do so with conviction in the expectation that his word will be believed. When Jones blurts out the information, it is reason-able for us to take it as evidence for the arch-rival's hiding-place because we know of the hypnotism and of the master criminal's interest in having the information made available to us. But Jones is not testifying because condition (2) is not satisfied. He has no authority himself to vouch for p, as will become apparent if he is asked how he knows it. Perhaps the master criminal is testifying through him; this would depend upon whether the master criminal intends us to come to our conclusion, via the utterance, on the basis of recognizing his intention that we should so conclude as wholly overt. In the absence of some such Gricean intention, we should not, I think, be entitled to treat the master criminal as himself stating that *p*. In any case, Jones is not testifying even if he satisfies condition (1) and possibly (3), because he clearly does not satisfy (2).

I conclude, therefore, that clause (2) is not redundant and that it plays an important role in our understanding of the type of evidence that testimony is. We said earlier that testimony is the evidence of persons and (2) shows in a schematic way what it is about persons that makes this sort of evidence special. In the case of Jones we are making certain inferences from Jones's utterance which rely in no way upon Jones's trustworthiness; this contrasts with the testimony case where we are not just believing that *p* because of something or other about the witness's utterance but we are *believing the witness*. As Thomas Hobbes puts it:

When a man's discourse beginneth not at definitions, it beginneth either at some other contemplation of his own, and then it is still called opinion; or it beginneth at some saying of another, of whose ability to know the truth, and of whose honesty in not deceiving, he doubteth not; and then the discourse is not so much concerning the thing, as the person; and the resolution is called BELIEF, and FAITH: *faith, in* the man; *belief*, both *of* the man, and *of* the truth of what he says. So that in belief are two opinions; one of the saying of the man; the other of his virtue. To *have faith in*, or *trust to*, or *believe a man*, signify the same thing; namely, an opinion of the veracity of the man; but to *believe what is said*, signifieth only an opinion of the truth of the saying.[28]

Our definition of testimony naturally concentrates upon the speaker or testifier, and what it is about his or her performance that constitutes it testimony, but a full understanding of testimony would be incomplete without some explication of the characteristic part played by the hearer. As the quotation from Hobbes brings out clearly, the recipient of testimony is in a very different position from the person in our example who believes what Jones says. When we believe testimony we believe what is said because we trust the witness. This attitude of trust is very fundamental, but it is not blind. As Reid noted, the child begins with an attitude of complete trust in what it is told, and develops more critical attitudes as it matures.[29] None the less, even for adults, the critical attitude is itself founded upon a general stance of trust, just as the adult awareness of the way memory plays us false rests upon a broader confidence in recollective powers.

[28] Hobbes, *Leviathan*, ch. 7, p. 57.
[29] Thomas Reid, *Inquiry into the Human Mind*, VI. xxiv, in *Philosophical Works*, 197.

Contrary to what we are inclined, unreflectively, to suppose, the attitudes of critical appraisal and of trust are not diametrically opposed, though in particular cases, one cannot, in the same breath, both trust what a witness says and subject it to critical evaluation. What happens characteristically in the reception of testimony is that the audience operates a sort of learning mechanism which has certain critical capacities built into it. The mechanism may be thought of as partly innate, though modified by experience, especially in the matter of critical capacities. It is useful to invoke the model of a mechanism here since the reception of testimony is normally unreflective but is not thereby uncritical. We may have 'no reason to doubt' another's communication even where there is no question of our being gullible; we may simply recognize that the standard warning signs of deceit, confusion, or mistake are not present. This recognition incorporates our knowledge of the witness's competence, of the circumstances surrounding his utterance, of his honesty, of the consistency of the parts of his testimony, and its relation to what others have said, or not said, on the matter.[30] It may also incorporate some reference to the inherent likelihood of what is reported, though, as we shall see in Chapter 10, this is more problematic than it seems at first blush. It is important to appreciate the complex relation between trust and critical appraisal, not least because of its significance for the understanding of transmission chains (as will emerge in Chapter 11).

But we are not done with problems about the term 'evidence', for there are certain difficulties of a rather different kind which seem to be implied by treating testimony as a form of evidence. If someone has evidence for a proposition *p*, it may seem that she cannot thereby directly know that proposition. This thought is supported, and perhaps created, by the close association of evidence and inference. Yet there is a way of talking of evidence in which we speak readily and intelligibly about the evidence of the senses and the evidence of memory, for instance, without implying that all memory or perceptual knowledge must be 'evidential' in the sense of being indirect or inferred. Of course, there are many puzzles with the concept of direct knowledge, but, if the category makes any sense at all, then there are many instances where we 'just know' by memory or by sensing/perceiving. I just know, if I know it at all, that yesterday my car broke down in a busy street with me at the wheel, and I just know that this is my Georgian silver teapot on the table in front of me. Similarly, as I will argue in Chapter 8, I can just know that there is a visitor at the door when my wife tells me so, or that there was no business mail for me today when the departmental secretary tells me so. In one sense, my 'evidence' is the deliverance of memory, sense, or testimony in these cases, but, in

---

[30] There is an interesting, if slightly odd, discussion of these matters in Locke's *Essay Concerning Human Understanding*, bk. iv. ch. xv. My list overlaps his six 'considerations'.

another sense, I do not use evidence to come to a conclusion in the fashion characteristic of inference.

Extended Testimony

So much for evidence and its ramifications. Let me return to my promise, in the early part of this chapter, to compare the idea of testimony as the content of a speech act of testifying with other ways of talking about testimony that are more or less remote from that paradigm. There are four main points I want to make.

In the first place, our definition allows that the speaker's authority need not be firsthand, and may, indeed, be many stages removed from the primary witness (if there be only one). But we saw earlier that the presentation of hearsay may take several forms. To consider only the simple case of hearsay once removed, the present speaker (the S of our definition) may straightforwardly testify that there is no mail for the doctor today by using the sentence 'There is no mail for the doctor today'. But he may also explicitly advert to the hearsay nature of the communication by saying 'The doctor's secretary says that there is no mail for her today'. On our definition, the first utterance counts as testimony that there is no mail for the doctor today, whereas it would be natural to count the second as testimony that the doctor's secretary *said* that there is no mail for her today. Certainly, it is at least testimony to that, but the question arises whether it is also testimony to the more substantial issue of whether there was mail for her. The answer to this depends upon the context. My inclination is to say that it is testimony to the substantial issue where that is the issue the speaker intends to address and where the speaker means by the utterance to endorse the secretary's report. Very often the speaker will be indifferent between two such sentences, one mentioning his source and the other not, and he would respond with annoyance if his audience replied to the second by saying 'Yes, but is there?' Annoyance would be evoked by the fact that such a reply would commonly be a criticism of the speaker's endorsement of his informant's message and of his assessment of the informant's reliability. (This is important for our discussion of transmission chains in Chapter 11.) I am not, of course, denying that such criticisms may sometimes be warranted.

By contrast, a speaker may choose a less committed form of words specifically because they do not want to endorse the more substantial claim. Where Robert is a notoriously unreliable secretary, S's remark need strike no note of endorsement; it may merely report the secretary's statement, in a spirit of 'take it or leave it'.

What are the implications of this elucidation of hearsay for our definition of testimony? It is clear that S testifies that p (i.e. that there is no mail for the doctor today) in the first case, where that is what he literally says, and that he does not testify that p where he refrains from saying that p because he does not want to endorse his informant's testimony to him. But what of the intermediate case where (in terms made familiar by H. P. Grice) we might hold that he does not *say* that p but he certainly *means* that p (or means$_{nn}$ that p, in Grice's terminology)?[31] I do not think that we would find it natural to say that his meaning that p was merely a matter of suggesting or implying that p, either conversationally or conventionally, since the endorsement of p is more overt and 'up front' than that characterization would indicate. It is not unusual to perform a speech act of X-ing that p by using some form of words other than the explicit performative, 'I X that p', nor is it unusual to perform one speech act by using a form of words more appropriate to another. Consider, for example, a speaker who utters the sentence, 'Allow me to say that I repudiate your allegation'. Although this is couched in the form of a request (a request to utter a repudiation), it is actually the repudiation itself. Closer still to our intermediate case, we may make one request with a form of words appropriate to another, as when we say, 'May I ask you to speak to the motion' or 'May I ask you to leave', neither of which is really asking permission to make a further, substantive request but is actually therein doing the substantive requesting.

If what I have been calling the intermediate case counts as testifying that p, for the reasons given, then I think we should treat the speaker in such a case as having stated that p even if they have not (in a favoured theoretical sense) said that p. Their endorsement of the third party's statement that p puts them in the position of stating that p, whichever form of words they choose, as long as their intention to so state is contextually clear. The relevance of this to transmission will be brought out in Chapter 11, but we can at least now say that transmission or hearsay chains can be chains of testimony in two ways. The first, or as I shall call it, the pure case, is one in which each member of the chain testifies that p (i.e. each endorses the message); the second, or derivative case, is one in which some members of the chain do not testify that p but only that the third party has testified that p. This derivative case needs in turn to be distinguished from other types of communications, but I will defer this until Chapter 11.

My second point about ways of speaking of testimony that are to some degree removed from our definitional paradigm concerns the fact that it is

---

[31] See H. P. Grice, *Studies in the Way of Words* (Cambridge, Mass., 1989). Earlier influential papers by Grice on meaning are republished in this posthumous collection, along with some later reflections on the topic. On a Gricean analysis of meaning, it is plausible to see the speaker in the intermediate case as aiming to bring about the audience's belief that p, or belief that the speaker believes that p, via the operation of some complex mechanism of recognition of intentions, rather than merely 'letting the audience know' that a third party has said that p. My point here is not dependent upon acceptance of a Gricean analysis, but that analysis illustrates the point nicely.

common, in ordinary parlance and in philosophical discussions, to use the term 'testimony' of material which is not an obvious product of the sort of explicit speech act of testifying that we have been considering. I have in mind what might be called 'documentary testimony'. Historians and philosophers of history, for example, refer to such documents as church registries of births and deaths, private diaries, confidential diplomatic minutes, newspaper reports, and so on as testimony. In some of these cases we are not really very far from what we have been treating as paradigm testifying since the only difference lies in the original speaker's or writer's ignorance that he will be testifying to us. The newspaper reporter is testifying in our defined sense inasmuch as he is offering his word to a contemporary audience of his presumed readers and is aiming to relieve their presumed curiosity about contentious or 'news-worthy' issues. He may not intend to be testifying to future historians but, inasmuch as he is testifying 'to whom it may concern', it does not seem to be stretching matters too far for us, as latter-day historians, to treat his observations as testimonial evidence for the resolution of our disputed questions and the furtherance of our inquiries. It seems plausible to deal in a similar fashion with registrations of births, deaths, marriages, and in general with matters of public record. Confidential documents such as diplomatic communications or the private record of conversations, or even private diaries which were never intended for communication to anyone, are perhaps more difficult to subsume under our definition but where we can legitimately create an author–reader situation it would seem natural to extend the notion of testimony to cover such cases as well, particularly where the document in question was concerned, for whatever reason, to set the record straight. The way in which this form of testimony can stretch the interpretation of clause (3) in the definition of natural testimony is paralleled in speech exchanges amongst contemporaries by those situations in which someone makes a casual remark, which may be a question or a request and hence not intended to be informative at all or may be a mere comment or remark with a truth value but no implication of audience ignorance or dispute resolution (as in the breakfast comment, 'This butter spreads easily'), but where the comment in question itself creates a context of inquiry or dispute. For instance, a question may reveal that the speaker believes something which the audience finds surprising or contentious and then testimony is called for—or, even, in extreme cases assumed—and where the remark is an indicative utterance it may assume the status of testimony in virtue of its creation of an issue. For instance, if an audience believed that Smith was on holidays overseas, and a trustworthy speaker commented casually upon Smith's eccentric behaviour in a nearby hotel, the audience might well treat the comment as testimony to his whereabouts as much as to his eccentricity. The speaker's comment has unwittingly created an issue about Smith's location and contributed to its resolution.

Thirdly, there is what we might call institutional testimony. This is the sort of thing mentioned, but not distinguished in any way from the ordinary giving of testimony, by H. H. Price[32] in connection with such matters as road signs, maps, the measurement markings on rulers, destination-markers on buses and trams, the author attribution on the title-page of a book, and so on. I also made reference to this sort of testimony in Chapter 1. From these we get what we might call *orientation information* and we get it so naturally and pervasively that we tend to think of it under the heading of observation rather than testimony. That is, we seem to find out for ourselves by merely looking or looking plus acting in such cases; none the less a moment's reflection shows that the information in question is really provided by others and it is a tribute to the strength of our implicit trust in them that we hardly notice it. Such institutional testimonies resemble our paradigm in being something like frozen speech acts. There is not after all such a very great difference between consulting a map and asking an experienced citizen for directions or placing ourselves in the hands of a professional tourist guide ('frozen speech acts' may seem particularly appropriate as a description of some of their performances). Sometimes, indeed, the facts conveyed (i.e. measurement facts) are partly constituted by conventional agreement but this does not remove them from the provenance of our definition since it is perfectly in order for an individual speaker to testify to the existence of a convention or to testify to matters which involve convention.

Fourthly, there is what we might call oblique testimony. Each of us knows for instance that we were born, and yet it is possible that some of us were never explicitly told this fact. Of course we were (presumably) told at some point about the facts of human reproduction and there are birth certificates that we could consult and may perhaps have had to produce on occasion. None the less no one needs birth certificates to sustain his belief in the fact of his own birth and when we heard how babies came about we may have received no assurances that it was also thus in our own case. We do not know of our birth solely on our own authority; we may know it as a sort of implication from the more straightforward testimony about the general facts of reproduction, the celebration of birthdays, the existence of birth certificates, and so on. Something similar may be true of such historical facts as the existence of certain central and significant historical figures, such as Napoleon or Julius Caesar. We have all sorts of testimonies *about* these men and their deeds but naturally we have no explicit testimonies that indeed Napoleon did exist and was not, say, a brilliantly sustained invention of French politicians. I suggest this category of oblique testimony with some diffidence because I am not entirely clear whether it really raises questions about our problem area, rather than certain sceptical doubts of a more general nature, but at least it seems possible

[32] H. H. Price, *Belief* (London, 1969), 113.

that we could believe or know some proposition on the basis of what is *implied* or *involved* in some testimony rather than itself attested.[33]

I want to conclude by mentioning some uses of the term testimony which seem to be even further removed from our definition. In the first place there is a use of the expression or its grammatical variations to refer to any sort of evidence at all. This is fairly clearly a transferred use and is of interest primarily in suggesting the centrality of testimony as a form of evidence. (It also seems to be relevant to Hacking's views mentioned in Chapter 1.) This extended usage, as when a detective says that the state of the victim's clothing testifies to the violence of the attack, can run over into sheer metaphor as when Shakespeare puts into the mouth of one of his characters the words: 'The bricks are alive this day to testify to it' (*2 Henry VI*, Act IV, Scene ii).

More interestingly there is the use of the term 'testify' in religious and quasi-religious contexts to specify the way a man's life or his deeds or some particular act (which can be an act of professing his belief) are to be treated as pointing to some transcendent reality. I am not sure how this employment of the term should be analysed but it seems plausible to suppose that we still have our definition at work here, although in a more heightened, dramatic, and mysterious form. The martyr, for instance, is sometimes said to testify or witness to his faith by death and I suggest that this means that his dying for his beliefs is a kind of evidence for what he believes. It would probably be widely conceded that his willingness to suffer great hardships and even death is evidence for the sincerity of the relevant beliefs; it is evidence, perhaps even testimony of sorts, *that* he believes, but many would insist that this is all it can be. None the less, I think it is plain that people who speak of the witness or the testimony of martyrs or the lives of men dedicated to certain ideals intend to convey by that language the idea that the words and deeds of the men (or women) in question stand to the 'realities' they believe in, rather as reports stand to the realities they are about. Of course, there are differences in the types of case that I am here treating under the one heading. There may, for instance, be important differences in the way the word 'testify' is used of martyrs, on the one hand, and of those who stand up at prayer meetings and testify to 'being saved' or to God's presence in their lives, on the other. A full treatment of these issues would take us further into the philosophy of religion than I intend to proceed but I will venture the opinion that the differences are not significant enough to yield different senses of 'testify'— the testifier at the prayer meeting is not only reporting on certain changes in his life-style but sees himself as reporting on divine actions.

It is one thing, however, to hold that the 'religious' use of 'testimony' or

---

[33] For an interesting discussion of problems in this area with special reference to history see G. E. M. Anscombe, 'Hume and Julius Caesar', in *The Collected Philosophical Papers of G. E. M. Anscombe* (Oxford, 1981), i. 86–92.

'testify' is intended to conform to, or legitimately extend, the sense of such terms, as defined by the speech-act model, it is another to hold that these intentions are successful, and another again to accept any of these testimonies as true. Whether this way of talking is ultimately intelligible will depend very much on the special competence and authority that it presumes the witnesses to have and, granting intelligibility, there is then the question of how we are to weigh the evidence presented. This last question, however, takes us beyond the topic of definition and looks forward to the problems of weighing and assessing particular testimonies, problems we shall examine elsewhere.

3

Objections and Clarifications

We need now to consider some further clarifications of the nature of testimony. These do not stem from the attempt to extend the speech-act analysis to documentary or institutional contexts (moving focus, so to speak, from the verb 'testify' to some of the wider reaches of the noun 'testimony') but more from problems in the scope of the definition. Some of these were already confronted as we worked our way towards the final analysis of natural testimony but we can now consider more fully certain philosophical difficulties they give rise to.

On my account the scope of testimony is very wide. Testifying is not an arcane procedure restricted to the lawcourts but a very fundamental act we engage in many times a day. Yet even those readers prepared to allow a category of natural testimony as a pretty common phenomenon, occurring as often as we give what would naturally be called 'reports', might feel some disquiet at just how wide a net my account of testimony casts. I have already done something in Chapter 2 to calm any fears the 'man in the street' might feel but even this proverbial denizen is often affected by philosophical theories, either directly or by subtle cultural processes. In any case, I shall boldly assume that more of my readers inhabit ivory towers than streets and will thus be aware of, or even moved by, certain philosophical objections that might naturally (or unnaturally) be made to the wide scope of my account. A discussion of these objections will be of importance to the later development of the epistemological argument, as well as having an immediate relevance to the clarification of my analysis and its import. Part of the point of what follows will be to exhibit just how fundamental a speech act reporting is.

Let me begin by returning to Thomas Reid's characterization of testimony as one of the 'social operations of mind'. As we saw earlier he defined these as operations which presuppose understanding and will but also 'intercourse with some other intelligent being'. Reid cites the exchange of testimony, the giving and receiving of commands, promising, contracting, and asking questions as amongst these operations.[1]

Reid's discussion of the social operations, though tantalizingly brief, is penetrating and original. He contrasts them with the 'solitary' operations and insists that they are not reducible to the 'solitary' operations, being

---

[1] Thomas Reid, *Essays on the Intellectual Powers of Man*, essay I, ch, viii, in *Philosophical Works* (Hildesheim, 1967), 245. All refs. to this work will be abbreviated to *EI*.

'original parts of our constitution'. He sees attempts to reduce or analyse them 'under the common philosophical divisions' as like the equally un-successful attempts 'to reduce all our social affections to certain modifica-tions of self-love' (*EI* 244). Reid complains not only of reductionism but also of a widespread philosophical neglect of these social-intellectual phenomena. He ties them closely to the existence of language, claiming that the primary orientation of language is towards expressing these social operations (*EI* 245). In a passage which remarkably foreshadows the sort of concerns with language characteristic of some contemporary speech-act theorists, Reid complains that, although every language has the resources to express questions, commands, and promises, as well as judgements, there has been no analysis of what is involved in the expression of the former, in striking contrast to the 'voluminous tracts' devoted to analysing the expression of judgement, namely, the proposition. Reid comments that, with regard to questions, commands, and promises, the expression of them has not even been given 'a name different from the operations they express'.[2]

Reid's thought here is a little opaque. One thing he may mean, and it connects with a modern issue in the philosophy of language, is that just as the range of speech acts we call assertions can be said to express a thought that we call a proposition so there is something intellectual expressed by the utterances we call questions, commands, and promises—something (or things) which we have no term for and have paid scant attention to. If this is what Reid means then it can no longer be said that the topic is neglected. Modern discussion of it takes J. L. Austin's distinction between illocutionary and locutionary acts as its starting-point, though there are also pertinent contributions from the tradition stemming from the work of the later Wittgenstein. We shall not enter into that debate here, except to signal support for P. F. Strawson's proposed schematism of the relation-ship between the meaning of what a speaker says and the force his saying has. On Strawson's proposal there will be certain basic categories of 'sayings', corresponding to basic types of locutionary act, and ranges of full-blooded illocutionary forces appropriate to each category. Strawson distinguishes two such basic categories, propositions (having the form, that *S* is *P*) and imperatives (having the form, that a person *Z* is to do some act

---

[2] The passage is worth quoting in full: 'In every language, a question, a command, a promise, which are social acts, can be expressed as easily and as properly as judgment, which is a solitary act. The expression of the last has been honoured with a particular name; it is called a proposition; it has been an object of great attention to philosophers; it has been analysed into its very elements of subject, predicate, and copula. All the various modifications of these, and of propositions which are compounded of them, have been anxiously examined in many voluminous tracts. The expression of a question, of a command, or of a promise, is as capable of being analysed as a proposition is; but we do not find that this has been attempted; we have not so such as given them a name different from the operations which they express.'(*EI* 245.)

Y), but leaves it open that there may be more, as would be the case, for instance, if the range of speech acts associated with questioning could not be accommodated by the imperative grouping but required a basic category of interrogatives.[3]

Reid would no doubt be delighted at the shift of interest from constatives (or propositions, in one sense of the term) to imperatives or directives and an associated interest in satisfaction conditions rather than truth conditions, but the contrast between propositions and other basic categories of sayings is not strictly parallel to Reid's contrast between the solitary and social operations of mind.

The most significant difference, for our purposes, is that many of the social operations will express propositions rather than imperatives or something else. Certainly requests, commands, and entreaties are social operations and do not express propositions but such social operations as accusations, warnings, and reports just as certainly do. What each of those latter *says* is capable of being true or false. Requests, commands, entreaties, on the contrary, do not give expression to how the speaker thinks the world is but to how he wants it to be. This simple point not only invalidates the opposition of the social operations to the expression of propositions but also a good deal of what Reid wants to say in this connection about the nature of testimony. His classification of judgement as one of the solitary operations and of the proposition as what is peculiarly involved in the expression of judgement may have led him to think that testimony did not express propositions. He does not explicitly say this (which is just as well, since it is palpably false) but he does strongly oppose judgement and testimony in ways which at least make it unclear what view he held of testimony and propositions (*EI* vi. i).

In his full discussion of judgement Reid rightly says that testimony is essentially social while judgement is not, but then he makes two highly dubious claims about the relations between the two. The first claim is that testimony does not express judgement; the second is that the public expression of an opinion in a matter of science of criticism is not testimony but (the expression of) judgement. In his own words,

A judge asks of a witness what he knows of such a matter to which he was an eye or ear witness. He answers, by affirming or denying something. But his answer does not express his judgement; it is his testimony. Again, I ask a man his opinion in a matter of science or of criticism. His answer is not testimony; it is the expression of his judgement ... (*EI* 413).

I want to contest both these claims, since both seem to run counter to the conclusions of Chapter 2, but it is difficult to know where to begin because Reid provides little in the way of argument of them. The distinc-

---

[3] P. F. Strawson, 'Austin and "Locutionary Meaning"', in Isaiah Berlin (ed.), *Essays on J. L. Austin* (Oxford, 1973), 60.

tion between social and solitary acts of mind (to which Reid adverts in the next paragraph after making the two contested claims) is, as we have seen, unable to support so strong a claim as the first nor does it seem to bear particularly upon the second. Reid does produce what may be intended as an argument for the first soon after when he says: 'In testimony a man pledges his veracity for what he affirms, so that a false testimony is a lie: but a wrong judgment is not a lie; it is only an error' (ibid.).

It must be conceded that there is a tendency in ordinary speech to reserve the expression 'false testimony' for what is produced by deceitful witnesses but this seems to have resulted from the influence of that family of uses of the term 'false' which expresses our interest in treacherous, disloyal, or dishonest behaviour. So we have 'false friend', 'false promise', 'played me false', 'false subject', etc. None the less, it is surely clear that the testimony a witness gives may be perfectly sincere and yet false (in the sense of not-true). Here Reid's view is opposed not only to my account but also (I make bold to affirm even against Reid) to common sense. It seems clear that false (i.e. mistaken) testimony will sometimes (at least) express judgement, namely false judgement. Indeed, so much seems required by Reid's own view of judgement which comes a little later in the chapter: 'I give the name of judgement to every determination of the mind concerning what is true or what is false' (*EI* 415). Reid may have felt that truthful witnesses *normally* get their testimony right, so that our primary interest is in whether they are honest, whereas the judgements we make on the basis of their reports are primarily open to the criticism of error rather than dishonesty. There is something in this, although much depends on the interpretation of 'normally' but, in any case, the view will not support a position as strong as that Reid adopts. Moreover, modern experience of the workings of the law and extensive psychological research on the reliability of perception, memory, and the giving of reports tend to indicate that there is a good deal of room for mistake and error and certainly undermine any idea that a witness merely records or registers neutral facts. I shall examine this evidence in a later chapter because, although it lends support to my case against Reid, dubious conclusions are sometimes drawn from it.

In the quoted passages there is, however, another point which seems to conflict with our analysis of testimony. Reid appears to think it obvious that when a man publicly offers 'his opinion in a matter of science or of criticism' this is not testimony; this obviousness can then support the view that testimony and judgement are mutually exclusive since this view explains why the 'opinion in a matter of science or criticism' is not testimony, namely, because it is the expression of judgement. We have seen good reason to reject the general view that an expression of judgement can never be testimony and hence an argument of this type carries little conviction. The premiss it relies upon, however, cannot simply be dismissed since it raises important questions about the nature of testimony. Is it true that those expressions of judgement that are opinions 'in a matter of science or criticism' cannot be testimony?

Reid's contrast is with the case in which a witness speaks to what he has seen or heard or, presumably, observed via one of the other senses. Perhaps his point is that, in the matter of testimony, a sharp distinction must be drawn between the sensory and the intellectual, between what is observed and what is thought or opined. So, someone may testify to a painting's being of a soldier dressed in a red uniform but only express a judgement as to the beauty of the painting or its market value or its date of composition or the type of paint that has been used in it. There is certainly something plausible about this sort of demarcation but it is not without difficulties. If we think in terms of formal testimony then something like the distinction Reid is making is marked in English law and allied traditions by the contrast between fact and opinion and the related contrast between fact and inference. A witness may testify to what he has perceived but his opinions drawn inferentially from his observations are, as a general rule, not admissible evidence. Part of the legal justification for this certainly resides in the idea that the point of the whole judicial apparatus is to provide as its output (by way of the jury's verdict or the judge's findings) precisely such conclusions or opinions and hence it is a sort of absurdity, a denial of the point of the proceedings, for the witness who is there to provide the raw material for the judge or jury's thinking to produce his own opinions and conclusions. On the other hand, the legal exclusion of opinion is by no means absolute nor could it be. To begin with, expert testimony is plainly opinion and has long been allowed in English law, although sometimes with certain misgivings and hedged about by restrictions. In line, for instance, with the justification mentioned above for excluding opinion, the general practice of judges is to prevent even an expert witness stating his opinion on an ultimate issue such as the reasonableness of a convenant in restraint of trade, the validity of a patent, or the construction to be put upon a document.[4] None the less, in a complex civilization like ours, expert testimony has come to assume a significant role in legal proceedings. It is, moreover, particularly interesting in the present connection, and in the light of our earlier discussion of hearsay, that an expert is allowed to adopt statements made in scientific works as part of his testimony although this is not only hearsay but often hearsay to opinion.[5] Secondly, non-expert witnesses may give testimony to matters of

---

[4] Cf. R. Cross, *Evidence*, 3rd edn. (London, 1967), 361. As Cross notes, the law is particularly concerned that the admission of expert opinion should not 'shift responsibility from the bench or the jury to the witness box'. Even here, however, there are exceptions to the general practice cited in the text. Cf. R. Eggleston, *Evidence, Proof and Probability* (London, 1983), 124.

[5] See Cross, *Evidence*, 365 and also Eggleston, *Evidence*, 130–1.

opinion where the factual and inferential elements in a belief are so bound together as to be practically inseparable. As one American judge has put it, a witness may give his opinion or impression when 'the facts from which a witness received an impression were too evanescent in their nature to be recollected or too complicated to be separately and distinctly narrated'.[6] Typical cases listed by Cross are claims about age, speed, weather, handwriting, and identity in general.[7]

It will be clear to the philosophical reader that the legal discussion of these matters has points of contact with complex debates within philosophy about the degree to which any viable distinction can ultimately be made between fact and theory, observation and inference, the sensory and the judgemental or intellectual. It may be that what a person can observe, no matter how 'brute' he may suppose the observation to be, is always a function of some beliefs he has, so that his observation can be represented as an outcome of an inference involving those beliefs and hence an 'opinion'. To revert to my earlier example of the painting of a soldier in a red uniform it could be argued that an eyewitness report of this would only be possible for someone who had the relevant concepts and the understanding that goes with them. By a familiar move such understanding is then equated with theoretical thinking which is inferential and so our witness is giving an opinion, as may be seen by contrasting his verdict with that of someone from a very different cultural background faced with the same painting but unable to make the 'inferential' move from, say, 'man in curious red clothing carrying an implement' to 'soldier in red uniform'. (A common example in the philosophical literature is the theory-laden observation of a Wilson cloud chamber and its operations.) I cite this philosophical manœuvre without intending to endorse it, for I do not find its argument wholly persuasive, but merely to emphasize the difficulties of sustaining too sharp a distinction between fact and opinion. None the less, I think a rough but workable contrast, of the kind the law envisages, can be made by learning from the philosophical debate without prejudging its eventual outcome.

One thing the philosophical discussion may be taken to show, at the very least, is that whether someone is offering a judgement or giving his opinion in a sense which would contrast with merely recording a fact must be heavily dependent upon context. (The strong philosophical claim can then be seen as the claim that this context-dependency is strong enough to eliminate entirely the notion of 'recording a fact' as a theoretically fundamental idea—but it may none the less have a practical validity in context.) This context-dependency is of two kinds. In the first place, and most importantly, there is the context of expertise and competence. To take the

---

[6] Justice Gibson cited in J. H. Wigmore, *A Treatise on the Anglo-American System of Evidence in Trials at Common Law*, vii, 3rd edn. (Boston, 1940), 12.
[7] Cross, *Evidence*, 368.

painting example again; let's suppose that it is by Sir Joshua Reynolds. Most of us would merely be offering an opinion, though not necessarily just guessing, if we were to say when the work had been painted (particularly if aiming at an order of precision like a decade). On the other hand, an expert on eighteenth-century paintings might be able to say authoritatively at once that it was painted in 1782 and, at current prices, was worth $500,000. He might, or might not, be able to decompose his judgement into the elements of fact and inference that, in some sense, make it up, but even where he can go beyond something like 'It has that late Reynolds look about it' *his* facts and inferences may be so loaded with expertise themselves as to put a lay audience in no better position to judge his conclusion. In these circumstances, the art expert can testify where the layman can only give an opinion. At the other end of the spectrum any native speaker is an expert (up to a point) on the meanings of utterances in his native tongue but most would be hard put to provide the 'facts' about those utterances upon which their semantic interpretations are based.

In the second place, there is the context of inquiry. As we have seen in the legal situation, the opinion of an acknowledged expert may be inadmissible where it concerns the ultimate issue which the tribunal itself has to decide upon; the law is particularly anxious that the witness should not usurp the function and responsibility of the tribunal itself and this anxiety is acute where the expert's opinion encompasses disputed questions for the resolution of which the tribunal has been created.[8] The point can however be generalized in a way that returns us to Reid's position and the concern that underlies it: an expert's view on some matter within his competence will be disregardable whenever his audience is, or ought to be, or is presumed to be or is aiming to be, equally competent to have an independent view of the matter themselves. Hence the opprobrium attaching to 'the argument from authority'. Locke, who regarded argument from authority as one of the 'wrong measures of probability'[9] (but thought himself to have 'a due respect for other men's opinions'),[10] seems usually to have had in mind the dangers of merely accepting the conclusions of other people's arguments, demonstrations, etc., when one was capable of examining the arguments themselves. The extract from Locke's *Essay Concerning the Human Understanding*, for instance, quoted in Chapter 1, continues as follows:

The floating of other men's opinions in our brains makes us not one jot the more knowing, though they happen to be true. What in them was science is in us but

---

[8] See Eggleston, *Evidence*, 124, for cases where an expert opinion may harmlessly be allowed on ultimate issues and for a slightly different account of the basis of the law's anxiety.

[9] J. Locke, *An Essay Concerning Human Understanding*, ed. J. W. Yolton (London, 1961), 606.

[10] Ibid. 55.

opinionatrety, whilst we give up our assent only to reverend names, and do not, as they did, employ our own reason to understand those truths which gave them reputation. Aristotle was certainly a knowing man; but nobody ever thought him so because he blindly embraced and confidently vented the opinions of another. And if the taking up of another's principles without examining them made not him a philosopher, I suppose it will hardly make anyone else so.[11]

In other words, if one is out to be a philosopher, to philosophize, to understand philosophy, one will not succeed by merely discovering the current or prevailing beliefs of the philosophical community or its outstanding members, and similarly for other branches of inquiry.[12] Of course, Locke loads the dice by talking of 'blind' embracing of other men's opinions but even so the point I am making about the context of inquiry is at least an element in his thought. The point may be illustrated by the painting example. If we are inquiring (either judicially or less formally) into the theft of the painting of a soldier in a red uniform it may be important that we know such things as who painted it, what it is worth at current prices, and other pieces of technical opinion which can form part of the basis of our investigation. Normally we will not have the relevant expertise about these artistic questions nor the opportunity to acquire it, so if the inquiry is to proceed we must here accept authoritative opinion. It is less clear, to say the least, that we could accept another's opinion, as if it were testimony, that so and so stole the painting in such and such a way where this opinion is based on the very same evidence that we are examining, although we might very well come, *on the basis of that evidence*, to agree with his opinion. The importance of the context of inquiry may be seen by changing our focus and considering an inquiry conducted by an art expert into who painted the picture (there is a dispute as to whether it is a genuine Reynolds). The expert may well accept the evidence of chemists about the composition of the paint if he needs such data but he will not treat the opinions of his fellow art experts about 'the ultimate issue', namely, the authorship of the picture, in the same way. Of course, even here, the situation is not as clear cut as our exposition has suggested since, as we saw in Chapter 1, a consensus of opinion by fellow experts cannot be lightly disregarded. Reid himself was, as we saw, most insistent upon the point, extending it even to mathematical proofs. Similarly our art expert will with reason be at least a little perturbed if he finds his judgement to be quite at odds with that of all his peers. He may, of course, stick to his guns but he will surely give the evidence what Reid calls 'a new and more rigorous examination'. In this we seem, however, to have a point of

[11] Ibid.
[12] Philosophy is not perhaps an ideal example since its conclusions seem so essentially unstable that many are tempted to hold that the subject consists of a set of skills rather than a body of truths. The bearing of Locke's point upon the understanding of some given science is none the less plain enough.

distinction between ordinary testimony and this sort of expert deliverance
for it is precisely possible here for the disconcerted art expert to consider
for himself the very evidence upon which the contrary deliverance is based.
Against Reid we should conclude that many statements on matters of
'science or criticism' *can* figure as testimony, depending on the speaker's
status and the context of the communicative exchange. We may acknowledge, none the less, that Reid is right to attempt some distinction between
testifying and merely opining.

The discussion of Reid has shown, against his philosophical objections,
that testimony can be mistaken as well as deceitful and has both vindicated
the category of expert reports and clarified its nature and limits. To that
extent the discussion has given support to my wide definition of testimony.
The realm of speech acts embodying the locutionary acts called propositions by Strawson is, however, wider than that of reports. If we think
of the speech act of assertion as covering a very broad range of 'sayings
that' or (so to speak) propositioning, but not as being identical with it,
then reporting will not be coextensive even with asserting, though it is the
dominant form of asserting. Assertions in soliloquy are not reports because
there is no audience (unless we are prepared to treat ourselves as both
speaker and hearer) nor are predictions or guesses (if they are to be treated
as assertions) nor usually are assertions of hypothetical propositions
though where the asserter is an expert on the matter under hypothesis and
asserts authoritatively then he may be seen as testifying. This last point has
quite general application. The whole category of expert testimony, as we
saw earlier, undermines the rather natural idea that reports can be given
only to what has been observed (either by the reporter or by someone at
the other end of a transmission chain upon whom he eventually relies).
Experts do not usually testify to what they have observed, though they
may do that too, but rather to an expert view or opinion they have
formed. The natural idea is in any case threatened, or at least subject to
modification, by the possibility, which surely exists, of mathematical testimony, since mathematical facts are not in any ordinary way observed.
Even predictions may be regarded as reports where there is sufficient
expertise backing them; the weather bureau's predictions are sometimes
publicized (in Australia, at least) under the heading 'Weather Report',
though this also includes the bureau's observations about the past twenty-
four hours. There is, I think, a sense of these forecasts as expert testimony
to present tendencies which will develop fully in the short-term future.[13]
Perhaps the temptation to treat expert forecasts as testimony should be
resisted on the grounds that, although a report need not (ultimately) stem
from an observation, it must stem from the determination of some fact

[13] Of course it may be that the reference of 'report' is not to the forecasts but to the
journalist's presentation of them, so that he is reporting on a forecast which is not itself any
sort of firsthand report.

about the past or present or some timeless truth, as in the mathematical case. The future will not do, it may be argued, because there are *now* no facts about the future to be recorded and passed on. There is, I think, something to be said for this restriction but just how compelling it is would depend upon the outcome of a very complex philosophical debate about the logical status of future contingent truths, a debate which has raged, for instance, around the interpretation of Aristotle's discussion of the possible future sea battle in *De Interpretatione*. There is no need here to settle or enter that debate; we shall merely note its relevance and the fact that even forecasts may not be entirely beyond the scope of the act of reporting.

There are other species of assertion which it might be misleading to call reports but which none the less strictly speaking are pieces of testimony or incorporate a report. Warnings, for instance, where they are species of assertion (the indicative, 'The ice over there is thin', rather than the imperative, 'Don't walk on the ice!') clearly cast the warner in the role of testifier to a fact presumed not to be known to the audience and pertinent to an interest of theirs so that we may see it as intended to resolve a question for that audience. The speaker is indeed doing something *more* than reporting and his act's principal purpose reaches beyond apprising the audience of the bare facts to the audience's appreciation of those facts as dangerous. This is why it can be misleading to describe him as reporting even though it is true.

This is perhaps the point at which to explore in more depth an issue briefly raised in Chapter 2 and which touches on our concern here with the scope of my analysis and with the centrality of reporting as a speech act. This is the issue of assertions about the existence and characteristics of one's psychological and sensational states. For ease of exposition, I shall adopt the terminology favoured by some philosophers and call them 'avowals'. Utterances such as 'I am in pain', 'It hurts awfully', 'My after-image is of a blue circle with a red square patch in the middle', 'I hate him', 'I love her', 'I am jealous of them', 'I feel nauseous', are just a few sample avowals. In Chapter 2 I claimed without extended argument that we were entitled to treat these as reports and, if so, they clearly form a common and rather significant kind of report, so emphasizing how basic reporting is. There is, however, room for debate about whether avowals are reports though I think that the case against treating them as such is, in the end, rather weak. Most of the considerations urged on behalf of treating avowals like 'I am in pain', 'My annoyance with you has almost subsided', or 'I am not envious of him' as not falling into the category of testimony merely stress certain special features of such reports and very frequently exaggerate the differences from what are allowed on all hands to be the genuine article. There is a familiar area of debate here which I cannot fully explore but which is worth some detailed treatment both because of its relevance to our topic and its intrinsic interest. The resistance to treating such assertions as reports stems from two rather different responses to the peculiarity (one might almost say the mystery) of our psychological life. In the face of the 'privacy' and subsequent 'privileged access' of our psyches, some philosophers want to naturalize our avowals by assimilating them to winces, groans, and the like, while others seek to supernaturalize them by endowing them with infallibility. In the first case they are not reports, nor even, it would seem, assertions, because they are not propositional at all; the speaker is not providing evidence for some state of affairs inaccessible to the hearer, he is actually exhibiting that state of affairs. In the second case he is telling the hearer that some inaccessible state of affairs obtains but he is so authoritative about it and it is so inaccessible 'in principle' that the hearer must accept what he says as true and this is not the usual situation with bearing witness.

I do not want to minimize the philosophical problems, both ontological and epistemological, that cluster around the nature of mind. None the less I find neither of the above responses (or sketches of responses, for I have made no attempt to present them in any complexity or subtlety) really satisfactory. The former has never been plausibly developed beyond Wittgenstein's cryptic remarks in the *Philosophical Investigations*[14] and the odds against doing so are, *for a great range of avowals*, surely astronomical. Whatever can be done for the assimilation of some utterances of 'I am in pain' to cries, screams, or groans, there is no future in extending the treatment to such palpably propositional expressions as 'I was initially irritated by his performance but now I feel only mild distaste'. Nor are the prospects bright for according quite different logical status to what is expressed by 'I was wholly irritated by his performance' and 'I am wholly irritated by his performance'—not to mention 'He is wholly irritated by his performance' where 'he' and 'I' have the same referent.[15] Again, what is to be said of insincere avowals, where the state of mind 'expressed' by the utterance does not exist, other than that they are falsehoods? If they can be false because the state does not obtain, surely they can be true when it holds.

This point helps to show up the weaknesses in the second line of response. Even granted that the subject is infallible about his mental states, we need not concede him impeccability. The subject can certainly say what is false, intending to deceive an audience into believing that things are as they are not. This surely makes such avowals very like (to say the least) false reports.[16] Moreover, the infallibility claimed for avowals does not usually extend beyond utterances about *present* psychological states so

---

[14] L. Wittgenstein, *Philosophical Investigations* (Oxford, 1953), para. 243.

[15] Or apparent referent since some have denied that 'I' is a referring expression.

[16] 'False' cannot here be used as it is in 'false promise'. It is not that the speaker does not want the world to conform to what he says, he knows it does not.

that there seems in this objection no room for rejecting past-tense utterances about the subject's psychological affairs as reports. The subject may not only lie about his past pains, palpitations, pleasures, and premonitions but he may be mistaken about them, as observers may sometimes be in a strong position to determine. Those who lie about the states of mind they have had may surely be caught out by finding their present remarks inconsistent with earlier ones and finding reason to detect motives for present insincerity, not to mention the matter of observing inconsistency between present remarks and past behaviour. Similar considerations apply to the possibility of mistake. Howard now claims that he enjoyed reading *Ulysses* some three years ago but Vincent recalls his saying then what an unendurable experience the reading was and Albert recalls the reluctance with which Howard went about his task, the frequent puttings aside of the weighty tome, the drowsy eye, and bored expression. The state of affairs in question, Howard's enjoyment, is not really then so inaccessible 'in principle'; we can't *have* (or have had) Howard's enjoyment but this does not mean that we cannot have evidence about its presence or absence independently of what he now says. Moreover, as so many philosophers have urged in recent years,[17] the case for the infallibility of present-tense avowals has been greatly overrated. About many of our psychological states we are, when enduring them, powerfully authoritative, and there *may* be some circumstances in which it is inconceivable that we are wrong about their presence or, more significantly, absence, but we are clearly fallible about many other mental states and there are not many avowals for which it is impossible to make at least a case for their fallibility. To illustrate: we are not even in a particularly privileged position in our declarations of the presence or absence of complex emotions such as jealousy or love. For such cases observers can certainly gain sufficient access to the realities to correct our claims. Something similar is true of the more dispositional cognitive states such as belief. In all instances where self-deception is a real possibility the observer may be in a better position to determine the question than the sufferer. We are of course less prone to self-deception about our sensations and less prone to inattention and other mistake-producing orientations, though there are many complexities even here that can put the observer in a better position than the sufferer. An observer may have good reason to think that the subject has misdescribed features of his experience—for instance, the subject reports that the after-image has five blue spots when every other subject has reported six and the source has six.

A thorough treatment of the topics of awareness, privileged authority, and the degree of incorrigibility appropriate (where and when) to the

---

[17] See D. M. Armstrong, *A Materialist Theory of Mind* (London, 1968), 100–13; R. Rorty, *Philosophy and the Mirror of Nature* (Princeton, NJ, 1980), 88–98.

subject's beliefs about his mental states is beyond us here. I have tried to do no more than show that some of the considerations which might be urged against treating utterances indicative of such beliefs as reports are less than compelling. It may finally be urged however that, although the infallibility or the incorrigibility[18] of avowals raises insufficient difficulties for the proposal to classify them as reports, none the less a related difficulty remains in that avowals, or many of them, have a kind of uncheckability which distinguishes them radically from normal reports. They may not be infallible or beyond some sort of external criticism but the criticism must always be indirect—it must proceed via other relevant utterances of the subject or via observations of his behaviour or via evidence about the public causes of his mental state. What it cannot do is reach directly to his sensation or feeling or thought and so there is a sense in which his 'report' cannot be open to the sort of direct checking that is always in principle possible with reports about the public world.

There are various avenues of rejoinder available here. One might, for instance, challenge the sharp dichotomy of public and private that seems implicit in the argument, insisting that our cognitive access as observers to the state of someone in agony or filled with hate or terror is just as direct as his own, even though fortunately our experiential state is not as his. We might, moreover, seek to reinforce such a response by recourse to familiar reflections on the public nature of the concepts in terms of which the subject has to think in framing his avowal. It may very well be that this challenge can be developed in such a way as to defuse the objection but its successful elaboration is, I think, unnecessary for my purposes. It is possible instead to concede the objection's assumptions and initial premisses about privacy and the lack of symmetry between the subject's direct epistemological route to the mental state and the observer's indirect one, but nevertheless reject the argument's conclusion. The form of the argument is:

(1) Avowals of mental states are directly uncheckable by an audience.

(2) Reports are necessarily directly checkable by an audience.

∴ (3) Avowals of mental states are not reports.

Clearly this is formally valid and we have conceded (1) for the sake of argument, but why should we accept (2)? If 'checkable' is given its ordinary sense then vast numbers of palpable reports would be ruled out as such, many of them amongst the most valuable we could have. Indeed, as audiences, we are particularly interested in testimony to events or states of affairs which are not only beyond our present ken but which could not be observed by us as things stand. Most events are like this—once the car

---

[18] Infallibility and incorrigibility are not the same but, for our purposes, there is no need to press a distinction between them.

crash has occurred there is no way that someone who didn't observe it can directly check on the observations of one who did. He can of course sometimes check on its immediate effects if he is quick enough but this is beside the present point since the analogous opportunity is available for mental states. The case is different with what we might think of as more permanent events, such as a bushfire, but even here the passage of time can make it impossible to check directly the occurrence of a fire or a carnival or a riot. Moreover, few things are so permanent that they do not change position or, eventually, expire or otherwise cease to exist and, when they do, perfectly reliable reports on their previous existence or whereabouts become uncheckable ('directly'). The vast majority of historical testimonies consists of reports of this kind.

Inevitably it will be replied that such impossibilities are not as pure as the impossibility of checking on the existence and internal properties of mental states. There is a sense, it will be said, in which we *might have been* present at the accident and had the same access to it as the present witness; there is even perhaps a sense in which we might have been present at the 1758 sighting of Halley's comet to see what the witnesses we now rely upon saw, or present at any of the remote historical happenings reports of which we cannot now directly check upon. There may be real doubt about whether those latter suppositions make sense: who would 'we' have been if such a supposition were to have been realized and what 'would have happened' to history to effect such a realization?[19] None the less, I suggest we once more extend (a perhaps too permissive) tolerance to the objector's idea that there is some utterly unrealistic but thinly ('logically') conceivable possibility that we could have checked upon such reports on the actually uncheckable. Why should we be so impressed by this remote possibility? True, we cannot even make this much sense of the idea that we might directly check on avowals. If mental states are partially individuated by the identity of their possessor then, although I could have and enjoy direct access to a pain just like Gertrude's, I could not experience and cognitively grasp just that pain she reports without being her. In common philosophical parlance I could have a pain qualitatively but not numerically identical to Gertrude's. On this, common sense and philosophical tradition seem agreed. I am not disposed to deny the validity of this consensus, though it should be noted that if telepathy is an intelligible possibility then it may at least cast some doubt upon the point, not by making understandable the idea that two persons could *have* the very same pain (numerically and not only qualitatively the same) but by raising the possibility that one might

---

[19] Certain issues about the identity of persons raised by Saul Kripke in *Naming and Necessity* (Oxford, 1972) come to mind as do the difficulties about time-travel discussed by David Lewis who is sympathetic to its coherence and Hugh Mellor who is not. See D. Lewis, *Collected Papers*, ii (Oxford, 1986), 67–80; D. H. Mellor, *Real Time* (Cambridge, 1981), 172–7.

gain direct access to the sensation, thought, or whatever, without being under the necessity of actually having or undergoing it.[20] But, setting this aside, we may still ask why the admission that there is the claimed difference between avowals and 'external' reports should have the consequences the objector's argument requires. After all, we are happy to accord the status of reports to claims (such as historical reports) which are *actually* quite impossible to check directly, so why should the additional feature of being conceptually or logically impossible to check directly have an effect upon an utterance's right to be classified as a report? We have seen that premiss (2) is simply false when given a normal ('actual') reading for 'checkable' so the objector must rewrite it as

> (2′) Reports are necessarily at least directly logically checkable by an audience.

(That is, it must be possible to imagine that the audience could have directly observed or accessed the situation reported.) It is hard to see what rationale there could be for accepting (2′). At most, the impossibility it relies upon serves to cast light upon an interesting feature of the epistemology of mental states, but the relevance of this to the standing of avowals as reports remains undemonstrated, not to say unmotivated.

An unmotivated adherence to (2′) is particularly baffling when it flies in the face of the linguistic data, as it surely does. We have no hesitation in using the term 'report' or related expressions in connection with mental states. 'The defendant reports that he had a severe headache on the night in question and several witnesses can be called to confirm his evidence'. Perfectly sensible surely and such language is clearly not restricted to the lawcourts. In Stanley Milgram's famous account of his experiments on obedience and authority,[21] he refers to follow-up studies in which the subjects were asked whether they believed that the 'victims' in the experiments were really getting the painful shocks apparently administered by the subjects. What the subjects say in the follow-up studies about their beliefs is treated as reporting on their states of mind. As Milgram puts it, what the subjects' responses to the questionnaire gives is their 'testimony on belief'. He summarizes the results by saying: 'Three-quarters of the subjects (the first two categories) by their own testimony acted under the belief that they were administering painful shocks.' Lest it be thought that the past tense matters in those sample sentences consider the sort of instruction that frequently occurs, or could occur, in psychology laboratories: Experimenter: 'I want you to report carefully what sensations you get and what feelings you experience when the lights change colour/when the sounds stop/after five minutes suspended in the water tank.' In the face

---

[20] It is more plausibly viewed as involving a form of mental isomorphism rather than identity, a high-powered version of empathy, fellow-feeling, or thinking.

[21] S. Milgram, *Obedience to Authority* (London, 1974), 172.

of such data we would need a very powerful theoretical case to deny avowals the title of report, but as we have seen there is no such case.

Another very interesting question upon which I have had nothing directly to say so far concerns morality. Can there be testimony to moral claims, to the rightness of actions, the goodness of policies, the wickedness of proposals? Many would be inclined to dismiss the possibility out of hand but the issue is more complicated than is often supposed and some of the bases for dismissal are rather dubious. To settle the matter conclusively is beyond us here, since that would call for a comprehensive account of the nature of morality, but the discussion can be taken a certain distance without too ambitious a foray into the foundations of ethics.

When I spoke of some of the motivations for returning a quick negative answer to the question about moral testimony as dubious, I had in mind various versions of what might be called 'primitive emotivism'. This is the meta-ethical theory which has it that all moral utterances (and indeed all value utterances) are no more than expressions and/or excitants of feeling. This would remove morality from the purview of testimony by removing moral utterances from the province of propositions altogether. It is worth reminding ourselves that this is no straw man. The theory was once enthusiastically, not to say ferociously, advanced by A. J. Ayer and, for all its simplicity, it has had a powerful cultural influence. Here is Ayer in full cry:

If a sentence makes no statement at all, there is obviously no sense in asking whether what it says is true or false. And we have seen that sentences which simply express moral judgments do not say anything. They are pure expressions of feeling and as such do not come under the category of truth and falsehood. They are unverifiable for the same reason as a cry of pain or a word of command is unverifiable—because they do not express genuine propositions.[22]

Extreme non-cognitivism of this sort certainly puts morality beyond the reach of testimony but it is itself distinctly implausible. To begin with, it is inadequate to the phenomena of moral experience since moral utterances are frequently produced in the absence of the sort of feelings emotivists invoke and in the absence of the desire or prospect of evoking such feelings in an audience. Again, even if the analysis were conceded for simple categorical moral utterances, it seems impossible to extend it to more complex utterances such as hypotheticals, and it can make no sense of what moral reasoning palpably occurs in ethical discussions. Such reasoning has to be treated as purely to do with the truth of factual assumptions or probable consequences of action but it is surely clear that more than this goes on in moral argument. We can appeal to such arguments as the generalization principle ('what if everyone did the same'), to consistency

---

[22] A. J. Ayer, *Language, Truth and Logic* (London, 1974), 144.

with moral principles and values (itself surely a value appeal), and to high-level moral principles ('the taking of innocent life is wrong') and moral concepts such as justice or courage.

All these appeals may be somehow phoney or, more plausibly, sufficiently different from appeals within other areas to be treated as 'non-cognitive', but what I have called 'primitive emotivism' is incapable of demonstrating this.[23] More sophisticated versions of subjectivism or emotivism may be able to handle these and other moral phenomena, though this is by no means certain. To do this they must allow at least that there can be genuine reasoning from high-level moral generalities or principles to particular moral claims, and genuine contradiction at the level of such moral claims. Their subjectivism or emotivism will be relevant rather to the status of the principles, the moral fundamentals, or frameworks. Some of the issues then raised will be relatives of those raised in the philosophy of science when the issue of theory choice, especially of the more fundamental sort, is discussed. What does seem likely, however, is that the more complex and refined the non-cognitivist response becomes, the more ground it will begin to share with objectivist theories. Whether such a streamlined version of subjectivism as Simon Blackburn's, for instance, is so very different from an Aristotelian ethic (or even from a suitably demystified intuitionism) is a moot point.[24] Certainly, Blackburn wants to concede the implausibility of denying the epithets 'true' or 'false' to ordinary (low-level) moral utterances and he seeks to give an account of how this is possible within the non-cognitivist constraints he sets himself. For such as he, there will be room for serious, decidable argument and debate within morality, for reasoning and rational comparison of values, for establishing and rejecting moral facts. There will be some sense in which a moral framework is a matter (ultimately) of choice but the choice is not arbitrary and unconstrained.[25]

If I am right about the concessions required of a serious version of non-cognitivism then dismissals of moral testimony on the ground that there is

---

[23] Similar considerations apply to that slightly different simplification, 'primitive subjectivism' which treats moral utterances as reports on current psychological states such as desires or feelings of approval. Here reporting a moral truth would be a mere species of reporting a psychological truth, i.e. a kind of avowal. Some philosophers who advocate the 'subjectivity of morals' hover between the two theories, cf. Bertrand Russell in *Religion and Science* (Oxford, 1935), ch. 9, repr. in abridged form as 'Science and Ethics' in P. Edwards and A. Pap (eds.), *A Modern Introduction to Philosophy* (Toronto, 1965), 297–302.

[24] See S. Blackburn, *Spreading the Word* (Oxford, 1984), 197–202.

[25] This is not to say that there will be no differences of principle between a refined subjectivism and even an equally refined objectivism such as that promoted by John McDowell in various publications. My point is only that there is much more convergence of outlook than the original oppositions of primitive emotivism and primitive objectivism would have allowed. One such difference remaining would concern the point of applying the predicate 'true' in morality and how this differs from its point in certain other domains. Some of the problems here have been explored by David Wiggins in 'Truth, Invention and the Meaning of Life', *Proc. of the British Academy*, 61 (1976), 331–78.

nothing to be reported seem unconvincing. None the less, there may be specific features of moral truths which rule out testimony to them. One such might be that they are already known to everyone so that the third condition of natural testimony is not met. One cannot genuinely report something to someone who already knows it. This, however, is only plausible, if at all, on a dispositional or capacity interpretation of 'know', for the existence of certain types of moral quandary shows that people can, as a matter of fact, be uncertain or even ignorant of what is morally right. It may be that the moral truth is accessible to their unaided thinking if only they could sustain the appropriate inquiry, but right now that may not be much help, even if true.

It may be best, at this point, to distinguish between the general and the particular, between moral principles and particular applications of them. Supposing that moral principles can be true, there seems to be no reason why someone who knows one such should not convey it to another who is ignorant of it. Indeed, the moral education of the young proceeds, at least in part, in just this way. True, some theorists of moral education would have it proceed otherwise but, in the first place, they characteristically do not think that there are moral truths, being themselves in the grip of some more or less primitive non-cognitivism, and, in the second place, most parents still pay little attention to them. There is much more, of course, to little Tommy becoming a moral being than his acquiring the information that stealing is wrong, that good boys and girls don't tell lies, and so on, but nothing in the nature of morality prevents such transmissions occurring.[26] Something similar, it seems, is true at the concrete level of moral action. When someone tells me: 'What you are proposing to do is unjust', this may come as a surprise and his so telling me may figure in my decision not to act as I had proposed.

Yet one may still feel some unease. Surely morality, unlike perception, is a predominantly, if not purely, rational activity. When someone tells me that what I am proposing to do is immoral, I do not react by asking for his credentials but for his reasons. When Jones tells Smith that his house is on fire it may be appropriate for Jones to ask how Smith is in a position to know this, to question his credentials or even his sincerity, but it would be absurd to ask for his arguments. With expert testimony the situation is a little different but even here, though reason has more sway, the audience is, by definition, in no position to assess the witness's reasoning but must

---

[26] Part of what more there is may well involve an appeal to the child's powers of reasoning and to his imagination. Some studies seem to suggest that very young children respond better to certain types of moral instruction and rebuke where they contain elements of reason-giving. The evidence is hardly compelling but it is interesting. See Nancy Eisenberg-Berg and Michael Hand, 'The Relationship of Preschoolers' Reasoning about Prosocial Moral Conflicts to Prosocial Behaviour', and Carolyn Zahn-Waxler, Marian Radke-Yarrow, and Robert A. King, 'Child Rearing and Children's Prosocial Initiations towards Victims of Distress', both in *Child Development*, 50 (1979).

be content with determining his credentials. What the present uneasiness with moral testimony amounts to, I suggest, is an uneasiness with the very idea of a moral expert.

Perhaps it will be conceded that normal adults stand in the position of moral experts to the very young, but this is necessarily exceptional. Once maturity is achieved, normal adults are peers with respect to moral expertise, which is to say that in the adult community there are no moral experts. Hence condition (2) of the definition of natural testimony does not apply in the (adult) moral community.

There is no denying the force of this objection but we need to be careful not to mislocate its source nor to exaggerate its power. One important source of the idea that there is something wrong with the notion of moral expertise is the fact that particular moral judgements are so much a matter of quite specific contexts and circumstances into the appreciation of which an outsider will often be unable to enter. This is one reason why the offering of moral advice is so frequently prefaced by phrases like: 'Well it's really up to you, of course, but I would be disposed to . . .'. Hence there seems to be a more than trivial sense in which an agent must personally take responsibility for his act in a way that precludes his appealing to what someone else told him. Recalling our discussion of expert opinion, we may say that, just as a judge or jury will often be dependent upon expert testimony but must not let it usurp the tribunal's own function of find-ing on the ultimate issue, so, in moral matters, the agent has a special adjudicatory task that he cannot abdicate. This connects with the point made earlier about there being more to a child's becoming a moral being than her learning certain moral truths from a moral authority. She must make those truths her own and build them into her life; to become a moral being in the full sense she must develop projective skills[27] in morality parallel to the skills one develops in becoming a mathematician or a fluent speaker of some language.

The mathematical analogy has been nicely exploited by Elizabeth Anscombe who points out that mathematical teaching is not primarily a matter of telling pupils mathematical truths but of inculcating the capacity to do mathematics, to construct and criticize proofs. As we shall see in a later chapter, this point about what it is *to be a mathematician* (in no matter how humble a way) is not incompatible with the transmission of mathematical knowledge by testimony, but it does put the role of auth-ority in mathematics in context and it shows its relative unimportance for

---

[27] Here as elsewhere in this discussion of moral expertise I am indebted to Margaret Coady's discussion in her unpubl. M.Ed. thesis, 'Authority, Reason and Education' (Univ. of Melbourne, 1972). The use of the term 'projective skills' in this connection is hers, though she has more sympathy than I with Peter Singer's interpretation of the notion of moral expertise which I discuss later in this chapter.

someone's being a mathematician.[28] The case is somewhat similar when learning a language. Here again one needs initially to take a great deal on trust and one can always encounter someone more authoritative than oneself on matters of vocabulary, meaning, or grammar, but speaking the language is a practical matter requiring projective skills, the capacities to apply, amend, and project the information and 'rules' one has acquired from others to the varied, sometimes unique, circumstances one confronts in the day-to-day business of communication. It is this sort of point that Aristotle has in mind when he says, 'It is possible to do something that is in accordance with the laws of grammar, either by chance or at the suggestion of another. A man will be a grammarian, then, only when he has both done something grammatical and done it grammatically; and this means doing it in accordance with the grammatical knowledge in himself.'[29] The moral agent needs the moral knowledge 'in himself' since that knowledge must be constantly exercised and interpreted in practice in the varied and special circumstances of his life. One may get through life with some mathematical knowledge by testimony and virtually no mathematical skills, for one can choose not to be a mathematician. But it is not possible to opt entirely out of being a moral agent.[30]

Yet, when all the necessary concessions are done with, it remains true that we (or at least some of us) do seek even as adults to benefit from the moral insights of others. As Aristotle has it, 'we ought to attend to the undemonstrated sayings and opinions of experienced and older people or of people of practical wisdom not less than to demonstrations; for because experience has given them an eye they see aright'.[31] Where such apparent insights clash with our own or with reasoning and argument that leads us to a different conclusion, we may disregard them. We are then somewhat like the man who thinks that a reported observation must be wrong because his own clear observation contradicts it or because he has arguments to show that it is very unlikely.[32] But we can be impressed (surely, on some occasions, rightly) by the moral beliefs and outlooks of certain people because of their credentials, even where the beliefs are 'undemonstrated', and where they cannot provide demonstrations. Their authority

---

[28] G. E. M. Anscombe, 'Authority in Morals', in *The Collected Philosophical Papers of G. E. M. Anscombe*, iii. *Ethics, Religion and Politics* (Oxford, 1981), 47–8. This is one of the few publ. discussions of this topic worth reading.

[29] *Nicomachean Ethics*, 1105ª 22–7.

[30] There are various ambiguities in the term 'moral agent' and I certainly do not mean it to be equivalent to 'saint'. None the less, this bare statement in the text would need to be elaborated to deal with the problem cases such as the psychopath or the total amoralist. I have views on this but cannot embark here on the discussion which would be necessary in a fuller treatment of morality.

[31] *Nicomachean Ethics*, 1143ᵇ 10–14.

[32] The problems raised by this sort of situation are discussed in more depth in Ch. 4 and later chapters.

may even be such as to override our initial inclination to a different view. Of course, there are dangers in relying upon the moral wisdom of others, even greater dangers, no doubt, than in relying upon the technical expertise of scientists and doctors or the perceptual expertise of eyewitnesses. Normal adults are not related to moral truths as the uninitiated are to an area of science or as all of us are to the facts of less than recent history. None the less, it is surely also dangerous to base our moral life upon an illusory ideal of total rational autonomy when the fact is that a good deal of our moral outlook is influenced by the example of others, by the way they live and the way they speak of what guides their behaviour. We do better to confront the matter directly and try to understand what moral expertise might consist in.

Here I have attempted no more than a sketchy preamble to such an enterprise, taking a cue from Aristotle's emphasis on the value of moral experience. Further work along these lines might proceed by discussing our capacity to recognize good and virtuous people and to detect moral wisdom in those who speak to us of the good life in general and of what to do in particular cases. Another path has been proposed recently by one of the most eloquent spokesmen for 'applied philosophy' and 'practical ethics', Peter Singer. Singer argues that, by dint of their training, clarity, and full-time thinking on the subject, moral philosophers have a claim to the title of 'moral experts'.[33]

I am not particularly enamoured of this explication of the notion of moral expertise, though I would not want to deny that hard, disciplined thinking about moral matters is a component in someone's being authoritative for us about moral issues. My disinclination to follow Singer's path springs not from any disparagement of the role of thinking (even philosophical thinking) in morality but rather from an appreciation of the significance of action and experience in this area. In an informal presentation of the Singer view I once heard, an analogy was drawn between the moral philosopher's expertise and that of a motor mechanic. No such example appears in Singer's paper and I do not know if he would accept it, but it seems in broad terms in harmony with the views he expresses. In any case it is worth pressing the analogy to see what is unsatisfactory about Singer's thesis. As everyone knows who has had to have car repairs done, there are motor mechanics and motor mechanics. The mechanic whose credentials consist entirely in a theoretical understanding of combustion engines and the like is not to be compared as an expert with the experienced veteran who has actually confronted the practical, multifarious problems of repairing over a lifetime, and successfully solved most of them. Both in turn need to be distinguished from the veteran incompetent or the experienced crook. A thorough training in the skills of analytical

---

[33] Peter Singer, 'Moral Experts', *Analysis*, 32 (1971–2), 115–17.

moral philosophy, at best, puts one in something like the position of the first mechanic and I, for one, would no sooner think of consulting your average moral philosopher over a genuine moral problem than of consulting a philosopher of perception about an eye complaint. Lest I be thought to disparage my own profession I should add that the moral philosopher would probably give far better value than the average economist, psychologist, or sociologist, and a moral philosopher with the appropriate insight and practical wisdom to go with his intellectual skills would be a very useful guide indeed.

In conclusion I think we can say that a reasonable case obtains for the view that there is testimony to moral facts. In conjunction with the earlier discussion of Reid and expert testimony, and of the problem of avowals, this helps to support the wide scope of my analysis and the associated idea that testifying is a fundamental speech act. We must turn now to the epistemology of testimony.

II

The Tradition

4

Testimony, Observation, and the Reductive Approach

David Hume is one of the few philosophers who has offered anything like a sustained account of testimony and if any view has a claim to the title of 'the received view' it is his. In what follows I shall examine and criticize Hume's position in the hope of throwing light on more general issues concerning the epistemological status of testimony. Hume's account of the matter is offered in his essay on miracles, section 10 of *An Enquiry Concerning Human Understanding*. There Hume, as we saw in Chapter 1, concedes the utility and evidential value of testimony: '...there is no species of reasoning more common, more useful, and even necessary to human life, than that which is derived from the testimony of men and the reports of eye-witnesses and spectators'.[1]

Essentially his theory constitutes a reduction of testimony as a form of evidence or support to the status of a species (one might almost say, a mutation) of inductive inference. And, again, in so far as inductive inference is reduced by Hume to a species of observation and consequences attendant upon observations, then in a like fashion testimony meets the same fate. So we find him saying immediately after the piece quoted above:

This species of reasoning, perhaps, one may deny to be founded on the relation of cause and effect. I shall not dispute about a word. It will be sufficient to observe that our assurance in any argument of this kind is derived from no other principle than our observation of the veracity of human testimony, and of the usual conformity of facts to the reports of witnesses. It being a general maxim, that no objects have any discoverable connexion together, and that all the inferences, which we can draw from one to another, are founded merely on our experience of their constant and regular conjunction; it is evident that we ought not to make an exception to this maxim in favour of human testimony, whose connexion with any event seems, in itself, as little necessary as any other (p. 111).

And elsewhere in the same essay he says: 'The reason why we place any credit in witnesses and historians, is not derived from any *connexion*, which we perceive *a priori*, between testimony and reality, but because we are accustomed to find a conformity between them' (p. 113).

---

[1] D. Hume, *An Enquiry Concerning Human Understanding* (Oxford, 1957), s. 88. All quotations hereafter from this work are taken from L. A. Selby-Bigge's 2nd edn. of the *Enquiries* publ. by Clarendon Press, Oxford. Bracketed page refs. in my text are to that edn.

This is the view that I want to contest and, as it is convenient to have a label, I shall call it the Reductionist Thesis and shall employ the abbreviation RT to refer to it. J. L. Mackie, as mentioned in Chapter 1, has argued plausibly that some such reductionism is essential to a concept of 'autonomous knowledge' which he sees as involved in traditional empiricism. Mackie is attracted to an RT programme, and to the concept of cognitive autonomy associated with it, but is uncertain of its viability and admits that it is only one ideal of knowledge 'latent' in our ordinary concept of knowledge. The 'autonomous knower', in Mackie's sense, is someone who 'should know whatever it is off his own bat'[2] and who relies upon testimony only when he has checked for himself the credibility of the witnesses he trusts. Although this ideal exercises a powerful fascination for us, I shall try to show that it is chimerical and that the programme it rests upon is, in principle, misguided.

My criticism begins by calling attention to a fatal ambiguity in the use of terms like 'experience' and 'observation' in the Humean statement of RT. We are told by Hume that we only trust in testimony because experience has shown it to be reliable, yet where experience means individual observation and the expectations it gives rise to, this seems plainly false and, on the other hand, where it means common experience (i.e. the reliance upon the observations of others) it is surely question-begging. To take the second part of the ambiguity first—let us call it RT″—we find Hume speaking of '*our* experience of their constant and regular conjunction'. And it is clear enough that Hume often means by such phrases to refer to the common experience of humanity and not to the mere solitary observations of David Hume. Our reliance upon testimony as an institution, so to speak, is supposed to be based on the same kind of footing as our reliance upon laws of nature (Hume thinks of this as an important premiss in his critique of miracles) and he speaks of the 'firm and unalterable experience' which has established these laws. It is an important part of his argument that a miracle must be a violation of the laws of nature and so he says:

It is no miracle that a man, seemingly in good health, should die on a sudden: because such a kind of death, though more unusual than and other, has yet been frequently observed to happen. But it is a miracle that a dead man should come to life; because that has *never* been observed in any age or country. There must therefore be a uniform experience against every miraculous event, otherwise the event would not merit that appellation (p. 115).

We may ignore, for our purposes here, the validity of this highly debatable account of a law of nature and the blatant question-begging of his '*never* been observed in any age or country' and yet gather from this extract the need Hume has to mean by 'experience', 'observation', and the like, the

---

[2] J. L. Mackie, 'The Possibility of Innate Knowledge', *Proc. of the Aristotelian Society* (1970), 254.

common experience of mankind. Clearly his argument does not turn on the fact, for instance, that *he* has 'frequently observed' the sudden death of a man 'seemingly in good health'—it is quite likely that Hume (like most of us) never had occasion to observe personally anything of the kind. And the point is surely clinched by his reference to 'uniform experience' and his use of the phrase 'observed in any age or country'.

Evidently then, RT as actually argued by Hume is involved in vicious circularity, since the experience upon which our reliance upon testimony as a form of evidence is supposed to rest is itself reliant upon testimony which cannot be reduced in the same way. The idea of taking seriously someone else's observations, someone else's experience, already requires us to take their testimony (i.e. reports of what they observe) equally seriously. It is ludicrous to talk of their observations being the major part of our justification in taking their reports seriously when we have to take their reports seriously in order to know what their observations are.

Hume's conflation of personal and communal observation can be further illustrated by a passage from the *Treatise of Human Nature* (bk. I, pt. iv, s. 2). Discussing our reasons for believing in the continued, independent existence of material things, he says:

I receive a letter, which, upon opening it, I perceive by the handwriting and subscription to have come from a friend, who says he is two hundred leagues distant. It is evident I can never account for this phenomenon, conformable to my experience in other instances, without spreading out in my mind the whole sea and continent between us, and supposing the effects and continued existence of posts and ferries, according to my memory and observation (p. 196).

Here we have Hume using 'my' observation when he is clearly not entitled to do so since there is probably no single person who has personally observed the complete path of even *one* letter from the moment it leaves the sender's hand to the moment it reaches its destination. Hume might have observed postmen, posts, ferries, etc., but his beliefs about what they do (his belief in the postal system) is dependent upon a complicated web of testimony and inference, prominent amongst which would no doubt be what he was told by his teachers or parents. And yet, 'my memory and observation'. How easy it is to appropriate at a very fundamental level what is known by report and what is known by personal observation. Similarly, that babies are born of women in a certain way is known to all of us and it is a fact of observation but very many of us have not observed even one birth for ourselves.

J. L. Mackie, who, as we saw earlier, is attracted to the reductive enterprise, realizes that any RT project must eschew covert reliance upon the observations of others. Mackie acknowledges that 'the greater part of what each one of us knows comes to him by testimony'[3] but thinks that

---

[3] Ibid. 257.

the success of a project like Hume's is essential to the viability of a certain concept of 'autonomous knowledge'. He is clear, however, that what I have called the RT″ form of it will not do and he proposes instead a version of the first part of what I have called the RT ambiguity—let us call it RT′. Here is Mackie's version of the problem:

Knowledge that one acquires through testimony, that is, by being told by other people, by reading, and so on, can indeed be brought under the heading of this authoritative knowledge, but only if the knower somehow checks, for himself, the credibility of the witnesses. And since, if it is a fact that a certain witness is credible, it is an external fact, checking this in turn will need to be based on observations that the knower makes himself—or else on further testimony, but, if an infinite regress is to be avoided, we must come back at some stage to what the knower observes for himself.[4]

Mackie is surely right to think that only some such version can avoid the criticisms we have made of RT″ so let us, on Hume's behalf, retract his incautious commitment to common experience and state the RT in terms of personal observations alone. My claim was that, so stated, RT′ is plainly false but this has yet to be shown. A Humean version of RT′ would run something like this:

We rely upon testimony as a species of evidence *because* each of us observes for himself a constant and regular conjunction between what people report and the way the world is. More particularly, we each observe for ourselves a constant conjunction between kinds of report and kinds of situation so that we have good inductive grounds for expecting this conjunction to continue in the future.

My justification for bringing in the idea of a kind of report correlating with a kind of situation (which is not, for instance, explicit in Mackie's version) is Hume himself: 'And as the evidence, derived from witnesses and human testimony, is founded on past experience, so it varies with the experience, and is regarded either as a *proof* or a *probability* according as the conjunction between any particular kind of report and any kind of object has been found to be constant or variable' (p. 112).

Now I characterized this sort of position as 'plainly false' because it seems absurd to suggest that, individually, we have done anything like the amount of field-work that RT′ requires. As mentioned earlier, many of us have never seen a baby born, nor have most of us examined the circulation of the blood nor the actual geography of the world nor any fair sample of the laws of the land, nor have we made the observations that lie behind our knowledge that the lights in the sky are heavenly bodies immensely distant nor a vast number of other observations that RT′ would seem to require. Some people have of course made them *for us* but we are pre-

---

[4] Ibid. 254.

cluded from taking any solace from this fact under the present interpretation of RT. So it was this general situation that made me speak of
RT′ as plainly false.

But the matter is perhaps more complex than such a characterization
would indicate, as can be seen by considering a possible rejoinder by the
defenders of RT′. This might run as follows: 'You are ignoring the very
important provision, made by Hume, and already noticed by you, that the
conjunction in individual experience is between kinds of report and kinds
of object. This cuts down the amount of observing that has to be done and
makes the project a manageable one for an individual.' I think I may
reasonably plead 'not guilty' to this accusation inasmuch as I intended the
list above (of conjunctions never checked personally by most of us) to be
more than a recital of particular conjunctions that RT′ requires us to have
personally checked. The list was supposed to be typical in the sense that it
indicated *areas* in which we rightly accept testimony without ever having
engaged in the sort of checking of reports against personal observation
that RT′ demands.

But, quite apart from this, there seem to me to be serious difficulties in
the very idea of finding constant conjunctions between (in Hume's words)
'any particular kind of report and any kind of object'. Hume wants these
conjunctions to be something like the kinds of conjunctions he thinks are
required to establish causal laws and even laws of nature. In such matters
the decisive constant conjunctions are between one kind of object and
another kind of object. But whatever we think about the idea of a kind of
object, the notion of a kind of report surely requires some explanation
in this context. Unfortunately, Hume does nothing to provide such an
explanation and since the matter is also of interest in its own right I
shall risk a digression to consider some possible interpretations and their
implications before turning to a different, and perhaps more decisive,
difficulty for the type of approach represented by RT′.

It seems to me that 'kind of report' may be meant to refer either to the
kind of speaker who gives the report or to the kind of content the report
contains. If it is the former that is intended (and some of Hume's remarks
seem to indicate this) then presumably the kind of speaker will not be
determined by such considerations as colour of skin or nationality or hair-
style or height. Rather, the relevant kind will have something to do
with authority or expertise or credentials to say. So the RT′ would go
something like: we rely upon testimony because we have each personally
observed a correlation between expert (or authoritative) reports and the
kinds of situations reported in a large number of cases.

But the major difficulty for this interpretation is that a man's being an
expert or an authority on some matter cannot be a matter of mere inspection in the way that his being white or tall is. That some man is an expert
on, say, geography or South-East Asian politics, is either known on the
testimony of others (by far the most usual case) or it has to be established

by observing some high correlation between his reports and the relevant situations in the world. If the former, then we are no further advanced upon the RT programme of justification since the same problem of establishing expertise must arise again and again. If the latter, then the notion of an authority or an expert no longer provides us with any specification of *a kind of report*. That is to say, we cannot use the idea of *a kind of report* as equivalent to *report of a kind of speaker* and then proceed to validate testimony along the lines of RT′ because the kind of correlation situation whose existence we would supposedly be investigating would have to be known by us to exist already before we could set up the terms of the investigation.[5]

This indicates that the business of establishing constant conjunctions between kinds of report and kinds of situation must begin with the interpretation of 'kinds of report' as 'reports of kinds of situation'. And certainly this seems to be a natural way of interpreting Hume's intentions at this point. An initial problem for this interpretation concerns the degree of generality that should attach to the content of a report before it qualifies as a kind of report. That is to say, some sort of decision would presumably be required as to whether or not the report 'There is a sick lion in Taronga Park Zoo' belonged to the kind, medical report or geographical report or empirical report or existence report. Perhaps it could be said to belong to all of them or to some and not to others but whatever was said it would be of considerable importance to the establishing of conjunctions, since a decision here is a decision about the actual identity of the conjunctions and hence, in consequence, about the degree of correlation likely to be established. For instance, if the report were treated as belonging to the kind 'existence report' then it might be that Jones had personally established quite a large number of conjunctions between existence reports and the relevant existence situations without this being any real reason for accepting the report in question. (Compare with: 'There is a Martian in my study', which is presumably well supported by Jones's personal experience of existence reports.) On the other hand, if it were treated as a medical report then Jones may have had very little personal experience of correlations between medical reports and medical facts yet this would hardly be a real reason for not accepting the report. In addition, Jones would, on Hume's hypothesis, now have a strong reason for accepting the report if he classifies it one way and no reason for accepting it if he classifies it another way. Since either classification is logically permissible, then it seems to be purely a matter of whim whether Jones has or has not good reason for accepting the report. Clearly some sort of non-arbitrary restriction on the

---

[5] It may appear that part of this difficulty could be met by recourse to the qualification 'report of a so-called expert' but this is mere appearance since we require some assurance that we are checking the reports of those who are not merely self-styled experts but widely acknowledged as such. This sort of assurance could only be had by reliance upon testimony.

scope of 'report of a kind of situation' is required to make this notion of any real value in the elaboration of RT'. Here, however, I shall pursue no further the interpretation of 'kind of report' and the difficulties involved in specifying clearly the sort of correlations required by RT' because, on the perhaps dubious assumption that the difficulties are soluble, I want to raise what seems to me to be a more fundamental problem.

This difficulty consists in the fact that the whole enterprise of RT' in its present form requires that we understand what testimony is independently of knowing that it is, in any degree, a reliable form of evidence about the way the world is. This is, of course, the point of Hume's saying: 'The reason why we place any credit in witnesses and historians, is not derived from any *connexion*, which we perceive *a priori*, between testimony and reality, but because we are accustomed to find a conformity between them' (p. 113). It is a clear implication from this that we might have discovered (though in fact we did not) that there was no conformity at all between testimony and reality. Hume's position requires the possibility that we clearly isolate the reports that people make about the world for comparison by personal observation with the actual state of the world and find a high, low, or no correlation between them. But it is by no means clear that we can understand this suggestion. To take the most extreme discovery: imagine a world in which an extensive survey yields no correlation between reports and (individually observed) facts. In such a colossally topsy-turvy world what evidence would there possibly be for the existence of reports at all? Imagine a community of Martians who are in the mess that RT' allows as a possibility. Let us suppose for the moment that they have a language which we can translate (there are difficulties in this supposition as we shall see shortly) with names for distinguishable things in their environment and suitable predicative equipment. We find however, to our astonishment, that whenever they construct sentences addressed to each other in the absence (from their vicinity) of the things designated by the names, but when they are, as we should think, in a position to *report*, then they seem to say what we (more synoptically placed) can observe to be false. But in such a situation what reason would there be for believing that they even had the practice of reporting?

Let us first of all concentrate upon the *speech act* of reporting as it would be natural for an observer to do and ignore for the moment documentary, oblique, institutional testimony and the like. We must suppose that the Martians constantly misinform each other about issues in dispute or unresolved issues of interest and never correct each other's misinformation on the basis of their own observations (since that would involve giving correct testimony in the correction situation). They always, for instance, tell each other the wrong time and date, give their names and addresses wrongly, say falsely what the weather is like outdoors, and give false information about where they have been and what they have been doing. On the supposition that they are reporting we cannot have the audience indifferent to the import of this misinformation; we must ask how they act upon it and how they react when their actions go astray in the face of recalcitrant reality; we must ask about their responses upon observing the misreported situations for themselves and we must question how it is that they then continue to misreport them. One thing they can't do, as we have noted, is report back, indignantly or sorrowfully, that the original testifier is wrong. Nor is it coherent with the attribution of any remotely plausible psychological life to the Martians to suppose that they rely upon these 'reports' for the conduct of their intellectual or practical affairs. We are, of course, envisaging a situation which is the stable plight of the community extending over a reasonable length of time; it may be that one could establish a no-correlation result for a very short period in which very few reports, all of them false, were actually made. Obviously, Hume's project is aimed at establishing something general about a more permanent phenomenon. Hence we must suppose that the Martians come to find many 'reports' in conflict with their own experience. They also find themselves constrained to falsify their own observations when communicating with others.

It is true that there is a great deal that they cannot or will not directly check upon and even quite a few reports whose falsity may have no practical consequences for the recipient, but it is also true that there is unlikely to be a firm consensus of falsehood about that corpus of unchecked misinformation. Suppose A hears a sound and asks B, who has just entered from the back yard, whether there is an animal in the yard. B knows from his observation that there is (or, strictly, was until very recently) no animal in the yard but says falsely 'There is a dog in the yard'. He might equally have given false report by saying, 'There is a cat in the yard' or 'There is a frog in the yard' or whatever. So the fact that ten people will all falsely report some situation or occurrence does not guarantee or even make it likely that they will all say even roughly the same thing. Indeed, they may all contradict each other and still say what is incompatible with a true report. On the assumption that they are not in collusion, it will be very unlikely that 'cohesive falsehood', as we might call it, will often emerge; it will naturally arise only when, in the face of some fact p, not-p, i.e. the flat denial of p by use of negation, is the natural way to misreport it rather than some proposition q, r, s, ..., which is incompatible with it. Consequently, the lack of cohesion in the various reports any individual gets to matters he has not himself observed gives him another reason not to rely upon these reports.

In summary, any Martian has four powerful reasons for not relying upon what others appear to be telling him: (i) he finds their 'reports' false whenever he checks personally on them, (ii) he finds reliance upon them consistently leads him astray in practice, (iii) he finds himself utterly unreliable in what he tells others and it is, at least, possible that he is not atypical, (iv) others often give chaotically divergent reports on those matters beyond his checking. It is therefore very hard to imagine the activity of reporting in anything like its usual setting with the Martians, for there would surely be no reliance upon the 'reportive' utterances of others. This conclusion emerges only from the consideration of the speech act of reporting but is strongly reinforced by reflection on the consequences of the no-correlation outcome for documentary and institutional testimony, e.g. road signs, maps, etc. With no reliance (or only confused and intermittent reliance at best) on the utterances of others, the Martian community cannot reasonably be held to have the practice of reporting; even the concept of fantasy would give us only a marginal and elusive grasp of what they are about. Martian 'reporting', we might think, is like a generalization of the fantasy games children play ('Mummy, there's a burglar in the house') which are not taken seriously by adults. These games are, however, parasitic upon fully fledged reporting which adults do generally rely upon and which give the fantasy a kind of point. In the case of the Martians, the generalization is so wide that the fantasy appears to have no point at all. In some respects the supposition that reports could exist in this sort of context is like the supposition that orders might never be obeyed. If there were Martians who uttered certain sounds in a tone of voice like the tone we use in ordering we might initially conjecture that they were issuing orders in making these sounds but this conjecture would be undermined if it were found that these sounds never had any effect that might be described as obedience upon any audience.

Alarming as these conclusions are for the Humean project, they arise from assumptions which are already too concessive. The situation with the Martians is even worse than the above discussion reveals since they are in trouble even about the content of the utterances that are alleged to be non-correlated reports. The question of the meaning or content of what they say in their alleged reports is of great importance because the task of looking for a correlation or conjunction of the Humean type is dependent upon knowing what state of affairs is supposed to correlate with the utterance. The principle of correlation has to be given by the meaning of the utterances because, after all, *any* utterance is correlated with or conjoined to *any* situation according to *some* principle of matching. So, even if we allow, for the sake of argument, that we can understand what it is for the Martians to engage in reporting, we cannot accept the coherence of the no-correlation story unless we can understand what Martian reports actually say. But it is precisely here that serious difficulties arise and to see how they arise we must look more closely at the supposed Martian situation.

It is clear from earlier chapters that a very high proportion of the statements made by a community over a sample period will have to be testimony statements. These utterances will contrast with such speech episodes as soliloquies, musings, and conjectures. In the Martian community a common vocabulary is employed across different speech acts so that, as with us, the same form of words may be used for either conjecture or testimony (e.g. 'He pushed her in') although there may also be speech-act indicators available of an Austinian or Searlean form ('I testify that ...', 'I conjecture that ...'). Suppose then that we encounter a Martian who uses the utterance 'Kar do gnos u grin' in the presence of a tree in a garden. Perhaps he waves a languid hand at the tree as he does so. We speculate that this utterance means, can be translated as, 'There is a tree in the garden' and, in particular, that 'gnos' means 'tree'.[6] We then find, however, that the Martian frequently uses 'gnos' in remarks in situations not involving the presence of a tree in his observational vicinity. Some few of these remarks we assess as mere conjectures (and I shall ignore the problems raised by the question of how this assessment is made) but the majority we decide to be testimony. So we find the Martian saying things of the form: 'Kar do gnos u grin', 'Kar do gnos u bilt', 'Kar do gnos u tonk', and we guess that these mean 'There is a tree in the garden', 'There is a tree in the study', 'There is a tree in the field', or whatever. We suppose him to be telling us about the location of trees that are beyond our observational range—what I shall call 'absent trees'. But then we find that there never is a tree in the garden or in the study or in the field and that in fact this Martian never uses 'gnos' to make a true statement when he is talking (non-conjecturely) to others about, as it seems, absent trees. Furthermore, whenever we are able to check upon the truth of Martian utterances, we find that no Martian ever uses 'gnos' to make at first hand a true report about absent trees though engaged, as we suppose, in constant attempts to do so or to appear to do so. Just as surprisingly, we find that no Martian ever contradicts or corrects another about absent trees on the basis of his own observation or the 'testimony' of others since, by hypothesis, no testimony ever matches the facts. When one Martian, having heard another report (as we interpret it) that there is a tree in the yard, looks for himself into the yard and sees none he never corrects or criticizes the first report, no matter how great the importance of the truth about the matter. Indeed, if called upon to say anything germane, he repeats the falsehood. If we preserve the hypothesis that we have identified the speech acts of reporting correctly (and we can see once more how this would naturally be threatened by the lack of connection between the putative reports and other significant behaviour) then we would have to reject our interpretation of 'gnos' as 'tree' or make some equally dramatic

---

[6] There is perhaps a problem in working out what he is up to and hence a puzzle as to how we are even entitled to speculate that his utterance means *this* but we may suppose that there is enough about his behaviour to permit us to conclude that he is soliloquizing in the fashion of one who is struck by the existence of that particular tree in that particular garden.

semantic adjustment. We would have to conclude that 'gnos' did not mean 'tree' or that it did not mean it unambiguously or possibly that the Martians have a device for negation which we have not yet uncovered (so that 'Kar do gnos u grin' really means 'There isn't a tree in the garden') or perhaps that the Martians are totally incomprehensible to us. Indeed, this last conclusion would be considerably fortified by the fact that the linguistic chaos described above is generated on behalf of not just one sound, 'gnos', that the Martians utter, but by every sound which is supposed to be a word and upon the reference of which the truth or falsity of an alleged report could turn!

It might be complained at this point that I have not described the Martian community in sufficient detail and I readily concede that my account of their circumstances is somewhat sketchy. Attempts to describe the Martian community in any more detail, however, are unlikely to improve the prospects for the Humean enterprise. Possibly one could fill out the particulars in such a way as to make marginally more plausible one or another explanation (massive mistake, massive deceit) for their non-veridical testimony but it is clear that either pattern of explanation runs into insuperable difficulties. These difficulties are primarily difficulties for the rational acceptability of any proposed interpretation of the meaning of their utterances which has all their reports coming out false but the problem should not be thought of as restricted to the linguistic realm. Holding fixed such interpretations as ' "gnos" means tree' also makes it that much harder reasonably to treat the Martians as perceiving, remembering, and reasoning. This is because there are subtle but none the less fundamental links between any thinker's perceptual, memory, inferential, and testimonial resources. We shall explore these more fully in a later chapter but here it is enough to note that the linguistic disarray produced by the no-correlation hypothesis generates puzzling questions for the interpreter about how the Martians perceive their environment, remember it, and reason about the perceptions, memories, and inferences of their fellows. True, we can have evidence that the Martians perceive, remember, and reason about their environment from the way they behave towards it—avoid obstacles, act on their surroundings, and satisfy desires—but all of this is jeopardized by their apparent incapacity to transmit true information and to correct one another's (apparent) mistakes. (This incapacity is quite different from and more damaging than that possessed by creatures lacking a language altogether.) What do they think of their fellow Martians' cognitive capacities, for instance, given that they must know that the fellow Martians are from time to time in a position to observe or infer the falsity of their testimony but never contradict the false reports. Instead, if anything, they confirm them, even in circumstances where deception has no point.

The transmission of information through a chain of witnesses should also be considered in this connection since it too must also preserve the no-correlation result. This is particularly puzzling from the point of view of any mechanism that might explain the no-correlation. Consider the situation: A's firsthand report that p will be false to the reported situation (not-p) but then B transmits the message to C who transmits to D and D gives it on to E. To preserve no-correlation each transmitter must correctly transmit the (false) message but this is hard to understand in a situation in which no firsthand reporter ever testifies truly. If we suppose, for instance, that no-correlation results from the desire to deceive then it is impossible to explain how this desire allows such effective transmission of the original message. It is hardly to be supposed that hearers always know that their original sources are lying and that linking testifiers are always accurate. Amongst other difficulties is the problem that this would require that they always distinguish correctly who is an original and who an intermediate witness. Moreover, such witnesses as B, C, D, and E will report that p, as transmitters of the message, but if asked what their informant told them must report (falsely) that he said not p. If the mechanism at work is deception then when asked if they believe what their informant said they will have to reply (if they reply at all), 'Yes', but if asked whether they believe that p they will have to say 'Yes' again. It is not clear that any sense can be made of this. On the other hand, if the mechanism is one of mistake rather than deception then we will have to suppose either that the misreporting mechanism only works for original witnesses or that it works for all and the mistakes keep cancelling out in the transmission process. The former suggestion is absurdly *ad hoc*, especially since the way intermediate witnesses gather the message they transmit is by the same sort of processes (seeing or hearing) as the original witness. The latter suggestion is equally absurd since it requires, for instance, that whenever B hears A say 'p' he mishears this as 'not-p' and then mistates 'not-p' as 'p' and yet for an original witness such as A only the one mistake can occur (either the misperception or the mistatement). These possibilities are more than fantastic, they strain beyond breaking point any possibility of natural expanation and disqualify themselves as background hypotheses available for the interpretation of Martian utterances.

I will not pursue these issues of detail further now; I am content if enough has been said of the Martians' plight to raise grave doubts about the task of identifying the contents of Martian-type reports and hence of investigating Humean correlations in such a world. The general point here is that, although making true reports with words is not the same thing as using the words correctly, none the less the ability to make true reports with words *is* connected with using the words correctly and this ability is something that can only be exhibited (even to the persons themselves) in the making of true reports.

There is a further point to be made about the connection of testimony with meaning. If we take it that teaching someone the meaning of words involves the giving of reports and testimony then the present form of RT′ is in even hotter water than before since the suggestion that no reports in fact conform to reality involves the claim that our imagined Martians never report to the Martian children the actual use of their words.

Here the idea that the Martians have a public language seems to get no grip at all. It may be objected that parents and others do not give testimony when they offer instruction in the language and certainly some of the deliberate inculcation of language skills to the immature will consist in training, coaxing, or drilling rather than reporting. In the very early stages of the child's progress the teacher simply makes sure that the child can produce certain sounds in the presence of relevantly highlighted objects. The doll is waved about conspicuously and the child is encouraged to repeat the sound 'doll' and so on. I doubt that such performances are as mechanical and as far removed from reporting as the objection requires and as words such as 'drilling' suggest. They are designed, after all, to appeal to the child's, admittedly immature, cognitive equipment and to elicit responses which are, to some degree, under the control of awareness and intelligence. Many theorists go so far as to talk of the child's making inferences and constructing theories. I think that there are difficulties in following such a path, especially that of theory construction, but the child *is* being called upon to recognize intentions or purposes in its instructor's behaviour and to grasp the connections the instructor intends to set before it. It is thus plausible to see such performances as a forerunner of testimony, a kind of proto-reporting (having some analogies with the oblique testimony discussed in Chapter 2), on the ground that the child is expected to gather from the adult cavortings that the adult intends the child to come to think that 'doll' is the word for this sort of object and this thought would have been the content of a straightforward report but for the fact that the child is not yet in a position to grasp it in such a form. Some support for this construal comes from the fact that such instruction is naturally supplanted by what seem to be reports, namely, reports on the meanings of words ('"Cat" means one of these' or '"Cat" is the word for a four-legged mammal with . . .') when the child has a little more grip on the language's resources. This suggests strongly that there is an intimate relation between the performing of such instruction and the giving of report; the instruction is, at least in part, a surrogate for reporting, a sort of proto-reporting. It may have more than this role but it has at least this role. Consequently, we can hardly find it plausible that the Martian community's reports utterly fail to correlate with reality whilst their linguistic instructional performances match pretty reliably. Not only would this pose a problem, as it were, of mechanism, since it would be hard to see how that which makes for the massive breakdown in reporting does not equally produce breakdown in the adjacent area of proto-reporting, but also, on Humean grounds, there is as little reason to deny a non-correlation story in the one case as in the other.

It might be argued that our only ground for treating the instructional routines as surrogate reports is their relation to such supposed reports as ' "Chair" means one of those' or even the instructional use of 'This is a chair' and the supposition is simply wrong since such utterances are not reports. But why not? Once we have overcome whatever prejudice might exist against expert reports there can be no reason to resist the idea that there can be reports on the meaning of words and other expressions of a natural language and on the grammar of that language. All mature speakers of such a language have the relevant expertise to a reasonable degree though, of course, some are more expert than others. If, as it is plausible though perhaps not compelling to suppose, meaning facts and other linguistic facts are constituted by conventions then this is no barrier to their being testified to. Amongst the things we often want to know when visiting a foreign country are details of its various conventions (eating, greeting, sporting, and so on) and there can surely be no denying that suitably placed people can report on such matters for us. It is not exactly clear what Hume thought constituted public meanings but there is no reason at all to suspect that he would not have allowed them to be matters of report. Probably, he would have accounted them matters of empirical fact open to both observation and report, such as that certain expressions are used in such and such ways in a certain community.

A more serious objection is that this stress upon the teaching of language by report and proto-report distorts the reality of language acquisition. Though these processes have some role to play in learning one's first language they are overshadowed by processes in which the child learns by observing the communicative activities going on around him or her. There is an area of empirical research here which is still in an early stage of development and which it would be foolish to pre-empt but it is worth remarking that whatever the child acquires by way of such observation is subject to the same constraints that we non-Martians are under in striving to understand the Martian conversations. The child is in no position therefore to acquire the language on a no-correlation supposition. Furthermore, even if we imagine that a natural language could be acquired with *no* explicit teaching, in the sense that the child simply comes to his own conclusions about the meanings and other grammatical properties of the common language, we cannot suppose that he is beyond the need of correction from those versed in the language. The problem which we have dramatized for the teaching situation arises just as dramatically in the correction situation. A community cannot operate a common language without the resources for correcting the inevitable divergences from correct use and the child's 'hypotheses' about the meaning and structure of the language are profoundly dependent upon the correctional testimony of the mature speakers. This point is worth remembering when it is claimed, as it sometimes is, that it is 'a merely contingent fact' that languages are acquired by teaching since the point about correction applies equally to 'hypotheses' the child is born with.

Let us summarize our progress to date. From Hume's account of testimony I extracted a reductionist thesis which had two forms. I argued that the second form, RT″, which justified testimony in terms of common experience, was circular and that the first form, RT′, which justified testimony in terms of individual observation, was simply false since our reliance upon testimony rightly goes beyond anything that could be justified by personal observations. I then considered the rejoinder that RT′ might be more plausible if great weight were put upon the observation of constant conjunction between kinds of report and kinds of object and I argued that much was unclear about what was to count as a kind of report, and hence what was to count as a correlation, for the purposes of RT′. In any case RT′ surely requires that any such investigation into conjunctions of reports with states of affairs might conclude that there were no such correlations between the two. The supposition that such a situation obtained was pursued for the purpose of *reductio ad absurdum* and I argued that in such a situation, (*a*) there could be no such things as reports, (*b*) even if there were reports, there could be no way of establishing Humean correlations or non-correlations since there could be no way of determining the contents of the alleged reports in order to correlate them, and (*c*) the idea of a public language seems undermined.

At this point, certain general objections to my line of argument need to be faced. It might be objected, first of all, that although I have shown that no interpreter could have acceptable evidence that the no-correlation result obtained, none the less this does not show that the no-correlation result is impossible or unintelligible. The objector might accuse me of showing indifference, in what has gone on above, to the distinction between, on the one hand, the impossibility of an interpreter's having reason to construe the Martians as reporting at all or, if reporting, as invariably reporting wrongly and, on the other hand, the impossibility of the Martians actually doing either of these things. Clearly, the former impossibility is weaker than the latter. It might further be suggested that my failure to distinguish here shows a regrettable attachment to some form of verifiability theory of meaning which certainly collapses any distinction between a factual proposition's verifiability and its intelligibility or possible truth.

I have little sympathy with logical positivism nor with any strong versions of verifiability theories of meaning, though it may be that, once we move away from the hard-line positivist position which has cognitive meaning depending upon the possibility of individual sensory verification, then there is at least some plausibility in what have come to be called anti-realist theories of meaning. Such theories have their own unclarities but

generally hold that we cannot understand what it would be for a proposition to be true or false unless we have some grasp upon what it would
be to find it true or false. A parallel point could be made about satisfaction
conditions and the like in the case of non-propositional speech acts. This
aside, however, one reply should be made at once to the objection, namely,
that my criticism of Hume is unaffected by it, in that my criticism need
rely on only the weaker of the claims distinguished in the objection. I
argued that Hume's RT project requires us to be able *to detect* a no-
correlation situation and this, I have tried to show, cannot be done. None
the less, Hume's project also requires that such a situation be possible and
it would be interesting to know if my argument rules this out. I suspect
that it does and I think this can be shown without entering into the debate
about the merits of anti-realism as a general theory of meaning.

If we look at the arguments I have used against the no-correlation
possibility it is true that they are often presented in terms of an outside
interpreter seeking to make sense of a community's utterances but this is
partly a device for making vivid what I have called the 'plight' of the
Martians themselves. In asking what 'we' can make of Martian utterances
I am asking what semantic properties they have or can have. To ask what
interpretations are possible of utterances is to ask what constitutes those
utterances as having certain semantic properties. The possibilities of communication and interpretation are not extrinsic to the existence in public
languages of semantic properties like meaning, content, and even truth, so
when we explore such possibilities and come up against their limits we
may legitimately see ourselves as showing the limits of application in
reality of those properties. My discussion of the plight of the Martians was
not only designed to show that an outside interpreter could have no reason
to assign meanings that led to the no-correlation result but that the
Martians themselves were in the same position with respect to their own
and others' utterances in Martian. There may be natural properties of
which it can be shown both that there are contexts in which no one could
have reason to believe that they are instantiated and that they none the less
could be instantiated in those contexts, but, for the reasons given, I
seriously doubt that the semantic properties of public languages are
such.[7]

This might be admitted but another line of objection developed as
follows: your case rests on there being every reason to reject interpretations of the Martian's linguistic and other behaviour which lead to the

---

[7] My remarks are specifically about public languages. I do not mean to deny the possibility
of private languages. Whatever sense can be given to the idea of a private language, the
possibility or indeed existence of such languages is irrelevant to the problems about testimony
here discussed since testimony essentially involves communication in a public language.
Wittgenstein's objections to the possibility of a (certain sort of) private language have never
seemed to me persuasive though I cannot be certain that I have understood the argument(s).

no-correlation result and it is certainly true that behaviour alone could never justify the meaning and speech-act attributions required by the no-correlation supposition, but perhaps we could have other reasons for the attributions. In particular, it has been suggested to me that neural evidence might, in principle, become available that would enable us to fix the meanings of Martian utterances in a way that made all their actual reports or even all their utterances come out false. If we supposed for instance that meanings were fixed by or supervened upon the totality of certain sorts of dispositions to linguistic behaviour then might we not, at least in theory, reach beyond the actual linguistic behaviour to the dispositions via neural evidence?

The basic objection to this proposal is not that it is far-fetched (which, of course, it is in the extreme) but that it is quite unclear what neural evidence could turn the required trick. It may be that certain brain states are, or are the bases of, the dispositions to linguistic behaviour that determine correct interpretations of Martian language, but which brain states or events these are is not to be determined solely by neurological investigation. The identification of the relevant neural states rather waits upon an appropriate interpretation of actual utterances and other behaviour. Given that we could have no grounds in Martian behaviour for speech interpretations that yield a no-correlation story then there is equally no ground for identifying appropriately meaning-related brain states that would yield that conclusion. Nor could we remedy this situation by extrapolating from any discoveries we might come to make in our own community about the neural bases of our own linguistic dispositions and behaviour, since the bridging claim that they must have the same types of brain states for the same dispositions (what philosophers call a type–type identity claim) is not logically necessary and is indeed empirically defeated by the evidence of their behaviour.

Even were the suggestion not basically flawed in this way, there is of course some difficulty in seeing how the Humean enterprise of justifying testimony (or any enterprise with a similar inspiration) could be saved by the existence of a possibility detectable only by such a method. The objection to Hume, after all, is that his method of checking correlations requires that it be possible for that method to yield a no-correlation result. The relevance to this of the fact that some other method, not actually available to Hume or to anyone else, might yield such a result is at least a little obscure.

We should perhaps recall here the point made earlier in our discussion of whether the Martians could even be construed as reporting, namely that the denial of the no-correlation possibility does not mean that no segment of reporting could be false. One might, that is, encounter early in one's investigations a chunk of utterances every one of which turned out to be a false report, but it is only against the background of a subsequently discovered even greater or more significant corpus of correct reports that this possibility could make sense to an investigator.

Am I then saying, in opposition to Hume, that there *is* an a priori connection between testimony and reality? An answer to this question would have to rely on a comprehensive theory of knowledge which could determine the conditions under which an a priori connection holds between some x and reality and hence not only whether there is such a connection between testimony and reality but also whether such a connection holds, say, between perception and reality. I cannot provide such a theory here, though I will discuss some of the issues it involves in Chapters 8 and 9, but I do not understand the idea that testimony could exist in a community and yet it could be possible to discover empirically that it had no 'connection with reality'. Hence, I suspect that the problem of justifying testimony, conceived in anything like Hume's reductive terms, is a pseudo-problem and that the evidence of testimony constitutes a fundamental category of evidence which is not reducible to, or wholly justifiable in terms of, such other basic categories as observation or deductive inference. This opinion I have not proved but if my argument so far is correct then there is no sense to the idea of justifying testimony by the path of individual observation, at least where this involves anything like a search for Humean correlations.[8] Testimony constitutes a serious stumbling block for the 'autonomous knower' of whom Mackie speaks since there must be at least the minimum connection between testimony and reality that the breakdown of the no-correlation possibility reveals. From what our discussion of that breakdown exhibited we may well conclude that the connection has to be quite extensive. If, as I claimed earlier, the ability to use language meaningfully is connected with the making of true reports then it is surely the *consistent* making of true reports that matters. None the less, I shall postpone a discussion of this stronger conclusion until Chapter 9 and there I shall also seek to clarify the relation of such a conclusion to the general philosophical problem of scepticism and my invocation of the concept of truth.

Now, of course, none of this generalizing means that there is no such thing as mistaken or lying testimony and it is, I think, the fact that there are conditions and circumstances under which we disregard the reports of witnesses which Hume sees as providing support for RT independently of his methodological doctrine that there can be no necessary connection between any one object (or kind of object) and any other object (or kind of object).

---

[8] I have not of course proved that our reliance on testimony may not be 'justified' in some other manner. Russell, for one, has attempted, in *Human Knowledge: Its Scope and Limits* (New York, 1948), to justify testimony by recourse to a principle of analogy and Price in *Belief* (London, 1969) by recourse to a methodological rule. I shall discuss their views in subsequent chapters.

Were not the memory tenacious to a certain degree, had not men commonly an inclination to truth and a principle of probity; were they not sensible to shame, when detected in a falsehood: Were not these, I say, discovered by *experience* to be qualities, inherent in human nature, we should never repose the least confidence in human testimony. A man delirious, or noted for falsehood and villany, has no manner of authority with us (p. 112).

Hume's argument is not fully explicit here but he seems to be claiming that since we sometimes discover by observation and experience that some testimony is *unreliable* (i.e. 'A man delirious or noted for falsehood or villainy has no manner of authority with us') then we must discover the general *reliability* of testimony by the same method. But this surely has only to be stated to be seen to be invalid, for the fact that observation can sometimes uncover false testimony does nothing towards showing that the general reliability of testimony depends upon observation in the way RT requires.

Furthermore, the fact that observation will sometimes lead us to reject some piece of testimony needs to be set against two other facts.

1. That other testimony sometimes leads us to reject some piece of testimony without personal observation entering into the matter. Consider, for instance, Hume's *very* example of the man noted for delirium or falsehood or villainy. Connected with this is the very important fact that our concepts of checking, verifying and falsifying are not inherently individualistic. The individual does the checking and verifying but this does not mean that she must rely exclusively upon her own personal observations. Suppose someone makes some allegations that are sufficiently important or disturbing not to be taken at face value. We subject them to scrutiny by cross-examining the witness and when this does not settle the matter we check on the witness's credentials. This latter task invariably involves trusting some other people whose credentials inevitably remain themselves unchecked. A surprising number of acute epistemologists have failed to see this point, just as Hume himself seems to ignore it in the passage quoted above.[9]

2. That testimony sometimes leads us to reject some piece of observation. There are many different sorts of cases here. In philosophical discussions about perception one is apt to hear quite a lot about people who

[9] Part of Elizabeth Fricker's argument for the view that testimony is 'a secondary and not a primary epistemic link' seems to depend on the assumption that the sort of evidence a person must have for the reliability of a witness if he is to be credited with knowledge of some reported fact has to be non-testimonial. See her 'The Epistemology of Testimony' in *Proceedings of the Aristotelian Society*, supp. vol. 61 (1987), especially s. iii, and particularly pp. 75–8. Her general position puts her close to Hume (with certain important qualifications) and her claim that 'testimony is not an autonomous source of knowledge' (p. 78) is very much in the spirit of the outlook I am criticizing.

'see' a table in front of them in optimum observational conditions but become convinced that there is no table there because everyone around them says there isn't. Less fancifully, this case springs from those in which the testimony of others assures us that we are or are not hallucinated. Furthermore, there are often situations where we accept correction of our ordinary misobservations from the reports of others: 'Look at that herd of cows', 'They're not cows they're rock formations'. Or we observe a scuffle between three men and the upshot is that one of them is stabbed. There were four of us observing it and I hold that the man stabbed himself but the others maintain stoutly that one of the other two, namely Smith, delivered the blow. I capitulate. Surely this could be the reasonable thing to do in some circumstances. Indeed, it would seem equally as valid, on Hume's line of argument, to claim that, since testimony sometimes leads us to abandon an observation, then we rely upon observation in general only because we have established its reliability on the basis of testimony. But I think Hume would hardly be happy with *this* employment of his mode of argument.

Finally, it is worth remarking on the fact that the points made in the last few paragraphs and indeed a number of those made in the earlier analysis of the RT programme are reflected elsewhere in our epistemological landscape. Consider memory. Sometimes an individual discovers that his memories are false because they do not adequately consort with his present perceptual experience. He may think he recalls a large flowering gum tree in a certain familiar park at a certain spot but when he goes there to admire it, there is no sign of its ever having been there, though he soon comes across it in a nearby golf course which he recalls frequenting. Here individual observation (plus or including a little inference) shows memory to be fallacious. In the passage quoted above from Hume there is at least the hint of a reductionist thesis about memory which might begin from such facts as this. (Hume says that the 'tenacity' of memory is discovered by experience to be a quality in human nature and he sees this as a step on the way to the justification of testimony.)

Any suggestion, however, that the general reliability of one's memory is to be established by present perceptual experiences cannot be seriously entertained since, unless we take its reliability for granted to some extent, we cannot even gather the empirical evidence which is supposed to make the case for or against memory's connection with reality. The position of the tree may have been misremembered but to establish this we have to accept at face value a large number of memory deliverances, such as, that *this* is the park in question, *that* the golf course frequented in the past, and *this* the previously encountered tree, not to mention the fact that present observation itself rapidly assumes the status of memory and must needs do so to count as empirical evidence for an RT type justification of memory.[10] Moreover, parallel to the case of testimony, we often correct memory by memory and correct or reject apparent observations which conflict with memories. So, I may seem to glimpse a friend in the corridor of a building but reject the evidence of sense because I recall that he is in another country. Here we have a more or less conscious intellectual process but the influence of memory on perception can be more direct, as when I believe that my friend is in another country and so actually fail to recognize him visually when, upon his unexpected return, he is before my eyes. There are also, of course, intimate relations between testimony and memory as epistemological sources; indeed, all our basic sources of information are closely interwoven. We shall scrutinize this more carefully in Chapter 9.

Let us conclude by asking whether the collapse of Hume's reductionist project and the undermining of its associated ideal of 'autonomous knowledge' leave room for any aspirations to a robust degree of cognitive autonomy. The development of post-Enlightenment commitments to freedom and autonomy, in both the intellectual and the practical spheres, has in fact been implicated in more or less extreme versions of individualism, but this connection is not inevitable. Just as the autonomous agent need not utterly renounce his dependence upon others, even at the deepest levels of his existence, so the autonomous thinker need not entirely renounce some degree of fundamental reliance upon the word of others but rather should deploy it to achieve a genuinely critical stance and a viable independence of outlook. One needs intellectual autonomy to achieve a feasible degree of control over the beliefs one acquires and to ensure that one's thinking is appropriately responsive to one's actual cognitive history and present intellectual environment. None the less, the independent thinker is not someone who works everything out for herself, even in principle, but one who exercises a controlling intelligence over the input she receives from the normal sources of information whether their basis be

[10] An analogy between the difficulties facing Hume's purported justification of testimony and those facing such a justification of memory is drawn by George Campbell in his perceptive essay *A Dissertation on Miracles* publ. in 1762 by Kincaid and Bell, Edinburgh. Campbell's critique of Hume is mostly concerned to vindicate theological reliance upon some miracles but his first three sections offer a penetrating critique of Hume's philosophical assumptions concerning testimony. Some of his comments foreshadow part of my case against Hume. He detects, for instance, the ambiguity inherent in Hume's use of 'experience' and accuses him of arguing in a circle if relying upon communal experience (which he calls 'derived') to justify testimony, and of restricting the scope of our knowledge absurdly if relying upon personal experience to turn the trick. The first point he handles well but the second is not properly developed. He does not discuss the language or correlation problems raised here at all. I became acquainted with Campbell's essay only when rewriting my original article 'Testimony and Observation', *American Philosophical Quarterly* (1973) for inclusion here as Ch. 4. The dissertation has recently been rescued from long and unjustified neglect by Lewis White Beck and repr. by Garland Publishing (New York, 1983).

individual or communal. The Humean picture of testimony supports an ideal of epistemic autonomy which is illusory, and which has, incidentally, been particularly harmful in educational theory. Once it is abandoned, we are free to construct a more realistic and serviceable concept of autonomous thinking.[11]

---

[11] There is an interesting discussion of cognitive autonomy in Frederick F. Schmitt, 'Justification, Sociality and Autonomy', *Synthese*, 73 (1987). I have benefited from reading Margaret M. Coady's M.Ed. thesis 'Authority, Reason and Education' (Univ. of Melbourne, 1972) and her paper, 'Autonomy and Individualism' in the *Cambridge Journal of Education* (1974). Another good article on intellectual autonomy, which deserves to be better known and which is sensitive to the difficulties faced by reductive approaches to the epistemology of testimony, is Anthony Quinton's paper, 'Authority and Autonomy in Knowledge' in *Proceedings of the Philosophy of Education Society of Great Britain*, supp. issue, 5/2 (1971).

5

Deciding for Testimony

In this and the next chapter I shall discuss respectively H. H. Price's and Bertrand Russell's attempts to vindicate our extensive reliance upon testimony. Both Price and Russell have the same starting-points as Hume and Mackie inasmuch as their problem situation is that of an individual endowed with memory, perception, and inferential resources who must somehow determine whether reports in a language he understands are sufficiently reliable to allow him vastly to extend his very restricted knowledge base. Their protagonists are seeking to 'justify' testimony at large (and not merely some contentious item of testimony), but, unlike Hume's hero, their efforts do not follow the inductive path of checking samples of reports by individual observation and generalizing to some larger reliability. I shall proceed in reverse chronological order by discussing first Price's theory and then Russell's.

Price's treatment of the problem occurs in lecture 5 of his book *Belief*. The book is a product of his Gifford Lectures but in fact this section was written after the lectures were given when Price realized that his failure to discuss the epistemological problems posed by testimony constituted a serious gap in his analysis of belief. Perhaps because of this, the argument and presentation of the chapter on 'The Evidence of Testimony' is rather diffuse and, at times, confusing. I shall try to present an orderly summary of his view, with incidental criticisms of a clarificatory nature, and then provide an overall assessment.

Price begins by giving substance to his claim that testimony is an important source of knowledge. A good deal of what he says will be familiar from Chapter 1. He points out that not only is a vast amount of geographical and historical knowledge, much of which seems as secure as anything we know, dependent upon testimony but much fundamental information which we do not so readily associate with testimony is indeed testimony-based, for instance, knowledge of one's own age and birthday, or of the date or of the day of the week. Moreover, reliance on testimony plays a part in our dependence upon signposts, milestones, maps, rulers, and destination notices on buses. Clearly testimony is a more pervasive phenomenon than we are accustomed to think and Price could have added that a great deal of what we regard as pre-eminently matters of observational fact is in reality the observation of others, for example, for most of us, that human beings have brains.

With the preliminaries completed, Price puts forward a principle which he thinks embodies 'something like' our underlying assumptions about testimony 'in the great majority of cases'. This principle, which I shall call '*A*', goes as follows:

> (*A*) What there is said to be (or to have been) there is (or was) more often than not.

What then is the nature of *A* and what ought to be our attitude to it? It certainly looks like some sort of factual claim, indeed, as Price says, it looks like an inductive generalization. Yet if we are to be guided by what Price calls Locke's 'Ethics of Belief' which enjoins us never to believe a proposition more firmly than the evidence warrants, we should be culpable of credulity (at least) in accepting it. In other words, it is, on Price's view, impossible to establish the truth of *A* as any sort of empirical generalization on the basis of an individual's firsthand observation and hence the Humean view mentioned earlier must be wrong. Why does Price think this? Because

the amount of testimony which each of us has been able to test and verify for himself is far too small to justify any inductive estimate of the 'overall' reliability of testimony in general: too small, that is, in relation to the enormous number and variety of all the beliefs he has, which are supported partly or wholly by testimony spoken or written, or conveyed in other ways (for example, by means of maps). Whatever estimate any one person tried to make of its reliability, whether favourable or unfavourable, he would not have nearly enough first-hand evidence to justify it. Indeed the habit of accepting testimony is so deep-rooted in all of us that we fail to realise how very limited the range of each person's first-hand observation and memory is.[1]

Price thinks that the situation would be easier to handle in a simple and primitive society than in a complex and highly educated community and, if so, I find it ironic that those developments so closely associated with the rise of an individualist ideology, namely, the development of science, literacy, technology, and the spread of education and communication, have not only made us more, rather than less, dependent on testimony but have also made our dependence harder to justify.

What then are we to make of Price's contention? Much is unclear about Price's thesis here but its general point is not. He is clearly claiming that where *A* is viewed as an inductive generalization it is too weakly supported by the observed facts to be acceptable. In addition he wants to say that the evidence of observation and memory are too weak to justify *any* inductive generalization about the 'overall' reliability or unreliability of testimony. Faced with the justificatory problem, an individual inquirer simply has no empirical evidence worthy of the name, for or against *A*, nor for or against certain variations on *A* such as, 'What there is said to be (or to have been) there is (or was) in at least one case out of every five'—an example which

---

[1] H. H. Price, *Belief* (London, 1969), 119.

Price explicitly considers.[2] Now Price is not denying that an individual can conduct some tests on the veracity and reliability of some pieces of testimony, although he rightly points out that the extent to which this is possible is frequently exaggerated. Indeed he might also have added that, in our normal practice, the verifications and falsifications open to an individual are heavily testimony-contaminated both in virtue of the fact that checking a report most commonly consists in checking it against one or several other reports and in virtue of the fact that checking on a report will often require a testimony-dependent identification of some crucial object that figures in the report. This point was made in Chapter 4 and was implicit in the discussion of Chapter 1; it will also figure significantly in Chapter 9. Let us suppose none the less, with Price, that some individual checking of the required kind can go on, then it may well be that this is inadequate to establish anything about the truth or probability or credibility of A but it is not clear from Price's account just why this is so.

The fact that the beliefs we have checked are only a small proportion of the total number of beliefs that an individual accepts unchecked on the basis of testimony does not by itself perhaps rule out a justification in such terms, since certain types of statistical inferences seem to proceed in this way and some inductions might also. To be quite clear about Price's objection we would need to understand which theory of inductive justification he is assuming but I do not think it profitable at this point to embark upon either totally speculative exegesis of Price or the perilous seas of inductive logic. As indicated earlier, I believe that we have independent grounds for objecting to an inductive justification of A (or whatever sentence is taken to register our conviction about the reliability of testimony) and, in any case, Price's position can at least be made plausible in an informal way. What needs to be emphasized is that Price is acutely aware of the tremendous variety in types of belief, types of testimony, types of testifying situation, and so on, that are encompassed by A and it is against that background that he views the 'smallness' of any testing as rendering it inadequate to justify A or anything like it. The situation may be compared to an American's trying to justify his confidence in the proposition that 'Most Australians are bad-tempered' by recourse to his observations of the only four Australians he knows or can, at the time, get to know. Suppose he finds that three of the four are bad-tempered. I think (hope!) that no one would count him justified in giving even modest credence to the general belief on this basis. It seems clear that with such a predicate, at any rate, we would be unjustified in treating such a sample as sufficiently representative or typical of the whole population to which inductive extrapolation is being attempted.

Two other points need to be made briefly about Price's anti-inductivist

---

[2] Ibid. 118. Hereafter, page refs. to Price's chapter will be bracketed after quotations in the text.

argument and about his formula A. The first is that, although Price often speaks as if the insufficiency of any individual's firsthand evidence for A is a matter of the poverty of the checking he has, as a matter of fact, done, it is surely apparent that his position requires that this be no mere historical accident. In other words, the problem is posed by an individual's *inability* to provide sufficient inductive support for A from his own resources alone; when Price describes situations in which there is vast disproportion between the checks an individual has made and his high degree of confidence in A (revealed in his practice rather than in explicit assent to A) then clearly these situations are meant to be typical of any situation the individual may find himself in.

Secondly, we may justifiably have some qualms about the phrasing of A. It seems inevitable that epistemological principles concerned with the reliability of some supposed source of knowledge will make use of the quantifier 'most' or something like it, which is to say that there seems to be something right about the move. On the other hand, what we mean by the reliability of testimony is poorly captured by A if A is so read that most of the testimony so far given in human history is capable of being false, yet this is possible if we take mankind's present history to be only a small proportion of its total history. Conversely, if we require the generalization to be true of any historical period at all then it seems we can imagine a period in which the generalization is false, although testimony is still broadly reliable as an 'institution', so to speak. For example, we can imagine a situation in which a group of conspirators have contrived to put most of the world's population to sleep and have reduced most of the remainder to servile silence. They then devote an intensive period of time to bombarding the servile silent with lying propaganda about what has happened. During this period A is false but this does not seem to show anything about the general reliability of testimony.[3]

No doubt much more could be said about A and its status but I want to examine Price's positive alternative to treating A as making a factual claim of an empirical kind. Price suggests that our attitude of predominant trust in testimony is indeed based upon a principle to which A is an approximation but that the principle should be interpreted not as a factual proposition which we believe but 'more like a maxim or a methodological rule' which we believe in. Consequently he reformulates A in the imperative mood and gives two versions of it—just for good measure.

(B) Believe what you are told by others unless or until you have reasons for doubting it.

(C) Conduct your thoughts and your actions as if A were true.[4]

---

[3] In connection with A, we should also recall that not every case of 'said to be' is a case of testimony.

[4] Price of course does not use the A, B, C tags and so where I write in C, 'A were true', he merely writes out A in full. Earlier in the chapter he had somewhat inconsequentially introduced a version of B reading: 'Accept what you are told unless or until you have reason to doubt it.'

Neither *B* nor *C* are subject to the assessment true or false (or at least not in the relevant way) so Price thinks that he has avoided the evidence problem which confronted *A*. None the less, he recognizes that such policies or maxims need to be assessed in terms of reasons for adoption and it is hard to resist the suspicion that our problem with testimony has hardly been advanced by a change in grammatical mood. This suspicion should surely be aggravated by Price's avowal that *B* and *C* are policies 'for forming beliefs' and that the two sentences are merely different ways of formulating the same policy. (This indeed might be contested but I will not dispute it here.) We should thus be clear that *C* enjoins us to believe *A*; moreover, it enjoins us to believe *A* even though there is no reason (or utterly insufficient reason) to believe *A* true. Now such a policy is very different from a policy for acting and raises very difficult issues in the philosophy of mind concerning the possibility of intending to believe. In what follows I shall assume that it makes sense to speak of a policy for belief and, even if the most this may come to mean is a policy for acting in such a way that you can reasonably expect to result in belief, it will still contrast with a *mere* policy for acting. Note also that if belief is construed as the possible outcome of a policy or even believing itself as an action then the expression 'rational belief' has a tendency to ambiguity, since Jones's belief that *p* may be totally irrational with regard to the evidence relevant to the truth of *p* but perfectly rational with regard to its function in promoting some policy. This is not, I suspect, a prospect which an agent who knows what he is about can contemplate with equanimity. Consider, for example,

(D)   Your mother does not have a fatal disease.

(E)   Conduct your thoughts and actions as if *D* were true.

Let *E* be proposed to certain children as a policy for belief by a doctor who recommends it to them precisely because, as he tells them, there is very powerful evidence that *D* is false but the consequences of following *E* will be generally beneficial to the mother. The first thing to note about this policy is that it is not independent of the truth value of the contained proposition since it is the justified belief that *D* is false which gives rise to the policy. The plausibility of such examples will thus be of no help to Price since his move to a maxim is precisely designed to avoid reference to the truth value of the contained proposition *A*. Moreover, the policy is not as readily intelligible as it seems. There is something paradoxical and perhaps even incoherent about a policy which recommends one to conduct one's *thoughts* as if what one knows to be true were false, where this is not just a limited instruction to suppose or imagine something. Of course, the normal justifications for *E* would more plausibly apply to actions rather than thoughts and would affect thoughts only in so far as the expression of certain true thoughts needed to be suppressed. But if it is urged that, for the behavioural simulations to be fully effective, the children must really cultivate false thoughts then it is none too clear how they are to go about doing it. Self-deception certainly exists but it is a very puzzling phenomenon to describe and this situation does not seem to qualify as an instance of it. The fact that thinking and believing are essentially directed towards the truth seems to undermine the alleged rationality of a policy for cultivating false beliefs. Furthermore, if it is true and known to be true that the mother has a fatal disease, then no policy which is justified in terms (or partly in terms) of her welfare could insist that this knowledge be totally 'forgotten' or disowned, for there would be occasions on which one would need to rely upon this knowledge in order to ensure that her suffering was kept to a minimum, in order to prevent others making the facts known to her and in order to be on the look-out for better treatments and even the possibility of a medical breakthrough which might produce a cure.[5] A policy which incorporates a disregard for truth in such a way as to make rational reassessment and modification very difficult or impossible has surely little claim to rationality.

These considerations should make us wary of the strategy, advocated by Price, of dismissing problems of truth and falsity by imperatival transformation of issues about beliefs into issues about policies for believing. Certainly in the mother example the contained proposition is false and (initially) believed to be false, whereas in the testimony case the problem is how to determine the truth value of A. But this difference does not show that in the latter case we are entitled to be indifferent to the truth value of A and the problem of determining it. After all, in the illness case it might be argued that, if policy E is advantageous on the assumption that D is false, it is surely also advantageous on the assumption that D is true, but it is therefore advantageous whether D is true or false and hence we really are entitled to be indifferent to the truth value of D. Yet the considerations mentioned in discussing the example surely show that this could never be desirable. Of course the situation might be different where it was known (somehow?) that there was no way at all of getting evidence for the truth or falsity of the contained proposition and I shall return to this question later.

How then does Price support the adoption of B/C? He seems at times tempted to support it by reference to goals of moral duty and social utility. So he claims that trusting the word of others 'is socially expedient and even socially indispensable' (p. 114) because without it we would have a Hobbesian state of nature, and also that it is morally demanded by 'precepts of charity' because we would not be treating people as ends in themselves if we did not concede to each 'a *prima facie* claim to be believed when he makes a statement' (p. 114). In the end, however, he does not seriously promote these considerations, so I shall say no more

---

[5] Although, of course, if we are allowing for this possibility we may have to redescribe our knowledge as the knowledge that the mother has an apparently fatal disease.

about them beyond remarking that it is not at all obvious that we would have much reason to believe that we were not *already* in a complex state of nature unless we believed that something like *A* were true.

Finally, Price offers reasons in support of policies *B* and *C* which involve knowledge as a goal but are not supposed to involve reference to the truth claims of *A*. Such a position inherits the difficulties discussed above but it also has quite specific problems of its own.

Price offers what he calls 'economic reasons' in support of *B* and *C* 'because they are concerned with the intelligent use of scarce resources'. The scarcity is a lack of sufficient firsthand observation for the goal we seek as cognitive beings, namely, knowledge. There are all sorts of questions we would like to be able to answer but lack the firsthand means to do so. Testimony does give us a way of getting such answers and very often it is the only means for getting answers; hence one must either accept it or remain in a state of suspended judgement. In Price's own words:

Each of us would like to know what happened before he was born and what is happening now on the other side of the wall. His own first-hand observations and his own first-hand memory will not enable him to answer these questions. If he cannot *know* the answers to them, he would still like to be able to hold the most reasonable beliefs that he can, on the best evidence he can get. And very often indeed the only evidence he can get is the evidence of testimony. He must either accept what others tell him for what it may be worth; or else he must remain in a state of suspended judgement, unable to find any answer at all to many of the questions which he desires to answer (p. 125).

It is of course true that unless we accept testimony there will be a whole lot of questions we cannot answer (and, as Price recognizes, a lot that we cannot even pose) and so it seems that we must either accept testimony or suspend judgement on these questions. But why should we not simply suspend judgement? It is not enough to rebut this alternative by pointing to our desire for answers because nothing that Price has said shows that it is epistemically better to 'have answers' than to suspend judgement. In the epistemically relevant sense of 'wanting answers' we do not want just any answers. Price's argument here turns on an equivocation on the term 'answer' for it is true that testimony provides us with answers in the sense of replies to questions, perhaps, but whether testimony provides us with answers in the sense of predominantly true replies to questions is another matter, indeed it is the matter of whether *A* is true. In other words, for the seeker after truth the question of whether he opts for testimony or suspended judgement can only be answered in terms of the reasons he can have for believing that the answers testimony provides are true more often than not (or whatever standard is regarded as adequate). But this seems to be none other than the original problem posed by *A*.

Price recognizes that the 'economic' policy won't work unless certain conditions are fulfilled; most of the witnesses must be honest, reliable, accurate, etc., and yet, 'it is logically possible that none of them are ever fulfilled' (p. 127). The real problem for his position, however, is not whether it is logically possible for the conditions to be unfulfilled but whether we have reason to believe that they are mostly fulfilled in fact, fulfilled sufficiently to provide support for such policies as *B* or *C*. He has already argued that we cannot have inductive grounds for such a belief and it is this rather than lurking logical possibilities which surely underlies the 'safety-first' philosophy which he describes as holding that 'if "safety-first" is one's motto, the wisest course would be not to accept testimony at all' (p. 127). Price, however, characterizes the 'safety-first' philosopher as objecting to such a policy as *C* not on the ground that there is no testimony-independent way of establishing *A* as an empirical generalization, but on the ground that the policy *C* is 'risky' because it will give us 'a mixed bag' of beliefs. With what is 'mixed bag' being contrasted here? Surely not with infallible knowledge or 100 per cent reliability because this was never in question. Nor were we at any point concerned with establishing a reliability rating of 90 per cent rather than, say, 75 per cent. Price says that even if we amended *C* to 'one case out of every three' instead of 'more often than not' the policy would still be risky, but we might well ask how he knows this. He cannot be relying on the mere logical possibility that any one of the pieces of testimony we accept may be false, but if not, then what is he relying on? It cannot be the fact that some percentage of testimony is likely to be true because no such fact has been established and Price sees no way of establishing it (hence the switch to the imperative mood). He thinks that 'the amount of testimony which each of us has been able to test and verify for himself is far too small to justify any inductive estimate of the "overall" reliability of testimony in general' (pp. 118–19). Consequently Price has no inductive reason to hold that it is true either. But if something like *A* is not a known fact then it is no good saying, as Price does, that someone who decides to reject *B* and *C* 'cannot value knowledge very highly if he does not even attempt to get it when there is a risk that his attempt will fail. He rejects the policy we are recommending because he does not really care very much for the end which it is designed to achieve'. Of course, we all know that testimony is, by and large, a reliable source of knowledge, in the sense that quite a lot of history and science and geography and common information is knowledge and it is precisely this that Price is presuming upon here. Yet on the premises Price is allowing himself (essentially the standardly individualist starting-point of traditional epistemology) he has no right to presume upon it for it is this fact that his theory is supposed to establish. If this is all that can be said for the theory of the methodological maxim then we must conclude that it is a failure.

There is, however, another way of viewing Price's theory. I do not suggest that this is an alternative interpretation to the one already offered because I do not think that it can really be found in Price's text. On the other hand, it is an interesting reconstruction from some elements in his treatment of the topic and it seems to be in the spirit of his project. What I have in mind is avoiding the circularity inherent in Price's actual discussion by treating the attempt to give reasons for adopting the policy for belief as a problem in decision theory analogous in some respects to Pascal's wager argument for belief in God.[6] So construed, Price's discussion of testimony exhibits analogies with William James's famous (or notorious) critique of W. K. Clifford's 'Ethics of Belief' in his paper 'The Will to Believe'. Price discusses James's paper later in the book when analysing what he calls self-verifying beliefs but it is a curious fact that although he makes much of the notion of an ethics of belief he nowhere mentions Clifford who not only coined the phrase but explicitly developed and defended the idea in a way that Locke, to whom Price attributes the notion, never did. Even more interestingly, Clifford's essay contains a long discussion of the problems posed for his view by our reliance upon testimony and although his discussion is rather garbled and superficial he does pose the problem in a way that finds an echo in Price: 'Are we to deprive ourselves of the help and guidance of that vast body of knowledge which is daily growing upon the world, because neither we nor any other one person can possibly test a hundredth part of it by immediate experiment or observation, and because it would not be completely proved if we did?'[7]

But enough of history—what of reconstruction? Well first let us look at a plausible decision-theoretic treatment of what is involved in Pascal's wager. Slightly different approaches to this have been made by Richard Jeffrey and Ian Hacking. Hacking, plausibly I think, finds three different arguments in Pascal, each involving rather different assumptions and each appealing successfully to a different decision-theoretic principle—dominance, expectation, and dominant expectation respectively. The argument from simple dominance makes the assumption, which some find implausible, that in the case where God does not exist there is nothing to choose between opting for God or against him in terms of pay-off or expected utility. I shall bow to such intuitions for my present purposes and ignore the dominance argument. The two other arguments may be presented in Jeffrey's diagrammatic way as in (1) and (2) below:[8]

[6] Or even Reichenbach's famous wager on induction. See H. Reichenbach, *Experience and Prediction* (Chicago, 1938), 348–57; 'On the Justification of Induction', *Journal of Philosophy*, 37 (1940), 97–103.

[7] W. K. Clifford, *Lectures and Essays*, ii (London, 1879), 188.

[8] I. Hacking, *The Emergence of Probability* (London, 1975), 63–72; Richard C. Jeffrey, *The Logic of Decision*, 2nd edn. (Chicago, 1983), 12–13. My matrices differ slightly from Jeffrey's because he doesn't take account of 'present fun' as a positive value and would, I think, differ from Hacking in referring to a chance of eternal bliss rather than to eternal bliss *simpliciter* as he does. Jeffrey does not allow infinity to be a value in a desirability matrix for theoretical reasons that need not, I think, affect our illustrative purposes since some huge number would do just as well.

(1) The argument from expectation (where it is an equal chance that God exists or not)

Consequence Matrix:

	S_1 God exists	S_2 God doesn't exist
A_1 Choose for (the Catholic) God	Chance of Eternal Bliss	Pious restricted life to no avail
A_2 Choose against (the Catholic) God	Certain Eternal Damnation	Present Fun

Desirability Matrix: $\begin{vmatrix} +x & -1 \\ -\infty & +1 \end{vmatrix}$

Probability Matrix: $\begin{vmatrix} .5 & .5 \\ .5 & .5 \end{vmatrix}$

Expected Desirability of $A_1 = .5x - .5$
Expected Desirability of $A_2 = -\infty + .5$

(2) The argument from dominant expectation (where God's existence is given a low probability)

Consequence Matrix as in (1) and Desirability Matrix as in (1).

Probability Matrix: $\begin{vmatrix} .000001 & .999999 \\ .000001 & .999999 \end{vmatrix}$

Expected Desirability of $A_1 = .000001x - .999999$
Expected Desirability of $A_2 = -\infty + .999999$

In (1), on the assumption, which seems immensely plausible, that x is greater than $-\infty$, A_1 is clearly the course to follow. In (2), A_1 is again the course to follow.

There are, of course, familiar reasons why this demonstration, though valid, is not persuasive, but let us see if the moves can be applied to Price's problem, and to begin with, let us assume that we must either choose to believe testimony reliable or not to believe testimony reliable, thus treating suspension of belief and positive disbelief as falling under the second heading. Our consequence matrix is going to be something like that in (3) below. This seems roughly right although there are some complications ignored, for instance, that the option A_1S_1 will include the discovery that some old beliefs thought true were really false.[9] Ignoring such complica-

---

[9] It is also tempting to follow Price and use the term 'knowledge' in column S_1 where I have used the expression 'true belief'. This temptation should be resisted if one holds, as most

(3) The testimony wager

Consequence Matrix:	S_1 A True	S_2 A False
A_1 Choose to believe testimony reliable (Adopt C)	Greatly extended 'true belief' and some new false beliefs	Great extension of error and some new true beliefs
A_2 Choose not to believe testimony reliable (Reject C)	Great failure to get available 'true belief'	Great safety from error

tions we must now ask what desirability and probability matrices are appropriate. Here we enter upon a very cloudy area indeed. There are two cultural considerations that will govern our assignments: (i) whether we can make a distinction between getting true beliefs and being safe from error as goals and, if so, how they should be compared on a desirability scale, and (ii) whether there is any greater probability attaching to S_1 or S_2. I take it that Price's rejection of the attempt to establish A is best construed as the verdict that S_1 and S_2 are equiprobable on the empirical evidence, but we could perhaps view his scornful remarks about the safety-first philosopher as a way of expressing his preference for epistemic boldness over epistemic caution.

There does seem to be a real issue here, as James noticed in 'The Will to Believe', and it is a point on which Clifford and James seem strongly opposed. Clifford's essay contains numerous strictures, of a rather florid kind, directed at those who do not guard themselves sufficiently against falling into error. It is hard to do justice to the full flavour of his prose by citing a brief extract but we may get some idea of his thought from the following:

Belief, that sacred faculty which prompts the decisions of our will, and knits into harmonious working all the compacted energies of our being, is ours not for ourselves, but for humanity. It is rightly used on truths which have been established by long experience and waiting toil, and which have stood in the fierce light

---

contemporary philosophers do, that true beliefs do not constitute knowledge unless they are acquired in the right way. Normally we think that testimony is such a right way but we cannot avail ourselves of that normal thought in the present context; rather, we face the situation where if we choose to adopt C and, *as it happens*, A is true then, *as it happens*, we acquire a lot more true beliefs. Compare Pascal's gambler who not only gets a chance at eternal bliss if he chooses for God (and God exists) but also acquires a new true belief—that God exists. It is at least doubtful that we should describe as part of his pay-off in A_1S_1 the acquisition of *knowledge* that God exists and I think it equally doubtful to use this honorific term in the context of the testimony wager.

of free and fearless questioning ... It is desecrated when given to unproved and unquestioned statements, for the solace and private pleasure of the believer; to add a tinsel splendour to the plain straight road of our life and display a bright mirage beyond it ... Whoso would deserve well of his fellows in this matter will guard the purity of his belief with a very fanatacism of jealous care, lest at any time it should rest on an unworthy object, and catch a stain which can never be wiped away ... It is wrong always, everywhere, and for anyone to believe anything upon insufficient evidence.[10]

James sees such passages as evidence that Clifford placed greater value on avoidance of error than gaining of truth and he argued that the imperatives 'Believe truth!' and 'Shun error!' were 'two materially different laws; and by choosing between them we may end by colouring differently our whole intellectual life'.[11] James's argument, if I have understood him and I am by no means sure that I have, is that these separate injunctions are normally in peaceful coexistence. It is true, as he points out, that we could shun error by simply avoiding belief altogether (if this were possible) but this, we might say, would be like someone who obeyed the rule 'Don't tell lies!' by refusing to talk at all. The caution against lying is only significant against the background of an interest in communication which is itself governed in a complex way by the injunction 'Tell the truth!'. Similarly with 'Believe truth!' and 'Shun error!' In our normal investigations we are moved by compliance with the former but compliance with the latter is a way of giving sense to what the former means. One could perhaps structure a quasi-learning situation in which a subject had the choice of answering certain Yes/No questions by the use of his senses or by tossing a coin. If there is nothing queer about the situation (his senses disoriented or whatever) then his decision to go in for coin-tossing is not a compliance with the rule 'Believe truth!' even though (we may assume) he will end up 'believing' some truths. His choice of the unreliable over the reliable procedure for finding the truth is precisely a violation of the rule to shun error and for that reason a failure to comply with the rule to believe the truth. James says none of this but I take it that he need not disagree, for his thesis really concerns the case where there is no reliable evidence available and yet we have to act; his essay is, in part, a defence of a sort of Protestant version of Pascal's wager. In such a situation he thinks we should place a greater value upon the chance of acquiring true beliefs than upon the prospect of being secure from error, all other things being equal. By contrast Clifford would go the other way. My sympathies are with neither side for I think that we should put an equal value upon these ends. Perhaps, as James says, 'the risk of being in error is a very small matter when compared with the blessings of real knowledge',[12] but the com-

---

[10] *Lectures and Essays*, ii. 182–3 and 186.
[11] W. James, *The Will to Believe and Other Essays* (New York, 1898), 18.
[12] Ibid.

parison is mis-stated, for the risk of being in error should be compared with the *possibility* of gaining more true beliefs. It is not at all clear that the risk of being in error 'is a very small matter' in the comparison.

With apologies for the length of this digression let me return to the desirability and probability matrices for the testimony wager. I would construct them as in (4) and I think my assignments are plausible:

(4) Desirability and probability matrices for the testimony wager

$$\text{Desirability Matrix:} \quad \begin{vmatrix} 10 & -10 \\ -10 & 10 \end{vmatrix}$$

$$\text{Probability Matrix:} \quad \begin{vmatrix} .5 & .5 \\ .5 & .5 \end{vmatrix}$$

Expected Desirability of $A_1 = 5 - 5 = 0$
Expected Desirability of $A_2 = -5 + 5 = 0$

So, on these assignments, there is nothing to choose between the options and although we will no doubt continue to rely upon testimony our faith will remain unjustified and unvindicated by the arguments used or implied by Price.

6

The Analogical Approach

I turn now to Bertrand Russell's discussion of what initially, at any rate, seems to be the same problem as that which exercises Price. Russell examines the matter, directly, in two places: first of all in *An Outline of Philosophy* and then in *Human Knowledge: Its Scope and Limits.*[1] The two discussions are similar in many respects so I will treat them together as one exposition but occasionally note where the treatment in one book diverges from that in the other. (I will refer to the earlier work as *OP* and the later one as *HK*.)

Russell thinks that testimony is essential to science and that the reliability of testimony is involved in our belief in the existence of physical objects—this is part of his broader point that the testimony of others is required to establish the private/public distinction. The reliability of testimony thus raises important and difficult issues which have not, Russell thinks, been done justice by philosophers. His own view is that the general truthfulness of testimony is a premiss in the early stages of science, but not in the finished structure where there is 'a general premiss which is needed to secure the probable trustworthiness of testimony' (*HK* 206). This general premiss turns out to be 'a principle of analogical inference' (*HK* 206).

Before introducing the analogy argument, however, Russell has a few preliminary moves which are worth attention.

1. He holds that our 'common-sense practice' is to accept testimony 'unless there is a positive reason against doing so in the particular case concerned' and the cause, though not the justification, of our doing so is an 'animal inference from a word or sentence to what it signifies' (*HK* 206). This animal inference is created by the process of language learning which Russell sees as, in part, the building up of habits of response to the stimulation of words.

If you are engaged in a tiger hunt and somebody exclaims 'tiger' your body will, unless you inhibit your impulses, get into a state very similar to that in which it would be if you saw a tiger. Such a state *is* the belief that a tiger is in the neighbourhood; thus you will be believing the testimony of the man who said 'tiger' (*HK* 206).

One may inhibit the impulse to belief, as when one disbelieves testimony, but the impulse still exists and if it ceased altogether one would cease to

---

[1] Bertrand Russell, *An Outline of Philosophy* (London, 1927), and *Human Knowledge: Its Scope and Limits* (New York, 1948).

understand the word 'tiger'. Of course there are less dramatic occurrences of the word 'tiger' such as 'tigers are found in India and Eastern Asia' and of these Russell says 'You may think you hear this statement without any of the emotions appropriate to tigers, and yet it may cause during the following night a nightmare from which you wake in a cold sweat, showing that the impulses appropriate to the word "tiger" survived subconsciously' (*HK* 206). I shall not delay on this somewhat primitive behavioural theory of understanding language. As it stands it seems unfairly to favour the morbidly sensitive amongst us and to have the curious consequence that none of us understand the word 'dodo', but perhaps some emendation in a Quinean direction could give the account more plausibility. For our purposes, the relevant claim is that we tend to believe testimony because the processes of language learning have conditioned us to respond to an utterance by believing what it states. This seems to me to be a dubious thesis about the origins of our attitude towards testimony since it seems more likely that an attitude of trust on the part of the child precedes and makes possible the acquisition of language and that it is this attitude of trust which should figure prominently in a causal account of our present attitude towards testimony. None the less, Russell's account may serve to bring to our attention the facts that we do have a tendency to believe what we are told and that unless our early language teachers had been mostly truthful with us we could not have acquired the language at all—a point which Russell makes explicitly later in the discussion.

2. Russell also stresses the importance of testimony for the drawing of the public/private distinction but he says little about this beyond claiming, in *HK*, that we arrive at the publicity of some event or object by an 'animal inference', from hearing thunder and my neighbour's saying 'thunder' at the same time, to the conclusion that my neighbour also heard thunder. Presumably, however, like other 'animal inferences' this reflex needs a rational vindication and in *OP* Russell notes, in passing, a paradox involved in any such vindication, namely, that we must be able to make the public/private contrast before we can determine that some phenomenon is a genuine public utterance and so a candidate for being a piece of testimony, in spite of the fact that the legitimacy of making the contrast at all is partially established by the reliability of testimony. In Russell's own words: 'We see moving shapes and interpret them as physical motions of his [the witness's] lips. This inference, as we saw earlier, is in part justified by testimony; yet now we find that it has to be made before we can have reason to believe that there is any such thing as testimony' (*OP* 9). Russell does not pursue the problem any further, saying, rather lamely, that this is part of the general problem of inferring physical objects from sensations and is not the most difficult of the logical puzzles concerning testimony. But the matter can hardly be left there since the facts noted seem to create a vicious circle in any attempt to justify our reliance upon testimony. Any

purported justification (and certainly the one Russell later provides) would seem to have to start with the knowledge of public facts like specific utterances by other human bodies and yet no such start can be made without assuming what is supposed to be proved, namely, the reliability of testimony.

These preliminary remarks, no matter how unsatisfactory, lead Russell on to what he takes to be the main issue. Curiously enough, however, this is not the issue one might expect. Having raised the problem of the general reliability of testimony, Russell goes on to try to answer the apparently quite different question of how we can know that we are ever being told anything at all (either true or false). In the early version of the argument in *OP* he simply treats the whole problem of testimony as the problem of determining whether certain of the noises others make are intended by them as assertions or not. In *HK*, however, the situation is complicated by the fact that he distinguishes two issues, neither of which is what one would expect to be the main issue, and then discusses only one of them, namely, that discussed in *OP*. The two issues he distinguishes are 'whether the testimony you hear is intended to be truthful' and 'whether it has any intention of conveying information'. Neither of these is the issue originally raised by Russell, which we could put in similar terminology to these as 'whether the testimony you hear is true more often than not'. Russell then goes on to discuss his second issue which he treats as a special case of the problem of the existence of other minds. His solution to the epistemological problem of testimony is then a principle of analogy which is designed to prove the existence of other minds and hence other intentions to communicate. It is not, he says, an inductive proof because it goes beyond experience and its principle, crudely, is: 'Given a class of cases in which A is accompanied or succeeded by B, and another class of cases in which it cannot be ascertained whether B is present or not, there is a probability (varying according to circumstances) that in these cases also B is present' (*HK* 209).

At the risk of a certain repetition let us distinguish four questions in this area and see where Russell's principle of analogy could be relevant and where not.

(*a*) How do we know that other human bodies have minds, i.e., go in for thinking, feeling, believing, having images, etc?

(*b*) How do we know that the production of certain types of noises, marks, etc., by other human bodies is accompanied by the relevant communication intentions, perhaps of a Gricean kind, that go with such speech acts as asserting, reporting, and testifying?

(*c*) How do we know that those who testify to us intend to tell the truth?

(*d*) How do we know that what we are told in testimony is reliable?

Russell clearly means his analogy principle to apply to questions (*a*) and (*b*), and whether or not the argument is effective its relevance to these questions is fairly clear or at least intelligible in the light of tradition. To take (*a*) by itself, the idea is that we know in our own case of an association between *B* (a certain sort of sensation, feeling, or thought) and *A* (a certain sort of pattern of behaviour and perhaps stimulus situation) and we observe *A* occurring among other bodies similar to our own and hence infer analogically to the (otherwise uncheckable) presence of *B* in association with those bodies. In the case of (*b*) Russell argues that 'the remarks we hear are so like those we make that we think they must have similar causes' (*OP* 10) and the individual knows in his own case that he talks because 'he means to convey something' (*OP* 9). There are, of course, notorious difficulties with this sort of argument but I shall not delay on them now; what I want to raise is the question of how such an argument could be relevant to (*c*) and (*d*). There seem to be two possibilities here:

(i) It could be relevant inasmuch as (*a*) and (*b*) need to be established before (*c*) and (*d*) can be posed.

(ii) It could be directly relevant, whatever, the upshot of (i), if some analogical argument could take us from something about our own situation to the general sincerity and veracity of most testimony.

With regard to (i) we have here a question as to the nature and pre-suppositions of testimony. Although there are not many philosophical discussions of testimony most of them (certainly Hume, Reid, and Price) take the existence of testimony in the community for granted and then raise questions about its epistemological status. Russell initially proceeds in the same way. If, however, one treats the very existence of testimony in a community as problematic then one would presumably have to show that there exists a language, or some other relatively sophisticated form of communication, which is used reportively in the group. Now whether one would thereby have to prove (*a*) and/or (*b*) would depend on how language and its reportive use should be characterized. Certainly it seems plausible to hold that a good deal that is 'mentalistic' would have to go into such a characterization—Gricean-type intentions at least seem plausibly required. To take an example of Russell's, the discovery that the Scottish ghost of the eighteenth century which kept on repeating: 'Once I was hap-hap-happy but noo I am meeserable', was in reality a rusty spit *just was* the discovery that these sounds were not intentionally produced for the purpose of conveying a thought in a certain way. On the other hand, the sort of mentalism that one would have to prove here is a matter for debate; it may be that there is not one other minds problem but several and some of the problems might prove more tractable than others and in particular it might be possible to establish that certain alien creatures were making noises with communicative intent without being able to establish much else about their mental lives at all. The whole question of the other minds problem and its relation to language is very murky (quite apart from difficulties with the analogical argument itself) as can be seen from the fact that some philosophers want to use the existence of communication, language, and even testimony to solve or help solve the other minds problem, which is to reverse the order of approach made by Russell. So Price, in an earlier work, used linguistic communication and in effect testimony as primary starting-points for an argument from analogy to other minds, and Austin uses the fact that other human beings testify to us about their mental states as a solution or dissolution of problems in this area.[2]

There is no explicit move such as (ii) in Russell but I should like very briefly to consider whether one could be developed. There is in fact something a bit like such a move in F. H. Bradley's references to the topic of testimony. His idea is that our belief in testimony is justified by an inference to a mental state in the witness essentially one with our own. As he puts it in 'The Presuppositions of Critical History', 'If we know that other men are we know it by an inferential judgement: and it is by a similar judgement that the matter of their testimony becomes ours.'[3] Bradley is primarily interested in the role of testimony in history and perhaps because of this he does little or nothing to show how this inference is supposed to proceed. The reference to the parallel between knowing that there are other men and knowing that their testimony can be relied upon indicates that he may have had in mind the use of an analogical inference in both cases.

How could such an argument proceed? Bradley claims that he can only trust what other men tell him if he can view them as observing on his behalf but they can only extend his personal experience in this way if they have the same mental outlook as he—Bradley talks of the need for an 'identification of consciousness' in this context. Presumably, as the investigator, I am meant to proceed by first observing the behaviour of others and finding analogies with my own behaviour such that I can infer an identity of outlook between me and them. But what behaviour will yield this conclusion? An identity of outlook is one of the hardest things to infer from behaviour without any initial or collateral reliance upon testimony. One way of telling that a man has a similar outlook to one's own is to ask him what he believes and another is to check on how he has reported to others events which you have both witnessed.[4] The first method is a direct

---

[2] H. H. Price, *Thinking and Experience* (London, 1962), 242–3; J. L. Austin, 'Other Minds', in his *Philosophical Papers* (Oxford, 1961), see especially 81–3.

[3] F. H. Bradley, 'The Presuppositions of Critical History', in *Collected Essays* (Oxford, 1969), 19.

[4] It might be thought that another way would be to check his reports against the facts but this would be to check the reliability of his reports directly and then to generalize from this reliability, rather than from similarity of outlook.

appeal to the man's testimony about himself and his beliefs etc., and would appear to be an unpromising way of establishing his reliability and sincerity as a witness. The second relies fatally upon the testimony of those to whom he has made the relevant reports. Furthermore, if these problems arise in checking 'identity of consciousness' in just one case, it seems a hopeless project for establishing the general reliability of testimony in a community.

I conclude that an inference along the lines Bradley may have had in mind is unlikely to bring Russell's problem any nearer a solution. Neither Price's nor Russell's theory of testimony can be regarded as successful.

Before closing the chapter, we should consider another line of argument for the justification of testimony from an individualist starting point that could well be suggested by the recourse Russell and Bradley have to the idea of analogy, namely, 'argument to the best explanation'.[5] I say that it may be suggested by the analogy argument just because several modern philosophers have moved in that direction when confronted by the difficulties of using inductive or analogical arguments to solve fundamental epistemological problems. The idea is that, instead of seeking forms of inference to get us from base propositions to problematic conclusions, we should treat the required conclusions as affording the best explanation of some uncontentious data. So, instead of trying to argue (say, by analogy) from known behaviour to the existence of other minds, we can treat other minds as the best explanation of the given behaviour.

I have many reservations about this tactic. One is that in such fundamental epistemological matters, it is often unclear what the criteria for 'best' explanations, or even 'good enough' ones, might be. But for testimony, there is a particular problem that is more pressing: the base propositions are already saturated with the material that is supposed to be separately delivered by an individualist version of the best explanation story. Since the data must be what is available to the individual, prior to any assumption of the reliability of testimony, this means that it will be either too impoverished for the idea of best explanation to get any grip, or, more likely, it will covertly incorporate a commitment to the reliability of testimony (in ways that we have already exposed and will examine more fully later). There is indeed a sense in which we may argue that the extensive reliability of testimony is required by the best explanation of the world that we experience; this is a sense that I shall exploit in the argument of Chapter 9 concerning cohesion and coherence, but *that* argument does not rest upon individualist premisses.

---

[5] I am here responding to helpful comments by David Lewis.

7

Scottish Fundamentalism

As we saw earlier, the eighteenth-century Scot, Thomas Reid, is one of the very few important philosophers in the European tradition to have recognized the epistemological significance of our reliance upon the word of others. We discussed in detail his views on the nature and definition of testimony in Chapter 3; here we must attend to his bold speculations about the parallels between perception and testimony and his efforts to vindicate our reliance upon the latter.

Reid's account of perception has probably been as closely scrutinized by philosophers as any part of his positive philosophical contributions but the analogy he draws between testimony and perception has been somewhat neglected.[1] Reid mentions the analogy in the *Essay on the Intellectual Powers* (hereafter *EI*) but principally to note a disanalogy and his most extensive treatment is in the *Inquiry into the Human Mind* (hereafter *IHM*).[2] Reid thinks that in perception we have both original and acquired perceptions and he compares this distinction with that between natural language and artificial language. The basic point of the analogy between perception and testimony is that both involve the operation of signs and that the signs operate in each case in similar ways. In original perception nature speaks directly to us through the signs of sensation affixing particular property types to particular sensation types and a tendency to believe in their present instantiation. We do not *infer* the nature and existence of the property instances from the nature of the sensation since there is no resemblance between the one and the other. We rather pass from the sensation to the perceptual judgement by the operation of a 'particular principle of our constitution' (*IHM* 195). An example (given by Reid) would be a certain sensation of touch signifying hardness in the body handled. Reid sees this paralleled in the case of communication by those 'signs in the natural language of the human countenance and behaviour' (*IHM* 195) which signify thoughts and dispositions of the mind and which constitute a natural language, without which, he thinks, artificial languages, such as English, could never have arisen. Again, we do

---

[1] Recently Gareth Evans drew attention to it in his book *Varieties of Reference* (Oxford, 1982), 236, and Keith Lehrer and John Smith discuss it in their paper 'Reid on Testimony and Perception', *Canadian Journal of Philosophy*, supp. vol. 11 (1985), 21–38.

[2] Thomas Reid, *Inquiry into the Human Mind*, ch. 6, s. xxiv. Page refs. will mostly be bracketed in the text and will be taken from Reid's, *Philosophical Works*, with notes etc. by Sir William Hamilton (Hildesheim, 1967).

not infer to the relevant states of mind from threatening or welcoming or alarmed behaviour nor do we somehow gather the connection from experience since 'previous to experience, the sign suggests the things signified and creates the belief of it' (*IHM* 195). This link is due, once more, to a particular principle of the human constitution.

Though Reid thinks the analogy is greatest in the above comparison there is also an analogy between acquired perceptions and communication in artificial languages. Acquired perceptions are indeed signs but their import is discovered by experience, though once discovered the sign operates like those of original perception and 'always suggests the things signified and creates the belief of it' (*IHM* 195). Again there is no inference, except in the initial stages, and the mind acts under the influence of general principles of the human constitution.

By artificial languages Reid simply means those that rely upon the will of human beings for the connection between sign and signified. This connection is discovered by experience with the aid of natural language and the progressive development of the artificial language itself and is dependent once more upon general principles of the human constitution. Once the connection is uncovered the mind passes naturally from the sign to the suggested reality and acquires the associated belief.

The language side of the analogy is clear enough in both its aspects, though more needs to be said about the general principles involved. The perceptual side has a certain air of obscurity about its details. In some respects, Reid's distinction between original and acquired perceptions echoes the distinctions between direct and indirect, immediate and mediate objects of perception but he would be hostile to any of the usual sense data or 'ideal theory' implications carried by such talk. None the less his theory clearly arises from the great seventeenth- and eighteenth-century debates about perception and part of its very considerable interest lies in Reid's attempt to combine a realist hostility to the theory of (sensory) ideas with an acceptance of the reality of sensations and of the insights of such predecessors as Berkeley. Reid does not, however, make it clear just what category of objects or properties original perceptions disclose. They are pretty clearly not supposed to be mental items though Reid skates close to this at times. Lehrer and Smith hold that the category is that of the primary qualities and they list motion, depth, extension, and hardness.[3] Reid certainly cites hardness, as we have seen, but, for Reid, depth is not an original perception of vision, though it is of touch. It seems moreover that there is some sense in which such secondary qualities as colours, smells, and tastes are originally perceived. Lehrer and Smith deny this because they take Reid's analysis of the secondary qualities to commit him to the idea that a property like red is a dispositional property of physical

---

[3] Lehrer and Smith, 'Reid on Testimony', 27.

objects and is known only as the cause of certain characteristic visual sensations.[4] (Reid holds that the physical nature of the cause is unknown.) But it is no objection to the view that my perceiving a red chair is an original perception to point out that red is the sort of dispositional property that Reid suggests. There are, moreover, cases of what Reid calls 'visual appearances' in which it can truly be said that the subject perceives something coloured but in which he is not confronted by any physical object which is that colour. In this connection Reid cites the phenomenon of colour constancy—we can see a white object and not notice that in the prevailing light conditions or background it really looks various shades of grey. Reid seems to hold that, if we do attend, then we see a grey visible appearance, i.e. not a sensation but something in the external world that has 'visible figure' and is grey even though the physical object is white. For these reasons it seems more plausible to hold with Timothy Duggan that the original perceptions are of what Aristotle calls the proper sensibles with the common sensibles treated as proper to more than one sense.[5] The Lehrer–Smith analysis seems directly to conflict with at least one explicit claim of Reid's, namely, 'By this sense [sight] we perceive originally the visible figure and colour of bodies only, and their visible place . . .' (*IHM* 185). Our topic here is not Reid's philosophy of perception so I shall leave the interpretive issue about original perceptions noting only that Reid's text is not entirely conclusive.

Our acquired perceptions are the result of experience and develop in accordance with a general inductive principle provided by our nature. Acquired perceptions range from such cases as the visual perception of depth to an expert's visual perception of weight difference in ships, to an expert's auditory detection of distance. Reid thinks, for instance, with Berkeley and Locke, that our visual perception of depth and distance is not direct (or, in his terms, original) but acquired as a result of correlating visual appearances with the results of tactile investigations. More clearly, the jeweller who perceives the difference between a true diamond and a counterfeit does so by relying upon the past conjunction of certain perceived properties (both original and acquired) and upon an inductive principle to do with the regularity of the course of nature.[6] So much for the perceptual side of the analogy, what about testimony?

If Reid is right about the analogy then a common picture of testimony and its epistemological status is quite wrong. This picture has it that all knowledge by testimony is indirect or inferential. We know that p when reliably told that p because we make some inference about the reliability

[4] Ibid.
[5] See the introduction to his edn. of Reid's *Inquiry* (Chicago, 1970), especially pp. xvi–xix. For a discussion of colour constancy see *EI* 332.
[6] For the way visual perception of depth is acquired see especially the *Inquiry*, ch. 6, s. xxii. Other cases of acquired perception are discussed in ch. 6, s. xxiv, and elsewhere.

and sincerity of the witness. Reid thinks that this is the wrong way about. Normally we accept what we are told as reliable, just as we accept 'the testimony of our senses' or 'the testimony of our memory'. The young child begins with a basic attitude of trust in its senses and in those who communicate with it and this is a condition of its learning (artificial) language and of progressing in understanding. It acquires information from natural language by relying unconsciously upon the particular principles which associate certain bodily behaviours with certain mental states. By this and other means it comes to understand the ways in which others use the artificial signs of a vernacular language. In doing so it relies to some extent on the inductive principle but more pertinently upon two general principles which Reid calls the principle of credulity and the principle of veracity. These seem to be merely the two faces of the one reality or as Reid calls them 'counterparts' (*IHM* 196). The combined effect of these principles is like the effect of the inductive principle in that it provides 'a kind of prescience' in this case of human actions rather than natural events. It guarantees a consistency of meaning in the use of language and a certain truthfulness in communicating. Reid claims that the principle of veracity, or 'the propensity to speak truth' is very powerful ('the natural issue of the mind') and operates even in the greatest liars 'for, where they lie once, they speak truth a hundred times' (*IHM* 196). The tendency to believe what one is told (principle of credulity) is strongest in the young child and is gradually tempered and qualified by the experience of dishonesty. Reid thinks that if nature had left the matter of the reliability of testimony an open question to be decided by experience alone then children would begin with incredulity and grow with wisdom and experience to be more trusting but 'the most superficial view of human life' (*IHM* 197) shows the process of growth to be quite contrary to this.

What Reid presents us with in pressing the analogy between testimony and perception is a picture of testimony-based knowledge which is, in some ways, similar to the treatment of mind, perception, and language found in some modern proponents of 'cognitive science'.[7] Reid has the same emphasis upon the innate contribution of the organism, though his appeal to the contribution of the 'human constitution' is not as extravagant as some. None the less, his account enables us to see the implausibility of treating all cases of testimonial knowledge as inferential or indirect. If we can have cases of direct knowledge in perception (as when I see a red apple close at hand in full daylight), then surely we can have cases of direct knowledge in testimony, as when I am told by a normally sighted, disinterested, and non-malevolent friend that there is a red apple on the table in the next room. It is no objection to this to cite the fact that I would not know unless the witness were visually competent, disinterested, and non-

---

[7] This is noted by Lehrer and Smith, 'Reid on Testimony', 37.

malevolent, since it is equally true that I would not know by my own perception unless similar conditions, such as normal lighting and properly functioning eyes, were fulfilled. In the perception case, it is enough (in conjunction perhaps with the satisfaction of a confidence condition) for my direct knowledge that the sensory information mechanism *is* function-ing properly and the contextual circumstances *are* normal; I do not need to determine in advance that this is so and argue from it to my perceptual conclusion. Similarly, we might conclude, from a perspective like Reid's, that it is enough if the communicative mechanism is functioning stan-dardly and contextual circumstances are normal (no particular reason for lying, etc.) for us to know directly that there is a red apple in the room next door.[8]

It may of course be possible to offer inferential support for a non-inferentially acquired belief. This is as true of testimony as it is of percep-tion and memory. In some cases, indeed, such support may strengthen the belief, in the sense of increasing one's confidence in the proposition involved. Here the extra support may make the difference between a case of belief and a case of knowledge. Reid is aware of this as the following remarks show:

And, as in many instances, Reason, even in her maturity, borrows aid from testimony, so in others she mutually gives aid to it, and strengthens its authority. For, as we find good reason to reject testimony in some cases, so in others we find good reason to rely upon it with perfect security, in our most important concerns. The character, the number and the disinterestedness of witnesses, the impossibility of collusion, and the incredibility of their concurring in their testimony without collusion, may give an irresistible strength to testimony, compared to which its native and intrinsic authority is very inconsiderable (*IHM* 197).

Yet a nagging doubt surely remains. Let us suppose that Reid has demonstrated his case for the analogy to the hilt. Does it really have the epistemological consequences claimed for it? It is one thing to show that we act as though we know without inference all sorts of things on the basis of what we are told and even that we do so in accord with an innate principle of credulity. It is another thing again to show that we are rationally entitled so to behave. Reid's psychological theory, it might be said, has some interesting and surprising things to tell us about how we think and communicate, even about how our make-up constrains us to behave, but it is psychology not epistemology. Hume, by contrast, is surely right to insist that an individual's trust in testimony is only worthy of the name knowledge where it rests upon the individual's perceptual experience of its reliability. We may not, as a matter of fact, proceed in this way but knowledge is normative and this is how we should proceed if we seek knowledge as a goal.

---

[8] The philosophical issues touched on here are discussed more fully in Ch. 8.

This style of objection rests upon the idea that the role of epistemology is to bring our most cherished beliefs before the bar of reason to see whether they are justified or not. Such justificationist enterprises look to some conception of reason or justification which is itself supposed to be independent of the beliefs, belief structures, and practices being arraigned before it. Contemporary philosophers are much less confident that any such trial is even theoretically possible than were their predecessors so the accusation of replacing epistemology with psychology is likely to be treated rather more lightly now than in the eighteenth or nineteenth centuries (witness Quine's project of 'naturalised epistemology').[9] Reid does not in any case merely produce a genetic or psychological account of our reliance on testimony and leave it at that. He fits the account of how this reliance arises from our constitution into a general epistemological framework of first principles which constitutes the positive side of his 'common sense' reaction against the scepticism he thought inherent in Hume and classical British empiricism. It is an assumption of this framework that if we construe the term 'reason' as narrowly as Hume, for instance, does and as it is in some respects natural to do, then it is not possible to vindicate our most central knowledge claims before such a tribunal. Where reason is construed as reasoning, i.e. moving from old beliefs to new beliefs, attempting to support some beliefs by calling upon others, or drawing out the consequences of holding certain beliefs, then Reid thinks this is quite clear since such reasoning cannot supply its own premisses.[10] Reid is moreover hostile to the idea that, even if we give reason a wider meaning, there is one pre-eminent form of it to which all reason-giving must reduce or conform. Here, as elsewhere, the tendency of his thought is firmly anti-reductionist, as can be seen clearly in his discussion of evidence in the chapter on the evidence of sense:

> Philosophers have endeavoured, by analysing the different sorts of evidence, to find out some common nature wherein they all agree, and thereby to reduce them all to one ... I confess that although I have, as I think, a distinct notion of the different kinds of evidence ... yet I am not able to find any common nature to which they may all be reduced. They seem to me to agree only in this, that they are all fitted by nature to produce belief in the human mind, some of them in the highest degree, which we call certainty, others in various degrees according to circumstances (*EI* 328).

The description of how our human constitution or natural faculties operate (the 'psychology') is made normative by Reid's invocation of the

---

[9] In addition, it is also none too clear what the successful completion of such a 'rational reconstruction' (supposing it to be possible) would show. That only those who have done (can do?) the reconstruction really *know*? Or perhaps others know vicariously if some philosophers can do it for them?

[10] His appeal to the impossibility of an infinite regress of reason-giving premisses occurs at *EI* 435.

ideas of first principles, self-evidence, and human nature. The self-evident first principles are very varied (consistent with his anti-reductionism) but our knowledge and reasoning depend upon them. They articulate as truths what might otherwise merely be descriptions of how we are prone to behave. One such principle, for example, is the perceptual one: 'That those things do really exist which we distinctly perceive by our senses, and are what we perceive them to be' (*EI* 445).[11] Another corresponds to the principle of credulity: 'That there is a certain regard due to human testimony in matters of fact, and even to human authority in matters of opinion' (*EI* 450). Reid thinks that the first principles are incapable of direct proof (they would not be *first* principles if they followed from more fundamental premisses) though in a broader sense of reason than that considered above they are deliverances of reason, namely that branch of reason traditionally called common sense.[12] The first principles do not, however, concern only necessary truths, nor does the acknowledgement of and reliance upon them deliver infallible certainties in particular cases, as the principle about testimony makes very plain. Moreover, their truth is susceptible to certain indirect proofs such as *ad hominem* and *ad absurdum*, those from the consent of the generality of mankind, the structure of language, the origin of the beliefs in our constitution, and the impracticality of denying them in real life. I cannot here enter in detail into these indirect arguments for the first principles except to note that they tend to rest upon two basic ideas: the absurdity of doubting beliefs that in practice you have no option but to act upon and the absurdity of denying one first principle but accepting others. This second point, which is somewhat undeveloped in Reid, stems from his belief in the coherence of the faculties of mind.[13]

In the case of testimony Reid could point to the futility and folly of abandoning our trust in communication. As we saw in earlier chapters, most of the arguments for being suspicious of testimony depend upon accepting its general reliability, although this commonly goes unnoticed. A case in point from contemporary discussion is the way psychological evidence designed to prove 'the unreliability of testimony' makes extensive covert use of the very 'faculty' supposedly undermined by the experiments. 'Eye witness testimony is unreliable',[14] announces one psychologist as he

---

[11] Perhaps this principle should be added to the inductive principle (another first principle) in the discussion of the analogy of acquired perception and testimony. Lehrer and Smith do as much, though Reid doesn't do so explicitly and they call it 'the principle of perceptual reality'.

[12] 'We ascribe to reason two offices or two degrees. The first is to judge of things self-evident; the second to draw conclusions that are not self-evident from those that are. The first of these is the province, and the sole province, of common sense . . .' (*EI* 425).

[13] See *EI* 439. The point is rightly stressed by Lehrer and Smith and will be discussed further in Ch. 8.

[14] Robert Buckhout, 'Eyewitness Testimony', *Scientific American*, 231/6 (Dec. 1974), 23.

reports to us on experiments not all of which he has done himself. 'As long ago as 1895', he tells us, such experiments were done.[15] All this would be laughable if it were not so common. We shall examine the significance of these and similar experiments in Chapter 15; here their inconsistencies illustrate once more both the unsuspected pervasiveness of our reliance upon testimony in practice and also one way in which the denial of one first principle runs foul of the operation of others. Our psychologist thought he could deny the general reliability of testimony in the name of something more solid, scientific observations. But these observations were only available, collatable, and presentable by reliance on testimony. The very word 'observation', as noted earlier, is most commonly employed in the sense of communal observation; most of what we regard as matters of observation are so only by proxy. It can also be shown that the very existence of language and hence of reports have implications for the reliability of testimony; some of these have been discussed earlier, especially in Chapter 4, and they will be more fully canvassed in Chapter 9. Here I shall simply note that although Reid does not argue thus it would be consistent with his programme to do so.

I want to turn again now to Reid's comparisons between perception and testimony. Although it is clear that Reid thinks of our reliance upon both perception and testimony as epistemologically primitive, as mediated by signs and as governed by formally similar principles, he does highlight certain disanalogies. The most striking is that the reliability of testimony depends upon the will of man and is subject to the defect of deception, a flaw which perception does not have. Indeed, as we saw earlier, Reid most implausibly treats testimony as if it could only fail through dishonesty. This is demonstrably false since a great deal of testimony consists of passing on perceptual information and, where it is mistaken, the mistake will, in all honesty, usually be transmitted. None the less there is the possibility (frequently enough realized) of deception and Reid insists that perception has no analogy to it. As he puts it: 'Men sometimes lead us into mistakes, when we perfectly understand their language, by speaking lies. But nature never misleads us in this way; her language is always true; and it is only by misinterpreting it that we fall into error' (*IHM* 199). It is for this reason that Reid stresses that the principle of credulity is strongest in children but less forceful (though still considerable) in adults, whose mature reason 'learns to suspect testimony in some cases, and to disbelieve it in others; and sets bounds to that authority to which she was at first entirely subject' (*IHM* 197). By contrast, he allows no such diminution in the strength of our trust in perception.[16] He is, of course, aware that we

---

[15] Ibid. 24.

[16] It is instructive in this connection to compare Reid's contrasting formulations of the first principles of perception and of testimony: 'That those things do really exist which we distinctly perceive by our senses, and are what we perceive them to be', as compared with,

are prone to a variety of what would commonly be called perceptual mistakes and indeed that we speak of the senses 'deceiving' us. Reid is, however, unsympathetic to this way of putting the matter and shows a strong tendency to minimize the errors due to perception. In his chapter on 'The Fallacy of the Senses' (*EI* II. xxii), he equivocates between arguing that the senses are not in general fallacious and that, strictly speaking, the senses are infallible but we make mistakes by incautious or short-term use of them.[17] This second position (which echoes Descartes's theory of error) is supported in part by treating perception as proper original perception. Such errors as mistaking a painting for the reality it represents or the size and distance of the heavenly bodies are put down to the operation of acquired perception. This is highly unsatisfactory since Reid now splits his unified theory of perception (and shows a certain amount of discomfort in doing so) and only succeeds in keeping the purity of one natural faculty by shifting the cause of error to another (that operating by the inductive principle). Since, on Reid's view, very few of our perceptions are original and the analogy with testimony (in 'artificial' languages) is with acquired perceptions, then these errors should be attributed to perception when pursuing the extent of the analogy. In any case, at the end of the chapter on fallacy of sense, Reid admits a category of strictly perceptual error which does deserve the title of deception, namely, errors occasioned by sensory disorder such as jaundice. It is also hard to see how certain illusions to do with original perception could be handled by the manœuvres Reid adopts—the Müller–Lyer illusion, for instance, does not seem to result from false inference, or some form of association culled from touch, or disordered eyesight.

We may safely proceed then by comparing the fallible reliabilities of perception and testimony without much concern for Reid's attempts to minimize the degree to which the former is prone to error. In fact, the admission of fallibilities in perception should reinforce Reid's view that individual perception is generally more reliable than testimony since the transmission of information via testimony usually involves perception twice over (in the witness and in the recipient). Not only can the witness misperceive but his audience can mishear or misread the message. Add to this the possibilities of deception and misremembering and the individual's perceptions appear much less risky epistemologically. There is certainly some force in these points but against them it should be said that the picture they present ignores certain features of our cognitive interactions

'That there is a certain regard due to human testimony in matters of fact, and even to human authority in matters of opinion' (*EI* 445 and 450). In the *Inquiry*, after speaking of the way the experience of deceit modifies the strength of our reliance on testimony, Reid adds, 'But the credit given to the testimony of our senses, is established and confirmed by the uniformity and constancy of the laws of nature' (p. 184).

[17] Perhaps Reid's tendency to bestow infallibility upon the language of nature stems from his piety towards its speaker, God.

with the world. It is a common modern criticism of eighteenth-century thought that it treats the subject too much as a passive recipient and recorder of data. Reid is less vulnerable to this criticism than many others but in the comparison of perception and testimony it is easy to lose sight of the fact that witness and audience are active explorers of a common world. This means that habits, expectations, and skills can not only produce error but can guard against it. Consequently, it may be more rational to rely upon the testimony of another than upon one's own perceptions in many common situations. The other may, for example, have better eyesight, better recognitional capacities for the subject-matter of the observation, be better placed, and less emotionally involved. There may also be more of him. Reid himself, as we saw in Chapter 1, cites the way a mathematician, who has made a discovery in his science and carefully confirmed it for himself, will still be anxious about its validity until he has had his judgement confirmed by the calculations of his mathematical peers. If they disagree with him he will return to a rigorous re-examination of his proofs.[18] The same sort of thing can happen in perceptual matters, though we are often in no position to make a second perceptual examination and can only consult our memory. Even where we can look again it cannot be decided a priori that we should trust our senses against the testimony of others. This is so because agreement with the perceptions of others is a prime test of the publicity of what is apparently perceived. Such an agreement can often be evidenced only by testimony (though it can sometimes be behaviourally indicated by 'natural language' or by other actions). The picture is thus very complex and can be complicated further if we hold that many (some would say, all) of the concepts in terms of which we make perceptual judgements are socially provided. If the notion of testimony covers such provisions then any claim about greater reliability would have to take account of a close mesh between perception and testimony at the level of thought itself. At the brink of such an issue we must, for now, halt our steps.

[18] *EI*, essay vi, ch. iv, p. 440.

III

The Solution

8

The Status of Testimony

We have seen the failure of a variety of attempts to justify 'reductively' our extensive reliance upon testimony. In treating testimony as epistemically more problematic than individual perception, memory, or inference, these attempts rest inevitably upon the sense of an individual's orientation to reality through others as somehow tacked on to his more fundamental orientation via his private intellectual powers. This implies that testimony is sufficiently separable from them to be capable of presentation for independent judicial arraignment. There is much to question in this picture. Some of these questions have already been raised and more will be discussed in subsequent chapters. Here I want to look closely at the way the picture matches or fails to match the linguistic, conceptual, and material status of testimony in comparison with these powers. What will concern us are the similarities and differences between testimony and the other sources of information as these manifest themselves in the logical grammar of our concepts and in our natural modes of thought and investigation. Although our interests here are by no means 'purely verbal' (in the pejorative sense) it will be instructive to begin with a scrutiny of the behaviour of certain verbs, especially the perceptual ones. Such an examination may not only help to reveal connections and disparities but should also throw light upon the structure these relations exhibit and thereby help to dispel certain natural misunderstandings about the status of testimony.

The verbs 'remember' and 'perceive', along with the particular verbs of perception 'hear', 'see', 'touch', 'taste', and 'smell', have the striking feature that their correct use requires a direct object that really exists. At least there is a common, standard sense of the expressions in which this is so. There is another employment of some of these verbs which has a different, though related, commitment, namely their use with a propositional object. Indisputably, there is such a use, but its nature and significance are by no means clear. It is most comfortable with 'remember', 'recall', and 'see' (and the generic 'perceive'), as in 'John saw that Lydia was upset', yet there is no comparable usage of 'touch that' at all nor does 'taste that' really get off the ground. 'Feel that' is common enough but frequently it is not perceptual but emotional. With 'smell' the that-locution is real but rare. 'Lydia smelt that John was afraid' makes sense though 'Lydia could smell that John was afraid' seems better. With hearing, the matter is complicated by the use of 'hears that' in connection with receiving tes-

timony but it is certainly used for the more directly perceptual cases as in
'Joan heard that Harold had shut the door'.

For these propositional uses of the perceptual verbs it is plausible to
hold that there is something parallel to the requirement of existence for the
direct object in the non-propositional uses. The parallel lies in the required
truth of the proposition introduced by the 'that-clause'. Let us refer to the
feature exhibited by the parallel as 'success grammar'. Where these verbs
have success grammar in either the object or the proposition form, the
discovery that the object does not exist or that the contained proposition
is false shows that the overall claim made by the sentence using the
perceptual verb is also false. 'John saw that Lydia was wearing her blue
dress' is simply false if Lydia was not in fact wearing her blue dress, just as
'John saw a blue wren' is false if there was no blue wren to be seen.[1]
Similarly, Joan did not hear that Harold shut the door if he did not do so
nor did Lydia smell that John was afraid if he wasn't.

It has been claimed that there are other senses of these perceptual verbs
in which they lack success grammar. Anscombe has argued[2] that there are
'intentional' uses in which it is correct to say that, for example, Macbeth
sees his dagger. She thereby hopes to do justice to the advocates and
opponents of sense-data whilst disagreeing with both. Where the parties
to the controversy share the assumption that the perceptual verbs have
success grammar but disagree on whether it is correct to talk literally of
'seeing' in such cases as hallucinations, Anscombe agrees with the sense-
data camp that it is correct but denies that this admission allows the
introduction of sense-data as existing entities. This is not allowed because
it is only correct for the intentional use of perceptual verbs in which their
objects need not exist (are 'intentional' rather than 'material'). I propose
no stand on this attempt to defuse the debate on perception and sensation.
It is enough for my purposes that there are central uses of the perceptual
verbs in which they have success grammar. Whether there are genuine uses
of the perceptual verbs where they take intentional accusatives either of
the objectual or propositional form need not concern us further. What is
of present interest is that although there are clear and central uses of
several perceptual verbs with the success grammar feature, it is plain that
'testify' is not such a verb nor, on the receiving end, is 'told'. John can
testify that *p* where *p* is false and Arthur can be told that *p* where *p* is
false, just as he can be told of something which does not exist.

How seriously, and in what ways, do these 'grammatical' facts bear
upon the epistemological status of testimony? One problem they create at
once is that the success grammar of perception and memory statements

---

[1] I am ignoring complications caused by reference failure and the possibility of truth-value
gaps for the propositional uses.
[2] G. E. M. Anscombe, 'The Intentionality of Sensation', in *The Collected Philosophical
Papers of G. E. M. Anscombe*, ii (Oxford, 1981), 3–20.

allows for and indeed calls for the use of 'seems' and 'appears' locutions which cancel the existence and truth implications while preserving a reference to the part played by the processes of perception and memory. So 'John seemed to remember', 'I seem to recall', 'I seemed to see'. These are most at home with the direct object verbs but are not out of the question with propositional object verbs. 'I seem to remember that you were present' is perfectly alright, though 'I seemed to see that he was upset' doesn't quite work. For cautious or disavowing 'perceive that' remarks we usually have recourse to 'thought' rather than 'seem'. 'I thought I saw that he was upset' or 'He thought he heard that the police had gone'.

Because we have no testimony verb which behaves like see or remember, we have no disclaiming device to operate on it in the way 'seems', 'appears', and 'thought' do in the case of perception and memory. John McDowell[3] has proposed a use of 'communicate' which is sensitive to some of the problems here but his proposal has its own problems which I prefer to side-step. Part of the puzzle is that we have no verb for 'receiving testimony'. When Reid speaks of the social operations of mind he lists both the giving and receiving of testimony as amongst them but, apart from 'trusting' which can refer to non-epistemic matters (or at least those not predominantly epistemic like trusting a dog or a friend), we have no single word for what the recipient of testimony does or undergoes in receiving it. (Sometimes the word 'hear' can do but it is, as already remarked, ambiguous.) It is not at all clear why this is so but since it is so it makes it that much harder to answer our question.

Let us coin a word for the receiving of testimony. The English word 'learn' is wider in scope since one can learn from (one's own) experience but a great deal of learning comes from the word of others so although its restriction to what we find out from testimony is a restriction, it is not a greatly artificial one. To show that we are using learn in the restricted way I shall write it in what follows in italics.

The ordinary English 'learn' has success grammar like 'see', or rather like 'see that' since learn takes predominantly propositional objects. We can speak of learning a poem but this seems merely to be elliptical for learning to recite a poem. 'Learning that' and 'learning to' seem related like 'knowing that' and 'knowing how'. If John learnt or learns that p then p is true. It may be objected that we can say such things as 'John learnt that his brother was dead from an army telegram but later found out that he was still alive.' Such things are said but to my ear they ring almost as false as 'The medievals knew that the earth was flat but now we know that it is not' and yet those who teach introductory epistemology courses know that such things are said often enough. I think that 'learn' clearly belongs

---

[3] John McDowell, 'Meaning, Communication and Knowledge', in Z. Van Straaten (ed.), *Philosophical Subjects: Essays Presented to P. F. Strawson* (Oxford, 1980), 117–39.

with 'know' and 'see that' as a verb with success grammar but, in any case, the most that the putative counter-examples can do is force us to admit that there may be a sense of such verbs which does not have success grammar and this allows that there is also a sense, and surely the dominant one, which does have it. It is upon that sense that I model my technical term *learn*.

The fact that *learn* does not take a standard direct object is the grammatical side of a fact noticed by one commentator on Reid's analogy between perception and testimony. In his book, *The Varieties of Reference*, Gareth Evans, who is in general sympathetic to the analogy, says, 'there are important differences between testimony and the senses notably in respect of the kind of information concerned (the senses yield non-conceptual information, whereas language embodies conceptual information...)'.[4] Exactly what Evans means by his distinction between conceptual and non-conceptual is not made entirely clear in his references to it in the book. Nor is his notion of information uncontroversial. Evans thinks that philosophers are prone to give too much weight to notions like belief and thought in their explanations of how we interact cognitively with our environment. No doubt these are very important, but for processes such as perception and memory, Evans thinks, we need to conduct our analyses in less sophisticated, less intellectualized concepts. These processes are, after all, shared with non-human animals and even insects for whom the application of higher level concepts such as belief is at least debatable. Allied to this consideration is the point that analyses of perception need to take account of the fact that we do not always believe that the world is as our senses represent it.[5] When we see one line as longer than another in the Müller–Lyer illusion we need not believe that this is how the lines really are. In Evans's sense of 'information' we are informed that one line is longer than the other but we need not believe it. (For Evans, information may be true or false, accurate or inaccurate.) Similar situations arise with memory. The phenomenon of 'déjà vu', for instance, is one in which some present happenings are experienced as if they had already occurred in the past and we feel as if we know what is about to happen next (especially what is about to be said next) because we have experi-

---

[4] Gareth Evans, *Varieties of Reference* (Oxford, 1982), 123. See also ch. 6, s. 3, and ch. 7, s. 4.

[5] There may be some scope for the application of the idea of non-conceptual information in the case of testimony if we are impressed by Reid's attempt to draw an analogy between 'original' perceptions and those 'original' testimonies given 'in the natural language of the human countenance and behaviour' (*Inquiry into the Human Mind*, ed. T. Duggan (Chicago, 1970), 195; see also the discussion in Ch. 7). What we gather from a smile or an angry gesture may then be thought of as 'spoken' in the natural language and *learnt* by the hearer non-conceptually in much the same way as a viewer non-conceptually sees a blue patch. To go down this path would involve an extension of our concept of testimony, the legitimacy of which would turn upon the plausibility and utility of extending the concepts of speech and language to 'natural' gestures and reactions. I suspect that there are too many difficulties in doing this, so I shall not follow Reid even though his suggestion retains some appeal.

enced it once before. Typically, we do not believe that these present happenings have been historically recycled, nor even that something very similar happened in the past, though that might be how we try to explain this eerie experience.

Because of facts such as the above Evans wants to say that information is belief-independent. Here Evans rejects the idea, favoured by some theorists of perception, that we should describe the phenomenon of belief-independence by reference to some belief-surrogate such as 'prima facie inclination to believe'. This manœuvre is defective, in Evans's view, partly because the idea of belief belongs with that of judgement and reasons whereas the operations of the informational system are more primitive. (It is also unclear just what a 'prima facie inclination' to anything could possibly be, in the absence of any actual inclination in that direction, but this is not a point pressed by Evans.)

In the case of perception and memory a subject's informational states are sometimes spoken of by Evans as 'seemings'[6] and the general thrust of his position is to treat perceptual 'seemings' as non-conceptual and sometimes even to write as if all informational states were non-conceptual. This cannot be his considered view, however, since as we have seen he thinks that testimonial information is always conceptual. More curiously he usually writes as if perception, certainly, and memory (one supposes) give only non-conceptual information but, on occasion, allows that they too provide conceptual information. So we find him saying that the distinction between remembering (direct object) and remembering that (propositional object) 'turns on the kind of information retained',[7] where it is clear that the former will go with non-conceptual information. It would seem natural surely to extend this idea to perception where the grammatical distinction equally exists. If 'informational states' can be specified as seemings then we can certainly have memory seemings of two kinds, as we saw earlier. It is less clear that we can have perceptual seemings of the two kinds for, as we noted before, the propositional seemings are more comfortably reported with a 'thought that' locution.

Perhaps the best thing to say is that Evans consistently held all strictly perceptual information to be non-conceptual, memory information to be either non-conceptual or conceptual, and testimonial information to be always conceptual. We would then need to give a different analysis of 'sees that' to 'remembers that'. This has some plausibility. Memory differs from both testimony and perception in being a way of retaining information rather than acquiring it and the information retained can itself come from either perception or testimony.[8] A subject can remember not only what he has been (conceptually) told but also his past (conceptual) beliefs, includ-

[6] *Varieties of Reference*, 123, 180 n., 227.

[7] Ibid. 267 n.

[8] Or for that matter, from inference, though for Evans an inferred fact need not, it seems, be information-based. (See ibid. 127).

ing those formed on the basis of his own perceptions, which could be recorded in the idiom of 'perceiving that'. It goes with this that the project of defining perceiving that in terms of perceiving things is quite feasible, whereas a parallel project in the case of memory is more suspect. For vision, at any rate, we may (following Frank Jackson) define 'S sees that A is F' by the set of conditions:

(i) A is F
(ii) S believes of A that it is A and F
(iii) S sees A
(iv) A looks F to S
(v) S believes of A that it is seen by him.[9]

Well-known facts about perception and belief require our use of the 'transparent' locution, coined by Quine, 'believes of—that ...' since the more natural 'opaque' locution 'believes that— ...' will not do. We need not, however, dwell on such details now. What we should note is that parallel conditions for (iii), (iv), and (v) are difficult to justify for an analysis of remembering that in terms of remembering things. I may very well remember that the battle of Hastings was fought in 1066, though I cannot, of course, remember the battle itself nor does it present a memory appearance to me in any way like the looks presented by vision. Equally I may remember that King Harold was shot in the eye by an arrow without anything like these conditions being fulfilled. Even where the thing that figures in the *memory that* can be remembered, it is not necessary to the propositional memory that it be so. I may remember that the first desk I looked at last week was priced at $4,000 without being able to remember the desk itself. Of course, 'remembering x' needs some clarification. Sometimes we use the expression 'remember' of a thing merely to register present recognition of something presented to us. This is related to but not quite the same as that use in which we recall something not present. It is, in any case, this second sense which interests us here and although an account of remembering things is beyond the scope of this work it is initially plausible that amongst the necessary conditions for S remembering A we should include:

(1) A existed (or occurred) in the past.[10]
(2) S believes of A that it existed (or occurred) in the past.
(3) It seems to S as if he has perceived A in the past.

These conditions may not be jointly sufficient but surely condition (3) may be unfulfilled when S none the less remembers that A was F. Roughly, condition (3) is a memory-impression condition but I may have no

---

[9] F. Jackson, *Perception* (Cambridge, 1977), 161.
[10] There are issues about how far in the past, cf. William James on primary memory in *Principles of Psychology* (Cambridge, Mass., 1890), ch. xvi.

memory impression of the first desk I saw last week and yet remember that it was priced at $4,000. I will recall that there was a first desk of course, but that is not to have a memory impression of it. Suppose I saw thirty desks in the week (looking for a birthday present) and was struck by the fact that the most expensive was the first and by its price but yet can recall no features of the desk itself. Or, to take a different example, consider a man struck with pretty complete amnesia. In his misfortune, he has forgotten his wife, though he can remember that he had a wife and that his wife was intelligent. That he has forgotten his wife may be proved by his total failure to recognize her when she walks into the room. (This shows a point of connection between remembering as recognition and as recall.) We may say that his memory impression is the impression of a belief.

There are further mysteries which could be explored here but enough has been said to support the following suggestion about differences between perception and memory. In perception (certainly in vision and probably also in the case of the other senses) perceiving things is more fundamental than perceiving that, but with memory the position seems reversed since memory is predominantly a matter of remembering that. In perception we observe our environment by a process of direct interaction with it which yields us much more in the way of what Evans calls 'information' than we cogitate upon, form beliefs about, and use as premisses in arguments and theories. In memory, our present interaction with our past environment is through the interaction which has already taken place and naturally a great deal of what we recall has already been thought about and conceptually processed in the past. When we talk of remembering things[11] we sometimes mean no more than a sort of systematic remembering that. The man who remembers that his wife was beautiful but does not remember her may simply be someone who does not remember enough facts about her. Martin and Deutscher seem to think that this is all there is to the distinction between direct-object remembering and propositional-object remembering.[12] They think that someone who can remember that he went down the street last Friday but does not remember actually going down the street lacks 'at least' more detailed remembering that certain things happened (in the sense of remembering that which goes with having experienced the event in question rather than having been told of it in the past). Yet at least some cases of remembering things do not seem to yield easily to this treatment. Some present observation can trigger a memory in a way that naturally allows for the form of description 'remembers x' without a great deal of detailed remembering that. So, a man may be watching a child swimming in the surf and recall his own swimming on the some beach at a quite specific

[11] Under 'things' I include processes, events, and episodes.
[12] See pp. 162–3 of C. B. Martin and Max Deutscher, 'Remembering', *Philosophical Review*, 75 (1966), 161–96.

date in the past without this being merely a conjunction of remembered facts. Often this will involve an image or some vivid sense of the familiarity of what is happening now with what happened in the past. In so far as one takes oneself to be remembering facts in such episodes (facts which could be reported in the idiom of 'remembering that') then they may, in certain circumstances, turn out to be no facts at all. Anscombe's case[13] of the man who saw a dummy which he took for a real man is to the point here. When he recalls what he saw he may say both that he remembers seeing a man and that he remembers that he saw a man, but we are in a position to know that both claims are false. None the less, he does remember something and we are in a position to say what it is, namely a dummy (or even, seeing a dummy). It seems wrong, however, to say that he remembers that he saw a dummy. Here there is direct-object memory without the (directly relevant) propositional-object memory.

It may be said that in Anscombe's case there are at least some propositions about the dummy that he truly remembers, i.e. he remembers that what he saw was clothed, say, in a red coat. Yet even this need not be so if we accept that memory is operating in Martin and Deutscher's example of the painter who unknowingly paints a scene from his childhood. Of him, we are at least tempted to say that he remembers the scene, in spite of the fact that he doesn't remember that it is a scene from his childhood or any other 'remember that' connected with it.[14]

Such examples as Anscombe's dummy and Martin and Deutscher's painter cannot be taken as decisive since there is no solid linguistic consensus about how it is best to describe them. Although there is certainly some pressure to describe the painter as remembering, it would not be absurd to resist the pressure by maintaining that, since the painter in no sense believes that this is a scene from his past, he is not remembering at all, though his past experiences are operating on him. One might even seek to prise the notion of remembering loose from that of memory at his point, saying that although his memory is at work he is not remembering. Someone who wanted to define remembering things in the way I suggested as 'initially plausible' might treat the example in some such way, since as a case of remembering it clearly violates condition (2) and perhaps condition (3), depending on the account of 'seems to *S* as if'.

This digression into the murky waters of memory has provided us with no solutions to the problems that beset that difficult topic but, in connection with Evans's claims, it has made some things a little clearer. We can see once more that there is intuitive sense to his view that memory as well

---

[13] G. E. M. Anscombe, 'The Reality of the Past', in *Collected Papers*, ii. 107.
[14] It is surely implausible to say that he remembers that a row of houses in the town is coloured green just because he paints it exactly how it was. But other cases are more difficult, for example, the common case of giving an argument or proof or illustration which you think original.

as perception can provide information without belief. Further, we are at least in a better position to assess his contention that a contrast between conceptual and non-conceptual information underlies the distinction between remembering that and remembering things. Evans calls the distinction one that is drawn 'colloquially' and it seems likely that it is not one distinction but several. It also seems likely that an important contrast often marked by the different locutions is between recollections of material that has been processed through the conceptual system and is recalled to some degree consciously in propositional form and, on the other hand, recollections of a less cerebral kind which often present themselves in imagery. The latter may be possible without conscious imagery as in (one construal of) the Martin–Deutscher painting example, but imagery seems centrally connected with remembering things, events, episodes, and so on, in a way that remembering that does not. If there is any room for the idea of memory impressions or memory experience (akin to sensory experience) it must be located here. That there is such room in any theoretically useful sense has been denied, and forcefully, but we do not need to settle the question here.[15] For our purposes it is enough that there is some room for non-conceptual memory information, though much less than in the case of present perception. Our purpose is to compare perception and memory with testimony and it is surely clear that there is no room for the non-conceptual element in the case of testimony proper. This is what underpins the grammatical fact that 'learn' and my technical term *learn* do not take direct objects except in the learn-how sense or in certain derivative ways.[16] Relatedly, we have no use for 'seems to *learn*' as a parallel locution to 'seems to see' or even 'seems to remember'. There is a good case for the existence of visual experience and phenomena, some case for the existence (sometimes) of memory experience and phenomena, but no case for the existence of testimony experience and phenomena other than the auditory and/or visual experiences necessary to the conveying of testimony.

Of course the existence of an epistemic locution with success grammar does not guarantee actual epistemic success to believers, at least not by itself. Certainly there are many cases where someone is either deliberately or accidentally misinformed. Hence there will be a locution to cover such happenings or the belief that they have occurred and the same locution will be available for cautious remarks about putatively genuine testimonial transactions. As in the case of 'seeing that' we may do best to use the 'thought that' terminology rather than 'seems that'. This is perfectly acceptable for the acknowledgement of misinformation as in 'John only

---

[15] By, for one, Professor Anscombe in a paper later than the one cited in n. 13. See 'Memory, Experience and Causation', in *Collected Papers*, ii. 120–30.

[16] The child who tells her father that she learnt geometry at school today means that she learnt that *p* and *q* and *r* . . . all being geometrical fact, or that she began to learn such fact, or that she learnt how to do certain geometrical tasks.

thinks he has *learnt* that *p*' or 'Mary thought she had *learnt* that *q* but of course *q* is false' or 'I thought I had *learnt* that *s*'. These are not denials that information has been conveyed, only that it is true. The cautious or tentative use with the first person sounds more dubious, as in, 'I think I have *learnt* that John is the murderer' but this may be because it would be more usual to express caution directly about the knowledge claim rather than the claim about its source, i.e. 'I think that John is the murderer'. When the source is what is under discussion one who has reservations about the testimony's reliability is more likely to use the available non-committal passive, 'I was told that John is the murderer.' None the less, 'I think I have *learnt* that . . .' or 'It seemed that I had *learnt* that . . .' appear to make perfect sense.

The conceptual issues which our discussion has raised and clarified about the relations between perception and testimony show that Evans was right to point to a contrast between the kind of information available from perception and from testimony and it gives some support to his characterization of testimonial information as always conceptual. We should, however, beware of drawing too hasty epistemic conclusions from this contrast. One such conclusion might be that there can be no such thing as direct or non-inferential knowledge by way of testimony and another might be that perception must have a more fundamental epistemological status than testimony.

Let us examine these propositions in turn. We might be drawn in the direction of the first conclusion by the thought that direct knowledge can only be appropriately invoked when we are faced with the contents of an experience. In support of this thought we might recall those theorists who have restricted the scope of direct knowledge precisely to awareness of sense-data. It may be admitted, indeed, that if there are sense-data and we know them, then at least some of our knowledge of them (perhaps all) will be direct. If Jones claims to know that she is confronted by a visual appearance as of a blue bird then we need seek no inferences of hers to support her claim to know. It is indeed the sort of thing which (whatever its ontological status) can be known directly. But we should not conclude that it is the only sort of thing which can be so known. After all, many of the things we know about our past are equally candidates for direct knowledge, even, perhaps especially, where there is no plausibility in the claim that we are undergoing memory experiences. Jones may know, without even the most subtle inferences, that yesterday she was in Melbourne though today she is in Sydney, and in normal circumstances it would be absurd to demand evidence beyond her avowal that she remembers. Moreover, the validity of certain mathematical inferences is plausibly held to be a matter of direct knowledge, though it is most implausible to treat it as even involving some special mathematical experiences, still less being constituted by them.

Another temptation which has perhaps supported the restriction of direct knowledge to such items as sense-data has been the traditional foundationalist stress upon incorrigibility. It is tempting to think that non-inferential knowledge being, in a sense, foundational, must be knowledge of propositions which are, in themselves, incorrigible or infallible. I do not want to be abruptly dismissive of this tradition of thinking, as it has become fashionable to be, but I do not find it persuasive at least in its pure and simple form. Moreover, it is only, at best, one possible form of foundationalism. It is surely coherent to suppose, as some modern foundationalists such as W. P. Alston have, that knowledge could exhibit a structure of more and less fundamental propositions without supposing that even the most fundamental exhibited such properties as incorrigibility. There is, of course, a trivial sense in which all knowledge is incorrigible or infallible, namely, that in which there is no way in which what is true can be legitimately shown to be false. But traditional, substantive incorrigibility required more than this, for it insisted that some basic propositions proclaimed their incorrigibility to the attentive eye, their infallibility shone forth from their visage. Whether such a feature is the possession of any proposition I shall not here inquire, but it seems clear that the usual arguments for the category of direct knowledge need invoke no such feature. Hence there is no need to restrict direct knowledge to the experiential or that immediately involving the experiential.

With that out of the way, however, another difficulty emerges for the idea that testimonial knowledge could ever be direct. After all, it may well be urged, the rational person does not believe just any and every thing he is told. His assent must be mediated by a consideration of the veracity of the witness, his reliability (competence to speak, in terms of our definition in Chapter 2), the probability of what he says, and so on. Thus mediated, our belief in what he says must count as inferentially based and likewise for our knowledge, where it is knowledge. Plausible as this argument seems, it is surely fallacious. The first problem with it is that it is at odds with the phenomenology of *learning*. In our ordinary dealings with others we gather information without this concern for inferring the acceptability of communications from premises about the honesty, reliability, probability, etc., of our communicants. I ring up the telephone company on being unable to locate my bill and am told by an anonymous voice that it comes to $165 and is due on 15 June. No thought of determining the veracity and reliability of the witness occurs to me nor, given that the total is within tolerable limits, does the balancing of probabilities figure in my acceptance. Or I find a stray dog with an identification tag attached to his collar. I ring the phone number on it (this happened to me recently) to be told that (*a*) the person speaking to me was not the owner, (*b*) that the owner was out and wouldn't be back until 5 p.m., and (*c*) that the owner often left the dog at home untied and he often got out and invariably found his way safely home. There is nothing hesitant or suspicious about the unknown communicant's responses and I entirely believe what he says without adverting to the premises about reliability, etc.—premises which I am here, as so often in speech exchanges, in no position at all to investigate or independently establish. It may be said that in neither of these nor many other cases that could be cited am I being rational in offering such ready assent. On the contrary, it would surely be irrational to the point of insanity to withold assent pending investigation of the respective premises. Of course, it is difficult to settle questions about the rational person and his or her standards, but it is hard to avoid the feeling that one's objector here is haunted by Cartesian or incorrigibilist standards of rationality and knowledge. We may partly shortcut further dispute along these lines, however, by turning to the second problem for the objector's argument.

   Much of the plausibility of his argument rests on the undoubted fact that testimonial transactions of the kind that are supposed to yield direct knowledge are dependent for their knowledge-yielding status on the truth of certain propositions which the objector casts in the role of premises to conclusions. If my telephone company informant is deceitful or incompetent or the claimed amount extravagantly unlikely then I will not know at all, no matter how ready my assent. I will not know either (or both) because the proposition I believe is false or my justification for believing it is defective. Hence it seems that I should first ensure that my justification is not defective, but if I do so successfully then what I end up with is precisely inferential knowledge. The trouble with this line of thought can be exposed by pointing out how readily it yields unpalatable conclusions for perceptual knowledge. When I believe unhesitatingly that there is a tomato on the table in front of me on the basis of visually perceiving it, I would normally be conceded the right to know this directly and it is precisely with such paradigms of direct knowledge that our objector wants to contrast testimonial knowledge. None the less, it is equally true for this case that its knowledge status rests upon the truth of such propositions as that the lighting is normal and my eyes functioning reliably, that no one has recently entered the room and placed a plastic copy of a tomato on the table, and so on. My knowledge rests on the truth of these and many other propositions but it is normally no requirement of my knowing that I have established their truth as part of my justification. The point has become familiar in recent discussions about the concept of knowledge and was first made explicit, I think, by J. L. Austin.[17] Most recently the point has been expanded and rechristened as the idea that knowledge is not subject to deductive closure, i.e. knowing that p does not

---

[17] J. L. Austin, *Sense and Sensibilia* (Oxford, 1962), esp. ch. x; cf. R. Nozick, *Philosophical Explanations* (Oxford, 1981), 204–7.

entail knowing all the entailments of *p*. As such it has been used by some
as a counter to certain sceptical arguments since they characteristically rely
upon the thought that, no matter how well placed we are to believe that *p*,
there will be some negative proposition *q* entailed by *p* such that I am not
well placed to determine its truth, and if I don't know that *q* then I don't
know that *p*. So suppose I know that I am looking at a tomato in my
kitchen. The proposition 'I am looking at a tomato in my kitchen' entails
that I am not a brain in a vat on Alpha Centauri, or less spectacularly that
I am not hallucinated. Yet I have taken no special steps to assure myself of
the truth of these latter propositions and so the sceptic will insist that I do
not know them and hence cannot know about the tomato.

Of course, the sceptic says much more and we shall not try to follow
him any further here. Nor shall we evaluate the non-closure move as a
reply to scepticism, though it should be noted that, even if effective against
certain forms of scepticism, it is not clear that every form of scepticism
relies upon the sort of argument it is designed to defeat. My point here is
merely to urge the far weaker consideration that for *A* to know directly
that *p* he need not have established the truth of various propositions that
q, *r* and *s*, which are entailed, or presupposed, by the truth of *p*. At least
this is true of our ordinary use of the verb 'to know'; I leave it open
whether this is precisely what the sceptic is out to reject. Clearly, in the
perception case, it is essential to the truth of *A*'s claim to know that the
tomato is on the table that no one has substituted a plastic imitation, that
the appearance of a tomato is not produced by *A*'s defective perceptual
apparatus, etc., but equally clearly he does not have to establish the truth
of these propositions and infer the known proposition (partly) from them.

Similarly with testimony: we do not have to establish the many propositions which, if false, would invalidate our ready assent to what we are
told, unless there is already some reason to believe that their truth is in
jeopardy. With regard, particularly, to such questions as the reliability and
honesty (here) of the witness, we can often take it that the testimony
mechanism is functioning adequately, just as we may usually take it that
the perceptual or memory mechanism is not malfunctioning. The analogy
should be taken seriously. In spite of the differences between perception,
memory, and testimony, they all provide techniques or 'mechanisms' for
acquiring true beliefs and, as we saw in Chapter 1, testimony has every
claim to the status of an important source of knowledge. That it is also a
fundamental source has been suggested by the failures of the individualist
reductive projects discussed in Chapters 4, 5, and 6 and by some of the
considerations deployed against those projects. There seems therefore to be
no barrier to accepting at face value the everyday facts which point to
there being many cases in which answers of the form, 'Jones told me', or in
my semi-technical vocabulary, 'I *learnt* it from Jones' are enough to support claims (directly) to know.

And yet. And yet. The nagging doubt remains that whatever the value of testimony as a justification for knowledge claims and whatever the case for there being instances in which knowledge by testimony is direct, none the less perceptual knowledge is necessarily more basic than testimonial. One point that must be conceded straight off is that the giving and receiving of testimony is only possible via perception (and, especially in the case of testimony chains, memory). We must *hear* the messages or *see* them written, in order for there to be testimony at all, and our informant must *remember* what he has seen or been told. Moreover, even allowing for complex chains of testimony, the source of testimonial information must ultimately be somehow perceptual or, in some special cases, intellectual.[18] In these ways, then, testimony is doubly derivative: it needs an epistemic origin other than itself and it needs an epistemic medium other than itself. But these facts do not demonstrate that testimony has an inferior epistemic standing to perception. They help to remind us of the *centrality* of perception, a centrality which probably lies behind the empiricist tradition's glorification of and even obsession with individual perception and its downgrading (if only by neglect) of testimony and reason. This centrality can be illustrated by reference to memory and inference as well as to testimony. Simplifying somewhat, we could say that memory as an information source makes past perceptions of the individual available in the present, testimony makes the past and relatively present perceptions of others available to those who did not perceive for themselves, and inference takes information from all these sources and yields unsuspected information latent in them, new possibilities and prospects for the direction of future perception. There are dangers in this picture, as in all simplifications, and we shall turn to them in a moment, but there is sufficient truth in it to show what could be meant by talk of perception as central and why the thought of it as such can be so powerful an influence.

One thing the picture illustrates immediately, however, is that this centrality grants no reductive priority to perception, nor what I shall call epistemological superiority. We have seen in Chapter 4 that the attempt to justify the epistemological power of testimony reductively in terms of perception (and inference) is unsuccessful. That attempt, even if successful, would not, in any case, have been a pure reduction to perceptual techniques, since it relied inescapably on inference and memory as well. Nor is it at all clear what could be meant by trying to justify our reliance on memory or inference purely in terms of a more fundamental reliance upon individual perception. Put crudely, inference needs perception to provide premises but it is none the less an independent and original operation of the mind. So, too, there is no memory without perception, but memory

---

[18] Or a combination of these, as in the example of the size of the football crowd discussed in Ch. 2.

is a power or faculty of the mind quite distinguishable from perception. Likewise with testimony. The giving and receiving of testimony is, as Reid calls it, 'a social operation of the mind' which presumes upon perception in the ways already indicated but which has its own epistemic autonomy. It is best, I think, to see all four as on a level though with perception at the centre.

Of course, much of this is metaphor, but it is important to deal with the dominant metaphors and combat those which are misleading. In fact, there is still something misleading in the picture I have presented by way of conceding a certain centrality to perception, and by bringing this out we can see again how important it is not to pretend a pre-eminence for perception which it really lacks. The picture treats the four sources of knowledge as if they could be quite isolated from each other and then asks questions about their epistemic relations. Useful as this may be, it can obscure the fact that there is a degree of interpenetration amongst all of them. We are familiar with this in the case of perception and it has led to the famous claim that all perceptual observation is theory-laden or inferentially loaded. Without fully endorsing much that seems to go with such philosophical slogans, we can agree with the truisms on which they are founded, such as the fact that what one perceives is often a partial function of what one expects to perceive, of what one already believes, and of the concepts one has. Into these factors, memory, inference, and the testimony of others enter essentially. A man sees the Queen visiting Melbourne University. He truly reports this to others who pass it on and it becomes common knowledge. His perceptions are at the source of the testimony but his belief that it was the Queen is dependent not merely on certain visual experiences but also on certain other beliefs which provided the identificatory framework with which he approached his visual experience and rightly interpreted it as an observation of the monarch. These framework beliefs would include perhaps the belief that the Queen was in Melbourne (testimony and memory), that she looked thus and so, usually wore such and such clothing (again testimony and memory), that her presence at the University could inferentially account for the high degree of security precautions going on in the vicinity and the even higher degree of grovelling. If there is no perception so pure that it is uncontaminated by testimony, memory, and/or inference, then the idea of making pure perception some kind of epistemological foundation-stone for any or all of the other three is absurd and the same absurdity will arise even if we allow only that most perception is so contaminated since what allowance could be made for pure perception would surely be too exiguous a base to build so ambitious a justificatory endeavour upon.

Yet the temptation to insist upon some epistemological superiority for perception (especially over testimony) persists. Surely, it may be said, if you have an outright clash between testimony and perception, or between perception and inference, or memory and perception, then the verdict must always go the way of perception. But is this really so? Certainly there seem to be plenty of cases in which the verdict may perfectly reasonably go against perception or what offers itself as perception. (Of course, if the verdict goes against it we may deny that it was really perception, just as we deny that something was really remembered or soundly inferred or really *learnt*. The point is that there are also ways of referring to the processes in question without inbuilt success grammar, and in those ways we can describe clashes between fair-quality perceivings and fair-quality testimonies or memories or inferences and prefer one of the latter to the perceiving.) Jones 'sees' an old friend at the end of the corridor and later tells others that she saw him, only to be told that the friend couldn't have been in the building because he left two days earlier for foreign parts. Prior to receiving this information Jones may have been utterly persuaded, on the basis of vision, that she saw her friend, but there are surely circumstances in which such conviction is rationally undermined by the testimony of others. Indeed, a dedication to perception at large (as contrasted with *my* perception) as a crucial determinant of rational belief or knowledge should itself endorse such undermining since testimony precisely makes available the perceptions, or apparent perceptions, of others, just as inference introduces order and the test of coherence to putative perceptions. Some readers may recall G. K. Chesterton's splendid story, 'The Man in the Passage', in which a number of persons present at the scene of a baffling crime non-collusively agree in reporting the presence of a man at the dark end of a nearby passage but give bewilderingly different accounts of what he looked like. Each is totally convinced by his own perceptions but they don't add up. Chesterton's detective, Father Brown, solves the problem with the hypothesis that there was a mirror at the end of the corridor and the features each witness reports so discrepantly are his own. The mirror has since been moved out of sight but testimony concerning its presence is decisive.[19] The report that there was a mirror at the end of the passage may be believable, in any case, but here it is decisive since its truth explains so much and reconciles the otherwise incredibly divergent perceptions (which present themselves, of course, as reports to others).

The discussion of these examples shows that the hankering after a primacy for perception is really a hankering after a primacy for *my* perceptions, or, more strictly, for the individual's own perceptions (whoever he or she may be). But why should such a claim have any appeal? Perhaps because it assumes the sort of egocentric predicament which forms one natural starting-point for much traditional epistemology as well as for much traditional scepticism. Yet such a starting-point is hardly attractive

---

[19] Actually, in Chesterton's story the details and moral are slightly different, but the story still makes my point.

here since, although the sceptic takes the egocentric position as his point of departure and also begins with the individual's 'perceptions', this hardly gives some honorific primacy to *perception* for this starting-point seems to lead inevitably to the sceptical conclusion that perception itself cannot be relied upon. (How, for example, do we know for sure that these are perceptions rather than merely dream impressions?) The fact that this egocentric assumption and the traditional sceptical challenge to perception go so naturally hand in hand should give us pause about the supposed attraction of the assumption.

None the less, the assumption has seemed to many to be compelling, regardless of sceptical worries, and it is worth digging a little further into the roots of its appeal. When one thinks of investigating knowledge in a systematic philosophical way it can seem somehow inevitable to start from the epistemically isolated self; beginning with the idea of an individual who initially lacks knowledge altogether, we ask what it would be for him to acquire it. It will seem natural from such a starting-point to focus upon the individual's perceptions or, more exiguously still, his sensations. The most austere beginning of all can be seen in Condillac's *Treatise on Sensations* where he imagines a marble statue gradually brought to life and knowledge, a process which begins with olfactory sensations and then opens the other sensory channels to the vivified statue's attention.[20] Since, for Condillac, attention itself is only 'exclusive sensation' the reductive empiricism of his starting-point is as stark as possible. The statue's mind was to be even nearer the bare, passive, empty cabinet than that of Locke's subject, though even Condillac's statue had to have some mental powers of analysis that rose above mere receptivity.

I have no wish to deprecate the interest of Condillac's thought experiment; indeed I think that, in the course of it, he makes some very interesting observations about sensation and about the relationship between the senses. None the less, it is surely clear that his starting-point is a product of cultural and philosophical predeliction rather than a priori inevitability. Even if we think it natural to start an examination of the nature of knowledge with the individual person there is a theoretical leap involved in treating the individual as Condillac does. In thinking of a person on the analogy of a vivified statue we are not merely avoiding loose assumptions and dangerous prejudice, we are employing prejudice and making assumptions. This can be seen even from the viewpoint of one such as Descartes who begins with the individual thinker and a restrictive method of doubt but who sees the thinker as endowed with far greater native powers than Condillac or Locke—hence the ongoing debate about innate ideas. One thing this debate can lead into is the idea of the subject as endowed with

---

[20] Cf. Étienne Bonnot de Condillac, *A Treatise on the Sensations* in *Philosophical Writings of Etienne Bonnot, Abbé de Condillac*, trans. Franklin Philip (Hillsdale, NJ, 1982).

powers and capacities as a member of a species so endowed and this in turn should shift the focus from the individual to the community. A statue does not belong to a species nor does it have naturally a communal life. But if we shift focus in this way it will be natural to see our starting-point as encompassing *our* knowledge and not exclusively *my* knowledge. There will then be no problem of the epistemological priority of *my* perceptions over *our* perceptions, though there will be plenty of room for discrepancies. I will know some things that are not common knowledge or even widely known and some of what *we* know will not in fact be known to me.

Further indications that the egocentric premiss owes much of its obviousness to cultural and ideological factors come from the fact that it has also been prominent within a specific political tradition in the derivation of moral and especially political duties, rights, and obligations. A good deal of social-contract theory begins with the isolated individual who is bereft of political, and often social, ties, obligations, or responsibilities and who must construct them on a basis of enlightened self-interest. Again, I do not mean to be merely dismissive of this way of thinking. Much of it is instructive and its variety of form is too striking to be captured entirely in some simplifying formula. None the less, not only is it clear that this tradition of thought faces many logical and conceptual difficulties but also that it is largely the product of the sort of individualist assumption we have been discussing, rather than an inevitable way to think about political obligation which thus requires and so justifies the egocentric premiss. As we saw earlier, Thomas Reid shows his awareness of this when he compares philosophical attempts at reducing 'the social operations of mind' with what he sees as similar attempts 'to reduce all our social affections to certain modifications of self-love'.[21]

It must be stressed that the fact that it is *I* who ask and try to answer the epistemological question is surely no bar to that question's being of the form 'What is the nature of *our* knowledge?' or 'How do *we* come to know?'[22] Equally, the fact that I ask the foundational moral and political questions is no bar to their being of a form which allows for answers in terms of a type of rationality wider than self-interest. That it is often natural and may be reasonable to treat the good of (at least some) others as equal to or more important than one's own good is not excluded by the fact that it is I who am engaged in asking the question. That the perceptions of others are as good if not better on occasion than my own and their transmission to me as valuable if not more valuable on occasion than my

---

[21] Thomas Reid, *Essays on the Intellectual Powers of Man*, essay i, ch. viii, in *Philosophical Works*, 244.

[22] The 'I' in the mouth of the traditional empiricist is, in any case, never quite as isolated as grammar suggests, since he usually presents himself as a representative reflector. None the less, the stance does have the exclusionary assumptions I am out to question.

own investigations are conclusions perfectly compatible with their being the outcome of my epistemological investigation. The question 'How can I share in knowledge?' is one only an individual can ask but this does not show that its answer must give priority to individual resources.

9

Language and Mind

From the conclusions of the last chapter and the results of earlier criticisms of individualist justifications of testimony, it begins to seem that the failures of such attempts are due not merely to defects in the particular programmes advanced but to more general, deep-seated faults. What is suspect is the very idea of an entirely individualist justification for the phenomenon of communal epistemological trust. The individualist projects we have examined have a tendency to rely covertly upon the validity of trusting others whilst attempting overtly to establish that validity. Moreover, we have available a perfectly general argument to show that this tendency is inevitable.[1]

The argument can be found in one of my objections to Hume. In Chapter 4 I argued that Hume's project was doomed because it assumed that, as a result of individual checking of reports against reality, we might find a total lack of correlation between the reports and the reported facts, whereas the existence of a language in which the testimony is given already guarantees *some* positive correlations. My argument rests on the idea that for someone to understand a language in use he must treat a good many of the reports supposedly expressed in it as true. This, at least, is all that is required to defeat Hume's argument; indeed, on my construal of Hume's programme, his argument is defeated if to understand a language requires the admission of only one true report expressed in it. If this is right then at least no individualist project, conceived in the spirit of Mackie's ideal of 'autonomous knowledge', can succeed in producing a justification of the reliability of testimony. Any such project must begin by assuming the existence of a public language in which the testimony to be scrutinized is to be made available, but the implications of this existence defeat the project and show the fundamental flaw in what I earlier called 'reductionist' justifications of testimony.

None the less, this leaves us with the question whether any sort of argument can be mounted to provide some justification or philosophical rationale for what is in fact our very extensive trust in testimony. In the absence of such an argument the thought may very naturally arise that,

---

[1] The argument does not of course show that there are *no* construals of 'individualism' or 'reduction' in terms of which some argument or other might be successfully mounted to justify testimony. It is hard to see what sort of argument could possibly do that. The most one can do is to show the impossibility of such projects understood against the background of traditional philosophical endeavour in the area.

although we must trust *some* testimony, neither the extent nor centrality of our actual reliance is rationally supportable. Perhaps the anti-Humean argument which puts paid to the hopes of individualist reductionism can be enlisted to combat this natural thought. The argument may not only serve to undermine the reductionist enterprise, it may, by a sort of inversion, serve, together with some related considerations, to underwrite less ambitious justificational hopes. We should not assume that the provision of a philosophical vindication of some practice must proceed along individualist lines. Certainly, this assumption has long played a dominant role in philosophy, as is vividly illustrated in Descartes's epistemology and even in most foundational theorizing about ethics where there is an overwhelming tendency to treat morality as irrational or somehow spurious unless it can be shown to be advantageous to the individual. But the deficiencies of this sort of approach need not cause despair, as they commonly do, about any attempt at a philosophical defence or supportive elucidation of some human practice.[2] Reductionism fails because its premisses already require testimony to have a degree of reliability, yet by exposing the necessity of that requirement and elaborating on its deeper implications we may do all that could be realistically expected in the way of justification. Such a justification may be expected to provide us with the kind of intellectual perspective on our practices of giving and receiving testimony that can make a sort of sense of St Augustine's talk of 'seeing' which we examined in Chapter 1. We may construe Augustine's emphasis upon the validating role of mental vision as expressing a concern for gaining an intellectual overview of some cognitive or epistemic practice. Such an overview may enable us to 'see' previously obscured connections and integrations within a field of such practices. To fulfil this role, the more positive employment of the line of argument presented in Chapter 4 needs substantial development, to which we shall shortly turn, but, initially, we must recall that in its negative role, the argument is effective if it demonstrates merely that linguistic communication commits a person to *some* degree of trust in the word of others. This would, however, be too limited a conclusion if the argument is to serve the positive role sketched above. The discussion of Chapter 4 has already indicated that the argument may have considerably greater scope than this and may serve to show that testimony must be generally reliable, but certain clarifications and cautions are advisable. Let us begin with a clarification.

The argument does assume that testifying (in the non-formal 'natural' sense of the expression discussed in Chapter 2) is a central and important speech act, perhaps an especially central one. I say that our idea assumes this because if the giving of report were something it was possible to treat

---

[2] There is, of course, nothing suspect about an 'individualism' which merely insists that our justifications be ones that individuals can understand and give.

as a secondary or minor speech act like adding, elaborating, or even surmising then it would be less plausible to claim that the understanding of communications in a language could turn on the general correctness of such secondary performances. Of course, a speech act like adding or surmising is called secondary, principally because it is in some way dependent on the existence of the more basic categories: a speaker is not in a position to add or amplify if he (or another) has not asserted or commanded. It is more difficult to say precisely what makes for a basic speech act beyond some complete non-dependency condition. Certainly, assertion seems to be a basic speech act, as does commanding. Here I am thinking of assertion and commanding in relatively unspecific terms so that assertion would not be restricted to acts of emphatic commitment (asseveration) but would include such acts as stating, warning, and of course, pre-eminently, reporting. Similarly, commanding would include formal superior—subordinate imperatives such as ordering, as well as advising, directing, and imploring. The idea behind such ranges can be plausibly explained by invoking the work of Paul Grice on meaning. Assertion covers the varieties of telling that and commanding the varieties of telling to.

Once the matter is put thus, however, it becomes obvious (if it were not already so) that reporting is indeed a central speech act. Reporting is not, of course, coextensive with assertion but it is probably the dominant form of assertion and is certainly more common than we are accustomed to think. I have argued the case for this in Chapter 3 and will not repeat it here, except to remind the reader that the fundamental significance of the direct speech act of reporting is emphasized by its connection with those other forms of testimony, such as institutional testimony, discussed in Chapter 2, which are related by various routes to the act of testifying and spread the impact of that act even more widely throughout the net of language and communication.

Given this centrality, what can we say of the prospects for extending my argument of Chapter 4 against Hume? Donald Davidson has deployed a line of reasoning in elaborating his project of radical interpretation which is, at least, related in spirit to the argument I am advancing[3] and both have affinities with certain ideas of the later Wittgenstein. The fundamental insight is that communication is only possible between beings whose outlooks overlap to some extent and the complex, relatively sophisticated communication characteristic of language-users is only possible where the communicants share a good deal of their outlooks. As Wittgenstein says in paragraph 242 of *Philosophical Investigations*, 'If language is to be a

---

[3] For Davidson's theory see the papers in his *Inquiries into Truth and Interpretation* (Oxford, 1984). Although the details of Davidson's programme are now widely understood, I was not familiar with them when I developed my position on Hume in my paper 'Testimony and Observation', which was written in 1968 though not publ. until 1973.

means of communication there must be agreement not only in definitions but also (queer as this may sound) in judgments'.

The context of Davidson's specific argument is his truth-conditional theory of meaning, the broad outline of which at least will be familiar to most philosophers. Although Davidson, at times, frames his discussion in ways that connect it directly with his semantical programme, the basic idea is detachable in the sense that a version of it (perhaps not as strong as Davidson's full-blooded version) can be supported with less controversial assumptions about language than his own. Consequently I shall not help myself to any of the assistance that may be forthcoming from the truth-theoretical semantics. Philosophical preconceptions will determine whether we treat the project of interpreting the speech of others (especially in its 'radical' form) as a task that we are somehow literally called upon to perform or merely as a picturesque way of dramatizing the problem of philosophically uncovering the assumptions and presuppositions that are built into our routine communicative practices. Much of the post-Quinean legacy of Promethean individuals theory-constructing away from peripheral nerve-hits should certainly be treated as fantasy, but not all of it should therefore be dismissed out of hand since some of the fantastic story can be instructive and Davidson's recourse to a principle of charity in the interpretive process, or the recourse others have to a principle of rationality or some related canon, may well survive an impatience with any literal reading of the story within which such principles are invoked. So there is much Davidsonian baggage (or apparent baggage) that we need not carry with us though we travel a similar route.

Davidson's argument, as it appears in several places,[4] may be summarized as follows. The task of radical interpretation is that of construing the utterances of others 'from scratch',[5] i.e. without the prior aid of semantic information about their language. We most naturally think of this as the job of interpreting the speech of a quite alien community, but, on Davidson's view, anyone confronts precisely this challenge with respect to what he takes to be his own linguistic community, since he can ask: how can I determine that *we* speak the same language?[6] To discover what others mean by their utterances we need to discover a great deal about what they believe and desire. For Davidson, this is related to the necessity of finding plausible T-sentences for the sentences of their language (sentences of the form ' "S" is true in L_A iff p') and for him we need therefore to determine what the aliens 'hold true' in making their utterances. But it is only against a background of shared belief that we can embark upon this enterprise and make sense of their supposed affirmations. As he puts it in 'The Method of Truth in Metaphysics',

---

[4] See 'Radical Interpretation', in Davidson, *Inquiries*, 125–39.
[5] 'Belief and the Basis of Meaning', ibid. 144.
[6] 'Radical Interpretation', ibid. 125.

First, consider why those who can understand one another's speech must share a view of the world, whether or not that view is correct. The reason is that we damage the intelligibility of our readings of the utterances of others when our method of reading puts others into what we take to be broad error. We can make sense of differences all right, but only against a background of shared belief. What is shared does not in general call for comment; it is too dull, trite or familiar to stand notice. But without a vast common ground there is no place for disputants to have their quarrel. Of course we can no more agree than disagree with someone else without much mutuality; but perhaps this is obvious.[7]

Elsewhere he writes: 'if we want to understand others must count them right in most matters'.[8]

All of this, as I suggested earlier, has affinities with certain themes in Wittgenstein's later writings. So, for instance, in paragraph 206 of the *Philosophical Investigations*, Wittgenstein says: 'Suppose you come as an explorer into an unknown country with a language quite strange to you. In what circumstances would you say that the people there gave orders, understood them, rebelled against them, and so on? The common behaviour of mankind is the system of reference by means of which we interpret an unknown language.' Although Wittgenstein's focus here is on orders rather than reports and on common behaviour rather than communality of belief, and although this focus is importantly related to distinctive views he holds in the philosophy of language and mind, there is every reason to think that the sentiments of this passage are very similar to those in the quotations from Davidson. Wittgenstein seems to have been hostile to the idea that assertion or reporting or something similarly descriptive was *the* central speech act, hence his tendency to stress ordering, commanding, and so on, and to make strong claims for the role of non-assertive language-games in human communication. He holds, for instance, that there could be a language whose use consisted entirely of orders and responses to them, with no role for reporting (cf. *Philosophical Investigations*, paras. 6, 8, 18), but whatever the tenability of this speculation (and I think it can be shown to be quite untenable) there is no reason to think that it casts any doubt on the idea that reporting is a central speech act. I think that he would have been equally happy to envisage a language composed wholly of reports and acknowledgements of them, so that there is no obstacle to substituting 'reports' for 'orders' and 'rejected' for 'rebelled against' in paragraph 206. Nor is his talk of 'common behaviour' really remote from Davidson's talk of a mutuality of belief and desire. As I interpret him, Wittgenstein had no wish to deny the reality or relevance of talk of beliefs and desires to the interpretive problem. His mentioning of the common behaviour of mankind is precisely a way

---

[7] 'The Method of Truth in Metaphysics', ibid. 199.
[8] 'On the Very Idea of a Conceptual Scheme', ibid. 197.

of non-mysteriously bringing considerations about common beliefs and desires to bear upon that problem. This is clear in some remarks about language which occur not long after the quoted passage, most notably in paragraph 242:

> If language is to be a means of communication there must be agreement not only in definitions but also (queer as this may sound) in judgments. This seems to abolish logic but does not do so.—It is one thing to describe methods of measurement, and another to obtain and state results of measurement. But what we call 'measuring' is partly determined by a certain constancy in results of measurement.

Here the centrality of common judgement, and hence presumably belief, to the existence of linguistic communication is explicit, nor is it fanciful to see the reference to 'constancy in results of measurement' as, in part, a reference to behaviour. It is not to our purpose here to determine in any detail Wittgenstein's position on the conceptual links between such ideas as truth, communal agreement, behaviour, language, and most importantly that distinctively Wittgensteinian notion, 'forms of life'.[9] We have seen enough, however, to vindicate the treatment of what I have called the Davidson argument as a specific application of an outlook on language, communication, and thought that not only has a precedent in Wittgenstein (and perhaps others) but is plausibly detachable, as claimed earlier, from Davidson's commitment to the truth-theoretical analysis of meaning, against which, of course, many critics have invoked precisely what they take to be the insights of the later Wittgenstein.

Returning then to Davidson we need to beware of a possible ambiguity in the argument as I expounded it earlier and as Davidson sometimes expounds it. It is one thing to argue that verbal communication pre-supposes a certain community of belief and, hence, given the existence of that communication, we must take for granted the correctness of most of the assertions (and reports) made in such communications. It is another matter again to claim that most of the beliefs so expressed must be true. In Davidson's earlier writings the two claims are not distinguished but there seems, at any rate, to be a clear difference between them.

(*a*) We must apply a principle of charity (or some similar interpretative maxim) in interpreting the speech of others, most notably an alien community,[10] so that agreement is maximized or optimized[11]

---

[9] Though it should be noted that in para. 241 agreement in *opinion* is contrasted with agreement in form of life. The latter is seen as fundamental to a common language whereas the former is not. It is not, however, clear how this paragraph relates to the next paragraph, quoted above, where agreement in *judgement* is seen as fundamental. Wittgenstein presumably intends some sharp distinction between opinions and judgements but both involve belief.

[10] But the device of an alien community is, for Davidson, merely a dramatization of our situation with respect to our fellows in the domestic linguistic community. See 'Radical Interpretation', in *Inquiries*, 125.

[11] Davidson uses 'optimized' rather than maximized in later writings and it is a better choice. See 'Thought and Talk', in *Inquiries*, 169.

amongst us and them. We must, that is, find their expressed beliefs mostly correct by our lights.

(b) We must apply a principle of charity in interpreting the speech of others so that agreement is not only maximized or optimized between us and them but between speakers from either community and relevant non-linguistic realities. We must, that is, recognize that most of their (and our) beliefs are true.

There is a further ambiguity latent in (b) depending upon how we take the expression 'recognize'. It would be possible for someone to distinguish between the necessity to hold other speakers' utterances correct by our standards and the necessity to think of their utterances as true, but to distinguish further the necessity that the utterances be true. It is a classical sceptical position to claim to discern a gap between beliefs that are fully justified by the approved communal or individual standards of rationality and beliefs that are actually true. The sceptic does not of course claim that fully justified beliefs (which I shall henceforth refer to as 'correct' to indicate that they have the best possible credentials or pedigree without begging the question about their truth) are not true; he merely claims to have discovered a gap between correctness and truth—a gap which he defies anyone to bridge. Whatever the merits of such defiance it does at least raise the surface possibility that it may be transcendentally necessary for any thinker to believe that *p* and yet *p* be false. Perhaps this is only a surface possibility for there may be some arguments to show that, for some cases of 'must', what we must think to be so is so. Another complexity frequently encountered in discussion of the principle of charity is that certain notions of shared belief and justified belief tend to be used interchangeably though they are, of course different. People can share unjustified beliefs and some justified beliefs are not shared. None the less the differences between justified and shared beliefs are not particularly material here. What I mean to capture with my talk of correct beliefs (as possibly contrasted with true beliefs) is the idea that our interpretations must proceed on the basis of a shared hold on established beliefs and methods for establishing them. There is then room for further discussion, in some of which we shall engage later in this chapter, of the areas in which there is lack of fit between what is shared and what is justified.

In the present connection, in any event, we should at least contemplate the possible differences between the following conclusions from the nature of communication (or the nature of interpretation):

(1) Most beliefs must be correct (i.e. the beliefs others express must either be ones we share or cohere with ones we share).
(2) Most beliefs must be correct and believed to be true.
(3) Most beliefs must be correct and true.

When set out thus it becomes (relatively) clear that, if there is any credence to the sort of gap the sceptic insists upon,[12] then (1) and (3) should be distinguished but it is less clear whether (2) marks a genuine alternative to (1). After all, the natural interpretation of the idea that there is a community of belief (and desire) between communicators can hardly be that they share a set of beliefs which they hold to be false! The absurdity of this does not arise from the impossibility of holding that some belief is false for one may well believe of others that some specific belief of theirs is false. Nor does it arise from the impossibility of holding that one has some false beliefs or other. What creates the absurdity is the idea that one might think of some specific belief or beliefs of one's own that it or they are false. The state of believing is precisely one of holding some proposition (sentence, if you like) to be true and to talk of a community *sharing* some large set of beliefs is precisely to talk of their believing the same (large number) of propositions to be true. I propose therefore to disregard (2) and hence to construct no midway possibility (c) between (a) and (b) but to interpret (b) as involving a commitment to (3).

If we can so distinguish between (a) and (b) the question arises as to which of them the Davidsonian argument establishes. Davidson certainly thinks he can establish (a), but where in earlier writings he takes his basic argument also to establish (b), in 'The Method of Truth in Metaphysics' he not only distinguishes them but he provides an additional argument, or an embellishment on the old argument, to move from (a) to (b). I call it an embellishment because it seems that Davidson thinks that his previous arguments are enough, properly understood, to establish both (a) and (b), but what he says in 'The Method of Truth in Metaphysics' apropos (b) is certainly not explicit in his early formulations. His acknowledgement of the problem goes as follows:

It may seem that the argument so far shows only that good interpretation breeds concurrence, while leaving quite open the question whether what is agreed upon is true. And certainly agreement, no matter how widespread, does not guarantee truth. This observation misses the point of the argument, however. The basic claim is that much community of belief is needed to provide a basis for communication or understanding; the extended claim should then be that objective error can occur only in a setting of largely true belief. Agreement does not make for truth, but much of what is agreed must be true if some of what is agreed is false.[13]

---

[12] It might be objected that, fortunately, we do not need the sceptic to raise the prospect of such a gap. Any realist about 'the external world' is committed to it since realism is committed to a gap between truth and warranted assertibility. This is a persuasive idea but, since it seems to me that the realism/anti-realism debate is even less well understood and charted than the scepticism/anti-scepticism issue, it would be best to pose the question with the aid of a premiss used by sceptics, though perhaps common to both sceptics and realists.

[13] 'The Method of Truth in Metaphysics', in Davidson, *Inquiries*, 200.

Davidson then proceeds to flesh out this last sentence by invoking the idea of an omniscient interpreter. 'We do not need', he says,

to be omniscient to interpret but there is nothing absurd in the idea of an omniscient interpreter; he attributes beliefs to others, and interprets their speech on the basis of his own beliefs, just as the rest of us do. Since he does this as the rest of us do, he perforce finds as much agreement as is needed to make sense of his attributions and interpretations; and in this case, of course, what is agreed is by hypothesis true. But now it is plain why massive error about the world is simply unintelligible, for to suppose it intelligible is to suppose there could be an inter-preter (the omniscient one) who correctly interpreted someone else as being mass-ively mistaken, and this we have shown to be impossible.[14]

This is a very strong conclusion and whether anything so strong can be extracted from Davidson's argument, even with the aid of omniscience, remains to be seen. Certainly the quotations indicate that Davidson him-self allows the appearance of a distinction between (*a*) and (*b*) and the need to establish (*a*) en route to (*b*), even if the same materials that establish (*a*) serve with an embellishment or elaboration to prove (*b*) as well. What I now want to do is to look at the case for and against (*a*). My own view is that a good case can be made for (*a*) but that the case for (*b*) is much more difficult to make and that Davidson certainly fails to make it.

It is possible to see three different arguments in Davidson's writings that seem designed to establish (*a*). At least Colin McGinn, in a criticism of Davidson's arguments,[15] discusses three and I will follow him for clarity of exposition without worrying unduly about the connections between the arguments. I shall label the arguments A, B, and C.

Argument A: interpreting the speech of others is essentially a matter of making sense of or 'rationalizing' parts of their intentional behaviour by ascribing the interpreter's own belief and value system to the others. McGinn does not actually attribute this to Davidson but says he has come across the argument in conversation. In a footnote, however, he quotes for comparison a passage from Davidson's paper 'Mental Events' in which Davidson says, 'In our need to make him make sense we will try for a theory that finds him consistent, a believer of truths, and a lover of the good (all by our own lights, it goes without saying)'.[16] McGinn might have referred to a passage in 'Psychology as Philosophy' which gets even nearer to argument A. There Davidson writes:

When we turn to the task of interpreting the pattern, (of a person's behaviour) we notice the need to find it in accord, within limits, of standards of rationality. In the

[14] Ibid. 201.

[15] Colin McGinn, 'Charity, Interpretation and Belief', *The Journal of Philosophy*, 74 (1977), 521–35.

[16] 'Mental Events', in D. Davidson, *Essays on Actions and Events* (Oxford, 1980), 222.

case of language, this is apparent, because understanding it is *translating* it into our own system of concepts. But in fact the case is no different with beliefs, desires, and actions.[17]

McGinn's basic objection to this is that the argument equivocates upon 'reasonable'. To understand the intentional behaviour of others we must see it as to some degree rational or reasonable but not necessarily 'by our lights'. 'You appreciate the reasonableness of an action', says McGinn, 'by putting yourself into its agent's shoes, not by forcing him into yours'.[18] McGinn is surely right to insist that we do not need to have the precise beliefs and motivations of the agent in order to understand how his action could seem reasonable to him. As McGinn puts it, 'empathy not charity' is what rationalization requires. None the less, the opposition between empathy and charity is here exaggerated. A sane Davidsonian will not say that understanding an intentional action requires an interpreter to have the precise goals and beliefs of the agent. That position is not just mistaken but clearly idiotic and simple justice rather than charity or empathy prevents us attributing such a view even to the most naïve Davidsonian. We can readily understand and explain the behaviour of someone who goes into a milk bar on a hot day seeking to buy a milk shake, even if we dislike milk shakes and believe that the shop doesn't sell them anyway. McGinn's target here is really a straw man and to be of any interest argument A and the objection to it would have to be made to cut much deeper. This can, I think, be done but it then comes much closer to argument C and is best considered in concert with it.

The same is true of argument B. Davidson believes that there is no separating the enterprise of, on the one hand, semantically interpreting a man's language, and, on the other, determining his propositional attitudes. Belief, desire, and meaning must be delivered as one parcel. Davidson deduces from this that we must begin the interpretive process by assuming general agreement on beliefs. 'We get a first approximation to a finished theory by assigning to sentences of a speaker conditions of truth that actually obtain (in our opinion) just when the speaker holds these sentences true.'[19] McGinn objects (*a*) that this applies, as stated, only to the preliminary stages of the investigation and does not therefore preclude the eventual attribution of preponderant error and (*b*) it ignores the equally available option of assuming *un*charitably that the alien's sentences held true by him are actually false. 'Falsity', avers McGinn, 'holds belief just as constant as truth, and affords an equally systematic rule for correlating sentences of our language with sentences of theirs in such a way (it is hoped) that the former will serve to give the meanings of the latter'.[20]

[17] Davidson, *Essays*, 239.
[18] McGinn, 'Charity', 522.
[19] 'On the Very Idea of a Conceptual Scheme', in Davidson, *Inquiries*, 196.
[20] McGinn, 'Charity', 523.

McGinn's (*a*) is fair enough, though again it suggests that the Davidsonian argument is not just that we must begin with a principle of charity but that the modifications to our initial magnanimity will themselves be fuelled by different applications of the principle. To press this point any further is to come to grips pretty directly with considerations and objections more usually raised in connection with argument C. McGinn's (*b*), however, can be dealt with immediately. The assumption of falsity just will not serve as 'an equally systematic rule' for the project of interpretation, since McGinn's claim that 'falsity holds belief just as constant as truth' is wrong. Truth and falsity are not of equal value in the enterprise of interpretation as the attribution of falsity does not fix belief in the decisive way that truth does. As Aristotle says in book II, chapter 6, of his *Nicomachean Ethics*, 'it is possible to go wrong in more ways than one . . . But there is only one way of being right'. Consider an interpreter faced with the alien utterance 'Gavagai'. He decides to proceed by the method of falsehood and so treats this sentence as expressing a false rather than a true belief. This requires him to see it as aimed at some truth but failing in one of an indefinite range of ways to hit the target. So the speaker utters the presumed sentence with conviction in the presence of a rabbit and McGinn's method has us hold that he has not said truly 'This is a rabbit' but rather falsely—what? Perhaps, 'This is not a rabbit'; but why choose this interpretation rather than the equally false 'This is a frog' or 'This is a cat', 'This is a tiger', 'This is a dog', etc. Even on the assumption, here made, that the utterance 'Gavagai' is a remark demonstrating an animal and identifying it as of a certain kind, clearly there are vastly more ways of fixing content by assigning falsity than by assigning truth. We may, of course, in specific cases have good reason to assign a particular falsity but that is obviously not to the point here. The method of falsity is just a hopeless general policy for radical interpretation.

This leaves us with argument C which seems, in any case, to offer the best reconstruction of what appeared most promising in arguments A and B. In essence the argument is that one cannot identify beliefs at all unless one located them in a wider pattern of beliefs, most of which must be true. It is the pattern which determines what the very subject-matter of the belief is. Moreover, if we couldn't identify beliefs then we couldn't identify meanings, since beliefs/desires/meanings are delivered together in the interpretive process. Hence, interpreting speech requires the general correctness of belief.[21]

Against this, McGinn offers both a counter-example and a supporting philosophical apparatus. The counter-example concerns the belief of (some of) the ancients that the stars were apertures in a vast dome through which penetrated light from a great fire beyond. Surely we can identify such a

---

[21] See 'Thought and Talk' which is quoted by McGinn.

belief and related beliefs without having to hold it and them true. Indeed, we clearly recognize such beliefs as radically false. Curiously, McGinn's example is merely an elaboration of one cited by Davidson to illustrate his own position—the belief of some ancients that the earth was flat. Of the flat earth belief, Davidson suggests that we should not be so ready to attribute it to the ancients since, if one of the ancients in question lacked the beliefs that, for instance, the earth is part of the solar system and that the solar system consists of large, cool, solid bodies circling round a very large hot star, then we may ask 'Is it certain that it is the earth that he is thinking about?' Davidson does not think that a definite answer is required here, as long as the considerations about patterns of belief can shake one's confidence that the ancients believed the earth to be flat. But can it? I don't myself find my conviction at all shaken, since there is enough else in belief-sharing between the ancients and ourselves (even about the earth) to make it clear that it is the earth they were referring to. I suspect that if there is any shaking to be done it may be about their understanding of the predicate 'flat' rather than the noun 'earth', but even here I doubt that a plausible case can be made out.

McGinn's elaboration of his own example and his rejection of Davidson's proceeds in a somewhat different way. He argues that what allows us to identify the ancients' beliefs about the stars as the beliefs they are, is not of course that they are true (they aren't) but that we can employ *our concepts* and *our (true) beliefs* to identify the objects that their beliefs are about. Here we can make use of the Quinean distinction between *relational* and *notional* belief attributions. This enables us to refer to the beliefs the ancients had without implying that they had our understanding of the objects of the beliefs. And certainly this is something we occasionally need to do. For instance, Smith may believe that the man in the false beard and dark glasses is a spy but unknown to him that man is in fact his brother. In terms of notional attribution it is *false* that Smith believes that his brother is a spy but in terms of relational attribution it is *true* that, *of* his brother, Smith believes that he is a spy. This notational convenience allows us to identify a belief an agent has in terms which need not be entirely acceptable to him. We can then say about the ancients that, of the heavens, they believed numerous falsehoods, and similarly of the earth.

Well, no doubt we can say this sort of thing, but what makes it true? Here McGinn has recourse to various currently fashionable causal theories—especially of reference and perception—and invokes the names of Kripke and Putnam. His basic idea is to hold that, just as perception and reference need to be analysed somehow in causal terms, so too do belief and even, it would seem, intentionality in general. The identity of any given belief, thought, or perception is at least partly determined by the identity of the object that caused it. His model is a certain view of perception and his claim is that a perceiver, Smith, might have two qualitatively identical perceptual experiences of quite different objects *a* and *b* in two possible sets of circumstances ('possible worlds') in which *a* and *b* are each uniquely *F* and perceived as such, and yet these would be two quite different perceptions—the difference consisting entirely in the fact that one is a perception of *a* and the other of *b*. McGinn concludes that Davidson's underlying conception of an intentional state is 'mistaken at root'. As he puts it, 'It is because we observe that people causally interact with objects in their environment in such ways as enable them to have thoughts concerning those objects, paradigmatically in perception, that we are prepared to assign those objects to their beliefs as comprising their subject matter, nothwithstanding the amount of bad theory they may bring to bear upon the objects.'[22]

I have several reasons for being wary of McGinn's line of argument and of his conclusions. One is a strong suspicion about the adequacy of the currently fashionable causal theories of naming and reference upon which McGinn's theory of intentionality and belief is modelled. These began, in Kripke's interesting work, as sketches for a picture of naming alternative to some others then fashionable, but have rapidly accelerated into 'causal theories' joining already existent causal theories of mind, perception, memory, and what have you. It is a matter passing strange that a notion so full of philosophical obscurity as causation should seem to offer so much by way of resolution of so varied a range of philosophical complaints. In particular, an explanation of reference and naming which relies on the causal history of expressions, to the exclusion of facts about speakers' thoughts, beliefs, understandings, and communicative intentions,[23] is not only open to palpable counter-objections such as Gareth Evans's 'Madagascar' example, but to a general problem about the specification of the right kind of causal connection. I think that these problems are very serious indeed but I shall here set them aside because, even if we assume that some causal theory has reasonable prospects of explaining names and some other referential expressions, it is a very far cry to McGinn's hopes for belief and intentionality.

To begin with, we should notice a serious ambiguity or unclarity in McGinn's project. Officially, the project has quite modest aims but its success is sometimes painted in much bolder colours. Officially McGinn is concerned only with *relational* beliefs and *relational* intentional states; unofficially he roundly proclaims his conclusions in unqualified terms about belief and intentional (mental) states. Such a slide is of the first importance since the relationships between notional beliefs and relational beliefs—or, more properly, notionally attributed and relationally attri-

---

[22] McGinn, 'Charity', 530.
[23] Kripke's account does include a reference to communicative intentions. See S. Kripke, *Naming and Necessity* (Oxford, 1980), 163.

buted beliefs—is by no means clear and is barely discussed by McGinn. He does say that 'in general if a notional attribution is true so is a corresponding relational'[24] but this merely tells us something about notational possibilities; it does not show that all beliefs are 'object or world-involving' (to use terminology that causal theorists are fond of) in that the identity of the belief depends upon some existing 'external' object. Indeed, such a thesis about all belief or intentionality is clearly absurd since many intentional states and beliefs are palpably what they are whether their 'objects' exist or not, or whether the propositions they express are true or false. It is perfectly possible to have true (or false) beliefs about non-existent objects or not yet existent objects or no longer existent objects, and in the first two cases, at any rate, no direct causal story can be relevant.

Furthermore, McGinn concedes, as he surely must, that his causal story gives no more than a necessary condition. As such, of course, it is compatible with the truth of some version of the principle of charity since its being necessary to determine what the aliens are referring to by adverting to the causal link (understood in terms of our concepts) leaves it open that we must treat most of their beliefs as true in order fully to determine such reference. In the case of names, for instance, recent discussion suggests that, granting some kind of causal link (between a 'baptism' and present usage), the status of a necessary connection, still allows some element of a descriptivist account of naming to make up the difference between necessity and sufficiency. At a minimum, the belief that you intend to use the name with the same reference as he whom you acquired it from; more full-bloodedly, that it is the name of a being of a certain kind (would I really be referring to Socrates if I thought he was an ancient insect?); but, in any case, some non-relational beliefs upon which the principle of charity at least has room to operate.

The thinness of McGinn's objection becomes even clearer if we shift from designation to predication and focus not upon what objects the alien beliefs are about but what they believe about those objects, i.e. what their beliefs actually are. Here the shift to a relational notation and an appeal to causal links can give no direct purchase on our interpretive problem. I do not mean to deny that interpretation can, even must, make use of knowledge, or suspicions, about causal links between the world and the mental states of those to be interpreted, nor that an interpreter does so by making use of his own identifications of items in the world even where these may not be fully congruent with the way the aliens identify those same items. But this is not something that Davidson or any other charitably inclined philosopher need deny. They can accept that such procedures get a purchase on what, in some sense, some alien beliefs are about, but this can only be a part, and by no means the most important part, of what the

[24] McGinn, 'Charity', 526.

radical interpreter requires. For all McGinn's criticisms show, the remaining part could be taken up by the principle of charity.

These considerations are reinforced by some related points made by Vermazen. He argues (1) that McGinn's objection is irrelevant to the interpretation of general beliefs and (2) that such general beliefs, connecting, as they do, predicates with predicates, play a vital role in fixing the meanings of one's words.[25] We can see what is involved here by returning to my earlier comments upon Davidson's remarks about the belief of the ancients that the earth was flat. Davidson wondered whether they really had a false belief about *the earth*, given their not having certain other beliefs about planetary objects and systems. This seems the wrong way to go about trying to acquit those ancients of error, for the problem of interpreting their claim is not really that of knowing what object they are referring to but of knowing precisely what they are saying about it. We need to know what they think the predicate 'flat', as used here, excludes. It is, at least, possible that their claim is such that it is compatible with the earth's being a huge sphere (just as a modern's remark that the city of Melbourne is very flat is perfectly compatible with the sphericality of the planet on which Melbourne rests and rests spherically). On the other hand, they may specifically or implicitly have meant to deny that the earth was shaped anything like a globe. Deciding between these alternatives is a matter of locating this belief on a map of their other beliefs and intentions, which is a matter of knowing what their beliefs are, what their predications mean, and what general beliefs they have. We need to assume a great deal of communality of belief with them in order to do this.

But how much need we assume? We may reject McGinn's critique but none the less see Davidson's principle as excessively charitable. McGinn's criticisms of argument C do not show that we can dispense altogether with a principle of charity but they do show (what should in any case be apparent) that we can tell what *some* beliefs of an alien community are *about*, and even what many such beliefs *are*, without having to treat those very beliefs as shared or true. This reinforces the reaction many have had to Davidson's principle, namely, that it is too strong or too ambitious. I think that it is too strong in two different respects. One concerns the claim about truth and that will shortly return us to his argument for establishing (*b*). The other concerns the extent and nature of the agreement required by the principle. Davidson often talks of *maximizing* agreement and here we must demur. As we saw in discussing Price's views in Chapter 5, the drive in epistemology towards the quantifier 'most' is understandable, but the claims actually expressed by this quantifier in such enterprises are actually

---

[25] Bruce Vermazen, 'The Intelligibility of Massive Error', *Philosophical Quarterly*, 33 (1983), 70–1. See also id., 'General Beliefs and the Principle of Charity', *Philosophical Studies*, 42 (1982), 111–18.

none too clear. Certainly it does not seem hard to imagine two communities who could understand each other's speech but between whom there were very large areas of strong propositional disagreement or divergence. This is certainly so for issues involving matters of high theory or ideology. For this reason alone Davidson's move from *maximizing* to *optimizing* agreement is an improvement. Others have suggested that instead of charity one should embrace a principle of rationality or one of avoiding the attribution of inexplicable error. None of the suggested titles (including charity) appeals much to me, but the fact they are all getting at, if they are to be acceptable, is that the interpretation of alien speech (and even the recognition of it *as* speech) turns upon acceptance of a certain similarity of constitution between ourselves and the aliens. And the same goes for the more radical interpretive enterprise that puts the individual in a position to have to interpret the speech of those who (it turns out) are fellow natives.

Although Davidson usually talks of agreement in belief he also stresses the role of shared desires and this is involved as well in Wittgenstein's talk of 'the common behaviour of mankind' as our 'system of reference' for understanding an unknown language. Here, again, one must beware of having too strong a commitment. It would be absurd to suppose that we could only interpret alien speech if the aliens were pretty much replicas of ourselves in what they wanted. Indeed we are not, in this, or most other respects, replicas of each other. A community's desires and beliefs will have a strong element of the cultural and the merely local in their causal determination. (This is part of what is wrong with F. H. Bradley's principle of 'the analogous' as a test for what is historically acceptable. See Chapter 10 for a discussion of this and of a related Humean view.) If we require the outlooks of others to be too like our own we lose part of the capacity to learn from them; if we insist on their dramatic dissimilarity we lose our capacity to understand them at all. If claims of uniformity of belief and desire within and between contemporary communities and across historical epochs are plainly contrary to the facts and to all sane expectations, so also are claims for radical dissimilarity and discontinuity. We must take it that the aliens inhabit the same physical universe as we do and are creatures evolved in broadly similar ways, whatever their cultural idiosyncrasies. In making sense of their utterances we can assume (and must assume) that they are interested in nourishment and reproduction, in some degree of co-operation and safety, in the appreciation of some kinds of beauty. Relatedly, they are equipped to recognize obstacles to the realization of their desires and opportunities for the pursuit of them, as well as the gross environmental features which are involved in both of these—distances, physical impediments, temporal direction, bodily sensations, sensory properties, and so on. This communality of constitution gives rise to some basic similarity of outlook and hence a considerable communality of beliefs and interests which, as Davidson remarks, is so obvious and banal in its operations as normally to merit no comment.

This very fact, however, makes it easy to overlook. It is significant that critics like McGinn fasten upon differences in belief that involve a good deal of explanatory theory; the nature of the heavens and their occupants is an issue upon which disagreement between communities (especially communities with very different levels of technological sophistication) is unsurprising and even predictable.[26] Similarly we may expect cross-cultural disagreement about the nature of human physiology but this does not license the thought that we might find human communities who did not believe that they had bodies and heads. There are philosophers who insist on working with so stretched a concept of theory that judgements like 'I have a head', 'This is my left hand', 'That is a hut', 'That is a rabbit', count as theoretical but, whatever insights stem from this manner of speaking, it is apparent that we can operate an intuitively clear distinction between fact and theory which will count very many beliefs as factual or non-theoretical and which these philosophers will at least have to countenance as far *less* theoretical than beliefs like 'The atomic weight of sodium is 22.991', or 'Rarely is an allosteric enzyme subject to only one mode of regulation'. It is consistent with this to concede that over time a theory may be so satisfactory and so explanatory that it becomes entrenched as a kind of fact, or that what is theoretical and explanatory for one group may seem, and even be, in a sense, factual for another group. So the atomic weights or chemical compositions of substances is theoretical and explanatory for laymen but merely factual and descriptive for practising chemists. Issues like these can certainly make a simple application of the principle of charity merely naïve. None the less, much of the so-called 'manifest image' of the world remains untouched as to its utility and truth value by the deeper discoveries of science, and were this not so science and other theoretical enterprises would be impossible. If we are to have our extensive disagreements with the aliens about science and ideology this must be true and must generate considerable agreement at the level of belief and desire and hence at the level of communication and report. We may conclude that when all due allowance is made for the overconfidence of some versions of the principle of charity, or its close relatives, there remains a solid core of truth to the claim it makes.

The above discussion itself strongly suggests a reasonable degree of reliability about the testimony of others, whether they be aliens or natives, but it is compatible with a good deal of error and unreliability. We can, however, improve the picture by other considerations and it is time to turn to these. In Chapter 8 we saw that we cannot treat an individual's perceptions, memories, inferences, and *learnings* in an isolated, atomistic fashion.

[26] Davidson himself at one point explicitly allows that divergences in theoretical beliefs are to be expected. See 'Thought and Talk', 169.

This applies both to the way we get into a position to exercise the powers in question and to the assessment of their results. An individual's present perception of something in front of him as an eighteenth-century mahogany architect's desk will be determined not only by the gross perception of certain colours and shapes but by the memories and inferences of both himself and others which are built into the conceptual and perceptual skills with which he approaches this particular cognitive encounter. But not only do specific exercises of such capacities presuppose an integration between informational routes, the beliefs acquired by such exercises are constrained to some degree by a goal of coherence between outcomes. The two considerations are related but distinguishable. Let us call the first cohesion and the second coherence.

Cohesion and coherence are closely related because our attitude to outcomes is all of a piece with that existing integration which makes for the operation of the particular channels of information. We could not treat extensive incoherence of outcome as a matter of indifference and continue to exercise the information-gathering capacities we have in a confident way. A parallel with sensory integration may be helpful. If our auditory information became radically discrepant with other sensory inputs we would not only lose hearing as a genuine sensory modality but the achievements possible to us through the other senses would diminish. Our hearing puts us in the way of exercising our other senses effectively, especially in the case of sight. This is connected with the fact we are sensory investigators and not mere sensory receptors. Hearing certain sounds I look to the skies, expecting some sorts of birds to be passing overhead, and see a flock of parrots, or hearing other sounds I look around in time to take effective steps to avoid an oncoming car. We can see the force of this if we ask what would be involved in considering seriously the case for some alien creature's having a perceptual sense beyond our own. A crucial determinant of any such claim is surely the criterion of achievement. A new sense must both add something distinctive to the range of achievements possible to the organism and cohere with the existing achievement capacities it has. The sighted man in the land of the blind can convince them that he has a further sensory power just because he can *do* so much more than they in handling the environment, though there is also a range of recognizable achievements common to them and to him.[27]

---

[27] The illustration from sensory integration is helpful but it is not meant to be comprehensively parallel. For one thing, those deprived of, or diminished in, one sense can make certain compensations by developing the skills of the other senses. The blind learn to hear things that the sighted do not. There are no ready parallels to this in the cases we are principally considering: sharper memory, for instance, will not tell you what is now happening in Washington, DC, if you are in London and cannot rely upon testimony. Sensory integration is also less total since we could tolerate quite a degree of discrepancy between taste and sight or taste and touch (though not, I suspect, between taste and smell). For more detailed discussion of the criterion of achievement and problems in distinguishing the senses see C. A. J. Coady, 'The Senses of Martians', *Philosophical Review*, 83/1 (1974).

In the wider context of the informational sources of memory, perception, testimony, and inference, the existing cohesion which makes for effective operation of such powers shows not only that they stand or fall together but surely that they stand successfully. Someone who sought to isolate an individualist basis in perception, memory, and inference, in order to test the reliability of testimony, would not only face the problems of language and understanding discussed earlier in this chapter but would have to discount an enormous amount of what goes into normal perception, inference, and memory. A private language and a private conceptual scheme may not be impossible (*pace* Wittgenstein) but, in any case, a great deal of the actual thinking, classifying, and recognizing that we do is heavily conditioned by our social existence and by the observations, constructions, memories, and theories of others. No doubt we have innate recognitional abilities but it is equally certain that one of our most fundamental innate endowments is the capacity to learn from others and an enormous amount of our recognitional success is dependent upon linguistic skill and information acquired from others. Here our language is of the first importance. That we 'carve' the world as we do is partly a matter of inevitable genetic disposition but, to a very considerable extent, it is also a matter of communal orientations and interests which each of us discovers by trusting the judgements, reactions, and trainings of others. This becomes clear when we note the conceptual distinctions which are made in one language and not in another. I do not urge this fact as any reason for gloom about translation possibilities, or as support for any form of conceptual relativism, but merely to illustrate the point that a good deal of what an individual recognizes, discriminates, and identifies in perception and memory is communally underwritten. As argued in Chapter 4, when we learn language we do so not merely by observing what others say but by trusting their saying of it and their powers of discrimination.

A particular application of this point, and a most instructive one, is provided by what Hilary Putnam has called 'the division of linguistic labour'. This draws attention to the ways in which the ordinary language user relies upon more expert fellow-speakers for his grasp of the sense of so many expressions in common circulation.[28] Most linguistic laymen, so to speak, get by perfectly well with such terms as 'gold', 'silver', 'amber', 'elm', 'mahogany', 'aluminium', in spite of remarkable deficiencies in the cognitive capacities that go with recognizing and distinguishing instances of these concepts. Most of us would have the greatest difficulty in telling elms from beeches, gold jewellery from imitations, silver from silver plate or even less worthy substitutes, amber from inferior beads, mahogany

---

[28] Hilary Putnam, 'The Meaning of "Meaning"' in *Philosophical Papers*, ii. *Mind, Language and Reality* (Cambridge, 1975), 215–71, esp. 227–9.

furniture from a variety of others, aluminium from molybdenum, and so on. We know *enough* about all of these, or about what Putnam called 'stereotypes' of them, to communicate efficiently most of the time on the topics involved, but this efficiency is fundamentally dependent upon our trust in those experts who can make the relevant identifications and distinctions with authority. Putnam speculates that all linguistic communities exemplify the division of linguistic labour so that it may well be 'a fundamental trait of our species'.[29] I think that this is very probably true but, in any case, its extensive application to the sorts of communities we live in and are familiar with is simply a fact of life. Consequently my dependence upon others for the very *recognition* of many of the most everyday items I encounter in perceptual experience (e.g. trees, fruits, metals) is a profound fact of what I take to be my individual epistemic resources. Needless to say, this fact is even clearer for those terms which are more evidently terms of art or theory and which many of us use by courtesy of the understanding of others, for example, electromagnetic fields, psychotic, condenser. It can be seen that the cohesion I began speaking of is built into the linguistic resources with which each of us structures and identifies much of the world which we encounter from day to day. It also seems a plain matter of fact that this cohesion, on the whole, is all the stronger and its contribution to cognitive and practical success all the greater in complex, technological societies like our own. (Of course this success must be discounted by the degree of confusion, fraud, etc., which the division of linguistic labour can generate.)

My discussion has points of connection here with recent debates within metaphysics and the philosophy of mind about the relation between wide and narrow psychological states. For instance, Tyler Burge urges, against what he calls 'individualism', that many psychological states that have traditionally been understood as totally constituted by facts about the individual ('narrow' states) really owe much of their identity to realities in the social or physical realm 'external' to the individual (the 'wide' conception.) For the conclusion about social constitution Burge relies, in part, upon a natural extension of the Putnam point about experts, except that the expertise in question is that possessed by the community at large. Whatever the overall merits, or even the precise shape, of this claim, there is clearly something to the idea that the actual thoughts an individual has cannot be seen as entirely independent conceptually of the linguistic community to which she belongs. It remains possible, however, that there are 'individualistic' elements to all psychological states and even some such states that are entirely individualistically constituted. Against this, some have ventured to suggest, in the spirit of what they take to be Wittgenstein's objections to private languages, that no thought contents can be individ-

[29] Ibid. 229.

ualistically constituted, and hence all psychological states are 'wide'. Interesting as this stronger thesis is, I am sceptical about its merits, and, in any case, have no need to rest any part of my argument upon it, since the cohesion I am appealing to is deep enough without recourse to this more radical version of social constitution.[30]

The other face of these considerations about cohesion is the fact that we operate informationally with a rather loose, but none the less real, ideal of coherence in the body of beliefs which we acquire in these diverse ways. This does not mean that we cannot admit any degree of conflict but where it is allowed we look for an explanation in terms of intelligible malfunction or misinterpretation. Such explanation need not, of course, invoke highly theoretical notions; often enough the invocation of such ideas as mishearing, malicious intent, tiredness, inattention, bad light, and so on will do. Moreover, what we look for we do not always find. Some of the clashes will be resolved against one of the sources even though we lack an explanation of its failure. 'I could have sworn I saw ... but I must have been wrong' is sometimes an inevitable if somewhat disturbing conclusion, as is 'I was sure I remembered ... but ...', or 'I could have sworn he was trustworthy ... but ...', or 'I was sure I did the sum correctly but ...'. We have sufficient slack in our outlook to be able to tolerate some inexplicable error or misinformation indefinitely (it is usually too much epistemological trouble to spend time finding out *why* misinformation or error occurred).

We can, moreover, tolerate some degree of incoherence in the outcomes themselves. There are cases in which what we are told does not conform to our individual experience but we jettison neither. Where *p* and *q* are in flat contradiction one should be jettisoned, but lack of coherence is a much weaker condition than contradiction and in many cases we are prepared to live with what we label '*apparent* contradiction' because of the practical or epistemic benefits. The uneasy theoretical truce in the foundations of quantum mechanics testifies to the power of such compromises but, at a more mundane level, so does the plight of a spouse who has evidence that her beloved partner is unfaithful but cannot accept this at its face value because of all the personal evidence it clashes with. If one does not have to act at once on the conflicting evidence one can wait to see how the conflict will resolve itself or be resolved by further evidence. Such situations are more common in intellectual life than intellectuals care to admit. Theorists cling to pet theories in the face of counter-evidence or counter-argument

---

[30] The individualism that is Burge's target is somewhat different from mine, though the two are conceptual cousins. Burge's critique is developed in a number of articles, most notably in 'Individualism and the Mental', *Midwest Studies in Philosophy*, 4 (1979); 'Other Bodies', in Andrew Woodfield (ed.), *Thought and Object* (Oxford, 1982); and 'Cartesian Error and the Objectivity of Perception', in Philip Pettit and John McDowell (eds.), *Subject, Thought and Context* (Oxford, 1986). For discussion of, and support for the more radical thesis, with explicit acknowledgement of Wittgenstein, see the editors' introduction to that last work.

that they cannot see how to refute but hope one day to be able to handle satisfactorily. Sometimes they are wrong to do so, sometimes not. We tend to decide that question historically rather than methodologically, i.e. by the outcome rather than by some methodological rule. This seems strange because the outcome may be largely determined by luck (there is a parallel here with the debate in ethics about 'moral luck')[31] but it reflects the fact that the correctness or otherwise of 'clinging' is a matter of judgement not of rubric.

None the less, coherence remains the ideal and our fairly generous capacity to tolerate incoherence or lack of fit testifies to the generally very satisfactory state of coherence which we continue to find and cheerfully expect between the different informational sources. The cohesion is not disturbed but reinforced by the way things continue to turn out. It is not that we somehow 'prove' from purely individual resources that testimony is generally reliable but that, beginning with an inevitable commitment to some degree of its reliability, we find this commitment strongly enforced and supported by the facts of cohesion and coherence. These facts could be different, just as the degree of cohesion and coherence could vary from community to community. Testimony is probably more reliable amongst an isolated community of dedicated monks than in a gang of fanatical conmen. Cultural values and physical circumstances will play their part in determining just how reliable local testimony will be and, once we abandon illusory justificatory endeavours which allow no rationality to any prior trust in any testimony, we can investigate the facts of such matters.

It may be argued that a degree of cohesion and coherence is insufficient to provide any additional vindication of testimony because, whatever assurances it gives, it does not provide us with any guarantee of *truth*. The considerations of this chapter may show that we are deeply committed to a quite extensive trust in the word of others, but this hardly takes us beyond the argument of Chapter 1 and certainly does nothing to indicate that we are thus committed because of the widespread truth of what witnesses say. It can be replied at once that the arguments of this chapter, if cogent, take us well beyond any of the conclusions of Chapter 1, if only because they demonstrate a depth to our commitment which was no more than hinted at there. Yet the question of truth remains to vex us.

One quick answer to it would suit nicely (for at least some of our argument), if it worked. This is the answer provided by Davidson's 'omniscient interpreter' argument which enabled him to move from claim (*a*) to (*b*) as noted on p. 160. We postponed consideration of this transition but this is a natural point to treat of it. Davidson argues that there is

[31] See the symposium between Thomas Nagel and Bernard Williams on 'Moral Luck', *Proc. of the Aristotelian Society*, supp. vol. 50 (1976), 115–51.

no absurdity in supposing an omniscient interpreter (hereafter, OI), who interprets the speech of others just as we do, finding enough basic agreement in beliefs to make sense of their speech. But in the special case of the OI there can be no difference between agreement in belief and truth. As Davidson puts it: 'But now it is plain why massive error about the world is simply unintelligible, for to suppose it intelligible is to suppose there could be an interpreter (the omniscient one) who correctly interpreted someone else as being massively mistaken, and this we have shown to be impossible.'[32]

There is a certain ambiguity about the interpreter's omniscience. If 'omniscience' means that the interpreter *knows everything* already then there is no need of interpretation. His position is wrongly construed as that of confronting a body of utterances the meaning of which is *unknown*. He is not initially in the position of needing to assume (*a*) in order to make sense of the corpus of utterances, so there is no question of getting from (*a*) to (*b*). If we suppose that the OI knows everything except the meanings and beliefs of the alien community then the argument will go through, but the OI's omniscience can now be seen for what it is. It is a device to conflate truth and what I have called correctness. As such we should consider carefully whether we can really understand this restricted sort of omniscience. Notoriously, the concept of knowledge has, besides the component of belief or some related attitude of assent, two crucial elements. One relates to the appropriateness of the way the agent has got himself into a position to believe the proposition in question and the other concerns the proposition's relation to the reality it is about. In short, the two elements are justification and truth. A great deal of modern epistemology and metaphysics, and indeed semantics, has been exercised about the relation between those two elements. Various forms of philosophical scepticism feed on the difficulties of making the justificatory element adequate to what appear to be the requirements of truth, while various forms of reaction to this have sought to soften those requirements by making the notion of truth (and hence of reality) less independent of the knower's justificatory apparatus than it initially seems to be.

I have neither the space nor the confidence to tackle these issues in any depth here but they are relevant to Davidson's use of the OI. The gap between (*a*) and (*b*) will be relatively easy to bridge, the weaker the requirements of truth can be made, since the OI will be someone who has ideal or perfect justifications for what he believes. Thus the communality of belief between him and those interpreted will ensure that their shared beliefs are just as sound, since they are at least supportable in this way no matter how they have actually been formed. If truth amounts to no more than such soundness or correctness then we have a demonstration that the

---

[32] 'The Method of Truth in Metaphysics', in Davidson, *Inquiries*, 201.

gap between (*a*) and (*b*) can be closed by the OI or that, suitably understood, there is no gap to close. If one's concept of truth is, however, made of the sterner stuff upon which the sceptical challenge, for example, is based, then this will not be satisfactory. It is the essence of the stronger view that no justificatory procedures can be guaranteed to reach right up to that mind-independent reality we hope to catch in our epistemic nets. This is the underlying significance of Descartes's malignant demon and of the permanent appeal of metaphysical realism (what Bernard Williams has called 'the absolute conception'). What the demonic doubt trades upon is that, however perfect our justificatory procedures are, it seems possible to imagine a gap existing or being created between their results and the way independent reality is in itself. On this stronger view the idea of an omniscient being has to be that of one whose relation to reality is such that he needs no justificatory procedures and *a fortiori* no interpretive techniques. Traditionally this has been the way in which the God of Christian natural theology has been understood. If we accept the stronger idea of truth we will thus be driven to conclude either that there can be no OI or that what is called an OI is not really an interpreter. On the weaker idea of truth, there can be an OI and Davidson's argument will go through, but only at the cost of assimilating justification so closely to truth as to make scepticism an uninteresting irrelevance. Perhaps this is a desirable outcome but I think that the sceptical challenge and the metaphysics that underpins it are more interesting than this allows, even if ultimately unsatisfying. In any case I should be wary of allowing a device like the OI to settle such complex issues merely by its intuitive surface plausibility. We surely do better to remain at the level of shared belief, with assumptions of correctness, without determining whether the concept of truth we have entitles us further to conclude that the beliefs, or a significant proportion of them, must be true. I am not so much interested in the normal use of words like 'correct', 'sound', 'know', or 'true', but in what logical space our conclusions in this chapter allow for the challenge of metaphysical scepticism. Our vindication of testimony shows it to have the same general kind of epistemic status as our other primary sources of information, such as perception, and it is perfectly natural and 'paradigmatic' to describe many resultant beliefs of all these as true and known to be so. But this can hardly constitute a rebuttal of broad sceptical doubts about our whole cognitive enterprise: these must be dealt with separately.

This concludes our treatment of the general justificatory questions about testimony. We have been concerned to examine the broad significance of testimony in our lives, its place in our epistemological landscape, the tradition of debate about that place, and finally, what can be said to vindicate the extensive significance we have claimed for our reliance upon testimony. This final task we have attempted to complete without succumbing to the individualist temptations that seem to have bedevilled other attempts at justification. Developing the line of approach used in Chapter 4, in the critique of Hume, we argued that an extensive commitment to trusting the reports of others was a precondition of understanding their speech at all. Here we found ourselves in partial sympathy with some of the ideas of Wittgenstein on linguistic communication, and of Donald Davidson on interpretation. Although Davidson's principle of charity, as sometimes formulated and understood, takes charity to excess, the core idea in it is defensible and adaptable to our purposes here. Moving beyond this, we argued that certain broad facts of cohesion and coherence imply the legitimacy of the strong commitment to trusting the word of others that is embodied in our actual cognitive procedures.

The position reached here fits into none of the original classifications outlined at the end of Chapter 1. We have seen reason to be dissatisfied with the Puritan and the Reductive responses and the attempted solution here proposed constitutes an alternative to the End of Epistemology response. It also constitutes an alternative to the Fundamentalist approach, at least in so far as that response relies merely upon an appeal to intuitively evident first principles.

We must turn now to a number of issues which are less concerned with the general status of testimony, its centrality and reliability as an institution, so to speak, and more with methodological questions about the credibility of particular types of testimony, or testimony in certain contexts or fields of inquiry. In the chapters comprising the section entitled 'The Puzzles', we shall examine perplexities to do with the credibility of astonishing reports, paradoxical claims about the inevitable decline of credibility in transmission chains, and finally a striking thesis about transmission and knowledge. In 'The Applications', we shall look at claims about the role of testimony in historical methodology and in mathematics. We shall also examine claims by psychologists about eyewitnesses that have some bearing on legal procedures, and finally certain difficulties posed for the law by the idea of expert testimony.

IV

The Puzzles

10

Astonishing Reports

> The most incredible thing about miracles is that they happen. A few clouds in heaven do come together into the staring shape of one human eye. A tree does stand up in the landscape of a doubtful journey in the exact and elaborate shape of a note of interrogation. I have seen both these things myself within the last few days. Nelson does die in the instant of victory; and a man named Williams does quite accidentally murder a man named Williamson; it sounds like a sort of infanticide. In short, there is in life an element of elfin coincidence which people reckoning on the prosaic may perpetually miss. As it has been well expressed in the paradox of Poe, wisdom should reckon on the unforeseen.
>
> (G. K. Chesterton in *The Innocence of Father Brown*.)

Chesterton's bland assimilation of miracles to striking coincidences will no doubt seem outrageously tendentious to those who criticize miracles in the spirit of Hume. Certainly, it ignores the special features of miracles which are believed to set them apart from other unusual events. None the less, it is no easy matter to say what those special features are, and, when a general critique of miracles is premised upon issues to do with the credibility of witnesses, the problem of the miraculous begins to look like a close relation, if not a special case, of the problem raised by the clash between reports and expectations. This insight, for so I believe it to be, goes back at least to Locke and is certainly a plausible construal of what is going on in one central strand of Hume's notorious critique. In what follows I shall not be concerned with miracles *per se* but with the astonishing and unexpected as subjects of report.

John Stuart Mill criticizes Campbell for conflating the miraculous and the unexpected in the latter's criticisms of Hume. Mill there makes use of the distinction (also to be found, in somewhat different form, in Hume) between events which are *contrary* to the uniform course of experience and those which are unexpected but *conformable* to this uniform course.[1] Much the same point is often put in terms of a contrast between what is contrary to the laws of nature and what is conformable to them, though unusual. This move has a good deal of surface plausibility but it is more difficult to give a plausible account of what would make it work. A principal problem is that reports of hitherto unexpected events can make

---

[1] J. S. Mill, *A System of Logic*, ed. J. M. Robson (Toronto, 1973), bk. I, ch. xxv, s. 3, p. 627.

us change our opinion about what 'the uniform course of experience' is, or which propositions we hold dear really are natural laws. We might recall, in this connection, the case of the King of Siam discussed by Locke and Hume. As Locke tells it, the King when informed by a certain Dutch ambassador 'that the water in his country would sometimes in cold weather be so hard that men walked upon it, and that it would bear an elephant if he were there' replied, 'Hitherto I have believed the strange things you have told me, because I look upon you as a sober, fair man: but now *I* am sure you lie.'[2] Mill tells us that the King should have suspended judgement instead of disbelieving, what we might call, the facts of ice. According to Mill, the King should have realized that the reports did not contradict 'universal laws which know no counteraction or anomaly, or the generalisations next in comprehensiveness to them',[3] but how was the unfortunate King to know this?

Mill rightly points out (in agreement with Campbell, Paley, and others) that mere antecedent improbability, in the sense enshrined in the calculus of chances, should not affect the acceptability of some report. If someone tells me that the last hand dealt to him in a game of bridge was AK953 of spades, QJ4 of hearts, K2 of diamonds, and AQJ of clubs, the fact that there are huge odds against just this combination of cards being dealt (I gather it is 635,013,559,599 to 1 against) provides no incentive at all to disbelief. After all, the same odds exist against any combination in a hand at bridge. (This point is at the heart of modern discussions in probability theory of what has become known as 'the lottery paradox'.) As Mill says, 'If we disbelieved all facts which had the chances against them beforehand, we should believe hardly anything'.[4] The matter is, or seems, somewhat different in cases to which Mill gives the general name of 'coincidences'. These are occurrences which strike us as really astonishing outcomes, like some of Chesterton's examples, or like someone's throwing a hundred dice in the air and all of them landing on the same face (an example of Laplace).[5] There is a strong temptation to hold that reports of such 'extraordinary' or 'astonishing' events are, if not unbelievable *tout court*, still to be treated with great scepticism because of their extraordinary nature. As Laplace says of his example: 'We would give no credence to the testimony'[6] of someone who reported the dice all falling on the same face. Perhaps not, but Laplace adds immediately, by way of emphasizing the point, that if we saw such an event ourselves we should only believe it 'after having brought in the testimony of other eyes in order to be quite

---

[2] John Locke, *An Essay on Human Understanding*, bk. IV, ch. xv, s. 5.
[3] Mill, *System*, 630.
[4] Ibid. 631.
[5] Pierre, marquis de Laplace, *A Philosophical Essay on Probabilities*, trans. F. W. Truscott and F. G. Emory (New York, 1951), ch. xi, p. 118.
[6] Ibid.

sure that there had been neither hallucination nor deception'. He seems wholly unconscious of any appearance of paradox in the fact that these 'other eyes' whose deliverances (via their 'other lips') reassure us about our own apparent perceptions are the very witnesses to whose testimony he has told us we would rightly 'give no credence'! When he goes on to conclude that it is better to believe the astonishing fact than give up the laws of vision, he shows that (misled perhaps by the metaphor of 'other eyes') he has forgotten that it is the testimony and not (primarily) the vision of the 'other eyes' which is at issue.

There are many difficulties lurking here but a central theme in the discussion both of miracles and coincidences goes back at least to Locke's discussion of what he calls 'the grounds of probability'.[7] This occurs in book IV chapter xv, of his *Essay Concerning Human Understanding* and in the subsequent chapter, entitled 'Of the Degrees of Assent'. Locke thinks that there are two general grounds of probability: (*a*) conformity with our own knowledge, observation, and experience, and (*b*) the testimony of others vouching their observation and experience. He offers several reflections upon the relations between (*a*) and (*b*). He says:

The difficulty is, where testimonies contradict common experience, and the reports of history and witnesses clash with the ordinary course of nature, or with one another; there it is where diligence, attention and exactness is required to form a right judgement, and to proportion the assent to the different evidence and probability of the thing, which rises and falls according to those two foundations of credibility, viz., common observation in like cases, and particular testimonies in that particular instance, favour or contradict it. These are liable to so great variety of contrary observations, circumstances, reports, different qualifications, tempers, designs, oversights, etc. of the reporters, that it is impossible to reduce to precise rules the various degrees wherein men give their assent.[8]

Here Locke acknowledges the importance of 'common observation in like cases' as a 'foundation of credibility' but, seeing no way of providing a criterion for deciding between the verdicts of general experience and particular testimony, he leaves the decision to 'right judgement'. Hume and Bradley on the other hand (and also, as we shall see, Laplace) take a different view. The division of opinion here goes very deep and although it tends to crystallize around the problem of miracles it is not restricted to this interesting but rather narrow issue. Hume, for example, not only denies any credence to reports of miracles, because they violate laws of nature and are thus contrary to 'uniform experience', but also to the reports of human acts, dispositions, etc., which although they would not normally be thought of as miraculous none the less run counter to that

---

[7] Probability, for Locke, is related to those propositions that are likely to be true but fall short of being absolutely certain. See ss. 3, 4, 5, of bk. IV, ch. xv.

[8] Ibid., bk. IV, ch. xvi, s. 9.

'uniformity in human motives and actions' which he supposes the study of history and contemporary society to reveal to us. In his own words:

The veracity of Quintus Curtius is as much to be suspected when he describes the supernatural courage of Alexander, by which he was hurried on simply to attack multitudes, as when he describes his supernatural force and activity, by which he was able to resist them. So readily and universally do we acknowledge a uniformity in human motives and actions as well as in the operations of bodies.[9]

Of course Hume's idea here is that acts of very unusual courage, benevolence, misanthropy, and so on, would be as miraculous as acts of turning water into wine or raising the dead. Not only is this a very implausible claim, given the comparison between our knowledge of natural processes and of what we might call 'human processes', but, further, the fact that Hume draws this analogy shows how strongly committed he is to the position that, for all clashes between foundations of credibility (*a*) and (*b*) then (*a*) shall either be decisive or at least heavily preponderant. The attempt to clarify and defend this commitment I shall refer to as the search for a criterion of the acceptability of testimony. In Hume, and other philosophers, it is fuelled by the desire to have a way of ruling certain types of testimony out of court without having to consider the particular circumstances of their deliverance. Hume's comments on the Ossian controversy of his own day, which concerned the apparent discovery of ancient epic poems among the Highland Scots, shows this commitment starkly in a context that has nothing to do with miracles. This is Hume's statement of principle: 'But as finite added to finite never approaches a hair's breadth nearer to infinite; so a fact incredible in itself, acquires not the smallest accession of probability by the accumulation of testimony.'[10]

F. H. Bradley adopts a very similar position in his essay entitled 'The Presuppositions of Critical History'.[11] Since Bradley's thesis is, in spite of certain striking characteristics of its own, very much a development of central strands in Hume's outlook and since, unlike the latter, it is rarely discussed, it is worth devoting close attention to it, especially since it has had a considerable, though often subterranean, influence. Bradley argues that we should reject all historical testimonies to the 'non-analogous', by which he means events and states of affairs which do not conform to 'our' experience of the present world. Bradley proceeds by first arguing that the non-analogous would be acceptable if only we could establish an 'identification of consciousness' with the witness who testifies to the non-

---

[9] *An Enquiry Concerning Human Understanding*, in L. A. Selby-Bigge (ed.), *Hume's Enquires* (Oxford, 1957), 84.

[10] David Hume, 'Of the Authenticity of Ossian's Poems', in *Essays: Moral, Political and Literary*, ii, ed. T. H. Green and T. H. Grose (London, 1875), 424.

[11] *Collected Essays*, 1–76. (Page refs. to this essay will hereafter be bracketed in the text.)

analogous; such identification is, however, impossible in history (though, he thinks, achievable in science) and hence the non-analogous must be rejected. Like Hume, Bradley is interested in the application of this argument to reports of miracles. Indeed, his essay is an attempt to provide a philosophical justification of the actual procedures of the new German school of biblical criticism associated with the names of Bauer and Strauss, who had applied what they took to be the methods of critical history to the New Testament and come up with the conclusion that much of the testimony therein could not be believed.[12] None the less, like Hume again but even more explicitly, he is also interested in providing a general criterion for the critical assessment of any testimonies, even those which do not involve what would normally be regarded as miraculous.

Bradley's banishment of the non-analogous from history is accompanied by a good deal of heart-searching because he realizes that there seem plainly to be cases in which we accept the non-analogous. As Bradley puts it 'our world is extended to fresh cases which (roughly speaking) have nothing analogous to previous phenomena' (pp. 27–8) and he instances mesmeric phenomena as a case in point: 'These may have no analogy in our own private experience; and yet we may receive the facts, on testimony, as no less certain than those which we find for ourselves.... Testimony rests on experience, and testimony goes beyond experience, and as it would seem, without the support of experience. How is this possible?' (p. 29). And in particular, asks Bradley, 'How is such validity possible, if, as we have seen, testimony must finally rest on an inference from personal knowledge and if personal knowledge is ultimately based on our own intelligent observation?'. His answer, as we saw in Chapter 6, is that, just as we know that there are other men by an inference, so we know that their testimony is reliable by an inference to their having similar outlooks to ourselves. Hence if 'we are justified in assuming the identity of their standpoint with our own' then we can be sure that they 'can see for us, because we know that they are able to think for us'. Consequently, I can accept testimony to the non-analogous where I can determine that a witness's mind is 'a cosmos like my own and subject to the same laws'. Where this 'identification of consciousness' can be established, and also the witness's integrity and will to observe and judge thoroughly, there we can accept testimony to the non-analogous. And, on the contrary, 'wherever the standpoint of the witness differs (wholly or in relation to the particular class of facts in question) from our own, or wherever its agreement is not known to us', there testimony must 'necessarily fail to establish a non-analogous case' (p. 30). The next step is then to deny that historical testimony can ever meet the requirement of 'identification of consciousness'.

---

[12] Bradley's position with respect to biblical history has recently been invoked and defended by Austin van Harvey in his book *The Historian and the Believer* (London, 1967), 70–7 and *passim*.

How does he try to show this? A good deal of his argumentation consists of an attempt to provide a general distinction between history and science, so that testimony can be legitimately accepted within science, even when it concerns the non-analogous in the past, yet be unacceptable within history. He is himself clearly unhappy with his treatment of this issue and it involves many confusions, incompletenesses, and apparent contradictions. I will not try to unravel all of it but will discuss an argument upon which he obviously places great store and then try to make some general points about the non-analogous.

The argument is an attempt to show that it is in general impossible to establish identity of standpoint in historical testimony. History deals, we are told, with 'conscious deeds and sufferings, the instinctive productions, and unconscious destinies of men and of nations' and hence is especially concerned with what is most changeable and developing in man's nature. Moreover, 'the historical witness is also the son of his time, and, in relation to that which bears most the stamp of the era, his mind is the reflection of the age in a mirror which shares its nature' (p. 41). His testimony, therefore, is given from a point of view which must be quite dissimilar to our own. By contrast, scientific testimony, even from the past, is such that 'we are able so to reconstruct the observers and the conditions of their observations, as to possess ourselves entirely of their faculties, and use them as our own. And the possibility of this consists in the fact that science abstracts . . . it uses, so to speak, not the whole but a part alone of the observer's consciousness' (p. 41). Science, for Bradley, seems then to be somehow ahistorical. As he puts it: 'The object of science does not transform itself in a ceaseless progress, and the subject of science can separate itself from the concrete development of the historical mind, and can remain practically identical while coexisting with standpoints generally diverse. But this with history is impossible' (p. 41).

Now it is beyond doubt that there have been changes in people's outlooks and styles of thought throughout the centuries, but it is also true that there are deep continuities, otherwise we could know nothing at all (analogous or non-analogous) about those who lived before us. We could not even decipher their utterances to see if they reported analogous happenings. It is merely arbitrary of Bradley to restrict such continuities to the area of scientific thinking, for it seems obvious that we can not only know *that* our ancestors at different stages thought differently from ourselves and one another but also, to a considerable extent, *what* these outlooks were like and what changes came about in them. Given that we can determine such questions, to a greater or lesser degree, then it would seem that some kind of identification of consciousness with the witnesses from the historical past is possible. It is, of course, not at all clear just how extensive Bradley requires the 'identification of consciousness' to be, but it cannot be total since we are supposed to be able to identify with people of the past when they are giving scientific reports, even though in other aspects of their thinking they differ from us. Again, Bradley's picture of science is astonishingly static. If it is arbitrary of him to restrict continuities of outlook to science, it is blind of him to find nothing but continuity of outlook within science. It is hard enough to see how he could have taken such a view of science in the 1870s, but it would be impossible today to ignore the 'historicity' of science, the existence of fundamental change, evolution, and revolution within the 'consciousness' of successive generations of scientists. The fact is that all human thought exhibits both continuity and change through history and if this fact is a barrier to the acceptance of non-analogous testimony in history then it will also be so in science.

Another difficulty with Bradley's position is that extensive or total 'identification of consciousness' is not even to be had amongst contemporaries, so that his systematic contrast of 'we' with 'they' is at least misleading. He might of course agree to this and disallow the acceptance of testimony to the non-analogous from any contemporary who did not have an identical outlook to his own. One might have thought this rather too great a price to pay for the immunity of a world-view. The fact of the matter seems to be that with both history, science, and the knowledge of ordinary life there is a crucial role for very plain mere observation, since no matter how interpreted our perceptions are by our theories or outlooks an area of commonly graspable observation is essential for the existence of any form of communication and understanding. It is precisely this function of observation which is under attack in Bradley's argument, for he wants the requirement of 'identification of consciousness' to be fulfilled *before* non-analogous observations are to be counted as observations at all.

My case so far has been designed to show that Bradley's argument against the possibility of an identification of consciousness in history is defective. I have argued earlier that our acceptance of testimony as a reliable source of true beliefs need not be based upon the prior establishment of any 'identification of consciousness' of this kind and it is some such supposed general need as this which underlies Bradley's critique. We need not deny, however, that in assessing particular pieces of testimony it may be relevant to know certain facts about the beliefs or the psychology of the witness. It is obviously relevant to what a man tells us that he is, for instance, insane, and it has been thought relevant to the credibility of certain records of telekinetic phenomena that the alleged witnesses were initially very sceptical about the possibility of what they later recorded as happening. Clearly, when some piece of testimony is in doubt or under challenge we will want to know what we can about the circumstances of its deliverance and production, such as the integrity and psychological stability of the witness, his capacities, the observational conditions at the time, his interests and beliefs insofar as they are relevant to the issue, whether there were other witnesses, and so on.

Historical testimony raises special problems with regard to this sort of assessment and Bradley suggests that, if we are unimpressed by the 'identification of consciousness' argument, we should still refuse to admit the non-analogous on the ground that, even granted identity of standpoint, we can never have enough assurance of the probability of what is reported to outweigh the improbability created by its being non-analogous. Bradley cites the facts that the historical event is gone and cannot be repeated for further observation, and that the historian cannot cross-examine his witnesses, as grounds for holding that an historian's 'reconstruction [of the supposed episode] will never be complete enough to take him beyond a mere probability; and hence since a probable conclusion must rest on analogy, that therefore the non-analogous is excluded for ever from the sphere of historical testimony' (p. 42). Bradley's move here may have an internal difficulty for the position he maintains about science, since scientific testimony to the unanalogous where it concerns the past may also be ruled out by the argument, but I will not press the *ad hominem* point. More interesting is the fact that he is here putting the claim that failure to correspond with our present experience of the world shows a reported event to be absolutely inadmissable as part of history. As noted earlier, a somewhat similar position is maintained by Hume, who not only denies credence to any reports of miracles because they violate laws of nature and are thus contrary to uniform experience but also to any reports of human acts, dispositions, etc., which run counter to that 'uniformity in human motives and actions'[13] which he supposes the study of history and of contemporary society to reveal to us.

The first thing that can be said about the Hume–Bradley criterion is that, even if it has a valid application to historical testimony, it does not take us very far as a principle for the sifting of testimonial evidence. As Collingwood pointed out, Bradley's criterion at best tells us what it is possible for us to accept but it gives no guide to the criticism of authorities which have passed the test of the analogous.[14] None the less, although the Bradley–Hume criterion would give us only a partial and negative characterization of the principles of critical history, it would, if valid, still be important as providing a rule which allowed us, or the historian acting on our behalf, to dismiss certain testimonies out of hand where what they report fails to correspond with our present experience of the world. Unfortunately, the validity of the criterion is very dubious; indeed, stated baldly in either Hume's or Bradley's terminology, the position seems quite absurd.

[13] Hume, *Enquiry*, 84.
[14] R. G. Collingwood, *The Idea of History* (Oxford, 1970), 239.

There are many historical happenings that are as certain as anything in history which are quite 'non-analogous' in our present experience, for example, sacrificial offerings of human beings, trial by ordeal, Socrates's acceptance of death rather than freedom because of his philosophical convictions about justice, the astonishing feats of Napoleon Bonaparte. This last case is notable for having evoked a masterly piece of philosophical pastiche from Archbishop Whately in 1819. His pamphlet *Historic Doubts Relative to Napoleon Bonaparte* is a very amusing and perceptive application of Hume's principles to the assessment of the available testimony about the life and deeds of Bonaparte.[15] Whately's essay deserves to be better known but I shall here merely quote from a section directly relevant to the discussion above. Whately claims that the reports of Napoleon's deeds are of matters at variance with uniform experience:

All the events are great, and splendid, and marvellous, great armies,—great victories,—great frosts,—great reverses,—hair-breadth scapes,—empires subverted in a few days; everything happened in defiance of political calculations and in opposition to the *experience* of past times; everything upon that grand scale, so common in Epic Poetry, so rare in real life; and this calculated to strike the imagination of the vulgar, and to remind the sober-thinking few of the Arabian Nights. Every event, too, has that *roundness* and completeness which is so characteristic of fiction; nothing is done by halves; we have *complete* victories,—*total* overthrows,—*entire* subversions of empires,—*perfect* re-establishments of them—crowded upon us in rapid succession.

To enumerate the improbabilities of each of the several parts of this history, would fill volumes; but they are so fresh in every one's memory, that there is no need of such a detail: let any judicious man, not ignorant of history and of human nature, revolve them in his mind, and consider how far they are conformable to Experience, our best and only sure guide. In vain will he seek in history for something similar to this wonderful Buonaparte, 'nought but himself can be his parallel'.

Quite apart from non-analogous certainties like the above, there are historical hypotheses which are worth serious consideration and may well come to be accepted if more data becomes available, such as the strong suspicion that Dr James Barry, an eminent military surgeon in Victorian England, was a woman, indeed Britain's first woman doctor, who amazingly managed to conceal her sex through a long military career.[16] Although there may be some plausibility in the Bradley—Hume criterion in the case of physical miracles, where there is a body of impressive articulated physical theory to support the talk of disanalogy, the same background is almost entirely lacking (*pace* Hume) when we try to apply

[15] Richard Whately, *Historic Doubts Relative to Napoleon Bonaparte* (1st publ. anonymously in 1819).

[16] For an interesting discussion of this hypothesis see June Rose, 'James Barry, the First Woman Doctor', *Listener* (26 Sept. 1973), 369–71.

the criterion to the sphere of the distinctively human which is the primary subject-matter of the historian. Collingwood saw this sort of point clearly, and although he was sometimes inclined to exaggerate the differences between the natural and the historical the contrast is striking enough in the context of the Bradley–Hume criterion. As Collingwood puts it:

The laws of nature have always been the same, and what is against nature now was against nature two thousand years ago; but the historical as distinct from the natural conditions of man's life differ so much at different times that no argument from analogy will hold. That the Greeks and Romans exposed their newborn children in order to control the numbers of their population is no less true for being unlike anything that happens in the experience of contributors to the *Cambridge Ancient History*.[17]

History conducted on the lines advocated by Bradley and Hume would seem to lack any capacity to absorb the strange and unfamiliar and would surely construe human history as much more static than most historians believe it to be. Yet even here, it might be urged, I am implicitly relying upon present experience in urging this point against Hume; it is just that I am interpreting my world as much more spontaneous, varied, and potentially surprising than Hume thought his to be. Indeed this may be so, but, if so, it shows the weakness of the 'non-analogous' criterion. If we take the criterion literally then it is absurd (there is no human sacrifice in my world so there can have been none in the past, reports notwithstanding) but if we treat it more tolerantly it becomes too vague to do the sort of work its authors require of it. On a tolerant interpretation, the principle would, for instance, allow me to credit human sacrifice in the past if I recognize in my world that some people are prepared to let others suffer in order to achieve important goals (Richard Nixon's sacrifice of Spiro Agnew perhaps), but now of course we no longer have a ready-made criterion because different people will assess such analogies differently and, indeed, reports of Alexander's amazing bravery and exploits may get a much more sympathetic hearing. The determination of matters like this will then depend a great deal upon how one interprets the present, that is, on how one sees the potentialities of one's fellow human beings for heroic or foolhardy behaviour under stress. But now the criterion of the analogous as a hard and fast test of credibility is beginning to dissolve, and it dissolves further when one reflects that the question of how one reads the present (of how one interprets one's neighbour's potentialities for heroism or for virtuous behaviour) may well depend in part upon how one learns from the past. It might be important to keep open the possibility that one's own time is exceptional with respect to certain widespread practices, dispositions, or beliefs.

Even so, although the criterion, tolerantly interpreted, will not do what

[17] Collingwood, *Idea*, 240.

Bradley and Hume want it to do, surely we can agree that there is some point in an appeal to probability and improbability in the assessment of testimony? Indeed there is, but I am not sure than the reference to analogy really helps us much here. The crucial point is surely that historical knowledge must form part of a general framework of knowledge such that we operate at least with an ideal of coherence in our system of beliefs. Consequently, if we come across a sixteenth-century treatise of meteorology in which we find interesting (but possibly non-analogous) astronomical observations interspersed with alleged observations of storms in which it rained frogs, then we will certainly do well to treat the latter claim sceptically on the grounds that it will not at all cohere with what we know now about the workings of the weather and the workings of frogs. But our response here is not conditioned only by the fact that we have never experienced frogs falling from the sky with the raindrops, for after all some of the astronomical observations may have no counterpart in our experience, even though they may fit neatly into our astronomical theories or at least be consistent with them and into the bargain be recorded by a number of different witnesses in a way that is mutually corroborating. I am not saying that therefore they must be accepted, only that they need not be rejected. Similarly, one does not have to accept Quintus Curtius's accounts of Alexander's astonishing courage but they are not all inconsistent with what we *know* of human nature, only with what we commonly encounter. Equally, we may find ourselves viewing the curious reported behaviour of the frogs more favourably if we have, or acquire, other reasons for dissatisfaction with our meteorological or zoological theories.

Quite apart from our attitudes to that area of the past which we dignify by the name of 'history', similar considerations apply to our assessment of the unexpected in the contemporary world. The practice and application of those investigations that have come to be known as 'the natural sciences' often carry with them an outlook or family of outlooks which is pertinent here. At one extreme there is that strident 'scientism' which cannot see truth or value in anything other than such sciences. This stridency is often most pronounced in the practitioners of what are termed the human sciences and we shall have more to say of this in Chapter 15. More moderately, there is the conservative scepticism which seeks to guard the remarkable achievements and impressive intellectual traditions of modern science against the ever present blandishments of credulity and superstition. This latter attitude is relevant to our discussion precisely because it is most given to producing a set of expectations about how things will turn out which are seen to embody the scientific attitude. Bradley's strictures on 'the disanalogous' may be seen as part of such an outlook, but in the concrete circumstances of scientific investigation, it can be as much a hindrance as a help.

To see how this can be, let us take an example from a relatively low-level and commonsensical area of science. The Australian scientist, E. G. (Taffy) Bowen tells a very interesting story,[18] in this connection, about a friend of his, a Captain Brett Hilder, who reported to Bowen his frustrating experiences with learned journals outside Australia to whom he had sent a paper on a curious phenomenon. This paper had been rejected out of hand by several journals with no reasons given. Hilder gave his manuscript to Bowen for comments that might help get it published but Bowen found nothing to improve. The problem was not with Hilder's presentation but with the surprising nature of what was presented. Here are the facts as Bowen told them to me:

Captain Hilder had been a sea-captain trading among the islands of the West Pacific for thirty years or more. He was a Master Mariner and among other things was one of the few skippers qualified to take his ship into Sydney Harbour or through the Torres Straits without a pilot. He was a founder member of the Australian Institute of Navigation and well known in maritime circles overseas. During World War II he trained as a pilot in flying boats and made many landings at night in waters adjacent to Japanese held islands, taking in supplies to the coast watchers. Altogether a no-nonsense character not given to whimsy.

The document he produced was quite extraordinary. It described a phosphorescent phenomenon he had occasionally seen from the bridge of his ship which took the form of long radial lines like the spokes of a wheel, radiating from a point beyond the horizon and rotating, sometimes in a clockwise direction, sometimes anticlockwise. The phosphorescence was not on the surface but appeared to be 10 or 20 feet down, and seemed to pass directly under the ship with no diffraction or other effects. The rate of rotation was quite variable and in one or two cases had stopped and reversed direction. In one or two cases also, the phosphorescence was not in the form of radial lines, but parallel lines moving past the ship rather like ocean waves.

The phenomenon was only seen at night but according to him was clear and distinct and seemed to stretch to the horizon. He gave a Table of 15 to 20 sightings he had made (and recorded in the ship's log) over a 20 year period. This Table gave dates and times, duration, latitude and longitude of the ship and so forth. The sightings were mostly in warm tropical waters and stretched in a wide arc from the China sea, down through Indonesian waters and into the Coral Sea.

He described several simple experiments he had performed to see if the ship was in any way responsible, e.g. stopping the ship, running the engine revs. up and down, switching the radar on and off etc. But none of these had any effect. He offered no explanation of the phenomenon but made vague reference to the possibility of magnetic effects—which was the only criticism I could make of the paper.

Frankly, I had great difficulty in accepting the story. But knowing the man, I had to believe that he had seen something and described it accurately. There was simply nothing to be done to 'improve' the paper. It was well laid out and well written; but it would simply not be believed by the great majority of referees who did not know the author. I had virtually no suggestions to make and the matter dropped.

---

[18] Private communication to the author.

About a year later, I happened to be reading a book on Dampier's voyages off the N.W. Coast of Australia and it turned out that Dampier had seen exactly the same thing and recorded it in his diary. This was about 100 years before Capt. Cook. Capt. Hilder was away at sea at the time and I cannot recall whether I told him about this.

Several years later, again by chance, I found a paper written in German in a German Oceanographic Journal, which referred briefly to the observation of phosphorescent wheels and went on to give a physical explanation.

It was that the phenomenon was due to under-water seismic activity. A single pulsating seismic source would give a set of concentric circles radiating from the centre—a phenomenon hardly seen except for the parallel lines mentioned by Hilder. However, two nearby seismic sources would give two intersecting sets of circles, and the moiré pattern between these would give a set of radial lines. Exceedingly small displacements of the two centres or a change in phase of the pulsations would cause the radial lines to rotate in one direction or the other.

This to me was a completely satisfactory explanation. I sent a copy to Capt. Hilder but our paths did not cross for a number of years and again the matter dropped.

The various referees from the journals were apparently rejecting Hilder's paper because its descriptions were 'disanalogous' with their experience and they could think of no explanation of the phenomenon. Bowen was prepared to take the matter more seriously because he knew Hilder and could vouch for his competence (in the sense discussed in Chapter 2). He also found some additional confirming testimony but would have believed Hilder anyway. He came across a possible explanation consistent with current scientific knowledge but I do not know if it is the right one and it does not matter for the present point.

This sort of case illustrates the dangers of scepticism about the unusual or unexpected report within science.[19] None the less, the suspicion remains that Hume, Bradley, and Locke had a genuine concern in focusing upon the area in which prior experience and testimony come into conflict and that Bradley and Hume were right to give some epistemic preference to experience over testimony. The genuineness of the concern is not in question but the nature and validity of the preference is far more dubious. We saw earlier that mere prior probability by itself is an unhelpful guide. Perhaps a richer sense of 'experience', as an arbiter of particular testimony, can be obtained by resort to Bayes's Theorem. This tells us how to calculate the probability of some event, given the occurrence of another event and certain background conditions. The formula can be set out as follows:

---

[19] The dangers are not of course restricted to areas of theory and speculation. A good illustration from a practical area is the way the British Admirality rejected an intelligence report prior to the First World War that German naval gunnery at long ranges was astonishingly good. The Admirality declared that the reported results were 'impossible' but then had to learn differently at Jutland. See Nicholas P. Hiley, 'The Failure of British Espionage Against Germany, 1907–1914', *Historical Journal*, 26/4 (1976), 887.

$$P(A/B\&K) = \frac{P(B/A\&K)\,P(A/K)}{P(B/K)}$$

where P is the probability operator, A is the 'unusual' event, B the testimony to it and K the background facts. So if some very surprising event is reported we may unreflectively think that the probability of such an event happening, given its having been reported and given the prior state of the world (including scientific laws, observed regularities, etc.), would be, say, .4, and yet have to reverse this initial reaction in the light of assignments we more confidently give to the other probabilities. For instance, we may set the probability of $B/A\&K$ (the report occurring, given the occurrence of the unusual event and the background facts) very high, say, .9, and that of B/K (the report occurring, given the background facts alone) relatively low, say, .1. We may then put the probability of the surprising event, given the background facts alone (A/K), as very low, say, .08. It is surely not hard to see how someone could reasonably make such assignments and yet the Bayes result will be .72. So our initial incredulity can be turned into reasonable belief by showing what our other views commit us to. Of course, the shift could just as easily go in the other direction, given plausible assumptions about the witness or the background or the degree of unusualness. For example, suppose the witness is known to be hysterically given to 'seeing things', of just the kind reported, then $P(B/K)$ will be very much higher than .1. It only needs to be .3 to give an overall result of .24, which makes the report incredible. What this seems to show is that Bayesian theory can help us with the consistency of our commitments, and perhaps with clarification of what they are, but it is ill-placed to provide any sort of criterion for the acceptability of astonishing reports.

In the context of our present inquiry this conclusion is reinforced by the consideration that, even if we don't know anything much about the witness (just as the journal referees and editors didn't know much about Captain Hilder), our broad philosophical assumptions about testimony and its epistemological significance will feed into the scales we use for the Bayesian operation or for any related probabilistic acceptability device. If we view testimony as a very weak evidential reed and our fellow observers as by nature grossly credulous we will come to very different conclusions from those whose fundamental epistemic outlook is more trusting. There is a continuum of attitudes to reports possible here. Let us call those at the end of the continuum, respectively, the Sceptic and the Gull.[20] No one is

[20] As Bruce Langtry has pointed out to me, there is an argument that one's fundamental attitude to testimony may be unimportant in some particular cases. Corroboration is the most typical sort of case. I may regard each of ten witnesses as highly unreliable but accept their joint testimony on the grounds that its truth best explains their agreement. Yet even here, I should say, attitude to reliability can play a significant role, since it may favour an alternative explanation of the convergence, such as collusion. The 'sceptic' will be more inclined to seek out and countenance such alternatives.

consistently a Sceptic or a Gull and I have argued that no one could be consistently a Sceptic. For one thing, as I argued in earlier chapters, a consistent scepticism about testimony would deprive one of any content to the contrasting notion of experience—what Locke called 'common observation in like cases'. In the context of Bayesian considerations it is tantamount to depriving oneself of any secure grasp on the background facts.

More restricted or localized scepticism or gullibility, however, is possible and, indeed, pretty common. Hume's arguments against the authenticity of the Ossian poetic epics were premised in part on the unbelievability of the reports of Scottish Highlanders, at least in such matters. His famous comment (according to Boswell) that he would not believe the poems genuine even 'if fifty bare-arsed highlanders'[21] should testify to it expresses a restricted form of the sceptical attitude. (Interestingly, he had earlier urged an investigator into the poems' authenticity to avoid the a priori and seek for testimonies to determine genuineness: 'These proofs must not be arguments, but testimonies... positive testimony from many different hands, that such poems are vulgarly recited in the Highlands, and have there been long the entertainment of the people.'[22] At the opposite extreme is the attitude of many modern social workers confronted with the very real and disturbing problem of sexual abuse of children by parents and other adults. It seems to have become a commonplace amongst these theorists and practitioners to adopt the principle that every report by a child of such abuse must be believed. 'A child never lies', said one of them fiercely on Australian television recently. Such believers not only carry the trust in testimony to extremes for one class of reporters but actually choose an improbable group to confer this favour upon. I do not mean that children are particularly wicked or even mendacious but rather that in addition to having more or less normal human tendencies to deceit they are, at certain ages anyway, possessed of a more than usual capacity for fantasy, as a reading of Richard Hughes's *A High Wind in Jamaica* would confirm. There is also a special problem about their understanding of complex language and of interview situations.

Less extreme versions of gullibility are provided from within science itself. In an amusing and important discussion entitled 'Pathological Science', the American scientist Irving Langmuir analysed the standing of a variety of enticing 'fringe' discoveries and hypotheses within and around the physical sciences.[23] Langmuir discusses such purported scientific breakthroughs as the Davis–Barnes effect, N-rays, Mitogenetic rays, and the Allison effect, as well as Rhine's experiments on extra-sensory perception and the Flying Saucer controversy. He then tries to draw some general

---

[21] Cited in Ernest Mossner, *The Life of David Hume* (Edinburgh, 1954), 418.
[22] Ibid. 416.
[23] Irving Langmuir, *Pathological Science*, transcribed and ed. R. N. Hall, *Report of the General Electric Research and Development Center* (New York, Apr. 1986).

conclusions about the nature of pathological science and offers the following list of 'symptoms' of its presence:

(1) The maximum effect that is observed is produced by a causative agent of barely detectable intensity, and the magnitude of the effect is substantially independent of the intensity of the cause.

(2) The effect is of a magnitude that remains close to the limit of detectability; or, many measurements are necessary because of the very low statistical significance of the results.

(3) Claims of great accuracy.

(4) Fantastic theories contrary to experience.

(5) Criticisms are met by *ad hoc* excuses thought up on the spur of the moment.

(6) Ratio of supporters to critics rises up to somewhere near 50 per cent and then falls gradually to oblivion.[24]

The list is impressive and undoubtedly rules out a good deal of bogus stuff but, as Langmuir admits, symptoms (1) to (5) might very well rule out serious new scientific developments. In discussion after Langmuir's paper, the case of Pasteur's germ theory was brought up, as was the case of the theory of relativity with measurements of very small fractions of a degree of arc in the neighbourhood of a bright disc of the sun, and also the Lane and Bragg theory that X-rays were electromagnetic waves.[25] In response, Langmuir does not try to show that there are differences between (some of) these and his target examples but retreats to the sixth symptom as the crucial one. 'The test of time is the thing that ultimately checks this thing' he says. But in his clarification of this test he seems to run several things together: (*a*) what appears to be the sense of the original expression of symptom (6), namely, the degree of acceptability of the theory to the scientific community over time—the pathological theories get a lot of initial support but in time this falls away 'to oblivion'; (*b*) healthy science may look odd at first, even by tests (1) to (5), but then solid, accurate results come to hand fairly quickly (within a few years) whereas with pathological science this quick establishment of the theory does not occur, though the theory tends to persist. There is no need to unravel the relations between (*a*) and (*b*) because, on either interpretation, the test of unacceptable, pathological science is not primarily logical or methodological but historical and sociological. It may well be true that 'the test of time' is the ultimate criterion but it isn't much help in assessing theories or reports at the time they are made or thereabouts. Langmuir's other 'symptoms' are perhaps useful hints about when to tread cautiously

---

[24] Ibid. 7.

[25] It is not clear that each of these satisfies all of 1 to 4. The germ theory seems clearly to satisfy 1 and 5 (on then current understandings of 'experience') and perhaps 2, 3, and 5. The fifth symptom seems much too subjective to be of great assistance anyway.

but hardly more. After all, a genuine explanation of a theory's experimental failure or other defect may well be thought up 'on the spur of the moment', and it will no doubt look 'ad hoc' if the theory is a genuine innovation whose connection with the rest of the theories prevailing in the area is uncertain.

These various responses to the very surprising, unexpected, or astonishing raise the general problem of why the fact that something surprises us should have any significance for probability calculations at all. The concept of probability remains one of the most puzzling in philosophy: although the mathematics are well enough understood the underlying idea of probability continues to evade any generally accepted analysis. Proponents of a 'subjectivist' analysis point to the way in which one's instinctive initial probability assignments (generated themselves by no more than feelings of confidence) can be rendered consistent but, as C. S. Peirce pointed out last century, judgements of 'likelihood' based merely on one's aversion to the unexpected are virtually worthless. Laplace was amongst those who refused to accept reports of large stones falling from the heavens upon the earth because the facts were supposedly contrary to experience. As Peirce remarked of Laplace and others, they refused 'to accept the evidence that stones fall from heaven (evidence proving that they do so daily), simply because their prepossessions were the other way'.[26] He cites the case of

a scientifically given English ecclesiastic who happened to be sojourning in Siena when a shower of aerolites were dashed in broad daylight into an open square of that town, (and who) wrote home that having seen the stones he had found the testimony of eyewitnesses so unimpeachable and trustworthy—that he accepted the fact, you will say? by no means—that he knew not what to think! Such was the *bon sens* that guided the eighteenth century—a pretty phrase for ineradicable prejudice.[27]

Peirce also instances the hostile reactions to the phenomena of mesmerism in the nineteenth century. That Laplace and like-minded scientists could go so wrong by taking the unexpected for the improbable is revealing. As Peirce was aware, this attitude to testimony had led to absurdities in the historical exegesis of ancient texts in his own day and has continued to exert a powerful (and, I venture to assert, a sometimes baneful) influence upon biblical exegesis. Speaking of Hume's method of 'balancing likelihoods', Peirce points out that contemporary German critics of ancient history had applied the method and thereby found themselves driven 'to deny the testimony of all the witnesses and to set down what seems likely in a German university town in the place of history. But wherever

---

[26] C. S. Peirce, 'The Century's Great Men in Science', in *Selected Writings: Values in a Universe of Chance*, ed. P. P. Wiener (New York, 1966), 269.
[27] Ibid.

those critical denials have been struck by the spade of the archaeological explorer, the attitude of criticism has made a laughable picture.'[28]

What then can be said in general about the assessment of testimonies to the astonishing? Strong claims of the Hume–Bradley type are difficult to sustain and weaker claims are hard to clarify and defend. Perhaps the most that can be said is that efficiency in the handling of information and advancing knowledge is best served by a certain lethargic bias in our basic framework of belief. Openness to the novel (Poe's reckoning on the unforeseen), whether directly encountered or as subject to report, is certainly a virtue, as I have argued earlier, but the wholly 'open mind' is not only unattainable in fact but undesirable in theory. We require a conceptual apparatus and related beliefs in order to construe our experience at all. (This point figured in our discussion of the facts of cohesion and the ideal of coherence in Chapter 9.) Hence the fact that a putatively reliable report clashes, or even appears to clash, with our incumbent belief system (using the word 'system' fairly loosely) gives us some reason for a cautious response to it. This caution will be the stronger where we have independent reason to be sceptical about this or that class of witness or the circumstances of their testimony (e.g. Government spokesmen 'briefing' the press on the details of a war their masters are currently waging). None the less, degree of coherence with what we already know or believe about the world always has some role to play in the assessment of the credibility of a particular piece of testimony. This factor, what we might call the plausibility of the reported matter, must always be weighed against the particular circumstances of the report. To adopt the terminology of the *Port-Royal Logic*, we must weight the internal circumstances against the external circumstances, where the internal circumstances concern the probability of the event reported in relation to what we know and the external circumstances concern the credit of the witness, degree of confirmation by other witnesses, the internal consistency of the narration, the type of testimony, the interest, relevant beliefs, and purpose of the testifier, and the abilities of the witness in relation to what he narrates.[29]

There is also another consideration which does not fit neatly into either of these categories and it is to do with the general requirements of explanation. When an investigator decides to dismiss testimony to the unusual there is some onus upon him to explain how the false or misleading testimony came about. This is a point stressed by certain critics of Hume, such as Paley,[30] and indeed implicitly acknowledged by Hume himself

---

[28] 'Letters to Samuel P. Langley and "Hume on Miracles and Laws of Nature"', ibid. 320–1.

[29] Antoine Arnauld, *The Art of Thinking: Port-Royal Logic*, trans. J. Dickoff and P. James (Indianapolis, 1964), ch. 13, p. 342.

[30] William Paley, *A View of the Evidences of Christianity* (London, 1953), 36. Paley there puts it: 'In adjusting also the other side of the balance, the strength and weight of testimony, this author has provided an answer to every possible accumulation of historical proof by

when he tries to explain apparently impressive testimony to the miraculous on the basis of the human tendency to love of the wonderful.[31] Hume undoubtedly overdoes this particular explanatory move since the force it has must be counterbalanced by the human tendency to love of the routine and familiar. Moreover, if the Humean point is made instead in terms of a more basic tendency to credulity, which operates in conditions favourable to the passions of the audience, then it must be realized that disbelief is subject to the same tendency, since disbelieving that *p* is equivalent to believing that not *p*.

Certainly, the critics have a genuine point, though it is not as decisive as they are inclined to make out. From the perspective of modern psychological theory, there may be available more persuasive explanations of false testimony than Paley and others were able to envisage—though, once more, at this level of generality, such a point can as easily cut one way as the other; to be effective it must be made more specific. In addition, the demands of explanation are not quite as severe as the critics claim since we, with reason, can tolerate, at least for a time, a degree of inexplicability about the phenomena we encounter or need to assess. The UFO phenomena spring to mind as a category of cases in which many of the sceptics are dismissive without being in a position to give a plausible explanation of the reports. Part of the problem is that there is unlikely to be *one* explanation of the great variety of circumstances in which such reports occur (except of course, the rejected explanation of truth) so that the problem of satisfying the explanatory requirement is a very demanding and time-consuming one. Another is that there are UFO reports and UFO reports. Some report strange visual and auditory phenomena for which they or others offer extraterrestrial explanations; others give reports which inescapably incorporate the extraterrestrials into the content—they claim to see and even be captured by green creatures who emerge from spaceships. One might accept that certain strange things had happened, as reported, to some members of the first group (as a result of one's assessment of the 'external circumstances') but have no explanation of what caused these strange happenings. One might none the less reject the explanations offered, on a variety of grounds concerned with explanatory adequacy. Here one would not be impugning their testimony only their theorizing, and one would be left with preferring no explanation (yet) to a bad explanation. For the second group, one might accept that something

telling us that we are not obliged to explain how the story of the evidence arose. Now I think that we *are* obliged, not, perhaps, to show by positive accounts how it did, but by a probable hypothesis how it might so happen. The existence of the testimony is a phenomenon; the truth of the fact solves the phenomenon. If we reject this solution, we ought to have some other to rest in; and none, even by our adversaries, can be admitted, which is inconsistent with the principles which regulate human affairs and human conduct at present, or which makes men *then* to have been a different kind of beings from what they are now.'

[31] Hume, *Enquiry*, 117.

strange had happened to some of them, though others were merely lying, but reject most of their descriptions of what took place. There would then remain the problem of explaining the falsity or inaccuracy of their descriptions. I do not suggest that this is impossible, in some cases it is not even difficult, but there may remain cases where we have no explanation and it seems reasonable to leave the matter there. The point is that the lack of a suitable explanation of reports, other than their truth, is a consideration against rejecting them, but it is only one consideration and it is defeasible in various ways. The explanatory requirement[32] is an ingredient in the overall verdict, along with the internal and external circumstances mentioned earlier. I think it very unlikely that any hard and fast rule can be laid down for determining the outcome of such assessments of so diverse factors—what is required, as Locke saw, is not a criterion but a judgement.

[32] Reverting to our earlier discussion of Bayes's Theorem we can see how the explanatory requirement can be expressed in its terms. If you have a good explanation of how a rejected report came to be made you can set $P(B/K)$ quite high and so tend to depress the value of $P(A/B\&K)$.

11

The Disappearance of History

'The action of time enfeebles then, without ceasing, the probability of historical facts just as it changes the most durable monuments.'

(Pierre, marquis de Laplace)

Having enunciated this thought, the eminent mathematician Laplace went on gloomily to conclude that the temporal process, together with the persistence of 'physical and moral revolutions', would end by 'rendering doubtful after thousands of years the historical facts regarded today as the most certain'.[1] Laplace's thought, or something very close to it, is found much earlier in John Locke's *Essay Concerning Human Understanding* and in John Craig's *Mathematical Principles of Christian Theology*.[2] Locke's essay was published in 1689 and Craig's curious treatise in 1699.

In Locke's discussion of this idea it is quite clear that we are confronting a general issue about the transmission of information and not a problem peculiar to History with a capital H. As Locke puts it:

. . . any testimony, the further off it is from the original truth, the less force and proof it has. The being and existence of the thing itself, is what I call the original truth. A credible man vouching his knowledge of it is a good proof; but if another equally credible do witness it from his report, the testimony is weaker: and a third that attests the hearsay of an hearsay is yet less considerable. So that in traditional truths, each remove weakens the force of the proof: and the more hands the tradition has successively passed through, the less strength and evidence does it receive from them.[3]

In what follows I shall principally discuss Locke's view and his arguments for it, though I shall also refer to Laplace's formulation of a probability argument for the position. For ease of exposition and to support my perhaps overdramatic title I shall call the view, 'the disappearance of history thought' or DOHT for short. (It does not of course maintain that history, or historical writing will literally vanish but rather that the evidential credentials of well-established facts will become negligible as they recede in the distant future. There will always be some historical

---

[1] Pierre, marquis de Laplace, *A Philosophical Essay on Probabilities*, trans. F. W. Truscott and F. E. Emory (New York, 1951), ch. XI, p. 124.

[2] John Craig, 'Mathematical Principles of Christian Theology', in *History and Theory*, Beiheft 4 (1964), originally publ. 1699.

[3] John Locke, *Essay Concerning Human Understanding*, bk. IV, ch. xvi, s. 10.

certainties, of course, but which ones they are will vary significantly with the passing of time.)

John Craig's argumentation will not detain us long but his application of the DOHT is worth at least passing comment. Craig purported to show, in his chapter on 'the rules of historical evidence', that the diminution in the reliability of the Gospel history of Christ, as it underwent historical transmission, would be such that it would vanish into imperceptibility in the year 3,150. He thought that, had we been restricted to purely oral testimony on the matter, then the vanishing point would have been somewhere near the end of the eighth century. Craig's purpose was not anti-Christian; he thought he could determine the rough date of the Second Coming. He reasoned that Christ would surely come before the evidences of his life and works perished but that he would not come until very near the vanishing point of 3,150. In support of the second clause he cited Luke 18: 8 where Christ says 'Nevertheless, when the son of man cometh, shall he find faith on the earth?' and Craig takes this to express a doubt about how probable the Gospel history will then be. Craig's sensitivity to Scripture impressed theologians as little as his mathematical calculations impressed probability theorists. Laplace commented pithily on the latter that 'his analysis is as faulty as his hypothesis upon the duration of the moon is bizarre'.[4] (Unfortunately I have been unable to trace this, undoubtedly spectacular, hypothesis.) None the less, what Laplace disliked was Craig's mathematics; as we have seen, he explicitly endorsed the guiding idea behind the analysis.

Yet surely the DOHT should be more disturbing than Laplace and Locke seem to have found it. That Locke had some slight misgivings seems indicated by his comment towards the end of his discussion. He says that he

would not be thought here to lessen the credit and use of *history*: it is all the light we have in many cases, and we receive from it a great part of the useful truths we have, with a convincing evidence. I think nothing more valuable than the records of antiquity: I wish we had more of them, and more uncorrupted. But this truth itself forces me to say, That no probability can rise higher than its first original.[5]

He goes on to attack the idea that some claim initially asserted with little evidence could become more probable by being often repeated. Of course, the idea that repetition conveys no increase in probability is quite different from the view that it decreases the probability, though the former follows from the latter. A few sentences later Locke once more asserts the DOHT and seems to see it as at least part of the reason for holding the weaker thesis about no increase in probability.

David Hume, in his confusing discussion of the problem, is explicit

---

[4] Laplace, *Probabilities*.
[5] Locke, *Essay*, bk. IV, ch. xvi, s. 2.

about the subversive nature of the DOHT. Hume's treatment of the issue occurs in his section of the *Treatise* devoted to the rather baffling topic of 'Unphilosophical Probability'. After mentioning Craig's argument which he misdescribes, perhaps with intentional irony, as 'a very celebrated argument against the *Christian Religion*', Hume says that

it must be confest, that in this manner of considering the subject, (which however is not a true one) there is no history or tradition, but what must in the end lose all its force and evidence. Every new probability diminishes the original conviction; and however great that conviction may be supposed, 'tis impossible it can subsist under such re-iterated diminutions.[6]

Hume thinks that he has a solution to the problem, or at least to a variation of the problem, and so he does not actually despair of history. His solution, however, requires premisses which are either false or highly debatable. The basic idea of his solution is that the most certain historical facts from the remote past have been transmitted in such a way that 'the links' which connect the past fact to the present impression, though 'innumerable', are none the less 'all of the same kind'. Hence, there is 'no variation in the steps' and 'the mind runs easily along them, jumps from one part to another with facility, and forms but a confused and general notion of each link'. In this way the vivacity of the impression is preserved and with it Hume's theory of belief which he sees the DOHT as endangering. It would take us too far into the shadows of Hume's psychologism to pursue his argument here but it seems to depend on the idea that the present knowledge of some historical fact requires both that the knower be directly acquainted with all the links in the chain of transmission and that he know them all to be of 'the same kind'. The former seems to me to be false and the latter merely to raise the question of transmission once again concerning the nature of the links.

I do not myself want to be committed in what follows to the view that when we reasonably believe some historical fact we do so on the basis that we ourselves are actually acquainted individually with some testimonial chain stretching back to the past event or situation in question. This idea is absurd, as Professor Anscombe has pointed out.[7] What seems compelling, however, is that when we have such beliefs we are committed to the existence of such chains and it is their nature which interests me in what follows and which interested Locke, Laplace, and the others. Their idea, as I see it, is that there is something about the nature of such chains which will make our historical beliefs rationally insecure. This is what produces the DOHT.

That the DOHT is a genuinely surprising thesis seems clear when we

---

[6] D. Hume, *A Treatise of Human Nature*, bk. i, part iii, s. 13, p. 145.
[7] G. E. M. Anscombe, 'Hume and Julius Caesar', *Collected Philosophical Papers*, i (Oxford, 1981), 86–92.

reflect that we do not appear to have less of a right to be certain now of the existence of Thomas Aquinas than Descartes had, or less entitlement to our belief that Julius Caesar was assassinated (Locke's example) or that Napoleon invaded Russia, than the respective contemporaries of those worthies had. Nor, coming nearer to home, is our conviction any less epistemically secure that Britain and Germany fought a war between 1914 and 1918 than it was for those people who believed it, on other's say so, thirty, forty, or fifty years ago. Nor does it seem any more believable that, barring cataclysm, those who live in 2083 will have less reason to accept such beliefs than we do now merely because they have acquired those beliefs from us and our successors. Yet, if the DOHT is correct, these firm convictions and thousands more like them are mistaken. We should obviously scrutinize very carefully the case for the DOHT.

In fact there are different cases or different versions of the case. I shall begin by presenting one that greatly impressed Locke but which does not seem to me to have much independent force (what I mean by 'independent force' should become clear). Locke claims that there is a rule in English law which 'if it be allowable in the decisions of right and wrong, carries this observation along with it, *that any testimony, the further off it is from the original truth, the less force and proof it has.*' This rule he cites as follows: 'though the attested copy of a record be a good proof, yet the copy of a copy, ever so well attested, and by ever so credible witnesses, will not be admitted as a proof in judicature.' And he adds approvingly, 'This is so generally approved as reasonable, and suited to the wisdom and caution to be used in our inquiry after material truths, that I never yet heard of any one that blamed it.'[8] Locke then immediately proceeds, in the passage quoted at the beginning of this paper, to extend the rule to cover all hearsay evidence and within a few sentences we have arrived at the DOHT. Locke's move from the somewhat limited case of document copies is probably based upon the idea that the document rule is only a special case of the more general restriction in English law on the admissibility of hearsay evidence. In any case, neither the specific nor the broad legal prohibition is as impressive an index of rationality as Locke believed.

In the first place, the rule about documents is today by no means so watertight as Locke suggests that it was in seventeenth-century English law. I cannot speak for the accuracy of his account of the state of the seventeenth-century law but the contemporary situation is summarized and illustrated by Cross as follows:

There is authority for the view that the copy of a copy is inadmissible, but there is also authority on the other side, and there seems to be no reason why the copy of a copy should not be received in evidence provided the witness producing it, or some other witness, makes it clear that the copy produced is a true copy of the first copy and that that copy was, in its turn, a true copy of the original. In R. v Collins it

---

[8] Locke, *Essay*, bk. IV, ch. xvi, s. 10.

was necessary for the prosecution to prove that the accused knew that his bank account was inoperative. The prosecution called an assistant bank manager who produced a copy of the unsigned carbon copy of a letter sent by his colleague to the accused informing him that his account was closed. The accused had been called upon to produce this letter and, as he had not done so, secondary evidence was admissible. But the Court of Criminal Appeal held that the letter had not been properly proved by the bank manager because he did not swear that the copy produced was a true copy of the carbon or that the carbon was a true copy of the original apart from the signature. Had the bank manager testified to these matters, it seems that the court would have considered the letter to have been properly proved by his evidence.[9]

In the English civil law there is now no restriction upon copies of copies . . . of copies of documentary records.

In the second place, the general inadmissibility of hearsay[10] evidence in the English law, upon which Locke may have thought the documentary rule rested, is itself not as compelling as laymen are inclined to believe. To begin with there are many systems of law in which a formal hearsay restriction has no place, and hearsay evidence is now admissible (with some marginal restrictions) in English civil law. Moreover, even within the English criminal law there are numerous categories of exception to the hearsay rule and there are as well many influential voices that favour either further relaxation or even abolition of the rule. As noted in Chapter 2, the exceptions to the rule are numerous and wide-ranging, although the principles (if any) underlying them are sometimes unclear.

In the third place, the transmuting of legal rules and restrictions, even from the law of evidence, into logical or general methodological prescriptions is fraught with danger. Prior to 1898 the English criminal law would not allow an accused to testify in his trial and prior to 1851 the civil law prohibited testimony being given by anyone who had an interest in the issue at trial—i.e. basically the plaintiffs and defendants. One can see some point in the prohibitions but it would surely be rash to generalize them in the way that Locke seems to be doing in the case of the hearsay (or more narrowly, the document) restriction. The rashness would not only be demonstrated by the fact that the subsequent abandonment of these rules casts some doubt upon the parallel claim for their wisdom, caution, and reasonableness but also by what the generalizations would commit us to. They would presumably go something like the following:

1. The testimony of anyone who speaks in his own defence against some allegation or criticism is necessarily evidentially weaker than that offered on the same matter by someone differently placed.

---

[9] R. Cross, *Evidence*, 3rd edn. (London, 1967), 498–9.

[10] Cross's definition of hearsay was cited in Ch. 3. His final, refined version goes as follows: 'express or implied assertions of persons other than the witness who is testifying, and assertions in documents produced in the court when no witness is testifying, are inadmissible as evidence of the truth of that which was asserted' (ibid. 387).

2. The testimony of anyone who stands to benefit or suffer directly from the outcome of the issue to which their testimony is directed is necessarily evidentially weaker than that offered on the same matter by someone differently placed.

There is a problem about the relations between (1) and (2). Both incorporate the idea that partiality may produce defective testimony but, where (2) alone would put the defender and his accuser on the same footing, the combined effect of (1) and (2) is to make the defender less believable than the accuser or anyone else who stands to gain from the outcome and to make both categories of witness less believable than anyone who has no stake at all in the outcome. If we symbolize the defender as D, the accuser or other interested parties as A, and the outsiders as O then in terms of the relation rationally less believable than ($<$) the combined effect of (1) and (2) is $D < A < O$ where $<$ is of course transitive.

But this just shows the dangers of treating legal rules in the way Locke treats the document rule. After all, the category A (the other interested parties) not only includes those who may have as great or even greater interest in having D convicted as he has in being acquitted, but it also includes all his associates who may have as great or greater interest in having him acquitted as he has himself. In fact, we are usually, in ordinary affairs of any moment, very interested in hearing what a person has to say in his own defence and on his own behalf and make no assumption that his accuser is more likely to be telling the truth than he. In this we are surely right. In themselves, the relations of defender or accuser confer no difference in credibility upon what is maintained and so the $D < A$ part of the generalization is unconvincing. Are things any better with the $< O$ part of the story? Here it may be thought that the 'outsider' who stands neither to gain nor to lose by the outcome must be more reliable because of his impartiality. It is indeed true that, considered purely in terms of these abstract relationships to the issue, he is less liable to the temptation to lie because we are assuming in our definition of the characterization 'outsider' that this is so. Yet two things need to be said about this.

The first is that very few actual people, if any, fit such a characterization. There are, of course, impartial people but they are not necessarily people who have nothing to gain from, or no interest in, the outcome of an inquiry, but rather people whose interest in and concern for the truth dominates whatever other interest they have in the proceedings. It may be doubted whether there are any 'outsiders' whose interest in the proceeding is so neutral that no description of it can be found which will rank, in the abstract, as a factor tending to bias. The most neutral observer is liable to have an interest in having his general outlook on the world, or certain aspects of it, reinforced by what he has experienced and this can lead to dramatic error. Years ago, the Harvard psychologist Gordon Allport, in his studies of this phenomenon, showed a group of subjects a drawing of several people on a subway train including a white man and a black man apparently engaged in a heated argument. The white man had a 'cut-throat' razor in his hand. After a brief viewing of the picture, about 50 per cent of the subjects reported that the razor was in the hand of the black man. This seems to be a case in which 'neutral' observers got things wrong because of an, as it were, subterranean, interest in conforming their particular experiences to their more general expectations.[11] This is clearly not a peripheral problem with testimony, as hardly needs demonstrating, though there are plenty of empirical studies to demonstrate it.

The second thing that needs to be said about the characterization 'outsider' is that the disadvantages that may arise from the partiality of an interest may be counterbalanced by the disadvantages that lack of interest may create. After all, a strong interest in some issue makes one pay a lot of attention to what is going on; the attention may be biased by the strength of the interest but the observation will not suffer from the dangers attendant upon casual concern. Lack of a strong interest in the issue or the outcome is liable to produce unfocused attention and lack of detailed observation. Roughly speaking, testimony can fail either through deceit or mistake and if partiality mostly induces deceit, indifference mostly induces mistake or inaccuracy. I conclude therefore that even the < O part of the generalized version of the nineteenth-century legal restrictions is un-convincing as a quite abstract proposition about categories of witness, and its implausibility should give us pause about Locke's generalization of the document rule.

In the fourth place, it is, as the above considerations might already have made us suspect, a debatable point whether the document and hearsay exclusionary rules are based on the sort of concern identified by Locke at all. Locke takes it that the rules express a concern that initially reliable evidence must become less reliable as it passes through more and more hands (or throats), but legal textbooks give a quite different analysis of the rationale for such exclusionary rules. We may best approach this by a brief comment on the exclusionary rule, which once prevented the accused from testifying. We treated this as embodying the idea that an accused's testimony was likely to be unreliable, but in fact the prohibition seems to have been predominantly brought about by the desire to protect an accused against the possibility of self-incrimination and, in particular, against the imputation of guilt which it was feared would arise from an accused's refusal to testify. Many lawyers opposed the abolition of the restriction for just this reason and in contemporary law there are still problems relating to the accused's testifying or failing to testify, such as the legitimacy of the judge's commenting adversely upon a refusal to

[11] See G. Allport and L. Postman, *The Psychology of Rumour* (New York, 1965), *passim* and for more discussion Ch. 15 here.

testify. Clearly, many pragmatic considerations, such as worry about how an innocent but nervous defendant would stand up to ruthless cross-examination, have a bearing on such legal rules.

With the document and hearsay restrictions the most plausible account of their legal justification seems to be that which invokes the desirability of all evidence conforming to the adversarial framework of the English criminal law, in particular, that all evidence be subject to cross-examination and to the solemnity of the oath (or its secular variant). By its nature, hearsay eludes these requirements in their usual sense because the witness who puts the relevant proposition before the court cannot be required to swear to its truth (she may not even believe it) and she is not in a position to be cross-examined fully on the circumstances in which her informant came to believe it.[12] Part of this anxiety about cross-examination comes from the desire to see fair play done and to ensure that there is little room for doubt that it is done but some of it does come from an interest in evidential reliability. The moral in this interest, however, is not that drawn by Locke. After all, an interest in having the opportunity to cross-examine on oath the original witness either of an event in issue, or more specifically of the first making of a copy, need not be prompted by any scepticism about the chain of transmission. It may rather be governed by a desire to test the veracity and competence of the original witness. And indeed this does seem to be the principal element in the rationalization of the hearsay rule both historically and by way of judicial elaboration, although the legal tradition contains a confusing and confused variety of assertions and arguments about the rationale for the rule. Lord Normand's summary of the case against hearsay exhibits the non-Lockean interpretation of the point of the rule very clearly, 'The truthfulness and accuracy of the person whose words are spoken by another witness cannot be tested by cross-examination and the light his demeanour would throw on his testimony is lost.'[13]

But the most telling evidence about the legal significance of the hearsay rule comes from the rationale for many of its exceptions. To illustrate from some of the categories mentioned earlier: the exception in favour of dying declarations for instance (which forms part of a wider range of exceptions on behalf of statements by deceased persons) seems plainly based on the idea that someone having a 'settled hopeless expectation of death' would not wish to die with a lie on his or her lips. Similarly, a declaration against interest (pecuniary or proprietary), on the part of a person now deceased, is admissible—subject to the usual baroque circumstances and interpretations—and the plain rationale of this lies in the idea

---

[12] Cross-examination as to material issues is not out of the question since it may be addressed to the circumstances of transmission and to eliciting more hearsay of an evidentially significant kind.
[13] Cross, *Evidence*, 479.

that someone who knowingly states something to his own positive dis-
advantage is unlikely to be lying. Confessions and admissions are likewise
admissible hearsay on the same sort of grounds, and the category of *res
gestae*, complex and strange as it is, seems allowed as an exception because
the causal surroundings of the utterance make it unlikely that the original
speaker was deceitful, the extreme case of this being one where the utterance was wrung from the speaker by the pressure of emotion or events.
More generally, it seems to me to be clear that the most plausible account
of the rationale of the hearsay exceptions is that they are believed to be
cases where the risk of the original statement having been falsely made is
minimal. There is no suggestion that such cases involve a diminution of
transmission risks. It should, of course, be noted here that one general
motivation for several of the exceptions may well be the desire to get hold
of evidence relevant to the matter at trial which would otherwise be totally
unavailable. This is particularly clear in the cases of deceased persons but
the law is reluctant to admit necessity as a rationale for any of the
exceptions.

It may be urged against me, at this point, that my criticisms are fudging
on a crucial issue concerning the interpretation of the term 'hearsay'. The
exceptions to the hearsay exclusionary rule and the campaign to abolish
the rule altogether are only concerned with a certain sort of hearsay, it
may be said, namely, hearsay at one remove. Where we have what is
sometimes called in the law, 'hearsay upon hearsay' there can be no
question of the English law admitting so dubious an article. Moreover, this
kind of hearsay introduces precisely the sort of chain of transmission on
which Locke's misgivings were concentrated.

In reply to this I would first point out that Locke's position is that any
hearsay, even what we might call primary hearsay (where the witness had
his information from the first observer or source), suffers from the decline
in evidential value to which he hopes to call attention. Admittedly, it is not
so great a diminution at one remove as at a thousand but its existence was
thought significant enough for Locke to see it as justifying the documentary exclusion rule about the copy of a copy.[14]

Secondly, it is false that English law has no truck at all with hearsay
upon hearsay, although it is true that it is less tolerated than primary
hearsay. One very important category of evidence which essentially
involves hearsay upon hearsay is that of reputation, evidence as to which is
the standard method of proving character. There are many curiosities
about the law's obsession with reputation but they need not concern us
now. The point is that, given the view that a person's character is best
ascertained by finding out what is widely believed about his character,

---

[14] For Locke the first copier is like the actual witness to an event so that his copy is like
such a witness's report. The second copier is then like the giver of primary hearsay, i.e.
hearsay at one remove.

then evidence about what is widely held to be his character must involve a degree of reporting what others report that others report, and so on. Similar considerations apply to attempts to establish questions of public rights where the deliverance of tradition and repute are crucial. A very good example of this occurred in a case before the Supreme Court of the Northern Territory in Australia in 1971 in an action by several Aboriginal clans against a mining company. The Aborigines sought to prove ownership and rights in a large area of land in the Gove Peninsula and this required that evidence of their practices and beliefs for the period roughly from the coming of the Europeans in 1788 to 1936, the date of establishment of a mission in the area which was argued to have changed their lifestyle. Two types of evidence were called, testimony from Aborigines as to what they had been told and expert anthropological evidence. Both were objected to as hearsay but the judge ruled the evidence admissible under hearsay exception clauses relating to public right[15] and to expert evidence. Both clearly involved hearsay upon hearsay. A characteristic piece of evidence, for instance, was for a witness to say, 'My father (now dead) said to me: this is the land of the Rirratjingu.' The father's own knowledge of this fact would itself partly depend upon his having been told similar things—though it would also depend upon the observation of certain behaviour and practices. As for the anthropologists, much of their expertise consisted in close familiarity with the oral traditions of the clans, but the judge ruled that this was an essential ingredient in their scientific knowledge and he was not prepared to regard such expertise as less admissible than the expertise of doctors or physical scientists.

Thirdly, much that is excluded by restrictions upon derivative hearsay surely constitutes evidence that a tribunal proceeding along rational lines should have before it. Glanville Williams constructs the following case in which evidence so excluded might have prevented a serious miscarriage of justice:

A and B, aged sisters, are both lying ill when they hear that their acquaintance X has been arrested on a serious charge. A realises that she saw X board a train at a place and time which were inconsistent with his guilt, and she tells this to B just before dying. B communicates this to C, the parson, just before she too dies. The information chimes exactly with X's alibi defence at the trial.[16]

Presuming the *he* survived long enough, what the parson could tell the court would surely be weighty, indeed decisive, evidence. Yet in fairness to Locke it should be said that the Law Reform and Criminal Law Revision

[15] The case in question is *Milirrpum and others* v. *Nabalco Pty. Ltd. and the Commonwealth of Australia*, 17 FLR 141, Blackburn J. in the Supreme Court of the Northern Territory. There were two separate grounds for admitting the evidence under the heading of public right, one concerned declarations of deceased persons as to public right and the other general reputation. (pp. 154–5)

[16] *Criminal Law Review* (1973), 139. (Also in Cross, *Evidence*, 481.)

Committees who recommended the abolition, subject to certain safeguards, of the exclusionary rule in the case of primary hearsay none the less favoured the continued exclusion of hearsay upon hearsay on the grounds that it was too unreliable. It is interesting in connection with Locke's document example, however, that they recommended that hearsay upon hearsay should be allowed in the case of documentary records, as it is already in the civil law.

I propose to leave the legal argument here for the time being. It has I think illustrated two things, namely, that an appeal, such as Locke's, to the wisdom of the law is at best inconclusive and that hearsay of one kind or another is an indispensable element in many legal proceedings. If history must disappear it seems that law must be at least seriously diminished. To DOHT we may have to add DOLT (diminution of law thought) and this without even having considered the considerable degree to which the very procedures of the law are dependent upon the reliability of legal history.

What of Locke's underlying philosophical argument, an argument which resurfaces in more mathematical terms in Laplace? 'No probability can rise higher than its first original', says Locke. And he goes on to say,

What has no other evidence than the single testimony of one only witness must stand or fall by his only testimony whether good, bad, or indifferent; and though cited afterwards by hundreds of others, one after another, is so far from receiving any strength thereby, that it is only the weaker. Passion, interest, inadvertency, mistake of his meaning, and a thousand odd reasons or capriccios men's minds are acted by (impossible to be discovered) may make one man quote another man's words or meaning wrong.[17]

Clearly, the basic philosophical idea here is that the later reports in a chain must suffer a decline in probability because the factors which can go wrong in the case of the original observer are not only repeated each time in each transmitter but have other factors such as 'mistake of meaning' added to them. It is this idea which attracted the attention of Craig, Laplace, and other theorists of mathematical probability. Assigning an initial credibility ratio to the original witness which was supposed to allow for the possibility of such mistakes (and of course for the possibility of deceit), these theorists then assigned credibility ratios to the later witnesses in the chain and by various mathematical calculations inevitably derived a lower ratio for the final credibility of the message.

The formulae used by different theorists are quite varied and illustrate once more the extraordinary disarray amongst probability theorists who write on issues to do with the probability of testimonies. Noting that the theory of testimony, or of the combination of the evidence of witnesses, has occupied a considerable space in the traditional treatment of mathematical probability, Keynes commented, 'It may, however, be safely

---

[17] Locke, *Essay*, bk. IV, ch. xvi, s. 11.

said that the principal conclusions on the subject set out by Condorcet, Laplace, Poisson, Cournot, and Boole, are demonstrably false. The interest of the discussion is chiefly due to the memory of these distinguished failures.'[18] On our present topic Keynes mentions half a dozen authors who have provided mathematical solutions and dismisses all but one of these. Forewarned by the list of distinguished failures and C. S. Peirce's sombre cautionary remark that 'this branch of mathematics is the only one, I believe, in which good writers frequently get results entirely erroneous',[19] I shall not adjudicate upon the merits of different mathematical proposals, nor indeed discuss them at all. It is an interesting question to what extent the probability we are concerned with when discussing the reliability and credibility of witnesses is susceptible of such 'Pascalian' treatment. Jonathan Cohen has argued that there is another kind of probability, which he calls 'Baconian', which is required to explicate many of the ideas of probability used in connection with legal proof and especially proof by testimony.[20] Cohen thinks that this non-Pascalian notion has quite wide applicability and his views may well have a bearing on our topic, but I mention them only because of this possibility and I shall not pursue the issues raised by his book any further. My reluctance to do so stems partly from certain doubts I have about Cohen's project and partly from limitations of time and capacity. My procedure will instead be to present an account of the materials upon which any theory of the probability of historical transmissions must operate. This account will differ from the Lockean perspective and will, I hope, do something to undermine or at least mitigate the scepticism of the DOHT.

Let me begin by making a general observation about the credibility of witnesses which does apply fairly directly to the various mathematical calculations with which probability theorists have tried to estimate the reliability of witnesses. To say the least, the idea of a witness having a credibility ratio for telling the truth in the way that a dice has a certain chance of coming up six is very curious. The mathematical tradition is full of talk about witnesses who tell the truth twice as often as they say what is false or who have a credibility ratio of .8 or whatever, but, as C. S. Peirce pointed out long ago, this kind of talk is very close to fantasy. It is not only that, in the case of real people, we have no way of computing such ratios. More importantly, the idea of such ratios fosters the illusion that people are like coins in having a quite general tendency to come down on one side or the other, a tendency which a long enough trial of their

---

[18] J. M. Keynes, *A Treatise on Probability* (London, 1963), 180.

[19] Peirce adds, 'it may be doubted if there is a single extensive treatise on probabilities in existence which does not contain solutions entirely indefensible': 'The Doctrine of Chances', in *Collected Papers of Charles Sanders Peirce*, ii, ed. C. Hartshorne and P. Weiss (Cambridge, Mass., 1960), para. 648.

[20] L. J. Cohen, *The Probable and the Provable* (Oxford, 1977), part I, pp. 5–47.

utterances would reveal. But people are not like that. They do not have quite general tendencies to lie, whatever the context or subject-matter, nor to make mistakes in abstraction from particular circumstances. Richard Eggleston reports that in his extensive experience of the law he found that witnesses who would not be prepared to lie to gain a personal advantage, and who were ready to speak awkward truths on matters which they thought relevant to an inquiry, would none the less lie about matters which they thought irrelevant to the facts in issue when the truth would prove embarrassing, as they believed, for them or for others. Eggleston argues plausibly therefore that, even as a working rule, the maxim, 'Falsus in uno, falsus in omnibus' misdescribes normal psychology, though in the law of evidence it has the prestigious endorsement of Wigmore and is implicitly followed in much legal practice.[21] I am not of course denying that we trust some people more than others but I do not think this licenses the talk about credibility ratios. This general point has some relevance to the issues raised by the DOHT and I will return to it later.

The first thing to notice about the Lockean version of the DOHT is that it gives a misleadingly unilinear picture of the transmission of testimony about historical matters. Restricting ourselves, for the moment, to oral transmission only, we can represent Locke's picture diagrammatically as follows:

(1) $p \sim Aap—Bap—Cap—Dap—Eap— \ldots Nap$

(where p is the fact or putative fact attested, $A, B, C, \ldots N$ are the witnesses in the chain, Aap means A attests that p, and $\sim$ is the source relation, typically observation, while—is the transmission relation). This is clearly a fairly simple testimony chain, yet even its simplicity conceals some ambiguity because it should be distinguished from a related but rather different chain in which the various witnesses merely testify that the previous testifier has told them that his predecessor has told him that his predecessor . . . that p. So we might have:

(2) $p \sim Aap—BaAap—CaBaAap—DaCaBaAap \ldots$

In its pure form (2) only operates with short chains for obvious reasons. We should not expect someone who is involved in a (1) chain to be able to produce a very lengthy (2) chain in support of the truth of p. Another possibility that might occur to one would be:

(3) $p \sim Aap—BaAap—CaBap—DaCap \ldots NaMap$

in which each witness but the first testifies that the previous witness has told him that p. However, all the steps subsequent to $BaAap$ in (3) misrepresent the communication since B did not himself endorse p as true, nor did C, D, and so on. Perhaps a better representation of something related to this that does happen is:

(3′) $p \sim Aap$—$BaAap$ & Bap—$CaBap$ & Cap—$DaCap$ & Dap ...
    $NaMap$ & Nap

These complications echo the discussion of hearsay in Chapter 2, and
what I there called the 'pure case' of hearsay or transmission is best
represented either as (1) or as a mixed case of (1) and (3′). What either
choice reflects is that appraisal and endorsement are at the heart of the
transmission of testimony, although this allows for differences in the
degree of endorsement and for feigned endorsements and so on. As we saw
in Chapter 2, this is the obverse side of the fact that the typical stance of
the recipient of testimony is that of trust. When I trust a primary witness
(say, one who purports to have seen an animal whose presence is unusual
in these parts), I am relying on the conviction that his word reflects an
exercise of certain visual and cognitive skills as well as his honesty. In turn,
I exercise certain skills in passing on the information which those who
trust me know or assume that I have. These include perceptual, memory
and verbal capacities, but also powers of appraisal which I have exercised,
no matter how informally, in my acceptance of the original claim. (The
gullible are those whose powers of appraisal are very weak.) The com-
patibility of appraisal and trust was argued in Chapter 2, but I shall take
these reflections no further now, since, in the context of the DOHT, I want
to concentrate upon the sort of transmission represented by (1). (Adjust-
ments could easily be made to accommodate (3′) or a combination of it
and (1).)

I said that the Lockean picture was too unilinear and what I meant by
this was that the transmission of public facts seldom proceeds in so
isolated a fashion as (1). Not only are there several such chains leading
from p but the individual chains are themselves more ramified than (1).
Where there are several simple chains like (1) the possibility of corroboration and of comparison of reports arises. Both of these afford the opportunity of confirming the truth of the report or of its kernel or at least of
securing no deterioration of its probability. Indeed, corroboration further
down the chain may increase the probability of the original report of a
single witness.

$$
(4) \quad p
\begin{array}{l}
\nearrow Aap\text{—}Bap\text{—}Cap\text{—}Dap \searrow \\
\sim Qap\text{—}Rap\text{—}Sap\text{—}Tap \rightarrow Eap \\
\searrow Wap\text{—}Xap\text{—}Yap\text{—}Zap \nearrow
\end{array}
$$

Using this very simplified model we would surely imagine that E is in a
stronger position with regard to having reliable belief that p than D, T, Z,
C, S, Y, B, R, or X. He may even be better placed that A, Q, or W. This
last suggestion may seem impossible but we can imagine circumstances in
which A is more confident that he has correctly observed that p when he
knows that Q and W have also, so that if *he* can be better placed by
corroboration then surely the hearsay corroboration that E receives may

put him in a better epistemic position than *A* in his uncorroborated state. Suppose *p* is the proposition that the lesser crested twit was in Cambridge in the early weeks of March. The bird is very rarely seen in Cambridge and even more rarely as early as March. It also has some resemblances to the more common, garden twit. *A*, *Q*, and *W* are all experienced ornithologists and although the sighting is indeed of the lesser crested twit they each, unaware of the others' sightings, have a certain diffidence in their judgements. They are confident enough to pass the message on and to do so without qualification. The chain of transmission goes, in each case, through expert mouths until the ornithologists down the line *D*, *T*, and *Z* each communicate their news to *E* who is editor of the ornithological magazine *The Early Bird*. He is somewhat doubtful when he hears from *D*, impressed when he hears from *T*, and quite convinced when he hears from *Z*. He would, of course, be less entitled to his confidence were *D*, *T*, and *Z*'s reports not the outcome of independent chains or were he to believe that they were not. But they are and he rightly believes so. We may even suppose that he has good reason to believe so. My point here is only that where such transmission patterns exist the later hearsay testifier may be in as good if not better a position than even an original witness. This seems to be a case where, contrary to Locke's claim, we can give a reasonable sense to the idea that a probability has risen in the course of transmission higher than its original. Let us call such patterns corroboration chains. A corroboration chain gives the final receiver additional grounds for confidence both that the original witness was reliable and that the chain of transmission was reliable. But it is still a fairly simple model. One way in which it can be complicated and, at the same time, made more realistic is by complicating the message, since it is, after all, exceptional for transmission to concern only one proposition; and another way is to exhibit chains of quite different messages which taken together make each more credible; another again, is to complicate the pattern of transmission of single messages, i.e. to complicate (1). We should also remember that a certain sort of non-corroboration can give us greater confidence in the authenticity of a message. Take the example of the military commander who sent a message back to headquarters through a chain of messengers. The message that eventually reached HQ was 'Send three and fourpence, we're going to a dance', but what he originally said, of course, was 'Send reinforcements, we're going to advance'. The story (I don't now recall where I read it) seems to support the DOHT but let's suppose the commander sent messengers by four different routes establishing four different chains and back at HQ they got four different messages as follows:

(*a*) Send three and fourpence we're going to a dance.
(*b*) Send reinforcements, we're going to a dance.
(*c*) Send three and fourpence, we're going to advance.
(*d*) Send reinforcements, we're going to advance.

The recipient of these messages would have no trouble, in context, in working out the real message and so the reliable chain, even if he otherwise knew nothing about the reliability of the different messengers in each chain. This example illustrates the sort of critical intelligence which historians use in assessing both documentary testimony and oral traditions. It is partly a matter of the broad or prior likelihood of any such message in the setting of a military campaign and partly the consonances and the dissonances revealed by comparison of the four messages. Indeed, if we go back to the first sort of complication mentioned, we find that where a message is more complex than that supposed in (4), or indeed in the military message, then historians tend to become suspicious of a very high degree of fit between different transmission chains. As Marc Bloch puts it:'criticism oscillates between two extremes: the similarity which vindicates and that which discredits'.[22] Bloch gives the example of the battle of Waterloo and says that while we would expect independent witnesses to agree on the great fact of Napoleon's defeat we would doubt their independence if they agreed exactly in their descriptions of battle details and even closely in the language they used. He is concerned with comparing original testimonies but the same point would apply to the purported independence of transmission chains for complex propositions.

I mentioned earlier that the picture could be made more realistic though more complex by considering the way in which chains of transmission of quite different facts could reinforce their respective credibilities. A simple enough case would be to suppose that an event like the 1983 Australian bushfires, astonishing in their extent and ferocity, had taken place amongst people more primitive and rude than even contemporary Australians are believed to be. Four different propositions might then come down by four different chains to an inquiring anthropologist of posterity: (p) huge fires burnt through great areas of forest near town M; (q) town M was covered in strange dark clouds and ash fell from the sky; (r) the summer of that year was terribly dry and hot; (s) there had been drought in the areas around M for several years before and including that year. These propositions (in this highly artificial example) would support each other and provide a form of corroboration if the chains were really independent. This kind of mutual support from different traditions is something which historians certainly appeal to.

It is time to complicate the simple transmission chain of (1). Clearly, when actual historical chains are produced they will tend to ramify in ways that make such patterns as (1) exceptional. One such ramification is (4), except that in all but its final stage it is a mere compound of patterns such as (1). In fact something like the following is not only possible but probably rather common:

[22] M. Bloch, *The Historian's Craft* (Manchester, 1954), 115.

$$(5) \quad p \sim Aap \overset{\displaystyle Cap \to Gap}{\underset{\displaystyle Dap \triangle Eap}{\overset{\displaystyle \diagup}{\underset{\displaystyle \diagdown}{Bap}}}} \begin{array}{l} Jap \dots \\ Iap \dots \\ Fap \diagdown Hap \dots \\ Kap \dots \\ Lap \dots \end{array}$$

On the face of it this looks as if it supports the DOHT because if we think of each vertical line as a successive 'era' then it looks as if what (5) adds to (1) is so many more opportunities of distortion or error in any given span of time. But interestingly (5) also adds a feature which counts against DOHT: two or more recipients at any one time (in any one 'era') will have learnt that p from different sources and two, or more, different recipients will have learnt that p from the same source. So, for example, K will have learnt that p from G and E, and K will also form with J and I a group who all have G as a common source. This then provides the possibility of a certain sort of cross-checking of the accuracy of the transmissions. K, for instance, can check for divergences in the stories he is told by G and E and check up on the consistency of G's narration of what is supposed to be the same attestation told to J and I, and he can also compare E's performances with H and L. This does not show that no mistakes can occur but it does show that more possibilities of correction and consolidation exist than Locke's picture of transmission allows. It also shows that we need not think of the various recipients in the chain of transmission as predominantly passive except for their contributions to error and deception. Certainly, where transmission takes place in a context of concern for getting at the truth and sifting evidence, we should think of the recipients as to some degree critical and intellectually active. Such contexts are preeminently those in which a science of history exists, but an awareness of the problems posed by conflicting testimony and some understanding of circumstances that promote or hinder reliability is presumably as old as humankind though, of course, the effects of different cultural situations should not be ignored. (Vansinna's comparison of the Rwanda and Burundi peoples in Africa is to the point here. He argues that their very different political arrangements made the Rwanda very conscious of and sensitive to history, whereas to the Burundi it was a nuisance. For the Burundi, as he puts it, 'It was in everyone's interest to forget about history.')[23]

If we now combine the ideas exhibited in (4) and (5) we get a picture with even more ways of ensuring reliability, since each of the individual chains in (4) may be construed on the model of (5) and, moreover, there may be and probably will be cross-overs from each of the chains to the others, thus allowing for more possibilities of comparison and checking.

---

[23] Jan Vansinna, *Oral Tradition: A Study in Historical Methodology* (Harmondsworth, 1973), 166.

To get a really complete picture we should add in the element of collateral corroboration illustrated earlier in the example of the bushfire. I shall not attempt to provide a picture of this state of affairs.

Another aspect of the oral transmission of history is that there are ways in which the reliability of the witnesses in the chain can be made very high indeed. Much oral tradition in societies without writing is strongly institutionalized so that specially selected people are given the privilege and onerous duty of being the custodians of the society's past. The histories are often in the form of songs or poems and they are learnt off by heart by specialists from specialists. In some societies, there are not only privileges for such people but heavy ritual sanctions against mistake.[24] It is an interesting aspect of the study of such communities that *accuracy* of transmission seems to go with *frequency* of transmission. It is readily intelligible why this should be so but it is worth noting because there may be a tendency to think (perhaps under the influence of the DOHT) that the more often a story is told, even by the same person, the more liable it is to be erroneous.

There is another important fact ignored by the DOHT and that is the possibility of checks on the reliability of an oral tradition which are themselves either utterly or partially independent of the tradition. Archaeology is one of the most important of these,[25] although there are serious problems about ensuring that the oral tradition does not derive illicitly from a later acquaintance with the archaeological remains. Vansinna gives a good example of archeological confirmation of an oral transmission. Nkole traditions

maintained that a certain site, which had clearly been occupied by an earlier people had served as residence for two different kings at some distance apart in the dynastic genealogy. Excavations showed that, unknown to the inhabitants of the region, a second site lay buried beneath the first one, which was very much smaller than the first. Thus the tradition was correct in maintaining that the place had been twice occupied, and very probably it also gave the correct names to the kings that were said to have lived there.[26]

Other disciplines such as astronomy, linguistics, carbon dating, and the study of handwriting, even entomology, can make important contributions[27] (though some are more relevant to written history). Astronomy, for instance, can provide information about an eclipse which may confirm claims in a particular oral tradition.

There is a quite different type of case which calls for consideration here. It is a type of case which gains its interest from an exploitation of one

[24] Ibid. 41.

[25] See Peirce, 'Answers to Questions Concerning My Belief in God', in *Collected Papers*, vi, para. 513, p. 350.

[26] Vansinna, *Oral Tradition*, 175.

[27] Ibid. 173.

part of Locke's position against another. Locke claims both that 'any testimony, the further off it is from the original truth the less force and proof it has' and that a better proof of some proposition is necessarily provided by 'a credible man vouching his knowledge of it' than by others 'equally credible' attesting it on his say so. But a testimony may be further off without passing through intermediate hands and this gives rise to the possibility that the original witness *at a later date* may give a less reliable report than someone who has his information from a chain of transmission emanating from that same original witness. And such a possibility is surely eminently realistic. Consider a man, A, who is the only witness of an assassination. Killer, victim, and bodyguard are all dead. A tells his account of the assassination to B in great detail while it is fresh in his mind, and B tells it to C and C to D and so on, in a transmission chain lasting fifty years at the end of which time M^{23} tells it to N^{23}. A in the mean time has never repeated his narration to anyone else—perhaps he was so shocked by the events he witnessed that he entered a Carthusian monastery. After fifty years, however, the circumstance arises for him to tell his story to Smith, who a day or so later gets the transmitted version from N^{23}. The details differ considerably and the question arises: whose report is the more reliable? Although it is true that the transmission has created possibilities of mistake, deceit, etc., it is also true that A's failure to repeat the story publicly over that lengthy period of time creates a general possibility of memory failure of a different but perhaps more alarming kind. If we know that A has excellent short-term memory but very bad long-term memory and, in addition, that all the transmitters in the chain are 'equally credible' to A, in the sense of having very good short-term memories, then we shall (in the absence of other information) surely advise Smith to credit N^{23}'s version above A's. Here we have a situation in which the original witness is less credible than witnesses many removed who owe all their information to him. Of course they owe it to an earlier report of his and he is indeed not only less credible than they but less credible than he was himself fifty years earlier. The example therefore does not refute the strict letter of Locke's position so much as cast a certain amount of doubt upon its spirit.[28]

I have proceeded against the DOHT by showing that transmission is a much more complex business than Locke and the others suppose. I want now to pursue the suggestion that even the most simple model of transmission has features which the DOHT cannot accommodate.

I do this partly because of the intrinsic interest that such an undertaking has and partly because it is relevant to an objection that may be made against my line of argument to date. This objection, which I owe to some comments of David Lewis, may be viewed as expressing a degree of

---

[28] This example and the point it makes was suggested by a remark of Joseph Raz.

scepticism about the way in which the complications of (4) and (5) really deflect the DOHT. No doubt the complications and the other considerations about critical intelligence, such as those to do with the use of ancillary evidence (like the findings of archaeology) suffice to show that Locke and the others had an impoverished conception of historical understanding and investigation.[29] None the less, so the objection runs, the DOHT may surely be refurbished to state an interesting sceptical or pessimistic truth about history as so enriched. For if we consider transmission as involving chains like some combination of (4) and (5), it will still be the case that the whole thing, considered as a process of information-conveying, of whatever internal complexity, will be subject to the inevitable decline in evidentiary value highlighted by the DOHT. Consider any such complex chain CH which embodies all the evidence there is for an historical proposition *p*. Suppose also that my arguments establish that CH *need not* involve any diminution in the credibility that attached to *p* in its initial communication by the first witness or even that it might involve an increase in credibility. (It should be noted that my view is not that history *cannot* disappear in fact, only that it *need not* disappear on account of DOHTian arguments.) However, it will be urged by the objector, the extant evidence for *p*, embodied in CH, must reduce in value simply by persisting through time and being conveyed through generations of communicators.

Now I cannot deny that this thought has a persisting power (which does not itself seem to diminish with time and reiteration by objectors—to this I can testify!). Yet I think it suffers from the same defects as the simple version of the DOHT it seeks to replace. Once more the idea of a simple unilinear chain has reasserted itself. The objector imagines CH as a complex whole which produces a message which is then passed on in a unilinear chain subject to the rigours of the DOHT or perhaps as itself a message which must be passed on in this way. But my critique of the DOHT is precisely aimed at subverting the necessity of such a picture. The point is that, for any position in time, the reception of CH, or its message, may be mediated by a chain of exactly the same credibility-maintaining form as CH itself. Such chains enable a community to have a hold on its history which is greater than merely unilinear chains would allow. These considerations seem to me to defuse the objector's attempt to repair the DOHT but lest the attempt still seem seductively appealing it will be instructive to look more closely at the simple, unilinear model of transmission and the features it can possess which are inimical to the DOHT.

The most striking difficulty here is that even with such simple transmission patterns as (1) it seems that there are circumstances in which they

---

[29] See, for instance, L. D. Reynolds and N. G. Wilson, *Scribes and Scholars: A Guide to the Transmission of Greek and Latin Literature* (Oxford, 1974), and esp. ch. 6 on 'Textual Criticism'.

can give rise to an increase in the reliability of the information conveyed. It may be, for instance that some member of the chain has a particular expertise in the subject-matter being reported and/or she may be a particularly good judge of the reliability of her informant and perhaps of other informants in the chain. Suppose that you are in the American West in the 1850s and it is important to know whether there are hostile Indians about. You are a member of a wagon train which has the redoutable Kit Carson as scout but you are also dependent upon several inexperienced people who perforce must do some of the scouting. They often report the sighting of hostile Indians and they genuinely see Indians but the question is whether they are right to see them as hostile (i.e. as belonging to, say, the ferocious Apache rather than the more pacific Cheyenne). They report, initially, to Carson but the vast majority of such reports he does not pass on to the wagon-master. He can tell from the associated descriptions of the Indians, from the nature of the countryside and the general incompetence of the reporters about such matters that their reports are unreliable. The witnesses tell other officials who pass the reports on undiscriminatingly to the wagon-master. He consults with Carson who tells him that the reports have little likelihood of being true. A new man joins the caravan whom Carson recognizes as a knowledgeable and trustworthy frontiersman travelling incognito (let him be the famous 'Uncle' Dick Wootton). The new-comer then reports a few days later that he has sighted a band of hostile Indians approaching the wagon train's projected path. He identifies them as Apache. It is not likely that there are Apache this far North but it is possible and, knowing Wootton's skills, Carson passes the information on to the wagon-master who knows nothing of Wootton's capacity other than that Carson has seen fit to trust his report. Let us symbolize Wootton as W, Carson as C, the wagon-master as M, and one of the inexperienced but improving scouts who has been getting instruction from Carson and proving a good pupil as I. For the wagon-master, the chains (6) and (7) below are less to be relied upon than either chains (8) or (9).

(6) $p \sim W—M$
(7) $p \sim I—M$
(8) $p \sim W—C—M$
(9) $p \sim I—C—M$

So, by passing through more hands, even in a unilinear chain of transmission, the testimony has become more credible. This clearly contradicts Locke's version of the DOHT quoted at the beginning of the paper and enables us to find a clear sense in which even the very strong claim denounced by Locke that a probability 'can rise higher than its first original' seems to be true. It is even likely that once I hears C tell M what I has told C then the claim that p becomes more probable for him.

There seems to be a parallel with expertise about sincerity. M may have more legitimate confidence in the truth of p in (8) above than in (6), in the case where C is someone he can rightly trust in the matter of determining the honesty of such as W.

It is natural to object to much of the above in the following way:

> Your counter-example to the DOHT does not show that unilinear transmission can avoid the problems posed for the DOHT, because it is not the *transmission* which succeeds in improving or preserving the credibility of the message. Rather, it is certain extraneous features of the situation in which transmission takes place, features such as Carson's *knowledge* of the abilities of the original observers, his *experience* of the surroundings, his *inferential* capacities and so on. These are not intrinsic to the testimony chain, but factors which operate on the message it produces.

In some respects, even if this objection were successful, it would concede quite a lot. It would rescue the DOHT as a thesis about transmission, understood narrowly, but surrender it as a thesis about much actual communication and husbanding of historical facts. Such communication commonly embraces precisely the 'extraneous' factors complained of.

None the less, the objection is misconceived in a more fundamental way. The idea of narrow or pure transmission with which it operates is not in fact a version of testimonial transmission at all. It is of the essence of hearing a witness and passing on what he has to say that you treat his communication as a worthwhile contribution to settling some issue. If you pass the message on as a piece of testimony, you have already judged it in a certain way, bringing powers of assessment and discrimination to bear upon it. You have, at a minimum, judged it in the way required by the definitional analysis of Chapter 2, which, *inter alia*, requires an assessment of the competence of the speaker. More substantially, you will judge how reliable the communication is and endorse it appropriately. This may range from the thought that the message is worth passing on, though with no great conviction as to its truth, to, at the other extreme, emphatic endorsement. No great degree of conscious deliberation need be involved in these processes and, characteristically, it is not. We operate with our *learning* skills as automatically as we do with our perceptual, memory, and inferential powers. Someone we trust, or have no reason to mistrust, tells us something important and we pass it on to those it may concern, frequently not even bothering to let them know that our information is second-hand. At other times, we may have some reason for caution about the message, but pass it on 'for what it's worth'. If we sound no note of caution we are properly understood to be giving some reasonable degree of endorsement to the message.

Of course, as always, there are peculiar cases that require some qualification to the account. As we saw in Chapter 2, not only can endorsement vary in degree, but circumstances may demand that a speaker subdue, or even suppress, his own critical faculties, and pass on what he has been told in a spirit of 'take it or leave it'. Standardly, this would either be contextually clear or made explicit by the speaker. In the legal context, for instance, a witness before the court may simply be asked to present what he was told (in a case where hearsay is allowed), in spite of his having made it clear that he does not trust his informant's word. This will most readily occur when an audience has reasons for wanting to form its own unmediated judgement on the worth of the third party's evidence. There are other deviations from the pure case of transmission, such as the link which preserves the truth unintentionally, and in spite of the agent's exercise of critical powers. As mentioned in Chapter 2, someone may seek to deceive an audience by passing on, as endorsed, a true communication which they have wrongly judged to be unreliable. This is necessarily uncommon, but it does happen, and it is no part of my case that it does not.

Let us return to our objector. At best, the objection models transmission on the deviant cases, especially the 'take it or leave it' type; at worst, it assimilates transmission to mere mimicry, like a series of parrots imitating each other. The objector's model does not apply to normal transmission, though it may seem to apply to certain transmission-related ways of preserving information, such as a series of copyists working to preserve an original document. Even here, however, there is more in the way of assessment going on than the model suggests, as the study of how actual scribes proceeded clearly shows.[30]

This concludes what I have to say about oral transmissions. It may be thought that I have discussed it too much for, after all, the greater part of historical transmission involves documents, records, history books, and other *written* testimonies. Moreover, these are surely more solid than oral tradition. I hope my discussion has shown that oral history need not be as weak a reed as those in literate cultures have tended to think but I am happy to concede the case that written records establish a security against memory lapses and similar possibilities of mistake which is a very important ingredient in the reliability of transmissions. Locke, Laplace, and others see the DOHT as applying to written transmission as well as oral, though Laplace, at any rate, recognizes the greater security afforded by printing as a very important factor. My concentration upon oral tradition was however dictated by two considerations (apart from its intrinsic interest which seems to me to be high), namely, (*a*) the strategic point that if the much greater reliability of documentary transmission is allowed then a case against the DOHT made in terms of oral history becomes that much stronger when applied to written history and (*b*) the important philosophical point that all written history is underpinned in certain complex ways by oral tradition. Let me turn to (*b*). When Locke is talking of a chain of copies of copies what he has in mind is something like this:

[30] Ibid.

(10) $x \sim A$ copies x producing x^1—Bcx^1px^2—Ccx^2px^3 ...

As Hume remarks of this sort of progression: 'each copy is a new object, of which the connexion with the foregoing is known only by experience and observation'.[31] When, however, we think in terms of documentary records now (for instance, of the documentary records of the First World War) we tend to think of the written evidence as itself preserved by methods which are not subject to the frailties of testimonial transmission. Modern techniques of preservation and copying have eliminated many of the possibilities which worried Locke so that it may seem that our diagram for the modern situation should just be the continued existence of x through time or, recalling the use of printing and photocopying techniques, something like the continuance of x and the continuance of its exact replicas and exact replicas of them and so on. None the less, the irrelevance of testimonial transmission in this context is only apparent, as we can see by asking how someone who is not acquainted with the original document knows that what he is given is indeed a copy or replica of the original. Perhaps he replies that 'it' says so in the document or on an accompanying document or in the book in which it is reproduced, or that he was told so by the librarian. The 'it' mentioned does not eliminate testimony but indicates that our man is relying on what I have elsewhere called institutional testimony—the sort of testimony that is enshrined in publishing practices as well as signposts and maps. Rather than go into that issue at any length now, let me just suggest that the modern transmission of documents and records involves a more complicated version of the following simple pattern for the transmission of a single document. (Think of it as a deed granting some sort of title or privilege to a village— the document is stored in the town hall and guarded by the official keeper. It is handed on from generation to generation and from time to time within generations it is hauled out by the keeper for inspection and for lending to interested parties whose credentials are well known.) Treating A as the original guarantor of the authenticity of the document x, K as the first keeper, K^1 as her successor, K^2 in turn as the next keeper, and B as the borrower who attests the authenticity of x on returning it to the keeper's care, we may see the second line of the diagram here as illustrating the way in which simple testimonies, often of an oral nature, will underpin the reliability of apparently straightforward documentary persistence (symbolized by the first line).

(11) x- -
     A attests x—K attests x—K^1ax—Bax—K^1ax—K^2ax—...

This diagram is not as perspicuous as it should be but I hope it begins to get the basic idea across. This idea requires us to allow a chain of oral

---

[31] Hume, *Treatise*, bk. i, part iii, s. 13, p. 145.

transmission to accompany and partially to underpin written transmission, so that Locke's worry is not totally irrelevant even to modern written history. Not only do the considerations already mentioned in connection with oral transmission apply here as well, but also another very important consideration which is that the piece of information to be transmitted is relatively simple, something like: 'This is the title deed entrusted to my care'. This contrasts with the oral transmission of, say, the memorized details of a battle. It is more like the great fact of which side won, or better still, that there *was* a battle. Of course even the perception and memory of such great facts may be subject to hyperbolic doubt but I think it fair to construe Locke's paradox as arising out of more everyday worries than that.

12

Dretske's Drinker

In a recent paper[1] Fred Dretske has argued that two very plausible epistemic principles are vitiated by counter-example. The first principle (A) concerns the closure of knowledge under known implication and the second (B) concerns the transmission of knowledge. Here I shall principally discuss the second but since I also treat briefly of Dretske's denial of the first, I shall begin by quoting his formulation of both.

(A) If S knows that P, and knows that P implies Q, then (assuming S accepts Q as a result of this knowledge) S knows that Q.

(B) If S knows that P then (given the satisfaction of certain conditions relating to S's sincerity, the willingness of S's audience to accept what S says as an honest expression of what he knows, etc.) S can bring his listeners to know that P (can *inform* them of P) by telling them that P (p. 109).

As Dretske says of B, 'It is hard to see how something like this principle could fail to be true if communication is possible and education occurs. For the way we know much of what we know is by hearing it from others who know' (p. 109). Plausible, and even compelling, as this principle sounds, Dretske challenges it with a counter-example.

George is a wine-lover especially fond of wines from the Medoc region of Bordeaux. His remarkable palate always enables him to distinguish Medocs from other wines and he is generally very knowledgeable about wines except for the alarming flaw that he thinks Chianti is a Bordeaux wine. He can tell a Chianti from a Medoc, of course (and, presumably, from other Bordeaux), but 'has the vague idea that "Tuscany" is the name of a wine-growing region in southern Bordeaux' (p. 110). George is served a rather ordinary Medoc at a dinner party and the following day, in response to a question about what wine was served, tells Michael only that it was a Bordeaux but a rather undistinguished one. Dretske argues that Michael does not thereby know that the wine served at the dinner party was a Bordeaux although George does know that and the further conditions of principle B are satisfied. Michael does not know because: 'For all he has been told, it might well have been a Chianti. George, in fact, would have said precisely the same thing had it been a Chianti. He often

---

[1] Fred I. Dretske, 'A Cognitive Cul-de-Sac', *Mind*, 91 (Jan. 1982). Page refs. to this paper will appear in brackets in the text.

has. Therefore, (B) is false' (p. 110). The basis of Dretske's objection is rephrased in more general terms a little later when he says, 'You cannot learn that *P* from someone who tells you that *P* if they would say that *P* *whether or not P*, and this holds even if the person happens to know that *P*' (p. 110).

The problem then for principle B is that Michael cannot know that *P* by way of George's testimony, because relying on George's word would yield the belief that *P*, *whether or not P*. It seems that Dretske is committed to an analysis of knowledge which employs as a necessary condition a subjunctive conditional to the effect that where *P* is not the case then the agent will not think that *P*. Robert Nozick has recently produced an analysis employing such a 'tracking' conditional and its most developed form makes reference to a method or way of believing. Nozick's statement of the relevant conditional, his clause (3), is as follows:

(3) If *P* weren't true and *S* were to use *M* to arrive at a belief whether (or not) *P*, then *S* wouldn't believe, via *M*, that *P*.[2]

The relevance of this to Dretske's example is that Michael, relying on George, would (according to Dretske) believe *P* even where *P* is not true. So the suggestion is that he wouldn't know, because he fails to satisfy some such condition as (3). There are presumably other ways than Nozick's of formulating a negative tracking conditional which would cast light on Dretske's use of 'whether or not'. I use Nozick's clause because, in the absence of an explicit formulation by Dretske, it provides a clear and fairly plausible explication of the intuition to which Dretske makes appeal. The explication is particularly plausible given the broad similarity of their approach to epistemology—a similarity acknowledged by Nozick in a footnote.[3] In what follows, references to (3) should be read as indicating Nozick's conditional or any other that could plausibly capture the intuition.

Once Dretske's intuition is brought into sharp focus, however, it no longer seems so obvious that it serves the purpose for which it was invoked. On the basis of this test George is supposed to know but Michael is not. Closer attention to the relevance of condition (3) to the example shows that it is implausible to treat Michael's plight as different from George's. My claim will be that Dretske's recourse to a 'whether or not' condition like (3) creates a dilemma for his treatment of George and Michael. If Michael does not know, for the reasons given by Dretske, then neither (for the same reasons) does George. If, however, George's knowledge claim survives the test of (3) then it is hard to see why Michael's is

---

[2] Robert Nozick, *Philosophical Explanations* (Oxford, 1981), 179. I have made Nozick's usage, in the quoted passage, consonant with Dretske's by symbolizing the known proposition with a capital rather than a lower-case '*p*'.
[3] Ibid. 689 n. 53.

not equally safe. Either they both know or neither knows. I think in fact that they both know but here I plead only for consistency.

Let us begin with George's position. It is crucial to the counter-example that George knows that the wine he was served was a Bordeaux. But does he? After all, if George would sincerely say that the wine he was served was a Bordeaux whether or not he was served a Bordeaux then he would think that it was a Bordeaux whether or not it was a Bordeaux. He often has. So there are cases in which George, using M (his taste-buds and taste experience) thinks that P even where P is not the case. Hence George fails to satisfy (3) and he does not know. But if George does not know in the first place, principle B is secure.

One might object to this (as I suspect Dretske would) that, although it is true that George would sincerely *say* that the wine he was served was a Bordeaux even if it were not, it is not true that he would *think* it was a Bordeaux even if it were not. This apparently desperate resort might be made more plausible, not to say swallowable, by the following explication.

The circumstances in which George would think that the wine was a Bordeaux when it was not are not relevant to the present case which is neither one in which he has been served a Chianti nor (apparently) one in which a Chianti is in the offing. Moreover, George knows, at least, that it is not a Chianti, since he knows from the taste that it is a Medoc. So the present circumstances are not such as to license our saying that George would think the wine was a Bordeaux whether it was or not. Drawing on the terminology of an earlier paper of Dretske's we might put it that there is in this case no 'particularised'[4] possibility that George would have been served a Chianti. Hence, in the circumstances of this case, it is unfair of me to conclude from the truth of, 'George would sincerely say that the wine he was served was a Bordeaux even if it were not' to the truth of 'George would think that the wine he was served was a Bordeaux even if it were not'.

But is this unfair? What is Bordeaux for the goose is also surely Bordeaux for the gander. Dretske may be right to insist on a particularized possibility for the case of George's knowledge but, in all consistency, the same must be said of Michael's situation as well. If the possibility of having been served a Chianti is ruled out for George by the circumstances of the actual case then why is that ruled-out possibility relevant to Michael's epistemic status in what is the same case? If particularized possibilities save George's knowledge, why don't they save Michael's? Or if they wreck Michael's, how can they fail to wreck George's too?

The interpretation of conditions like (3) is, in general, problematic and is especially so in epistemological contexts. Given possible situations ('worlds') in which George will think he has had a Bordeaux when he has

[4] Fred I. Dretske, 'Conclusive Reasons', *Australasian Journal of Philosophy*, 49 (1971), 11.

not (and so mislead Michael) the question is whether such worlds are so related to the actual world as to make (3) true or to make it false. My own inclination, subject to some misgivings about the incomplete description of the example, is to say that George does know and so does Michael. More generally, however, I cannot see that reliance upon a subjunctive conditional such as (3) can fail to cut equally both ways. Dretske makes it seem otherwise by interpreting the conditional one way in the case of George and another way in the case of Michael. None the less, there are certain ways of thinking of Michael's situation which can tempt us to believe that he does not know although George does. I shall discuss them in turn.

(*a*) It may be suggested that, *for all Michael knows*, George was served Chianti and so falsely reported that he had a Bordeaux. This makes Michael's position very different from George's and ensures that he does not know that George was served a Bordeaux. But this objection is question-begging because it assumes, in the premiss beginning, 'for all Michael knows . . .', that Michael does *not* know that George was served a Bordeaux. It is indeed part of the description of the example that George knows, prior to his conversation with Michael, that the wine is not a Chianti, whereas, prior to that conversation, Michael does not. This can hardly be relevant, however, since Michael knows very little that is pertinent to the dinner party prior to his conversation with George. For all Michael knows, prior to the conversation, George was not even served a wine—yet clearly this does not prevent his knowing it after the conversation.

(*b*) It may be claimed that if Michael were to learn the truth that George thinks Chiantis are Bordeaux he would surely no longer know (or perhaps even believe) that George was served a Bordeaux on this occasion. Hence he does not now know it. Defeasibility examples like this, usually aimed at undermining justification conditions, are common in the philosophical literature on knowledge but their effects on intuition are notoriously variable. One thing is generally agreed: not all cases in which there is some evidence which if the subject knew of it would destroy his entitlement to knowledge do in fact defeat his claim. My own intuition is that Michael's status as a knower remains undefeated but, in any case, this type of objection cannot help Dretske. The problem is that the objection is two-edged since there is also a truth which, if George were to learn of it, would place him in an analogous situation. This is that one of the styles of wine which George firmly believes to be a Bordeaux is not a Bordeaux.

(*c*) It may be urged that there is a crucial difference in the status of the evidence that George and Michael have for their common belief that the wine was a Bordeaux. George's evidence is that it tasted like a Medoc and he knows that all Medocs are Bordeaux, so it is plausible to think that he would not have this evidence for his belief unless his belief were true.

Michael's evidence is that George says that the wine was a Bordeaux and this we might suspect is evidence he would have even if his belief that it was a Bordeaux were false, i.e. in the circumstance that it was a Chianti. This objection, although not explicit in the paper under discussion, has the advantage that it mirrors a condition for knowledge given in Dretske's earlier paper 'Conclusive Reasons' (i.e. if S knows that P on the basis of evidence E then E would not be true unless P were).[5] Similar difficulties to those already encountered arise for this suggestion. It is not clear how we can treat as true the claim, 'it is possible that Michael should have had this very evidence but his belief have been false', without making it true also that 'it is possible that George should have had exactly the evidence he had but his belief have been false'. We could treat Michael's evidence as merely some utterance of George's to the effect that some wine he had at a dinner party was a Bordeaux, but then why not treat George's evidence equally abstractly as some taste sensations which he identifies as belonging to a type of wine which he believes to be a Bordeaux? To do so is to allow that in both cases the evidence might remain the same and the beliefs be false. We are presumably prohibited from taking this path by the requirement of particularized possibilities but, if we particularize the possibilities, it is no longer at all clear that Michael's actual evidence could have obtained unless his belief were true.

It should be noted that Dretske's denial of the unrestricted validity of principle A is relevant to the issue of whether George knows. To subvert A, Dretske uses a variation on the George–Michael counter-example. I find it unconvincing but that will concern us shortly. The point here is that if we give up A then one crucial prop for the belief that George knows that the wine was a Bordeaux is undermined. The prop is the idea that George must know that the wine was a Bordeaux *because* he knows that it was a Medoc. I think it is clear that Dretske is relying on this to persuade us that George does know that it was a Bordeaux—he refers, for instance, to George's knowledge that it was a Medoc as 'the evidence he had for thinking it was a Bordeaux' (p. 111). Yet if George knows (1) that the wine he had was a Medoc, and (2) that if it was a Medoc, then it was a Bordeaux, and accepts therefore that it was a Bordeaux, he may, according to Dretske's own views, none the less not know that it was a Bordeaux. And perhaps he does not, if he would hold the view that the wine he drank was a Bordeaux even where it had been a Chianti.

What then of Dretske's critique of principle A? George forgets that the wine was a Medoc but remembers that it was a Bordeaux and tells Susan as much, adding that it was therefore French. Dretske holds that Susan does not come to know thereby either that it was a Bordeaux or French. Nor, says Dretske, does George know that it was French, even though he

---

[5] Ibid. 12.

knows that it was a Bordeaux and that its having been a Bordeaux implies that it was French. So A is false.

In so far as the success of this argument against A turns on the view that George originally knew that the wine was a Bordeaux, the argument is doubtful since, as I have argued, that view may be untenable on Dretske's own principles. Even allowing that George originally knew it was a Bordeaux, Dretske is in no position to hold that he still knows it at the later date. As Dretske himself says, the later George is in 'precisely the same position that Michael was earlier. From all that George's memory "tells' him the wine they served could have been a Chianti. And if it was a Chianti, it was Italian, not French' (p. 111). Nor Bordeaux, of course. Here Dretske seems to have forgotten that Michael is not supposed to know that the wine was a Bordeaux. Clearly if, for all George's memory 'tells' him, the wine could have been a Chianti, then George does not know, when talking to Susan, that the wine was a Bordeaux. For this reason alone the counter-example must fail to touch A.

Finally, there is the question of how an adequate transmission principle should be formulated. Any plausible principle of this kind should refer not only to sincerity but to the speaker's competence as a witness and yet there is no explicit reference to this in Dretske's presentation of principle B. Testifying is just one speech act amongst many which has a competency condition.[6] Utterances about the future are not promises unless the speaker has certain powers to influence the future and someone who is blind cannot testify to what he has seen even if he happens to utter the truth about what has occurred. Similarly, in a court of law, only an authority of a certain kind can give the relevant expert evidence. It may well be that Dretske intends to capture this in his claim that S knows that P. If so then S's knowledge entails his competence about P-matters and this is precisely why it is so hard to accept that his listeners do not know when they trust him. The crucial question, on this way of viewing matters, is whether George is really competent about Bordeaux wines. If we decide that he is then we will treat his views and utterances, where true, as knowledge and his listeners will come to know from them. The fact that on the rare occasions[7] when he is mistaken they will be also merely exhibits the truth that no source of knowledge is infallibly reliable. On the

---

[6] In this discussion of competence I have had to ignore many of the complications that are involved in a fuller treatment of the transmission principle. For instance, competence about P-matters looks part of a jointly sufficient set of conditions but it may not be necessary since it may be enough for someone to show a related competence, e.g. about who has trustworthy competence about P-matters. This raises the general question of hearsay testimony. Cf. Ch. 2.

[7] Dretske says that George has 'often' declared a wine to be a Bordeaux when it was not. Perhaps it is best to treat this 'often' as rhetorical exaggeration, since if George is wrong so frequently it becomes very much less plausible that he knows in this case. If the 'often' is rhetorical, my point about rare occasions stands. If not, George is at least clearly incompetent about P-matters.

other hand, if we decide that George's Chianti defect is sufficient to disqualify him from competence about Bordeaux we will find it perfectly intelligible that an audience cannot come to know from his utterances on the subject, even where they are true. What will remain puzzling is how someone who lacks competence about Bordeaux wines can himself know such things as that the wine he had was a Bordeaux (without knowing it on the authority of another). One way to describe George's plight, as Dretske presents it to us, is that he knows the wine was a Bordeaux but is not generally competent about Bordeaux. I am not sure that this is a coherent suggestion for someone who purports to know at first hand but, if it is, then a properly formulated transmission principle remains untouched by the counter-example. The fact that George knows will not be enough to satisfy the transmission principle, he will have to be competent as well.

This last point may seem to leave Dretske's position relatively unscathed. It remains true, on this understanding of the matter, that George has knowledge which ends with him and so there is still a cognitive cul-de-sac. It was one of Dretske's chief aims to show that there could be an 'incommunicable piece of knowledge'. But there are two problems with this response. Firstly, the cul-de-sac was principally worrying just because it provided a counter-example to an otherwise acceptable transmission principle mirroring our well-founded reliance upon testimony. It does not do so, however, since an adequately formulated principle is immune to it. Secondly, the idea of a knower who lacks competence being thereby unable to pass on his knowledge becomes itself so much less surprising in the light of the amended transmission principle. After all, if we recall the sincerity conditions specified by Dretske, it is not at all surprising that violations of those conditions result in incommunicable knowledge. The compulsive liar cannot pass on his knowledge and, more significantly, neither can the notorious liar, even when he is telling the truth. Such dead ends need not constitute a serious epistemic traffic hazard.

V

The Applications

13

Collingwood and Historical Testimony

No Egyptologist has ever seen Ramses. No expert on the Napoleonic wars has ever heard the sound of the cannon at Austerlitz. We can speak of earlier ages only through the accounts of eye-witnesses ... No-one would dream of denying the element of truth in these remarks. Nevertheless they demand considerable modification.

(Marc Bloch, *The Historian's Craft*, 48.)

Although there are many different philosophical hares that could be started by the use of the term 'historical fact' I am interested in pursuing one that is related to the historian's attitude to testimony. By way of preliminary, however, I should say something about my use here of the word 'fact'. A contrast that sets off my use best is probably that between fact and theory. Some of the complexities that lurk beneath the deceptively still surface of this contrast have already been discussed. As we saw in Chapter 3, any such distinction is at once methodological and epistemological, in that it concerns the structure of inquiry as well as the structure of secure belief. As far as inquiry is concerned, it is plausible to suppose that an investigation begins with a problem or a puzzle, the delineation of which requires certain data in the form of propositions that are known to be true, or are taken for granted or commonly agreed upon as sufficiently secure to provide a grounding for the inquiry. It is to cover such data that I am using the word 'fact' and hence it will not refer to just any true proposition. Theories, however, stand as the outcome of inquiry and involve generality and inference and classification in a way that facts do not. It is interesting that the term 'datum' came into use in English at the same time (the middle of the seventeenth century) that the word 'fact', which had meant 'a deed or action', acquired the sort of meaning that interests me here. This seventeenth-century sense is defined by the *OED* as

Something that has really occurred or is actually the case; something certainly known to be of this character; hence a particular truth known by actual observation or authentic testimony, as opposed to what is merely inferred, or to a conjecture or fiction; a datum of experience as distinguished from the conclusions that may be based upon it.

This definition incorporates the idea that the facts are *known* to be true and it may be that the notion of data is less demanding, inasmuch as the data may be taken for granted or assumed, rather than known to be true. This difference of fit between fact and datum will not concern me greatly, since the distinguishing of facts from theories within any given inquiry should be sociologically possible without decisively determining whether all of the facts are really known. Clearly it would be possible to redescribe the situation by talking of 'putative facts' or something of the sort.

As examples of the sorts of things I mean by the term 'historical facts', consider the following propositions drawn pretty much at random from historical writings:

(*a*) 'The Treaty of Frankfurt was signed on 10 May 1871 and shortly after 30,000 Prussian troops entered Paris and stayed a short time.'

(*b*) 'Among prominent members of the Paris Commune of 1871 were a number of non-Frenchmen.'

(*c*) 'In September 1830, there were three days of street-fighting in Brussels.'

(*d*) 'Charles Albert succeeded to the throne of Piedmont in 1831.'

(*e*) 'Pius IX, on being elected Pope, pardoned all political offenders in the Papal States.'

As regards the other side of the contrast, there may be very different kinds of theory, indeed, many different kinds of historical theory. We may want a theory to fill certain narrative gaps in the facts, as when Herodotus speculates about the identity of the traitor whose information enabled Xerxes to destroy the Greeks at Thermopylae, or we may construct a theory about the motivations and reasonings of certain individuals in order to give one sort of answer to a question about why certain events took place, the occurrence of which is otherwise puzzling. Again, we may produce a theory to explain certain facts in terms of forces or tendencies or conditions such as economic pressures, patriotic fervour, or even dietary deficiencies.

No doubt the picture can be further complicated by, for instance, discussing the role of speculations, suggestions, guesses, and judgements in history, but a working distinction between fact and theory, sufficient for our purposes, has I hope emerged. If we now proceed to ask the deceptively simple question, 'How are historical facts come by?' or 'Where do historians find their data?', we shall move from preliminaries to an area of controversy and to my central concern in this chapter.

It is tempting to suppose that, since the historian is seeking truths about the human past, his facts will be provided for him by those who lived in the past, were engaged in the particular drama he is investigating, or were directly or indirectly observers of it. After all, if they do not provide it for him how else will he discover it? *He* cannot participate in or observe the events since they are, by definition, no longer accessible to such involvement. Consequently, the recorded testimony of the times would appear to be essential historical data, the very stuff of history. This natural assumption, however, has not only been challenged for its over-simplification and misleading implications but has actually been rejected out of hand, most notably by R. G. Collingwood. His views are worth examining not only because he presents the most drastic critique of the natural assumption but also because of the influence he has had upon historians reflecting on the nature of their study.

Collingwood's first line of objection against what he calls 'the common sense theory' is historical, in that he tries to show that the actual development of history and the current practice of it count against the theory. The common sense theory he defines as follows:

> If an event or state of things is to be historically known, first of all someone must be acquainted with it; then he must remember it; then he must state his recollection of it in terms intelligible to another; and finally the other must accept the statement as true. History is thus the believing of someone else when he says that he remembers something. The believer is the historian; the person believed is called his authority.[1]

This statement of the target occurs in Collingwood's British Academy Lecture for 1936, 'The Historical Imagination', but in other writings a related target or cluster of targets is attacked under the heading of 'scissors and paste history', the connection being that this is a form of writing about the past which more or less puts into practice the 'common sense theory'. Roughly speaking, Collingwood thinks that the study of the past has developed from being merely scissors and paste (or SAP, as I shall abbreviate it) in the ancient and medieval worlds, through critical history emerging about the seventeenth and eighteenth centuries, which he thinks of as only a more sophisticated form of SAP, to its culmination in the nineteenth and twentieth centuries in a genuinely scientific history which owes nothing to the methods of SAP. In simple SAP (Croce's 'chronicle') you have the collection of testimony spoken or written with the collector exercising some degree of judgement in selecting, editing, and occasionally rejecting as unreliable. In sophisticated SAP you have a more critical attitude involving a systematic examination of the credibility of authorities and an attempt to establish principles whereby such credibility could be assessed. In scientific history, or history proper, which has only emerged fully fledged in the last hundred years, you have an imaginative reconstruction of the past which proceeds by a dialectical method of question and answer from 'sources' of its own determining, which are 'put to the torture' to yield scientifically certain conclusions.

Now it is clear that even simple SAP does not embody the common sense theory as starkly defined by Collingwood in 'The Historical Imagination'. Although still too respectful to testimony for Collingwood's tastes, simple SAP already exhibits a degree of selection from and criticism of

---

[1] R. G. Collingwood, *The Idea of History* (Oxford, 1970) 234–5. Page refs. to this work will be bracketed in the text and accompanied by the initials *IH*.

texts and authorities which is not allowed by the common sense theory. The SAP man, according to Collingwood, has to ignore testimony that is irrelevant to his narrative and to choose occasionally between conflicting stories. None the less, even if we amended the theory so that it conformed to the practice of simple SAP, Collingwood would still reject it, as he rejects SAP, because it is not an adequate theory of history as we now know it.

In the first place it ignores the fact that the historical past has left traces other than testimony. In particular, archaeology has provided the historian with one way of transcending SAP by showing the importance of what are sometimes called, no doubt misleadingly, 'unwritten sources'. Hence the study of coins, inscriptions, surviving artefacts, and habitations allows the historian information about the past which is at least partly independent of testimony. In the second place, the 'scientific' historian when he uses testimony has a quite different attitude to it from the SAP man. It is not merely that he is more critical of his authorities and more aware of the need to establish reliability, for this does not distinguish him from the sophisticated SAP; it is rather that he is interested in false or spurious testimony or even the absence of testimony just as much as in reliable testimony. This shift in attitude Collingwood attributes primarily to Vico. As Collingwood puts it:

if in some source you found a statement which for some reason could not be accepted as literally true, you must not on that account reject it as worthless. It might be a way, perhaps a well-established way according to the custom of the time when it was written, of saying something which you, through ignorance of that custom, did not recognize as its meaning (*IH* 259).

The meaning involved here may be of several different kinds although Collingwood does not bother to distinguish them. It may be that the falsity of the testimony derives from our treating as literal an utterance which is intended as metaphorical or satirical or ironical or in some way symbolical and our failure to see this may involve misunderstanding a particular speaker's linguistic intentions. It may involve more than this if the speaker's performance conforms to some standard social forms (other than might be involved in ordinary contextual irony or metaphor) as when the speaker is exercising some office or going through some more or less conventional performance. Thus we may discover interesting facts about a culture by realizing that some apparent testimony is not testimony at all. Vansinna reports the case[2] of a young Rundi who recited his own verse compositions portraying himself as the killer of many enemies with lance and bow. The story seemed to be intended as a factual account with quite a lot of detail about names and places. When challenged about the truth of

---

[2] J. Vansinna, *Oral Tradition* (Harmondsworth, 1973), 89.

the recital, however, he was not the least bit disconcerted and freely admitted that he had not killed anyone. The performance belonged to a social category common in a number of African tribes and known among the Rundi as 'amazina'—poems of praise which need have no basis at all in fact though they have a factual air about them. Perhaps we can imagine some future historian of our society puzzling over the pages of *Private Eye* and, if lucky, discovering that not only is some of the magazine intended literally and some not, but that the reader is meant to have to work hard at some of the reports in order to determine which way they are to be taken. He might thus gain considerable insight into some aspects of our society. Again, we may be able to determine the meaning of a record or report in the sense of its social significance or role, even where we are uncertain of its reliability as a report of fact. It may be of interest to know that a certain story about the past is intended to provide legitimacy for present political claims, although it is difficult or impossible to determine its truth or falsity. Somewhat similarly, we may be able to determine, or at least conjecture, something interesting about the past precisely because of a lack of testimony. From the fact that the Kuba have an oral tradition about the first European to visit their country but no record at all of the second, even though the first was a merchant who merely travelled through and the second was an official who came to take over their country, we can surmise that they did not at the time realize the significance of their second visitor.[3]

So much for the illustration of Collingwood's objections: what about their force? It must be admitted that they show 'the common sense theory' to be inadequate as a theory of history. They show, that is, two things about history that the 'common sense theory' conceals from view:

1. There are other sources of historical information than printed or oral testimonies, other relics of the past, other data. (It is a further debatable question as to how 'independent' of testimony these sources are.)

2. The historian is more than a mere recorder of tradition or of the data mentioned in (1). He is also a theorist who can arrive at plausible, probable, and perhaps even certain views about the past, by reflecting on the data, or even the absence of data, in the light of his understanding of human beings and whatever contemporary knowledge is relevant to his problem (e.g. carbon-dating procedures, linguistics, etc.).

Yet none of this will serve to eliminate the appeal to testimony as a, or even the, basic source of historical data. In terms of Collingwood's classifications, he has shown that there is more to history than SAP but he has not shown that SAP is not an essential part of history. In terms of my initial distinction of fact and theory he has shown that there are more facts than testimonial facts and that there is a lot of theory, but he has not

---

[3] Ibid. 98.

shown, at least by the arguments discussed so far, that the testimonial facts are dispensable or unimportant. None the less, Collingwood's persistent declarations make it clear that he proposes a radical rejection of SAP in any of its forms.[4] So he says in expounding and obviously endorsing Croce's distinction between chronicle and history: 'Chronicle then is the past as merely believed upon testimony but not historically known ... History so far from depending on testimony has therefore no relation with testimony at all' (*IH* 202–3). And in 'The Historical Imagination' he writes: 'I am now driven to confess that there are for historical thought no fixed points thus given: in other words, that in history, just as there are properly speaking no authorities, so there are properly speaking no data' (*IH* 240). Elsewhere he asserts that belief in testimony 'stops where history begins' (*IH* 308). Plainly he needs arguments other than those so far examined to support such a position.

There is, I think, one argument only that Collingwood uses for his more radical claim, although it assumes a number of different forms which can appear to be quite unrelated. His basic argument (I shall call it 'the main argument') consists of the claim that all historical knowledge is essentially inferential and systematic and that it is the historian's imaginative reconstruction or re-enactment of the past which provides the criterion of historical fact. 'There is nothing other than historical thought itself, by appeal to which its conclusions may be verified' (*IH* 243). Consequently, reliance upon testimony (or for that matter upon pots and tombs) cannot be treated as providing the historian with data.

Before confronting this thesis head-on let us approach it through a claim which Collingwood presents as independent of the main argument, but which in the end needs to be stated in terms of it. This is the argument from the autonomy of the historian as a scientist. As Collingwood puts it:

If anyone else, no matter who, even a very learned historian, or an eye-witness, or a person in the confidence of the man who did the thing he is inquiring into, or even the man who did it himself, hands him on a plate a ready-made answer to his question all he can do is to reject it: not because he thinks his informant is trying to deceive him, or is himself deceived, but because if he accepts it he is giving up his autonomy as an historian and allowing someone else to do for him what, if he is a scientific thinker, he can only do for himself. There is no need for me to offer the reader any proof of this statement. If he knows anything of historical work, he already knows of his own experience that it is true. If he does not already know that it is true, he does not know enough about history to read this essay with any profit, and the best thing he can do is to stop here and now (*IH* 256).

Even without its devastating final flourish this argument might appear to rely overmuch on an appeal to discipline chauvinism, yet Collingwood's claims about autonomy are at once more elusive and more interesting than

---

[4] Although there are rare moments when his rejection is somewhat muted, cf. *IH* 276.

such first impressions would suggest. The notion of intellectual autonomy raises complex issues which require separate treatment, but Collingwood seems to have the idea that history as 'a science' provides its practitioners with an ideal of intellectual autonomy such that each of them must somehow do everything for himself. Or if this sounds tendentious let me put it in Collingwood's own words: 'By autonomy I mean the condition of being one's own authority, making statements or taking action on one's own initiative and not because those statements or actions are authorized or prescribed by anyone else' (*IH* 274). These are elevated sentiments but I am afraid they do not bear close examination. No SAP man has accepted testimonies into his account of the past merely *because* the statements are authorized or prescribed by someone else; even the veriest SAP discriminates between the testimony of Julius Caesar and that of a twentieth-century African tribesman with respect to the state of Gaul in 55 BC. Conversely, no amount of exercise of self-assertion can turn bad or irrelevant evidence into good and pertinent evidence or convert fantasy into fact. Some of the oddity implicit in Collingwood's stance here emerges in the following remarks:

A statement to which an historian listens, or one which he reads, is to him a ready-made statement. But the statement that such a statement is being made is not a ready-made statement. If he says to himself 'I am now reading or hearing a statement to such and such an effect', he is himself making a statement; but it is not a second-hand statement, it is autonomous. He makes it on his own authority. And it is this autonomous statement that is the scientific historian's starting point (*IH* 275).

To this one need only reply that whatever makes propositions useful as premises within an inquiry it is not the mere fact that the inquirer can state that he has heard them uttered or seen them written. A physicist is in no more or less secure possession of some experimental fact p by virtue of being able to say truly, 'I am now seeing the sentence "p"' or 'Jones is now uttering the sentence "p"', although, of course, if he is going to believe that p on someone else's word it will be necessary that he hear or read some sentence that expresses p. If we have here a sufficient condition of autonomy then an SAP man can make himself autonomous at very little cost, whilst observing exactly the same procedures as before. He only has to be a bit more long-winded.

Yet behind the muddle of this mechanical recipe for autonomy there lies what I have called the main argument and it is in terms of this that Collingwood's case against SAP and for autonomy must finally be understood. If the study of history is an inferential, systematic, evidence-regarding form of inquiry, in which the historian's imaginative re-enactment of the past is the criterion of historical truth, then it will be plausible to claim that SAP fails to live up to this standard and the historian's autonomy will consist in his exercise of the skills and powers of imaginative re-enactment.[5]

Collingwood's most vivid presentation of his thesis is in the form of an elaborate illustration, a detective story entitled 'Who killed John Doe?' In this story John Doe is found stabbed at his study desk and Detective-Inspector Jenkins of Scotland Yard must solve the crime with the help of the local constable. John Doe was in fact killed by the rector whom he had been blackmailing over a youthful indiscretion of the rector's wife. The detective-inspector reasons to the identity of the killer in a way that exhibits the programme of imaginative reconstruction and the logic of question and answer by means of which the historian determines the facts of history. As Collingwood describes the detective's thinking, it is supposed to rely not at all upon testimony, although it uses the fact that certain testimonies are given as a premiss to argue from. The detective dismisses the testimony of an elderly spinster that she killed John Doe because he had made a dastardly attempt on her virtue and the testimony of the village poacher that he had seen the squire's gamekeeper climbing in at John Doe's study window. He has no interest in these protestations, although he is intrigued when the rector's daughter confesses to the crime. Her young man, Richard Roe, is 'a medical student and presumably knew where to find a man's heart and had spent Saturday night at the rectory within a stone's throw of the dead man's house' (*IH* 267), so probably she suspects him and is trying to protect him. Richard Roe had in fact been out in the middle of the night (there had been a thunderstorm and his shoes were muddy in the morning) but he refused to say where or why because, as it turned out, he was trying to protect the rector. The detective reasons to the identity of the killer and his *modus operandi* from such clues as a lot of ashes and metal buttons in the rectory dustbin (the rector had to burn some incriminating letters and his gloves because they got paint on them from Doe's freshly painted garden gate) and certain paint smears on the cuff of a conventionally clerical jacket which was shrunk from a recent wetting and had been given by the rector to a deserving parishioner the day after the murder.

Collingwood thinks that here he has presented a paradigm of autonomous thinking which is not only independent of SAP type testimony but does not in its most important phases (the argument to the innocence of Roe and the guilt of the rector) even rely upon the detective's own statement about others' statements. As he puts it:

The essential points were that Richard Roe got his shoes muddy while going away from the rectory, that no mud was to be seen in John Doe's study and that the circumstances were such that he would not have stopped to clean or remove his

---

[5] Collingwood thinks that this will also provide a way of differentiating history from natural science and hence a link between the individual's autonomy and the autonomy of the discipline.

shoes. Each of these three points, in its turn, was the conclusion of an inference, and the statements upon which they severally rested were no more statements about other people's statements than these three points themselves. Again the ultimate case against the rector did not logically depend upon any statements made by the Detective-Inspector about statements made by other persons. It depended upon the presence of certain objects in a certain dustbin, and of certain paint-smears on the cuff of a jacket made in the conventional clerical style and shrunk by wetting, and these facts were vouched for by his own observation (*IH* 276).

There are three points to make about this claim in the context of the detective story and a fourth point about the relation of the detective's reconstruction to that of the historian's.

1. Collingwood's desire to show that his sleuth's clearing of Roe and discovery of the rector rest at no point upon autonomous statements of the form 'A told me that *p*' may well show his uneasiness with the mechanical account of that sort of autonomy which I previously criticized. None the less his sleuth's reasoning is still plainly dependent upon the initial construction that he put upon the rector's daughter's confession and Collingwood must indeed construe that as the detective's statement about another person's statement, but twice-removed, i.e. 'The constable tells me that the rector's daughter told him that she murdered Doe'. And further-more, of course, the detective-inspector believes that one of these con-tained statements is true though the other is significantly false.

2. More interestingly, Collingwood's claim about the detective-inspector's reasonings concerning 'the essential points' is simply false. The vital conclusion that Roe got his shoes muddy while going away from the rectory rests on the premiss that his shoes were muddy in the morning and this is said in Collingwood's telling of the tale to be known on the authority of the rectory parlourmaid whose testimony seems simply to have been accepted, in just the way that the wretched SAP chaps accept the ready-made statements of their authorities. Furthermore, another key fact, that there was no mud in the study, occurs in the narrative with no indication of how the inspector discovered it. Since he seems to have been called into the case rather late by the chief constable one may suspect that this was due to testimony also. There were no doubt photo-graphs of the body, but hardly of every inch of floor space near the body, and if the inspector did not find this fact out from the police who first arrived on the scene he may have winkled it out of Doe's parlourmaid, who cleaned the room the next day.[6]

I draw attention to these mistakes because they are more than mere slips. They show the way in which, even in a highly artificial piece of fiction deliberately organized to eliminate reliance upon testimony from

---

[6] This would then make two instances of failure to realize his hero's reliance on the testimony of servants, from which we may well learn something about the social life of an Oxford college at the time.

the essentials of the story, such reliance none the less persists and escapes attention since it is such a pervasive feature of the reality that the fiction is aimed at illuminating.

3. At another level again there is a great deal of material in the fabulous murder story that is highly testimony-contaminated even though it is treated by Collingwood as part of the inspector's personal observations. I have already mentioned the proposition that there was no mud on the study floor. Consider now the following propositions:

'Richard Roe is a medical student.'

'There was a thunderstorm that night between 12 and 1.'

'The metal buttons—found among the ashes in the rectory dustbin—bore the name of a famous glove maker in Oxford Street *whom the rector always patronized*.'

'They smoke all over the rectors' house' (and therefore Richard Roe would not have gone into the garden merely for a smoke).

'The girl and Richard had the drawing room to themselves ever since dinner' (and so Richard would not have had a rendezvous with her in the garden).

'John Doe is a blackmailer' (stated by Collingwood to be known 'at the Yard').

All these propositions, and more that could be cited, are known to the inspector on the testimony of others and figure in his imaginative reconstruction of the crime to a degree that seems indispensable. Some of these propositions might have been known to the sleuth by observation if the story were different, e.g. if he had also been a guest of the rector's and observed the smoking habits, the occupancy of the drawing room, and heard the thunderstorm, but, of course, he might also have observed the crime if the fictional world had been different and then he would no longer have had a problem of evidence and inference. In any actual crime puzzle or any plausible fictional simulation it is too much to hope that every such datum will be personally observed by the investigator and in any event it is difficult to comprehend how this or any similar story could be amended to make it a matter of the sleuth's own observation that, e.g., Richard Roe is a medical student, that the rector always patronizes a certain glove shop, and that John Doe is a blackmailer. Furthermore, it would defeat Collingwood's purposes to seek such recondite emendations since the strength of the fable is supposed to lie in its being typical of the scientific methods of criminal detection.

4. And finally, since the fable is intended to throw light on historical reasoning, we should be alive to the striking difference between such tales and real historical episodes. This is of course that the detective's investigation is more or less contemporaneous with the events he is exploring so that he can observe and remember and interrogate and preserve and even experiment in a way that the historian cannot. Collingwood does contrast

the methods of criminal detection and scientific history but not on these grounds. Instead, he points out that the law has to come to a quick decision and hence can be content with *less* than the rigorous proof available to a scientific historian! Of course it is true that the historian does have some advantages over a contemporary investigator in virtue of the lapse of time and some of its consequences. People caught up in some complex series of events may find it harder to get an overview of what is happening than those who investigate the events fifty (or more) years later. There is no doubt a great deal now known about the complex phenomena of the First World War which was not accessible to any given individual involved in that conflict. But part of the reason for this is that an historian will have more data available to him than a contemporary witness of the events. If he is lucky, for instance, he will be able to consult *both* German and British war records, secret files, contingency plans, political memoirs, etc., which would have been available to no single individual at the time. But although there are respects in which the lapse of time can give the historian certain advantages over the contemporary investigator, the fact is that much of what Collingwood fastens upon in the fable as distinctive of historical method is, on the contrary, only available to a contemporary investigator. In particular, the great stress he lays upon the inspector's own observations and their function in his inferences and reconstructions is possible only because the inspector is *not* doing history. Forgetting, for the moment, our criticisms of the amount of testimony and testimony-saturated 'observation' that Collingwood ignores in the detection tale, let us just list some of the facts which the inspector, or the constable, supposedly 'observes' and which the historian could only know were someone to tell him:

'Various people confessed to the murder, including the rector's daughter.'
'Richard Roe was staying at the rectory on the night of the crime.'
'John Doe was found lying across his desk with a dagger in his back on Sunday . . .'
'There was a thunderstorm that might between 12 and 1.'
'The rector took cyanide when he saw which way the inquires were going.'
'John Doe was a blackmailer.'
'Ashes from writing paper and leather were found in the rectory dustbin the day after the murder.'

Clearly this list is not exhaustive and yet equally clearly it shows that, even if we ignore objections (1) to (3) about the amount of testimony involved in the sleuth's actual procedures, we should still have to reject the suggestion that the fable lends weight to Collingwood's claims about the role of testimony in history. Hence his repeated contentions about the systematic, inferential, re-enactive, reconstructive nature of historical thought do no more than establish a role, and no doubt an important role, for *theorizing* in history. Far from such a role doing away with such data as are provided by testimony it seems to presuppose such data. It may be possible to theorize about the significance of the rector's daughter's confession and to arrive at some other truth by treating it as false, but we cannot even begin on such a trail unless we accept the truth of the report that she actually made the confession. It may be possible to speculate about Caesar's fortunes in Britain on the basis of what he fails to say in his writings, but we can only do so on the basis that they are his writings and that he truly testified to having invaded Britain at all.

Collingwood's picture of historical knowledge (for all his talk of proof, evidence, etc.) is dangerously close to fantasy or fiction. Indeed, he welcomes the analogy up to a point and sees the historian and the novelist as both engaged upon works of a priori imagination. He sees the most important difference[7] as lying in the fact that 'the historian's picture stands in a peculiar relation to something called evidence' (*IH* 246). But surely historical evidence includes the transmitted testimony of previous generations (though it may include much else)? Not so, says Collingwood, the evidence is anything present and perceptible (and it must be present and perceptible) which the historian can use as evidence. But this of course is not very helpful. If we are told that the only difference between *A* and *B* is that *A* stands in an unspecified relation *R* to something called *e* and we then ask, 'What is *e*?', we are entitled to regard our question as unanswered if we are told that it is anything which the historian can treat as *e* since it is still quite unclear what the historian is doing in treating something as *e*. Of course, it is not '*e*' but 'evidence' that is in question and the latter is an English word that we all more or less understand. Collingwood cannot take much comfort from this fact because testimony is a perfectly acceptable form of evidence as so understood. Furthermore, the idea that *x* is evidence for *y* because of the way some individual or group uses *x* is quite unclear. It is of course possible to treat notions like evidence as inquiry-relative and hence related to the activities of individuals and groups inasmuch as they conduct and initiate inquiries. In such a way of thinking about evidence there would simply be no evidence that Smith lived in Dugong Avenue unless someone had raised, directly or indirectly, a question about where Smith lived. The evidence which comes into existence with the question, however, had already existed under another title and was not created by the inquirers. There already were sightings of Smith entering and leaving the house in Dugong Avenue, listings in telephone books, electoral rolls, etc., and documents of ownership or occupancy. There is an important sense in which the relationship of these facts to the answer to the question is not at all dependent on the use made of the facts by the investigator or some group of investigators. The investigator's use of the facts will determine whether he gets

---

[7] The others are not very plausible and I will not consider them here.

the answer or not, but certain facts will support a certain conclusion independently of whether an investigator avails himself of them. Suppose certain investigators pay no heed to the sightings of Smith entering and leaving number 23 Dugong Avenue, and hold that he lived at number 41 Bunyip Crescent. Suppose, further, that they are asked why they ignore the sightings and they reply that this is simply their practice as investigators. Such a reply may show why they ignore the sightings but it does not show why the sightings do not really support the conclusion that Smith lived at 23 Dugong Avenue. To this extent, at least, that *x* is evidence for *y* is an objective matter and yet Collingwood's explanation of evidence seems to leave little or no room for this. Perhaps an appeal could be made to the 'peculiar relation' in which the historian's picture stands to the use made of present perceptions as 'evidence', but Collingwood really provides no account of this relation.[8]

What Collingwood seems most often to be trying to do is to make the historian's data depend wholly upon the historian's theorizing imagination, and when this enterprise becomes too subjective he introduces some sort of check upon the proceedings by talking about present perceptions described in terms of marks on the paper page, buildings, spoken noises (*IH* 244, 247), and so on. But this anchorage of the theorizing is only effective if the anchoring facts are not mere facts about present experience, minimally described, but facts about the past. That they are facts about the past cannot altogether be determined by the historian's imaginative re-enactments since the re-enactments can only have a genuine role in inquiry if they are built upon facts that are independent of them and, where possible, tested against other similarly independent facts. Even with a detective story the investigator may have a coherent and plausible theory of the crime only to find that it is at the mercy of one naggingly recalcitrant fact. He may of course settle for his theory *pro tem.* and hope that the recalcitrant fact can be accommodated somehow, but he cannot simply decide that it is not a fact because it does not fit his theory. Collingwood suggests that if an historian has convinced himself, after a study of the available evidence, that Henry VII murdered the princes in the tower, then the discovery of an autographed document confessing the fact would not verify the theory but only raise a new issue—the question of its own authenticity (*IH* 243). This shows some awareness of the fact that the authenticity of the document cannot be determined solely by the theory it supports, and if its authenticity is independently established then the theory that Henry VII murdered the princes is (other things being equal) strongly supported. And the emergence of such documents might be

---

[8] It may be that some remarks about the idea of the past as an innate idea are meant to tell us more about the 'peculiar relation' and if so then the relation between present evidence and picture of the past is determined by *our* mental constitution and not solely by the practices or mental constitutions of historians.

regarded as even more significant where their claims falsified a theory like the one about the princes in the tower. In any case, the fact that the document's authenticity would have to be established cannot illustrate the specific role of scientific history and its imaginative re-enactments since Collingwood admits that sophisticated SAP historians are alive to such problems and equipped to handle them. What Collingwood should rather have said is that an admittedly authentic confession by Henry VII is not even relevant as evidence unless it fits the historian's prior imaginative reconstruction of the facts upon which it seems to bear. So we find him saying, just after raising the Henry VII example, 'The web of imaginative construction is something far more solid and powerful than we have hitherto realized. So far from relying for its validity upon the support of given facts, it actually serves as the touchstone by which we decide whether alleged facts are genuine' (*IH* 244). But any historian who held on the basis of 'imaginative constructions' that Henry VII *did not* murder the princes would surely have to treat the discovery of an authentic confession of Henry's as a fact which counted against his theory, even if he hoped to salvage his theory by producing some reason why Henry had lied.

At this point, however, it might be urged that my treatment of Collingwood has been too unsympathetic and that there are ways in which his position could be construed or reconstructed so as to make it more tenable. I shall briefly consider two such possibilities, the first that there is an underlying metaphysical view in Collingwood's position in terms of which his theses may be defensible, and the second that, although Collingwood's stated position is too extreme, it can be reinterpreted so that his critique of testimony, though weaker, is still important.

The underlying view, which might with some plausibility be regarded as supporting Collingwood's rejection of testimonial facts, is the idea that no facts are interpretation-free. This is an idea which fits naturally, though not exclusively, into an idealist metaphysics and so would presumably have been congenial to Collingwood. We find it reflected in the writings of historians influenced by Collingwood. The following quotation from E. H. Carr is typical: 'The belief in a hard core of historical facts existing objectively and independently of the interpretation of the historian is a preposterous fallacy.'[9] We find something similar manifested in certain contemporary philosophies of science and theories of knowledge and in the philosophical movement known in Europe as hermeneutics. I cannot provide a full treatment of this idea here but I intend to comment briefly upon its relevance to my discussion of Collingwood.

It may be that Collingwood's claims and arguments about history are intended themselves to support the broad metaphysical view and, if so, my objections above to these claims and arguments are objections to that way

---

[9] E. H. Carr, *What is History?* (Harmondsworth, 1964), 12.

of supporting the broader view. Inasmuch, however, as the broad view is supposed itself to bolster Collingwood's specific claims and arguments in respect of history then it seems to me very dubious that this is so. Even allowing that there is some sense in which no facts are interpretation-free or theory-neutral, it will not at all follow that the facts of history are loaded with just those interpretations or theories in which Collingwood is interested, namely those produced by the historian's imaginative reconstructions. The most thoroughgoing 'interpretationist' must allow for different levels of interpretation, otherwise there would be no sense to the notion of interpretation. It may be, for instance, that of two people observing a Wilson cloud chamber only one can observe it *as* a Wilson cloud chamber; none the less, the fact that it is a Wilson cloud chamber can only involve interpretation if this is an interpretation of other facts which do not involve *that* interpretation, such as the fact that it is a scientific device. Once this point is taken, the question whether the broad view supports Collingwood's claims about historical facts will simply reduce to the question whether his specific arguments and claims about history will stand up to the kind of criticisms that I have made of them.

The second 'sympathetic' approach to Collingwood's objections to testimony might proceed by moderating Collingwood's claims in a direction indicated by E. H. Carr who, at one point, argues that historical facts, of the kind illustrated earlier, should be treated as the 'raw material' of history rather than as part of history itself. Another suggestion of Carr's, in the same spirit, is that they be regarded as mere facts about the past and not in themselves historical facts: they become historical facts only when they are drawn by an historian into an interpretation which 'is accepted by other historians as valid and significant'.[10] In so far as Carr's somewhat obscure suggestions are anything more than harmless terminological proposals, they seem to embody the two ideas that history, as a study, involves much more than the compilation of 'raw materials' and that these extra elements of selecting, interpreting, theorizing, imaginatively reconstructing, and so on, are what is really important.

I have already accepted the view that the data of history include more than testimony and that there are important elements of selection, judgement, and theorizing in historical work. Here I will only stress that nothing follows from this about the insignificance of testimony or the triviality of facts (even facts which have not yet been elected into the historians' 'club').[11] Rather, claims about comparative importance must depend for adjudication upon what criteria of importance are emphasized. I do not propose to embark upon a discussion of possible criteria here but

[10] Ibid.
[11] Ibid. Carr believes that nothing can be an historical fact unless elected into 'the select club of historical facts' by historians. The franchise may strike the reader as somewhat restrictive.

will content myself with the reminder that there are dangers in minimizing the importance of 'facts about the past', some of which dangers are manifested in Collingwood's pronouncements about 'scientific' history.

I conclude that Collingwood's attempt to discredit historical facts (data) and the historian's reliance upon testimony is unsuccessful. It seems that, just as we cannot dispense with observational and experimental data in natural science, so we cannot do without testimonial data in history. Of course, not *all* observation and experiment is reliable, and particular observational claims and experiments can be subjected to critical scrutiny and rejected, and similarly with testimony, particular instances of which may be found mistaken, spurious, or deceitful. The parallel with observation is relevant precisely because what is a piece of testimony to us is often a piece of observation on the part of our informant, just as our observations may be testimony for him.[12] In science and in ordinary life we work with a social concept of observation that is broad enough to include the observation of others. (It is this which leads Collingwood into some of the mistakes in his detective story.) 'It is a fact of observation' we say confidently, even where we are reporting no observations of our own. If we extend this courtesy to our contemporaries why not to our ancestors?[13]

---

[12] A point stressed by John Passmore in 'The Objectivity of History', *Philosophy*, 33/125 (Apr. 1958), 100–1.

[13] I do not say that there are no interesting differences between testimony from the past and testimony from the present. With regard to methods of assessing particular testimonies there are at least three areas of difference: (*a*) the possibility of interrogation of a witness, (*b*) the possibility of checking by personal observation, and (*c*) the possibility of checking with other witnesses. One can exaggerate the availability of these resources in the case of current testimony but (*a*) and (*b*) are not available at all with historical testimony, except for the most recent past, and (*c*) is much more restricted than with contemporary testimony. The historian may, of course, use analogues to (*a*) and (*b*), such as the reports of interrogations and the checks provided by archaeology. There are important issues here but further investigation is beyond the scope of this book and does not seem likely to affect its main contentions.

14

Mathematical Knowledge and Reliable Authority

The relationships between mathematical truth and the human intellect raise problems as baffling and complex as any in philosophy. Most have been so abundantly debated and discussed as to need no recalling but there is one problem which is seldom mentioned and even less often thoroughly discussed. It concerns the status of mathematically true beliefs which are believed on reliable non-mathematical grounds and, in particular, the ground of reliable testimony. It is, I think, commonly assumed that such beliefs cannot have the status of knowledge but this assumption is seldom made explicit and defended by argument. I believe, to the contrary, that such beliefs can constitute knowledge and in what follows I shall try to disarm philosophical resistance to this idea.

One of the few explicit treatments of the issue occurs in an interesting article on knowledge by Bernard Williams,[1] who claims that if someone believes a true mathematical proposition, p, on good authority but cannot mathematically demonstrate the proposition then he does not know that p. Let us call this the main claim. There are, as we shall see, related but weaker theses; none the less, I shall begin with and concentrate upon the main claim because it is, I suspect, the one most commonly assumed. I shall, moreover, direct much of my attention to Williams's discussion. Amongst others[2] who accept the main claim is Roderick Chisholm in the first edition (1966) of his *Theory of Knowledge*. Chisholm's explicit commitment is wider than Williams's, for he is concerned quite generally with necessary truths and the a priori, but his position would seem to involve emphatic endorsement of the main claim. He says, 'If what we know is a necessary truth—if we may formulate it in a sentence prefixed by the modal operator "necessarily" or "it is necessary that"—then our knowl-

---

[1] B. A. O. Williams, 'Knowledge and Reasons', in G. H. von Wright (ed.), *Problems in the Theory of Knowledge* (The Hague, 1972), 1–11. Quotations from this will have the page refs. bracketed after them in the text. Williams does not explicitly bring knowledge of logical truths within the scope of the main claim, although it is plausible to do so and some versions would certainly include them. I too shall discuss only the mathematical case but my criticisms could be adapted to deal with the wider claim. By talking of 'the main claim' I do not mean to imply that Williams's article is only or predominantly concerned with the issue discussed here.

[2] It seems that A. J. Ayer implicitly accepts the main claim in his reply to Williams's article in von Wright, ibid. 12.

edge is not *a posteriori*'.[3] Interestingly, in the second edition of his book
(1977) Chisholm has qualms about this and, with misgivings, entertains
the possibility that necessary truths may be known a posteriori on the
basis of reliable authority (his example is a logical theorem for the truth of
which we have the word of reputable logicians) but he does not finally
commit himself on the problem except to insist that if the main claim is
not true then a weaker cousin of it surely is.[4] I shall discuss the weaker
claim later but I shall begin with Williams's treatment of the main claim.

Williams says that the main claim commands widespread assent and
perhaps because of this he offers nothing in positive support of it beyond
the assertion that 'access to mathematical truth must necessarily lie
through proof and that therefore the notion of non-accidental true belief in
mathematics essentially involves the notion of mathematical proof' (p. 9).
Before examining this assertion a brief digression into certain matters of
general epistemology is called for. In his article Williams is concerned
to defend a particular approach to the theory of knowledge which, as
we noted in Chapter 1, is characteristic of much recent epistemology.
Abandoning that tradition, or family of traditions, which seeks to analyse
knowledge in such a way that he who knows some proposition, *p*, has
some understanding or insight which guarantees the truth of *p* (be it by
way of reasoning, intuition, or whatever), Williams endorses the family of
views which is concerned to define knowledge 'externally' in terms of the
way the belief in question is connected naturally with the relevant state of
affairs external to the knower. Causal theories are obvious candidates here
but Williams prefers the more general category of 'non-accidental connection'. Theories of this type preserve something of the form of the traditional insight picture but entirely alter its spirit. We could treat both
theories as offering three-condition definitions of knowledge but with
contrasting entries for the third condition:

Insight theory:

   (1) *A* believes that *p*.

   (2) *p* is true.

   (3) *A* has an insight into the connection between his belief that *p* and *p*
       (reasons or intuitions or some 'couldn't be otherwise' or 'couldn't be
       doubted' story).

Externalist theory:

   (1) *A* believes that *p*.

   (2) *p* is true.

   (3) There is some non-accidental or appropriate causal connection
       between *p* and *A*'s belief that *p*.

---

[3] R. Chisholm, *Theory of Knowledge* (Englewood Cliffs, NJ, 1966), 74–5.

[4] R. Chisholm, *Theory of Knowledge*, 2nd edn. (Englewood Cliffs, NJ, 1977), 47.

We may now return to Williams and mathematical knowledge. Earlier I quoted Williams as asserting that 'access to mathematical truth must necessarily lie through proof, and that therefore the notion of non-accidental true belief in mathematics essentially involves the notion of mathematical proof' (p. 9). Even on the assumption that, as Williams thinks, some version of the 'non-accidental true belief' formula will figure as an ingredient in an analysis of knowledge, the above assertion will not take us far. To begin with, it is ambiguous. On one interpretation, it may be taken as asserting that there could be no knowledge of mathematical truths unless *some* people had proved them but this seems perfectly compatible with their passing such knowledge on to others—the non-accidental true belief so transferred will 'essentially involve the notion of mathematical proof' but not at first hand.[5] Similarly, one might hold, for instance, that access to contingent colour truths necessarily lies through vision but this does not prevent the transmission of colour truths through testimony. A man can, for example, know truths about the colour of the Golden Gate Bridge, or a rare Australian parrot, or a Renoir painting in Boston, even if he has never left England and has never seen colour photographs of these things, and if he has seen the relevant photographs he can know from a reliable witness that, and how, they misrepresent the colour. Certainly, Williams believes that testimony can, in certain circumstances, be a source of knowledge (either by way of explicit reasoning from reliable report or by the 'right sort' of causal track between fact, report, and belief). This is a consistent and even predictable consequence of an externalist stance on knowledge which seeks to anchor it in reliable connections between beliefs and the world, whether or not those connections present themselves as such to the knower. Even the insight tradition should feel some embarrassment at refusing the accolade of knowledge to at least some cases of information gained from testimony, although Plato, for one, operating, as we saw in Chapter 1, with more austere standards than most modern philosophers accept, seems to have been, in this respect, more heroic. I shall have more to say about such austerity later.

If this interpretation of the Williams assertion makes it evidentially irrelevant to the main claim, the other available interpretation, that no one can have the right sort of access to mathematical truth unless he has himself mathematically proved the truth, is clearly insufficiently independent of the main claim to offer it support; indeed, it seems to be no more than the main claim in slightly different clothing. On any straightforward understanding of 'non-accidental' (and certainly on Williams's) both the belief of the man who has proved p and that of the man who has it reliably from him are non-accidental, as we can see by comparing them with the

---

[5] This is in fact Chisholm's 'weaker cousin' of the main claim and is perhaps not as uncontentious as it appears. We shall look more closely at it later.

belief of the man who simply guesses or opines that p. Hence the reference to 'non-accidental' in the assertion only serves to reassert the main claim. Perhaps there is a suggestion, in the assertion that the main claim follows from a general thesis, to the effect that necessary truths can only be known by a priori methods. The trouble with this is that, not only has Kripke's work on identity made this general thesis far from obvious, by showing that there is a case for holding that at least some necessary truths can be known a posteriori but the apparent transmissibility of mathematical knowledge by testimony already stands as a striking counter-example to the general thesis, which it requires some further argument to overcome.

Williams has no positive argument for the main claim and perhaps, like other philosophers, thinks its truth just obvious. Unlike other philosophers, he is aware of at least an appearance of paradox or oddity in its consequences so he provides a defusing argument to cope with this appearance. The problem arises from the fact that Williams believes that testimony can provide knowledge in certain circumstances and in the mathematical example there seems to be some truth that the recipient of the expert testimony non-accidentally or reliably learns. What can this truth be if it is not the truth of p? And if he reliably learns the truth of p, surely he must know that p? Williams's answer is that the recipient does not know that p, the item of knowledge he has is the knowledge that p is a mathematical truth.[6] Williams adds in amplification:

> It will seem paradoxical to take apart in any way knowing that p, and knowing that p is a truth of a given science. To be a truth of a given science is to be, in a special sense, a part of *knowledge*; and to know that a proposition has that status is to know that it is, by the standards of that science, to be counted as *known*, as opposed to its being, for instance, a matter merely of plausible conjecture (p. 9).

Knowing that p is a truth of a given science is an instance of what Williams calls 'impersonal knowledge'.

It is not at all clear that this provides a genuine escape route from paradox. To begin with, Williams seems to have mislocated or, rather, underestimated the paradox. It is indeed unacceptable to separate knowing that p from knowing that p is true, but if mathematical expert, Smith, tells me that some mathematical fact, that p, is true (and it is—since the example is at least one of true belief), then is it not also paradoxical to claim that I can thus know that p is a truth of mathematics without knowing that p is true? Consider my position: I know that p is a truth of mathematics and am somehow to be disqualified from concluding that

---

[6] Chisholm appears to have a similar move in mind when he suggests that 'it may well be' that someone who seems to know a logical principle on authority does not really know it because he does not really 'accept' *it*, rather what he 'accepts' (and presumbaly, in this instance, knows) is 'the contingent proposition to the effect that a certain formula in a book expresses a logical principle that is true'. Cf. Chisholm, *Theory*, 2nd edn., 47.

part of this knowledge is that p is true, but, on the face of it, knowing that p is a truth of mathematics is just knowing that p has been established as a truth by mathematical reasoning. It is hard to see how any account of knowledge can block the entailment from 'A knows that p is a truth of mathematics' to 'A knows that p is true' to 'A knows that p'. Moreover, the puzzle remains if we substitute history or physics or biochemistry for mathematics, since Williams does *not* seek to escape from paradox by relying on the idea that p can be a 'truth' of a given science or a part of knowledge, in the sense of knowledge in a given field, and yet turn out false. Such a move would be irrelevant to the present issue because it is conceded that p is true and it is, in any case, unclear whether Williams thinks that an item of 'impersonal knowledge' can be false. If this were the way Williams thought of the problem then it would be strange for him to single out mathematical knowledge for special treatment since it is the body of knowledge in which established propositions are least susceptible to turning out false. What is special for Williams about impersonal knowledge is, rather, its impersonality; some proposition can be an item of impersonal knowledge without being an item of personal knowledge for any given individual.

Can this last point help Williams? He argues for the point by showing that two plausible propositions about impersonal knowledge entail a palpable falsehood. Let 'Kip' stand for 'it is known that p', in the required body of knowledge sense, and 'Kap' stand for 'A knows that p'; then (1) and (2) seem very plausible:

(1) If Kip then, for some a, Kap.
(2) If Kip and Kiq, then Ki (p and q).

But (1) and (2) together entail the certainly false (3).

(3) If Kip and Kiq, then, for some a, Ka (p and q).

The unwanted conclusion (3) follows if we are allowed to treat (p and q) as a substitution instance for p. Whatever the interest of this paradox, however, it is hard to see how it can be taken to support the proposed ban on inferring 'A knows that p' from 'A knows that p is a truth of mathematics', since both propositions are statements of personal knowledge.[7] Of course, the content of the second piece of personal knowledge is an item of impersonal knowledge so that there is at least a question as to how we move from the second piece to the first but the answer to this question is unaffected by the paradox. In fact a plausible answer is to hand and it is precisely the denial of Williams's blocking move, for the answer is that if A knows that p is a truth of mathematics (and p is true) then A knows that p

---

[7] Actually, for Williams, the order of support is, or should be, somewhat the other way since he claims that (1) cannot be defended by relying upon the idea that 'anyone who truly asserts or, at least, who *knows*, that Kip must himself know that p "since" we have already seen in the mathematical case that it is false' ('Knowledge and Reasons', 10).

is true and if A knows that p is true then A knows that p. Williams has presented no argument against this very plausible transition.

Williams is actually in an even worse position than this. His attempt to drive a wedge between 'A knows that p is a truth of mathematics' and 'A knows that p is true' has, I have argued, nothing to recommend it but it is, in any case, beside the point. His claim that mathematical knowledge cannot be gained by testimony but only by individual proof is quite independent of how the testifier acquires his belief. Imagine the situation in which B is a great mathematician and has proved the truth of p for himself and then tells it to A who knows of B's prowess and, being entitled to trust him, does so. Here we seem quite remote from the 'it is known that p' paradigm, even though p is indeed a truth of a particular science, just because B clearly has personal knowledge that p and is passing it on to A. The distinction between personal and impersonal knowledge is not to the point. Both A and B will know that p is a truth of mathematics but it is more fundamental that they both know that p, although one knows it from the other.

It is worth noticing that, if we are looking for other things that A knows about p, it seems hard to resist the view that he knows that B knows that p. Certainly, A has justified true belief that B knows that p, there is no Gettier trickery in the example, and there is a reliable ('non-accidental') causal connection between the fact of B's knowing that p and A's belief that he does. But if A *knows that B knows that p* is true how can we block the inference to A *knows that p*? After all, on any definition of personal knowledge, A's knowledge that B knows that p entitles A to conclude that p is true (although like all entitlements A may be unaware of it). In Hintikka's terminology, if A knows that B knows that p then A virtually knows that p. Consequently, as Hintikka points out, there is a paradox in such claims as: 'John knows that p but I don't.' They are, as he puts it, epistemically indefensible.[8]

To salvage the main claim Williams could (and perhaps must) abandon the view that A *knows* something important about the truth of p as a result of B's testimony. If, for instance, he holds that A can only *believe* that B knows that p and can only *believe* that p is a truth of mathematics then no incoherence will result from the conjunction of these views with the main claim. This, however, seems most implausible, especially if one allows, as Williams rightly does, that testimony yields knowledge in other areas. At the very least a compelling story is needed about why mathematics should differ in this respect from history, physics, geography, etc., which, after all, have their own proper methods and evidential procedures. Plato's more radical and difficult doctrine that testimony cannot provide knowledge in any area at least faces no problems of this kind, but, as we

---

[8] Jaakko Hintikka, *Knowledge and Belief* (Ithaca, NY, 1962), ch. 4.

saw in Chapter 1, the consequences of adhering to it are more sweeping than Plato may have realized. It may be important that such an epistemology has a tendency to restrict knowledge to mathematical and logical propositions on the ground that pure intuition and a priori reasoning can alone provide the sort of insight that (infallible) knowledge requires. Such an outlook would indeed support the main claim but subscription to it requires a cost greater than that which most of us, including Williams, are now willing to pay.

There is one aspect of the transmission of knowledge which should be mentioned since it has some relevance to Williams's defusing argument. It would be fair to say that Jones did not know that p, even when it was true and he had been told it on good authority, if it was also true that Jones did not understand what he was told. The limit case is where 'p' is in a language that he does not understand at all, but there are degrees of understanding, either because some expressions are understood and some not or because some expressions are only partially understood or for other reasons altogether. A man can, of course, be a vehicle of information that he doesn't understand, as when a courier passes on a coded message without knowing the code. It may be that the popularity of the main claim arises from the feeling that the recipient of testimony to the truth of a mathematical proposition is in some way deficient in *understanding*, whereas someone who has proved the proposition surely understands it.[9] With reference to Williams's defusing argument, we might well be tempted to say of Jones that he knew that p was a truth of mathematics but not that p was true. This temptation arises only because Jones, not understanding 'p', cannot even *believe* that p, although he can believe that 'p' expresses a truth which is part of mathematics and so can know that 'p' expresses a truth which is part of mathematics. This may allow us to say that he knows that p is a truth of mathematics but does not know that p, although I would prefer to stay with 'knows that "p" expresses a mathematical truth'. Consequently, the point about understanding will not really help the proponents of the main claim unless they are prepared to say that the recipient of mathematical testimony that p cannot believe that p. They do not, however, want to say this—Williams[10] sets his example up in terms of the recipient's truly believing that p—and it would, in any case, be most implausible since much mathematical information is not difficult to understand.[11] Consider such propositions as: 'There is no

---

[9] This possibility and its ramifications were brought to my attention by Margaret Coady.

[10] As Dr E. J. Craig has pointed out to me there is further evidence that Williams cannot be relying upon the move about understanding in the fact that he does not want to 'take apart in any way knowing that p, and knowing that p is true', whereas this would be a possible response to the situation where 'p' is not understood—at least as possible as separating 'knowing that p is true' and 'knowing that p is a truth of a given science'.

[11] Wittgenstein, it is true, held at one time that mathematical truths could not even be believed on the basis of report but his argument for this conclusion is very obscure and he

greatest prime number' and 'Between every number (greater than one) and
its double there is at least one prime number'. Surely one can understand
these without being able to prove them. Similarly, there is no problem in
understanding Goldbach's conjecture that every even number greater than
two is the sum of two primes, although no one at present can prove it.

The notion of understanding is difficult, interesting, and important, and
it raises issues that go beyond the scope of this book. I have used, without
analysis, a relatively narrow and simple idea of understanding which ties it
to the comprehension of sentences and other actual and possible communications. It can hardly be denied that this concept is commonly employed
and that it has the sort of consequences, e.g. the connection with belief,
that I relied upon in my argument above.

Two objections may however be made against my employment of the
idea. The first is that a theory of understanding is correlative to a theory of
meaning and my procedure reveals an unargued commitment to a realist
theory of meaning, whereas on an anti-realist theory (stressing the importance of verifications and, in the mathematical case, proofs) the main
claim could be defended by departing from Williams and holding that a
mathematical proposition is neither understood nor believed by someone
who cannot prove it. One immediate problem with this rejoinder is that
it seems to constitute a *reductio ad absurdum* of the suggested anti-
realist theory, since it is surely absurd to claim that no one understands
Goldbach's conjecture. Moreover, the absurdity is magnified by the reflection that the understanding of a proposition must surely *precede* the
discovery of a proof for it. Suppose that someone, after working for years
on the problem, discovers a proof of Goldbach's conjecture tomorrow; the
current suggestion would have it that he has only understood the conjecture, and hence the problem it posed, *after* he has discovered the proof and
so solved the problem! A theory of meaning with this consequence is
surely incredible.

Yet there are more telling forms of anti-realism. A weaker but more
plausible anti-realist theory might hold that to understand, or at least
'fully' understand, a mathematical proposition one need only know the
kind of thing necessary for a proof of it, rather than being in possession of
an actual proof of it.[12] Along these lines we might weaken the main claim
so that someone could know a mathematical proposition on good authority as long as he knew the sort of thing needed to prove it. There is an
initial problem in knowing how much strength the weakened claim is

seems, in any case, to hold that they also cannot be believed on the basis of proof. (Cf.
Remarks on the Foundations of Mathematics (Oxford, 1964), para. 106–12.

[12] Such a position seems implicit in Michael Dummett's version of anti-realism and was
explicitly adopted by him in his William James Lectures at Harvard. See lecture-notes
available from the Harvard Philosophy Dept., pp. 25–8 of lecture 5. See also Michael
Dummett, *The Logical Basis of Metaphysics* (Cambridge, Mass., 1991) 161–2.

meant to retain. Does anyone now know, for instance, the sort of thing necessary to prove Goldbach's conjecture? If our answer is 'No' then the claim is still very strong and seems to inherit most of the difficulties of the simple anti-realism which it modifies. If our answer is 'Yes', then not only is the main claim considerably weakened, since we can now know a mathematical truth on authority as long as we have fulfilled some other condition well short of being able to demonstrate its truth mathematically, but it is a formidable task to give a plausible specification of what that condition might be and why it should have such significance. Presumably, the weakest interpretation of the condition would allow that it is a necessary condition of ('fully') understanding some mathematical truth that we can prove some mathematical proposition, that we know *that* much about mathematical proof. I very much suspect that something rather stronger than this is sought by contemporary anti-realists but even so weak a condition faces the prima facie difficulty that the ancient Egyptians, for instance, seem to have believed, understood, and even possibly known certain geometrical truths, such as the relation between the volume of a truncated pyramid with square ends and its dimensions, without access to mathematical proofs of any sort.[13] We cannot pursue such difficult issues further here, but it is worth remarking that it may be possible to maintain a general anti-realist stance in the theory of meaning whilst abandoning any idea that an individual can only understand a mathematical proposition via some explicit grasp *he* has on the notion of mathematical proof. If we take our reliance upon others seriously at a fundamental epistemological and semantical level (cf. Putnam's principle of 'the division of linguistic labour'), then perhaps all we need and can plausibly demand in the way of anti-realism is a theory in which an individual's understanding of a mathematical proposition is grounded upon the knowledge others possess of the workings of mathematical proof.

Something of this idea may lie behind Chisholm's 'weaker cousin' of the main claim which I mentioned earlier, although Chisholm makes no reference to a theory of understanding but rather seems to be relying upon an epistemological intuition. Chisholm holds that we can only allow that someone knows a necessary truth on the basis of testimony if some 'ultimate authority' somewhere 'knows some proposition *a priori*'.[14] His remarks are fairly cryptic but he seems to be relying upon the idea that testimony is essentially a passing on of information which has at some point been independently established. In the spirit of his discussion, we might say that if *A* knows some mathematical proposition, that *p*, because

---

[13] See J. F. Scott, *A History of Mathematics* (London, 1958), 2–9 and especially p. 7. For what it is worth, Scott and other historians of mathematics commonly refer to the Egyptians' beliefs as 'knowledge' and not only in the sense of knowing how. The possible relevance of Egyptian geometry was drawn to my attention by Professor W. C. Kneale.

[14] Chisholm, *Theory*, 2nd edn., 47.

B has reliably informed him of it, and *B* has it reliably from *C*, and perhaps so on (depending upon problems about declining authority), then somewhere the chain must end in an *N* who has proved that *p*. (I say that this is in the spirit of Chisholm's remarks because he makes no explicit reference to proof and yet my use of the notion here seems not to distort his thought.) In putting the matter thus I am strengthening Chisholm's claim since he says only that the ultimate source must know *some* proposition a priori. This would certainly be too weak as a sufficient condition but since Chisholm is only offering a necessary condition this may not matter; what is true is that the evidential chain argument he produces seems to establish something stronger. Whether it establishes something as strong as my version above is debatable. Suppose the proof of *p* is very complex and involves proving that *q* and that *r* along the way. Surely the 'chain' from *N* to *A* may be such that *N* has proved that *q* and *M* has proved that *r* (neither having the foggiest idea that *p*), and further along the chain *C* has proved that *p* from the reliable information that *q* and that *r*, though *he* has proved neither. We could, of course, say that a chain of the kind suggested by my version operates between *A* and *C*; this is true, but the interest of the more complex chain lies in the light it throws upon the idea of 'independently established', for *C* is still clearly dependent upon testimony in a way that the original argument does not envisage and hence in discussing the basis of *A*'s knowledge we would at least be tempted to go beyond *C* to *M* and *N*. Such complications are important for the general theory of testimony but I mention them here only to qualify my agreement with the 'weaker cousin' version of the main claim. So qualified, the 'weaker cousin' claim seems to be correct, though so distantly related to the main claim as to be perhaps beyond the range of genuine kinship.

I said that two objections might be made against the way I employ the idea of understanding. Having discussed the first at some length, I shall be briefer with the second. As the first drew attention to the possible relevance of rather technical issues within the theory of linguistic meaning so the second, by contrast, urges the need for a wider notion of understanding. Even when we invoke the theory of linguistic meaning, our horizons are still too pragmatic, it may be said, and what is required is a fuller, richer notion of understanding, tied to the demands and perspectives of organized bodies of knowledge. In terms of this richer notion it could more plausibly be maintained that only the man who has proved the mathematical truth really understands it and that it is this sense of the term which is relevant to a possible defence of Williams's defusing argument. Some philosophers concerned with the epistemologies of Plato and Aristotle have argued that we need some such rich notion of understanding to appreciate some of the Greek discussions of knowledge. (We touched upon matters related to this point in Chapter 1.) At present we lack sufficient guide-lines for this fuller concept to do proper justice to the complaint, but it is hard to see how the concept could be relevant to the problems of knowledge which concern Williams and so many other modern philosophers. It is correspondingly hard to see how it could lead to the view that lack of this sort of understanding of propositions such as 'There is no greatest prime number' prevents someone knowing them. It could, I suspect, only be made relevant by changing the topic and constructing, or perhaps retrieving, a concept of knowledge quite different from that which is the target of Williams and other modern epistemologists.[15]

I should call attention to one qualifying remark made by Williams, the exact import of which is unclear. Just before the passage I quoted in the third paragraph of this chapter, Williams says, 'Concerning mathematical propositions, for instance, save of the simplest kind, there is strong pressure behind the Platonic view that the distinction between knowledge and true belief lies in the possession of an *aitias logismos*, a chain of proof' (p. 9). The qualifying reference to the 'simplest kind' of mathematical propositions is probably intended to make an exception to the proof requirement on behalf of intuitive or direct knowledge rather than on behalf of testimony. I take the point to be that some, simple, mathematical propositions are known non-discursively or non-inferentially by the firsthand mathematician rather than that they can be known to another on the basis of testimony alone. Presumably, the firsthand mathematician knows such simple truths in a special mathematical way ('mathematical intuition' perhaps) the operation of which supposedly disqualifies them from being transmitted as knowledge by mere testimony. If, however, the qualifying remark is, as seems most unlikely, intended by Williams to allow that knowledge of the simplest mathematical propositions can be gained by testimony alone, then there is a problem about why the two types of mathematical fact behave differently with respect to testimony. Moreover, even if a satisfactory answer could be given to this, the main claim would still encompass numerous ordinary, readily intelligible mathematical propositions, like the ones mentioned concerning prime numbers, and would still be vulnerable to the difficulties already raised.

The main claim is concerned with the authority of human testimony and claims to mathematical knowledge. Viewed in one way the problem it raises is connected with the broader problem of the nature of mathematical proof, or what we might call mathematical evidence, and there have arisen interesting criticisms of the traditional picture of such proofs as wholly non-empirical. Hilary Putnam, for one, has urged that there is a

[15] Cf. M. F. Burnyeat, 'Aristotle on Understanding Knowledge', in E. Berti (ed.), *Aristotle on Science: The Posterior Analytics* (Atti dell'VIII Symposium Aristotelicum; Padua and New York, 1981). Also J. M. E. Moravcsik, 'Understanding and Knowledge in Plato's Philosophy', *Neue Hefte für Philosophie* (1978).

sense in which mathematics is 'quasi-empirical'[16] and, more interestingly
still, it has been argued that there is at least one mathematical theorem the
proof of which essentially involves the use of computers and dependence
of an empirical kind on their reliability. This theorem is the four colour
theorem which states that every map on the plane or sphere can be
coloured with no more than four colours in such a way that neighbouring
regions are never coloured alike. The four colour problem puzzled mathematicians for more than a hundred years and was only solved by a proof
of the theorem in 1977 by Appel, Haken, and Koch.[17] This seems, however, to make an ineradicable appeal to the results of a complex computer
operation. As Thomas Tymoczko[18] has argued, the point is not merely
that computers were used to prove a particular lemma but that there seems
no other way in which the lemma could be proved. He concludes that the
proof therefore fails directly one of the plausible criteria for a mathematical proof and indirectly another. The direct failure concerns *surveyability*,
since there is a part of the proof that mathematicians cannot survey, and
the indirect failure concerns *formalizability*, since our belief that the proof
is formalizable rests, in part, on the conviction that the computer has
obtained its results by formal methods. As Tymoczko puts it, 'we believe
that the formal proof exists only because we accept the appeal to computers in the first place . . . our only evidence for the existence of that
formal proof presupposes the reliability of computers'.[19]

If Tymoczko is right then the notion of mathematical proof may itself be
flexible enough to include something like the sort of dependence that is
involved in accepting reliable testimony. To see this is to see an analogy
between the mathematician's dependence upon reliable computers and the
layman's reliance upon the authoritative mathematician. Indeed, I suspect
that there are three levels of analogy here, relating the way mathematicians
rely upon each other's proofs in the course of proving something else
(although they think they can independently check such proofs if need be),
the way they rely upon the computer (where they cannot independently
furnish a proof), and the way the layman relies upon the expert mathematician. The existence of such analogies, although there are, of course,
points of dissimilarity too, may go some way towards eliminating the
feeling that the purity of mathematical proof requires adherence to the
main claim.

The upshot of our discussion is that no good reason has been found for
accepting the main claim and no promising directions in which such a

    [16] H. Putnam, *Philosophical Papers*, i. *Mathematics, Matter and Method*, 2nd edn.
(Cambridge, 1979). See esp. Ch. 4, 'What is Mathematical Truth?'.
    [17] K. Appel, W. Haken, and J. Kock, 'Every Planar Map is Four Colourable', *Illinois
Journal of Mathematics*, 21/84 (Sept. 1977), 429–567.
    [18] T. Tymoczko, 'The Four-Colour Problem and its Philosophical Significance', *The
Journal of Philosophy*, 76/2 (Feb. 1979), 57–83.
    [19] Ibid. 72.

reason might be sought have emerged. If it were to be asserted that the main claim is just obviously true, I should reply that, on the contrary, if anything is obviously true it is that the main claim is *not* obviously true. A strong case has been made in this book for the view that our reliance upon testimony needs to be given a fundamental role in any theory of knowledge. If we could have knowledge on the basis of what we were told in every area except mathematics (and perhaps, logic) then this would constitute an important restriction on the epistemological role of testimony. The main claim, however, needs proof and lacks it. In the absence of proof its importance is reduced to that of a curiously persistent prejudice, the grip of which calls for explanation in terms of the history of thought.

15

The Witness of Psychology

There was things which he stretched, but mainly he told the truth.
That is nothing. I never seen anybody but lied, one time or another,
without it was Aunt Polly, or the widow, or maybe Mary.

(Huck Finn: Mark Twain, *The Adventures of Huckleberry Finn*, 1.)

Professional psychologists have been concerned with questions to do with
the reliability of testimony, and particularly with what they call eyewitness
testimony, ever since the early years of this century. The beginnings of this
interest are often traced back to Binet's seminal work on suggestibility at
the turn of the century,[1] though some of the nineteenth-century investigations into perception and memory certainly paved the way for later developments. From the very start, the psychological theorizing has had a
distinctly practical orientation since psychologists were well aware that
their claims had relevance to legal processes and moreover showed the zeal
of dedicated reformers in urging this relevance upon a sometimes less than
fully sympathetic legal profession. As early as 1908 Hugo Münsterberg
used experimental results to criticize what he saw as deficiencies in evidentiary rules and trial procedures in his book *On the Witness Stand*[2] and
the tradition has continued, with occasional lulls, up to the present time;
indeed, the 1970s and 1980s have seen a 'great leap forward' in the
quantity of such research and recommendations.[3]

   The basic interest and even some of the basic insights of this work are
probably as old as human communication itself and certainly as old as the
writing of history. Thucydides was worried by 'the want of coincidence
between accounts of the same occurrences by different eyewitnesses, arising sometimes from imperfect memory, sometimes from undue partiality
for one side or the other',[4] and, as we saw in Chapter 1, Plato used the
setting of a jury trial to warn against putting too high a value upon
testimony. It has been the burden of this book that reliance upon the word
of others is an absolutely fundamental epistemological attitude which is far

---

[1] A. Binet, *La Suggestibilité* (Paris, 1900).

[2] H. Münsterberg, *On the Witness Stand: Essays on Psychology and Crime* (New York,
1908).

[3] There is a good bibliography in G. L. Wells and E. F. Loftus (eds.), *Eyewitness Testimony: Pyschological Perspectives* (Cambridge, 1984). See also the editors' preface, 'Eyewitness Research: Then and Now'.

[4] Quoted in J. Marshall, *Law and Psychology in Conflict* (New York, 1966), 1. The
quotation is from the Crawley trans.; the Jowett version sounds slightly less sceptical but the
point is much the same.

more pervasive in ordinary life and in specialized theory than we normally recognize and that, furthermore, the philosophical justification of this trust is not to be found in the sources commonly cited. Whether my own somewhat indirect justification fares any better I shall leave to the reader's judgement, but it may be thought that the psychological literature represents a challenge not only to legal practices but to my own epistemological conclusions. I think it can be readily shown that this thought is mistaken but, even so, the psychologist's critique of testimony bears in a number of ways upon a philosophical interest in the topic and also deserves some examination in its own right.

The psychological literature on testimony, eyewitness identification, and the like has recently shown a tendency to more caution and even self-criticism,[5] but for a good deal of its life this literature has been marked by brashness, didacticism, and hyperbole. Moreover, the conclusions these tendencies produced are still influential upon the lay public and many in the legal profession.

The most striking general feature of the deliverances of the psychological tradition on testimony is its almost messianic positivism. James Marshall is by no means exceptional when he writes: 'The atmosphere of the courtroom is not normally such that one could expect to find the truth of a situation; at best one finds only a rough approximation. The courtroom is not a laboratory.'[6] Marshall links these remarks to a perfectly intelligible criticism of the adversarial system and to that trial by media which is so characteristic of the American trial context (and increasingly of the Australian) but the quotation reveals an underlying ideology in which only the laboratory is a fit setting for truth. The silliness of this outlook should hardly need demonstrating (the truths of simple perception, elementary calculation, rudimentary history, and subtle personality investigation, as in Shakespeare's plays, constitute decisive refutation straight off), but quite apart from its evident falsity the way in which its adherents depart from it in practice is equally striking. Marshall spends a good deal of his time pursuing truth by quoting authorities (Wellman, Cardozo, Wigmore, etc.), and by engaging in primitive moral philosophy. His case is not untypical in its emphases, though it is perhaps at the extreme end of a continuum in its expression.[7]

It is salutary to note such underlying assumptions before proceeding to more detailed analysis, if only because discussions in the area of law

---

[5] See especially H. E. Egeth and M. McCloskey, 'Expert Testimony about Eyewitness Behaviour: Is it Safe and Effective?' in Wells and Loftus (eds.), *Eyewitness Testimony*, 283–303. Several other essays in that volume also show a new sense of caution as do quite a few contributions to S. M. A. Lloyd-Bostock and B. R. Clifford (eds.), *Evaluating Witness Evidence* (Chichester, 1983).

[6] Marshall, *Law and Psychology*, 5.

[7] But see also G. Allport and L. Postman, *The Psychology of Rumour* (New York, 1965), ch. 4. For the 'primitive moral philosophy', see Marshall, *Law and Psychology*, 1–2.

reform so seldom advert to them. This, in itself, represents a public relations triumph for the positivist or scientistic ideology. The 'findings' of psychological *science* are represented as the outcome of quite neutral cognitive processes operated by beings of a superior intellectual and moral status whose interest in the outcome and applicaton of their inquiries is wholly 'scientific', i.e. beyond discussion. A curious paradox results when this picture is confronted with the actual claims of the tradition, since these claims are predominantly dismissive and disparaging of basic human capacities for arriving at the truth. Only the psychologist stands aloof, above the fray, Promethean and triumphant—but how? After all, many of the frailties and fallibilities he purports to uncover are apparently part of the human condition and is he not human? Does he not use perception, memory, inference, testimony? Is he not biased, partial, full of expectations and ambitions—even in his professional work? Does he lack a psychology?

Perhaps I will be told that these are empirical questions and the answer to them waits upon laboratory investigation. If so, might I propose a new research programme for psychologists—the investigation of the psychology of psychological research. A rich area, I suggest, and surely given extra stimulus by the unmasking of Sir Cyril Burt and the dawning realization that scientific fraud and sloppiness are more widespread than once suspected. Such a research programme has literally endless possibilities, since the psychology of the investigators will need to be investigated in turn and so on. But enough of such frivolity. The answers to my questions, though empirical, are obvious and require little if anything in the way of experimental endorsement.[8] What is really revealing is that so few psychologists or their audiences ever ask such questions or acknowledge the obvious facts that constitute answers to them. I should make it clear that I am not criticizing psychologists for possessing human faculties, nor for having philosophical and evaluative assumptions, but rather for pretending an absence of them. All sciences have philosophical and evaluative presuppositions and the human sciences have them to a striking degree. This is not a defect but a condition of growth. Some awareness of one's assumptions is also a condition of healthy development and certainly some of the persuppositions are more ephemeral and dubious than others.

It is time to turn to cases. The psychological investigation of human testimony, up until very recently, has concentrated upon establishing what its practitioners have chosen to call the unreliability of testimony. Here are the conclusions of one such investigator, propounded in *The Scientific*

---

[8] Though they may well find experimental expansion or refinement. To be fair, there are some studies in this area and there are anti-scientist voices raised from within the psychological profession, including some that make quite radical criticisms of the discipline and its self-image. See e.g. David Faust and Jay Ziskin, 'The Expert Witness in Psychology and Psychiatry', *Science*, 240 (1988), 31–5.

American: 'Eyewitness testimony is unreliable. Research and courtroom experience provide ample evidence that an eyewitness to a crime is being asked to be something and do something that a normal human being was not created to be or do.'[9] The author is Robert Buckhout, writing as recently as 1974, and his article contains details of experiments done by himself and colleagues, as well as other experiments dating back to the 1930s. Buckhout's discussion makes many sensible points about conditions under which testimony can mislead and I do not (for the moment) want to dispute any of his detailed evidence. What I want initially to object to is the form his conclusion takes. The claim that testimony is unreliable amounts to a sweeping rejection of it as a form of evidence. Just how drastic the rejection is supposed to be is never made clear by the critics, but since 'unreliable' means *unworthy of being relied upon* a remark like Buckhout's constitutes, on a natural reading, a pretty wholesale rejection. But any such rejection is absurd to the point of idiocy. This is exhibited in Buckhout's own article, as we can see if we ask why we should believe any of the results Buckhout *reports* to us about the experiments on testimony he says he has done and witnessed, or if we ask how Buckhout came by all sorts of information he relies upon in his work and quotes to us as definitively known. Buckhout tells the reader, fully expecting to be believed, that various results were obtained in a classic experiment in the 1930s by Jerome S. Bruner and Leo Postman at Harvard. This is only one of numerous pieces of hearsay that Buckhout produces to support the unreliability thesis.[10] I do not myself object to the hearsay—it is part and parcel of all scientific work, especially in the social sciences[11]— but Buckhout's own reliance is fatal to his unreliability thesis. Testimony cannot be unreliable if its reliability is required to prove that it is unreliable.

At this point I am likely to be charged with lack of sympathy for the psychologists concerned. No doubt they have expressed their conclusions incautiously, even badly, but what they should have said is not that testimony is unreliable, *tout court*, but that it is not always reliable. Such a conclusion is safer and palpably more plausible but it is hardly exciting. If the charge of unreliability is weakened to that of mere fallibility then it will readily be acknowledged as true but scarcely be in need of experimental confirmation. The psychological work on testimony will then appear to be another case of spending lots of research money establishing what was already a truism. Surely something stronger than mere falli-

---

[9] Robert Buckhout, 'Eyewitness Testimony', *Scientific American*, 231/6 (1974), 23–31.
[10] Ibid. 25.
[11] As we have noticed earlier the fact that this is so is often masked by talking of 'observation', 'observational fact' and so on without noticing that the sense of these expressions is communal. I can't resist quoting Marshall who notes that 'rumour is a form of hearsay' (p. 14) without realizing that so is a great deal of scientific evidence.

bilism was intended by all those confident publications? This 'something stronger' turns out, I think, to be the view that testimony is less reliable (or more fallible) than we all thought and less useful for certain purposes, especially in the law. This would certainly fit with one way of using the expression 'unreliable', since when we say that something is not worthy of being relied upon, the acceptability of this remark depends a lot on context, particularly that of purpose and expectation. A bicycle which is perfectly reliable for the purpose of travelling safely a few hundred yards to the shops may be quite unreliable for winning the Tour de France. Similarly, on expectations, it is pertinent to tell someone that, contrary to his expectations, his car cannot be relied upon to get him around unless it receives a certain amount of mechanical attention from time to time. So in the case of testimony research we find that the psychologists are operating with certain background assumptions of this kind. These are commonly implicit though, as we shall see, they are sometimes made explicit and they usually concern the common man and often the legal process. There are levels of expectation and suitability at work in the psychological literature I have read and I will consider them in order of generality, moving from the more to the less general.

1. The assumption of epistemological super-realism

This is the idea that 'we' (and the courts) are supposed to believe that testimony and *a fortiori* perception put us on to the world exactly as it really is. The psychologist then points out triumphantly, citing experimental results, that this is not so. This thesis hovers, it seems to me, between a relatively unexciting truism and a piece of, probably false, metaphysics masquerading as an experimental conclusion. The truism is that all our information comes to us through channels which select, specify, adapt, and transform. This is little more than a definitional point about a channel of information, perhaps about information itself, but it is easy to misread it or transform it into a metaphysical thesis either of a sceptical or an idealist nature. So it is thought that because we see via mechanisms with distinctive features so we do not see what is really there and that no two of us see the same thing. Marshall quotes approvingly another author as telling us that 'the correspondence between percept and object is never absolute' and goes on to say that what

this means to the layman is that all of the physical aspects of our environment vary to each individual in terms of his own experiences. What you and I see when two cars proceed down a street and collide is not the identical cars, streets and collisions, but cars, streets and collisions fashioned from our respective experiences with them.[12]

12 Marshall, *Law and Psychology*, 9.

This seems to be intended literally but so taken it is absurd, since the contrast between our visual experiences will only have the required point if we do see the very same cars, streets, and collisions, even though we may experience them very differently. Of course, none of us can see *everything* that is before our eyes; notoriously, we do not see the backs of opaque objects or the microstructures of things before us or currently non-realized dispositional properties. Again, we often misperceive our environment because of expectations that go astray, bad light, or bad temper, but we are not permanently cut off from the truth since we equally frequently correct these mistakes—otherwise we and the psychologists would never be in a position to offer dire warnings about the unreliability of the senses. And, of course, we correct misperception by accurate perception, so the reality which the misperceptions miss is well and truly captured by the accurate perceptions. No metaphysical scepticism can rest upon the facts of incomplete or errant perception, whether they be noticed by ordinary people or psychologists. The same point applies to any form of idealism in which reality is something we make up or, in the fashionable jargon of sociology, construct. Scepticism and idealism (and, for that matter, realism) are metaphysical theses to which experimental and empirical evidence are irrelevant. Whether they are true or false or even ultimately coherent is a matter for philosophical argument. What should be incontestable is that there is a clear non-metaphysical sense in which perception, memory, and testimony do put us unequivocally and 'absolutely' in touch with reality, i.e. there are definite truths which are based directly on these information sources. With regard to this level of expectation and suitability there can be no question about the reliability of perception and testimony.

2. The assumption of passive recording

This is made very clear by Buckhout and he thinks that it plays a mischievous role in court proceedings. In court, he says, 'a witness is often asked to play the role of a kind of tape recorder on whose tape the events of the crime have left an impression. The prosecution probes for stored facts and scenes and tries to establish that the witness's recording equipment was and still is in perfect running order'. Both prosecution and defence, according to Buckhout, 'succumb to the fallacy that everything was recorded and can be played back later through questioning'. Buckhout thinks that this reflects a mistaken nineteenth-century view of perception and memory, 'which asserted a parallel between the mechanisms of the physical world and those of the brain'.[13] This view is mistaken because

---

[13] Buckhout, 'Eyewitness Testimony', 23.

'the observer is an active rather than a passive perceiver and recorder, he reaches conclusions on what he has seen by evaluating fragments of information and reconstructing them'.[14] The desire for accuracy is one of his motivations but so is the desire to conform to the expectations and values of others.

A good deal of Buckhout's critique of the passivity picture is correct and timely. We had occasion in an earlier chapter to criticize even so penetrating an analyst as Thomas Reid for treating testimony in a fashion (at times) which seemed to rely upon a similarly unsatisfactory model of mere passive registering. None the less, Buckhout, like many others who make the point, seems to think that the critique excludes any element of passivity or registration or recording from the process of information acquisition. This is clearly not so. That we are active, selective, interpretive in what we perceive and recount is not only consistent with our also being in part passive, receptive, and recorder-like but it actually seems to require it. Unless we register quite a lot we cannot act, select, and interpret at all. The real story is quite complex and multi-layered; neither the picture of wholly passive registration nor that of furiously active invention is adequate.

Two other points need also to be noted about the tape-recorder analogy. In the first place, the recorder does not itself give a totally full and faithful replication of the world around it since its machinery and structure determine that there is a good deal it will not record, e.g. visual, tactile, gustatory, and olfactory information, as well as auditory information beyond its range. In the second place, in so far as the tape recorder is not selective, it can, by that very fact, be misleading or inaccurate. When a great deal of sound is being produced close to a very sensitive recording device then a softly spoken conversation may be impossible to decipher when the tape is played back, even though it has, in a sense, been faithfully recorded. An honest ear and eyewitness to the conversation is likely to be much better value than the recorder as a result of his or her selectivity.

These two points are important in the present connection because exposure of the tape-recorder fallacy need not show that testimony is just unreliable in a court of law by the standards appropriate to a tape recorder. That a human witness and a tape recorder will often give different results is not necessarily a point against the human witness. For some purposes it would be good if witnesses were like tape recorders, for others it would not. Apart from the advantages of selectivity mentioned, there are also the advantages of background knowledge and other human skills which make for better understanding than a machine can give. Knowing Jones well, I may be able to tell at once from his manner, gesture, look, and tone that some remark is humorous or ironical, where the tape recorder will register a neutral but potentially sinister utterance.

---

[14] Ibid. 24.

There is the further point, of course, that in real courtroom scenes some human witness is always necessary to testify to the evidentiary setting of a tape recording—who was being taped, where, when, and how. I conclude therefore that the assumption of passive recording needs criticism and exposure but that this does not in itself show some unreliability in testimony.

3. The assumption of very great accuracy

This may be linked to (2) but need not be. When the idea is promoted that experiments show testimony to be less reliable than we all thought, the clear suggestion is that we thought it was generally very accurate indeed. Unless this were so then findings like an accuracy rate of 74 per cent for identification of a perpetrator in relatively good viewing conditions—i.e. no head covering and twenty seconds visibility—would demonstrate reliability rather than unreliability (and many studies show better percentage results than this one, depending on context and task).[15]

We need to ask: is this assumption widely shared and, as a proposition, is it true or false? As to the first, the claim is often made in the psychological literature that jurors and other laymen are far too trusting of eyewitness evidence. Here we need to look more closely at the detailed evidence but there is such a welter of it that it is hard to know quite how to proceed. The question splits into at least two parts: (*a*) how much reliance can be placed on testimony of various sorts, and (*b*) how much *is* placed upon it?

To begin with (*a*), it is important to distinguish the 'various sorts', though this is seldom done in the literature I have read. The testimony we confront in everyday life covers a vast range of subject-matter, situation, and context, and it invokes a variety of different skills and tasks. The same is true of the lawcourts. For understandable reasons, there is a strong tendency in the psychological work to use the term 'eyewitness testimony' principally for evidence of suspect identification and also, though with less emphasis, certain associated matters such as the identification of what we might call 'suspect events' or 'suspect intervals'. So there has been quite a lot of work on witnesses' estimates of how long a time a dramatic crime-like event took. But witnesses give vast amounts of information to courts other than this sort of thing—important as it can be. People tell us, surely with a high degree of reliability though not with infallibility, who they are, what work they do, where they live, how old they are, details of their familiar environment, their spouses' and children's names, ages, occupa-

---

[15] See R. C. L. Lindsay, G. L. Wells, and C. Rumpel, 'Can People Detect Eyewitness Identification Accuracy within and across Situations?', *Journal of Applied Psychology*, 66 (1981), 79–89.

tions, and similarly for their close friends and colleagues (much of this, of course, being hearsay but none the less valuable for that). They also *identify* familiar acquaintances, friends, colleagues, lovers, spouses, offspring, and old enemies with remarkable accuracy. This accuracy is still pretty remarkable about their personal belongings. All of these areas can provide vital information in daily life and in the course of a trial, yet my reading uncovered no reference to such competencies. I speculate that we rightly place very substantial reliance upon such testimony.[16]

No doubt, it might be replied, and it is salutary to note such facts, but what of the areas the psychologists have concentrated upon. Here, I think, the overall situation is rather unclear, though one should, at the outset, acknowledge that the psychologists have done a service to the law by creating more of a public conscience about suspect identification than once existed. None the less, there is much to query about the experimental work, even on its strongest ground. Some of it, indeed, reminds me of Wittgenstein's concluding remarks in his *Philosophical Investigations*: 'in psychology there are experimental methods and *conceptual confusion*'.[17] (Lest I seem to be endorsing the implicit arrogance of this utterance let me hasten to add that work in my own discipline sometimes makes me feel that in philosophy there is *only* conceptual confusion.)

Certainly, a good deal that I have read in this area turns upon conceptual and interpretive manœuvres that are highly questionable and, although more caution might have removed these deficiencies, there is, I think, a sense in which the data of psychology are essentially contestable. I shall return to this point but first I shall try to show the sort of thing I mean about the research areas in question. It will not be possible to present a wide-ranging survey but I will present what has struck me as characteristically problematic. Consider first an experiment to which Buckhout refers and calls 'a classic experiment'.[18] It was done in the 1930s (if Buckhout's testimony is to be believed) by Jerome Bruner and Leo Postman at no less prestigious an institution than Harvard University. In it a group of observers 'were shown a display of playing cards for a few seconds and asked to report the number of aces of spades in the display'.[19] They were allowed only a brief glance and most reported seeing three aces of spades in the array of twelve cards, all of which were aces. Most observers reported seeing only three aces of spades but our wily psychologists knew better. As Buckhout puts it: 'Actually there were five; two of them were coloured red instead of the more familiar black. People are so

[16] That it is testimony can hardly be denied but it is not only overlooked in the literature but denied by implication. Researchers as careful as Wells and Loftus, in discussing a case in which a man suffered a great deal through mistaken identification, note that he was acquitted because of a strong alibi 'and other *circumstantial* exonerating evidence' (*Eyewitness Testimony*, 2, my italics). Yet alibis are essentially testimonial.
[17] L. Wittgenstein, *Philosophical Investigations* (Oxford, 1953), Part 2, xiv.
[18] Buckhout, 'Eyewitness Testimony', 25.
[19] Ibid.

familiar with black aces of spaces that they do not waste time looking at the display carefully'.[20] In the caption under a reproduction of the display Buckhout, or his editor, writes: 'Because people expect aces of spades to be black, not red, they tend to see only the black ones and to miss the atypical red ones. Thus do prior conditioning and experience influence perception'.[21] Thus, we might also say, in paraphrase, do prior conditioning and expectation of the appropriate experimental outcome influence psychological research. It is clear that this 'classic experiment' shows virtually nothing about witness reliability. The experimenters have treated the blackness of an ace of spades as a merely accidental though common feature of it and simply failed to consider that it may be, or may be reasonably considered by their subjects to be, an essential or definitional feature. In fact, it is very plausible to hold that the phrase 'red ace of spades' reports not an unfamiliar ace of spades but an impossible card. (I should not advise Messrs Buckhout, Bruner, and Postman to produce red aces of spades in some of the poker schools I know of.) Given the meaning-assigning conventions of the card pack there can be no red aces of spades, though of course someone can manufacture a card with the structural features of the ace of spades but the wrong colour. The psychologists must have thought (if they considered the conceptual aspects of their experiment at all) that the card families were defined by their structural features alone, but this strikes me (and, more importantly, would have struck the subjects) as foolish. Hence, since there are only three (unambiguously definite) aces of spades, most of the subjects were right.

In one of Trankell's well-known experiments with a staged crime we find another slightly different type of example of ambiguity.[22] Trankell staged a bogus crime during one of his lectures. A student confederate entered while the class was in session and, after behaving in a way that could be seen as offensive to the lecturer, was evicted by Trankell who followed him out of the theatre. Verbal exchanges continued between the two outside the theatre and they were visible for a while to at least some of the class, but then, when they were out of sight, noises, including the sound of two shots (fired in fact by a laboratory assistant), were heard in the lecture room, followed by a moan ending in a scream. Trankell then returned to the room and in public view rang the university janitor asking him to come and take care of the student. There are further details which need not concern us now, nor need we discuss the morality of these deceitful and potentially traumatic manipulations, though it is interesting, I find, that the moral dimension worries psychologists so little.[23] What I

[20] Ibid. 25–6.
[21] Ibid. 25.
[22] A. Trankell, *Reliability of Evidence* (Stockholm, 1972), 33–7 for description of 'crime'.
[23] Perhaps this is less true since the fuss created by Milgram's experiments. See S. Milgram, *Obedience and Authority* (London, 1974); cf. S. Patten, 'The Case that Milgram Makes', *Philosophical Review*, 96 (1971), 350–64.

want to look at is one of the conclusions Trankell drew from the interview
and questionnaire data he compiled after the 'crime'. This concerns the
audience's reports of what took place when Trankell and the troublesome
student proceeded to leave the lecture room. The students were asked:
'How many times do you consider Trankell pushed S on their way to the
door?' Trankell admits that this question is loaded (suggesting an answer
of at least once) but he thinks it is all the more necessary to ask since
'similar questions are easily found in police interrogations and during the
hearing of witnesses in court'.[24] Triumphantly he announces that only 'six
out of the twenty-seven witnesses who took part in the interrogation gave
the correct answer to this question (that is to say that S was not pushed at
all)'.[25] Ignoring, for the moment, the fact that *we* have only Trankell's
word for what really happened (we are not told by Trankell whether the
student corroborated it), it is interesting to go back and read Trankell's
description of the incident. He says: '... the lecturer got up and took the
student by the arm. The student also rose from his chair, shook off the
lecturer's hand but went with him slowly towards the door, protesting
sulkily: "But why? ... huh? ... I can go by myself ... damned dictatorial
attitude!"'.[26]

Two men are becoming heated with each other, or seem to be; one
seizes ('takes') the other by the arm and the other, rising, shakes off the
dismissive hand with a sulky protest about his capacity to leave under his
own steam. Did the first push the second? Well it depends what you mean
by a push (just as it depends what you mean by an ace of spades).
Certainly, one could not see either the answer 'none' or 'one' as clearly
false; the question is too ill defined for that. Even the answer 'two' might
be within acceptable bounds, depending upon a more detailed description
of what occurred—perhaps Trankell took S rather fiercely by the arm
and tried to regain his grip when shaken loose. Trankell does not tell us
any of that but then he was no doubt under great stress at the time and
psychological evidence indicates that people under stress are not reliable
reporters. It turns out that five of the subjects did not answer because they
said they could not see or could not remember how the expulsion had been
carried out—or perhaps (may we speculate?) could not be sure what the
questioner meant by 'push'—and another four said one push. This leaves
only twelve out of twenty-seven getting the wrong answer, under the
powerful stimulus of a loaded question, as compared with the original
estimate of twenty-one out of twenty-seven. If the answer two is allowed
by the ambiguity of question and situation then another five come in from
the cold, so that those fairly clearly wrong reduce to seven out of twenty-
seven. The unclarities inherent in several of Trankell's procedures can be

---

[24] Trankell, *Reliability*, 43.
[25] Ibid.
[26] Ibid. 36.

seen in his praise of one of the subjects, L. A., who is called impartial and objective. She does not speak of 'pushing' in her account of the expulsion and is lauded for her 'uncommon abilty to register reality'[27] by the author. What he does not comment upon is that she describes the student as having 'been thrown out of the room'.[28] Perhaps this is only metaphor, but on the face of it her description is stronger by far than 'pushed'.

Turning now to a more recent practitioner of the art we find Elizabeth Loftus claiming, on the basis of a test administered to a group of subjects, that jurors and witnesses are insufficiently aware of the difficulties of cross-racial identifications. The test consisted of a multiple choice question with four alternatives and Loftus found that only 55 per cent of the respondents got the right answer but, as Egeth and McCloskey point out in their review of some recent research in the area, Loftus's phrasing of the test made it too complex and difficult to understand. This is the test:

Two women were walking to school one morning, one of them an Asian and the other white. Suddenly, two men, one black and one white, jump into their path and attempt to grab their purses. Later, the women are shown photographs of known purse snatchers in the area. Which statement best describes your view of the women's ability to identify the purse snatchers?

(a) Both the Asian and the white woman will find the white man harder to identify than the black man.

(b) The white woman will find the black man more difficult to identify than the white man.

(c) The Asian woman will have an easier time than the white woman making an accurate identification of both men.

(d) The white woman will find the black man easier to identify than the white man.[29]

Although (b) is supposed to be 'the' right answer, it is not at all clear what (c) is to be understood as saying. Even more alarming is the paper cited by Egeth and McCloskey in which Loftus and a colleague (Deffenbacher) asked subjects their opinion of the cliché 'they all look alike to me'. Since the saying is a gross exaggeration of a genuine difficulty it is heartening to find that only 20 per cent of the respondents marked it as true but, as Egeth and McCloskey comment: 'It is less encouraging to note that this is the alternative the authors of the study deemed correct'.[30]

Apart from these interpretive flaws, which I suggest are *endemic* to the research work in this area, there are also other methodological problems. I mentioned at the outset the strong ideological bias (scientism) explicit in

[27] Ibid. 52.
[28] Ibid. 51.
[29] E. F. Loftus, *Eyewitness Testimony* (Harvard, 1979), quoted in H. E. Egeth and M. McCloskey, 'Expert Testimony about Eyewitness Behaviour', in Wells and Loftus (eds.), *Eyewitness Testimony* (Cambridge, 1984), 296.
[30] Egeth and McCloskey, 'Expert Testimony', 302.

much of the earlier work. This not only produced a good deal of preaching but much exaggeration of the solidity and uniformity of the psychological results, both experimental and theoretical, which lay behind the preaching. This phenomenon goes back a long way. In 1909, John H. Wigmore published a humorous, if at times heavy-handed, critique of Münsterberg's book in the *Illinois Law Review*,[31] in which he pointed out that there was by no means the consensus amongst psychologists on the various aspects of testimony research which Münsterberg's broadside against the legal profession would suggest. Wigmore not only pointed to differences of methodology between different psychological schools[32] concerned with the area but to considerable scepticism and dispute within the psychological profession about the significance of the results said to be obtained. He also cited contradictory results from distinguished practitioners. Stern had claimed to show the 'law' that lapse of time affects the memory not only by weakening it but also by falsifying it.[33] Wigmore pointed out that Jaffa's results showed that the average number of errors in testimony taken on the same day as the event was 9.7, and taken five weeks later was only 7, which he took it, 'exactly contradicted' Stern's supposed law.

The tendency of the social sciences to present a misleadingly unified front when on show to the public, especially in an advisory capacity, has perhaps moderated a little in the past eighty years or so but it has hardly disappeared. In some respects there are even more pressures in that direction with the huge expansion of professional services based upon these studies. Certainly, the phenomenon of contradictory results is still a feature of the testimony research area though, as far as I can tell, it is only in recent years that this has been fairly publicly discussed by psychologists. The general and legal public are still largely unaware of such conflict.[34] This can be illustrated with a few examples. It is widely maintained in the literature[35] that stress experienced during the event being reported on reduces the accuracy of the testimony given, yet the empirical support for this claim is dubious. A thorough review of the literature on stress by Deffenbacher yields nine of the nineteen relevant studies showing that increases in arousal improve eyewitness accuracy. Deffenbacher suggests a way of making the results consistent (essentially by the hypothesis that

[31] J. H. Wigmore, 'Professor Muensterberg and the Psychology of Testimony', *Illinois Law Review*, 3/7 (Feb. 1909), 399–434.

[32] Particularly the Stern school of certainty-measurement and the Jung–Wertheimer associationist method.

[33] Wigmore, 'Professor Muensterberg' (cit. n. 31), 426.

[34] Three papers which make reference to it are: B. R. Clifford, 'A Critique of Eyewitness Research', in M. M. Gruneberg, P. E. Morris, and R. N. Sykes (eds.), *Practical Aspects of Memory* (London, 1978); D. M. Saunders, N. Vidmar, and E. C. Hewitt, 'Eyewitness Testimony and the Discrediting Effect', in S. M. A. Lloyd-Bostock and B. R. Clifford (eds.), *Evaluating Witness Evidence* (Chichester, 1983); and Egeth and McCloskey, 'Expert Testimony'.

[35] See Loftus, *Eyewitness Testimony* (cit. n. 29).

performance is poor at high and low levels but better at intermediate levels) but the hypothesis has not yet, to my knowledge, been tested.[36] 'Weapon focus' is another factor cited by some psychologists[37] which is supposed to interfere with eyewitness accuracy. This is the supposed tendency of someone threatened with a weapon to focus on the weapon and pay little attention to the appearance of the assailant. Egeth and McCloskey, writing in 1984, say that there is virtually no evidence for this phenomenon.[38] Finally, there is the 'discrediting failure effect', reported by Loftus in 1974, which is of particular interest because, unlike much else in this field, its results were genuinely surprising. She found that, in a juror simulation study, the subjects seemed not to disregard discredited eyewitness testimony, thus apparently showing undue reliance upon testimony. Other studies do not support this conclusion and others again, attempting to replicate Loftus's research, seem flatly to contradict it.[39] As Saunders *et al.* say in summary, 'the body of empirical research bearing on the discrediting failure effect is contradictory and ambiguous'.[40] I cannot resist mentioning that the discrediting material presented by Loftus to her subjects took the form of a summary of the defence attorney's case! It was put to the subjects that counsel for the defence showed various things about the witness's poor eyesight and it would not be surprising if the 'jurors' did not give this full weight as a discrediting. Once more, conceptual and perhaps ethical naïvety are to be found in the experiment rather than in the subjects. It is only fair to add that Saunders *et al.* pick this point up.[41]

Talk of the discrediting failure effect returns us to point (*b*), concerning the factual issue of how much reliance is actually placed on testimony.

Whatever the facts about the unreliability of testimony of a certain sort in certain settings (and our verdict should be, I suggest, 'not proven' at the least), we also need to ask whether the various experiments on the individual's capacities of perception, memory, and accuracy are addressing the relevant question for the law. As Wigmore stressed so long ago, the crucial question is how judges and juries assess the testimony presented to them. Here what evidence there is from the psychologists does not give too much cause for alarm. There are some areas in which suggestive and possibly pertinent work has been done. The research on confidence may be one.

---

[36] Cited and discussed in Egeth and McCloskey, 'Expert Testimony', 297.

[37] Loftus, *Eyewitness Testimony* (cit. n. 29), 223–4.

[38] Egeth and McCloskey, 'Expert Testimony', 297.

[39] M. A. Myers, 'Rule Departures and Making Law: Juries and Their Verdicts', *Law and Society*, 13 (1979), 781–97; N Hatvany and F. Strack, 'The Impact of a Key Discredited Witness', *Journal of Applied Social Psychology*, 10 (1980), 490–509; H. I. Weinberg and R. S. Baron, 'The Discredible Eyewitness', *Personality and Social Psychology Bulletin*, 8 (1982), 60–7.

[40] Saunders, Vidmar, and Hewitt, 'Eyewitness Testimony', 60.

[41] Ibid. 61.

Some evidence suggests both that the confidence of a witness is not a good indicator of his reliability and that jurors are overimpressed by confidence,[42] but even here one would need considerable assurance that the conceptual layers built into the notion of confidence have been properly unravelled before instructing jurors positively to disregard witness confidence. There is a world of difference between the brash assertiveness of the man who never contemplates being wrong about anything and the quiet, unaggressive person whose opinions are often qualified and diffident but who is here quite certain and unshakeable about what was seen. There is no guarantee that either is wrong or right but I should be inclined to discount the firmness of the former and be rather impressed by the resolution of the latter—yet both may be called 'confidence'. I have not made a full examination of the work on confidence but from what I have so far encountered in the literature I should be surprised if such distinctions had been sufficiently allowed for.

Clifford has argued that there is a paradigm disarray in the field of eyewitness research. Stripped of jargon, what this means is that there is a deep uncertainty about just what sorts of areas to study. There may well be a great gap between the realities of courtroom and police station and results obtained in laboratory conditions with photo displays (one of Marshall's being absurdly said to contain '115 possible items...to be recalled'),[43] or with mock crimes and university students who by now probably know what to expect when the 'crime' occurs and are not under genuinely urgent constraints in their reportings afterwards. Yet better paradigm test situations are hard to come by since there are powerful moral and legal arguments against turning actual courtrooms and juryrooms into psychological laboratories. These arguments are all the more powerful for being opposed by the relatively feeble body of results which psychological investigation has so far produced.

Finally, there is the question whether psychologists working in this area should be called as expert witnesses. This question is partly one of how reliable their findings are and here my view is that, where the findings go beyond common sense and what is already known to lawyers, then they are too controversial and unsubstantiated to be introduced as expert evidence. Even if they were both more interesting and better established there would still be a problem and it is a problem that arises within the whole category of expert evidence. This is a problem we shall be in a better position to address in the next chapter.

[42] G. L. Wells, R. C. Lindsay, and T. J. Ferguson, 'Accuracy, Confidence and Juror Perceptions in Eyewitness Identification', *Journal of Applied Psychology*, 64 (1979), 440–8.
[43] Marshall, *Law and Psychology*, 44.

16

Experts and the Law

MOUSE. Who are you?
FOX. I'm Robin Hood.
MOUSE. You don't look like Robin Hood, but if you say you are then
  it must be true, because Robin Hood wouldn't tell a lie.

(Characters in a Warner Brothers cartoon.)

The English law has never been altogether happy with expert testimony but increasingly it has had to learn to live with it. What began as something of a shotgun marriage has persisted as a cool and occasionally testy liaison, in which legal authority has striven mightily to keep expertise in a subordinate role. Elsewhere, notably in the American jurisdiction, the relationship seems more like open concubinage with all the shifting complexities of power and dominance that image suggests.

As I argued in Chapters 2 and 3, perfectly normal lay testimony already contains an element of expertise (captured by the competency condition in our definition) so that expert testimony, as a category, should present no difficulties of basic principle. Within the tradition of English law, none the less, a special problem of principle arises because of the hearsay restriction, since (as we saw in Chapters 1 and 2) a great deal of expert evidence will involve hearsay simply because of the collaborative and ramified nature of scientific and other intellectual and skilled enterprises. It will also involve something closely related to opinion evidence, which is also (as we saw in Chapter 3) subject to restrictions.[1] Certainly, experts give the court the benefit of their (and others') experience in the form of conclusions or generalizations from that experience. If this is opinion, it is valuable and often necessary opinion, and differs in several respects from the sort of opinion the courts are understandably anxious to exclude. Again, as we saw earlier, some generalizations from lay experience are admissible, such as estimates of age, identity, and speed. (A topic whose admissibility is much debated in this connection is drunkenness.) Other general facts can gain admission under the heading of judicial notice when they are sufficiently notorious.[2] In none of these cases is the witness (or the court) providing mere speculations or personal inferences or usurping the func-

---

[1] It may also trespass upon the prohibited areas of 'similar fact' evidence but the nature and rationale of this prohibition is too curious and complex for present investigation.

[2] e.g. the court in the *Case of the Oxford Poor Rate* in 1857, took notice that Oxford University was 'a national institution created for a great national purpose, the advancement, namely, of religion and learning through the nation' (1857) 8 E. & B. 184.

tion of the tribunal to come to its own conclusions on the facts, but I shall not discuss this further since I have given my view of the relation between testimony and opinion in Chapter 3. I shall, however, return to one issue arising from this.

We may conclude, then, that the complications introduced by the hearsay and opinion elements in expert evidence present no major barriers of basic principle to the acceptability of expert evidence. True as this is, it would be seriously misleading if seen as the only truth about the matter. Most significantly, the lay witnesses' expertise does not in general present itself to the tribunal, judge, or jury, in any mysterious trappings. Most of us know what it is to have decent eyesight, normal memory, common experience, and standard conceptual equipment; we have a fair chance of detecting whether witnesses who purport to be relying on them are really so endowed. Not so in the case of real expertise. Here, there are difficulties in determining whether a potential witness really has the relevant quali-fications and, even more seriously, whether his qualifications are in an area of genuine knowledge. On the first point, the courts have generally held, surely correctly, that formal qualifications are not necessary for expertise, but it is a much cloudier question just what sort of background is nec-essary. On the whole, the courts have looked favourably upon practice and experience and not insisted upon the skills acquired by theoretical study of 'an organised branch of knowledge'.[3] As Eggleston points out,[4] there are many cases in which expertise gained by practical experience in a non-theoretical context has been rightly utilized by a court. An experienced hotelkeeper, for instance, who had watched the trade at a particular hotel with a view to making an offer to purchase, was called to testify to the likelihood of a representation as to takings at the hotel being true. In another case 'experienced cattlemen deposed to the risk involved in putting young horses in the same field as horned cattle in marsh land'.[5]

There seems to be little point in distinguishing too much between ad-missible evidence involving generalization from special experience or practice and that expert evidence which is identified with some systematic body of theory. There is some pressure in the legal tradition to make a division of this kind however. Indeed, a threefold division now seems mandatory in Australian courts concerning admissible generalizations from particular experiences. Eggleston, commenting on the *Clark* v. *Ryan* decision in the High Court of Australia, says that Australian courts now seem required to distinguish between the non-expert witness who can testify as to ordinary matters of observation such as speed, the specially

---

[3] The phrase is that of Menzies J. in *Clark* v. *Ryan* before the High Court of Australia. His endorsement of this strict requirement is exceptional. See R. Eggleston, *Evidence, Proof and Probability* (London, 1978), 128–9.

[4] Ibid.

[5] Ibid.

experienced non-expert witness who deposes to facts and probabilities within the area of his special experience, and, finally, experts proper. As Eggleston argues, a sharp separation of the second and third categories is unreal and creates dangerous confusions in the law of evidence. Eggleston's basic objection to the Australian High Court's attempt to reserve the term 'expert' to someone who has gained his skill in some 'profession or course of study' is not only that it miscontrues the English authorities it quotes[6] and is seriously at odds with the precedents, but that adopting its recommendation forces the law to resort to gobbledegook in order to try to explain the patent admissibility of the evidence of the experienced non-expert. Witnesses in this category not only give an opinion but usually rely in giving it both upon hearsay and upon evidence of 'similar fact'. Since the illusion must be sustained that only experts can do this it is necessary to pretend that such witnesses are deposing only to personally observed facts. Rather than yield to communal self-deception it is better to classify them along with those experts whose skill has been gained from an 'organised branch of knowledge'. In agreeing with Eggleston on this, however, we must be careful not to claim that there is no point at all in distinguishing between experts of different kinds and, in particular, between the two categories in question. Let us, as a labour-saving device, call the specially experienced expert who has no background in an organized branch of knowledge, or no formal educational qualifications of pertinence, an empiric, and the contrasting expert, a scientist. I stress that these are terms of art and are not meant to imply either that empirics are in any way fraudulent (as some uses of the term do imply) nor that scientists are marvellously reliable (after all, scientists here may include literary experts). None the less, they seem appropriate labels since the term 'empiric' once had currency precisely to describe those who, especially in the practice of medicine, abjured abstract theory and relied solely on observation and experiment; and the word 'scientist', though it now has somewhat narrower scope, would once have suggested anyone devoted to some more or less systematic branch of theoretical learning.

Now one point of contrast between empirics and scientists is that scientists, due to their heavier investment in theorizing, are going to be less readily intelligible to the layman. They will think and speak in a

---

[6] Menzies J. seems to have relied ultimately upon the classic judgment of Lord Mansfield in *Folkes* v. *Chad* which is frequently cited (or garbled) but not so commonly understood. What Lord Mansfield actually said was, 'in matters of science, the reasonings of men of science can only be answered by men of science'. This is often taken to mean, as by Menzies J., that only men of science (from 'an organized branch of knowledge') can give expert evidence, but not only does this go beyond the literal meaning of the Mansfield dictum, it also ignores the point of the remark in context. Lord Mansfield was agreeing that a new trial had been properly ordered because expert evidence by an engineer at the original trial had come as a surprise to one of the parties. Lord Mansfield was saying that if your expert is a scientist then your opponents should have the opportunity to test and oppose his evidence by calling another scientist.

vocabulary replete with technical terms and theoretical assumptions not easily accessible to an outsider. This will be less true, if true at all, of the empiric (recall Eggleston's examples of the hotelkeeper and the cattlemen) whose expertise is not only largely untainted by theory but is seldom entirely remote from ordinary experience. Consequently, the first problem posed by the scientific expert for the courts is the problem of intelligibility. This is not just the problem of understanding what information the scientific expert is trying to convey, though that is serious enough. There is also the problem that the expert herself is likely to be strongly tempted to the sin of advocacy in proportion as she realizes that the unadorned presentation of her scientific information is likely not to be understood and, indeed, to be misunderstood.

There is also the fact that, the more esoteric the scientific expert's evidence becomes, the more authoritative it is likely to appear to the lay person. Not only is there a natural tendency in this direction but there are also cultural pressures in Western society towards according an honorific status to the scientific—more in the narrow sense than in my technical sense but carrying over to it. In what follows I shall generally use 'science' in the narrow, more popular sense, in which physics is the paradigm science but the issues raised by the wider sense will be discussed under the heading of neo-science. To the degree that an expert can parade as (in the popular sense) a scientist, to that degree can his opinion have a weight and authority that it may not deserve, not just because he may not be a particularly good specimen of 'homo scientificus' but also because what he testifies to may be much more contestable than the deferential lay person is inclined to believe. To a considerable extent, indeed, the adversarial system acts as something of a check on these tendencies, and that is one of its virtues. However, it is a virtue that carries with it the danger of a corresponding vice. A case which involves a battle of opposing experts is liable to bewilder or bore a jury or a judge and make it likely that the decision will be made in disregard of what legitimate expert information could have been utilized.

Part of the problem about the status of the scientific expert concerns the image that the lay person is likely to have of science, scientific processes, and the scientist himself. At least up until very recently, the image of the scientist was thoroughly Promethean: he had outwitted the gods and stolen the divine secrets which he had put to work for human benefit. He did not yet know everything, but what he knew was quite secure and certain and he would come to know more and more. He had not yet made life perfect by his applied knowledge (his 'technology'), but he was working on it. In its essentials this is, of course, very much a nineteenth-century outlook, but its survival power is remarkable. The image persists in the popular mind in spite of the undermining effects, on the theoretical side, of the revolutions and revisions of twentieth-century physics and biology, and

on the practical side, of the technologies of death, destruction, and dena-
turing which powerfully evoke the darker, punitive side of the Promethean
legend. Amongst intellectuals these undermining events have had much
more impact, as indeed also amongst the educated and semi-educated
young. Sometimes the reaction has gone to what are, in my view, alarm-
ingly irrational extremes but, in any case, theorists of science are much
more realistic about the degree of uncertainty and provisionality in current
pure science, about the differences between different kinds of scientific
theory, about the influences of religious (including irreligious), political,
and other ideologies upon scientists and science, and about the ambiguous
values inherent in the applications of science.

This more sceptical but more realistic vision of science and scientist does
not mean that the scientific expert has no role to play in the courts. It does
mean, however, that the courts will fail to make proper use of scientific
experts unless they have this more adequate understanding of what scientific expertise is like. One reason why juries can become confused or
cynical about expert evidence when they find a clash of opposing experts,
or confront other uncertainties revealed by cross-examination, is that their
imaginations are dominated by the Promethean image discussed above.
Even a slightly more subtle picture of science would make such confronta-
tions potentially less shocking. It is surely the responsibility of the court
and the legal process, on the one hand, and the expert witness himself, on
the other, to ensure, as best they can, that juries do not expect too much of
science in the courtroom. The task is in many respects just that of getting
them to think of the expert scientific witness as more like the ordinary
non-expert witness and the empiric, since conflict and uncertainty amongst
these should create no shock or surprise.

Saying this much is not, however, to say very much and it is to remain at
a level of relatively unhelpful abstraction. There remains the specific and
often daunting question of how to assess particular scientific experts and
their evidence. This splits into at least three questions: (1) whether the
witness is indeed expert in the field; (2) whether the field is a genuine area
of science; (3) whether, given a positive answer to (1) and (2), his particular depositions are credible. Similar questions arise about empirics and,
to some extent, about ordinary witnesses,[7] but they do not create as acute
problems. All three of these questions pose difficulty for a legal tribunal
since they seem to be questions that only an expert can answer. Hence the
spectre of a vicious logical regress arises. To discover whether Smith is
really an expert physicist I do not, of course, have to depend only on
Smith's assertion that this is so (though I might find reason to do so in
some situations), since I can ask other people about it. At some point,

---

[7] Question (1) is just the question of competence discussed in Ch. 2; question (2) seldom
arises for an ordinary witness but perhaps would for a witness claiming extra-sensory
powers; question (3) is a standard one.

however, I must be satisfied that I have reliable information from sources who know how to determine whether people are expert physicists. Clearly, I cannot determine the matter directly, in the sense of checking for myself on the truth of the information about physics which he gives me, for that would require that I too be an expert physicist. Equally clearly, finding out from other expert physicists whether Smith is one requires my settling the question whether they are and so on. In addition to worrying about who shall guard the guardians we must worry about who shall certify the certifiers. We have here an analogue, in the legal sphere, of an epistemological problem discussed in Chapter 4 concerning our reliance on testimony in general. There we saw that one difficulty for the reductivist project, which required that kinds of report be individually correlated with kinds of (reported) situations, was created by the ambiguity of the expression 'kind of report'. It could be treated as report of a kind of speaker or report of a kind of situation. Both interpretations had their problems but the former turned on the issue of expertise and was, roughly, that where 'kind of speaker' meant, as it naturally would appear to, expert of a certain sort, then the project was self-defeating since no checks on the general reliability of experts could begin until it was discovered who the experts were, and once this was discovered there was no further check on their reliability left to make. In the present practical context, we may equally wonder how the non-expert court can get into a position to determine the apparently expert witness's credentials without becoming so expert itself as to render his expertise unnecessary.[8] On the other hand, while it remains (more realistically) non-expert it faces the regress mentioned earlier.

There are ways of sofening this paradox in the context of practice and perhaps of eliminating it entirely. We have certifying bodies and institutions and their various certificates and, typically, the courts require that the witness be shown to have some relevant certification from such bodies. Doubt can arise, of course, about the credentials of supposedly expert institutions (as admissions officers in universities and similar institutions are well aware) but usually the courts do not doubt such credentials. Were they to require for every such certifying body some proof of its credentials, it is hard to see what could be forthcoming, other than more of the same. In fact their attitude is one of trust in most such bodies and, given that the general reliability of testimony is not in doubt, this attitude can be given an indirect justification. Unless we take a thoroughgoing sceptical stance we can assume that it is, for instance, in the nature of scientific expertise to be communal. There are leaders and initiators in the various sciences but

---

[8] Or relatively so. The matter is complicated by the fact that it is not just his expert opinion on relevant generalities that is needed but sometimes his expert observations on particular facts to which the court lacks access.

their work is recognized, criticized, expanded, carried forward, by a group who understand what the initiators have done and are doing. Such a group will have an interest in protecting the standards of inquiry in the area of science they practise, in exposing pretenders to the expertise that gives a focus to their lives, and, especially if their expertise has direct practical value for the outside community, in providing certification or warranties of expertise. One would therefore expect there to be such bodies as boards, colleges, universities, which fulfilled these functions (amongst others). No doubt they will not be infallible; the occasional fraud will go undetected even for a long time and there will also be the problem, to be addressed shortly, of the fraudulence or doubtfulness of whole areas of putative scientific expertise. None the less, the community of scientific experts is, for the reasons given, a good litmus agent for the presence of the relevant expertise. Their failure to approve a witness's credentials by way of certification or the like, or, better still, their positive condemnation of such credentials, is at least good reason for the court to reject him as an expert.

But now the problem becomes more manageable. We still have to be able to determine that some group is a body of scientific experts or represents such a body but this problem is not as acutely regressive as the earlier one since we, as non-experts, can have non-expertly assessable evidence for this. What I mean is that the lay person can reason to the conclusion that there will inevitably be expert bodies with the sort of features discussed above and he can then observe the existence of what appear to be just such bodies. Various people tell him that they are members of the expert bodies and that the bodies really are expert, others tell him that their sons and daughters are being trained by such bodies in some expertise or other, and so on in a complicated web of testimony. Given that it is (as we have earlier argued) reasonable to treat testimony as generally reliable, then it is, other things being equal, reasonable to believe these attestations. This point is reinforced by the consideration that experts are, in the nature of the case (and here we echo our earlier transcendental deduction from the nature of expertise), highly sensitive to the possibility of fraudulent experts and even more to the possibility of fraudulent bodies of experts. Hence one would expect a dubious expert body to have evoked controversy, or at least some substantial criticism of its bona fides, and in the absence of any such one can presume authenticity.

All this is rather broad brush stroke but it is, I think, a fair picture for all that. The detail is inevitably more complex and ambiguous. No institution is altogether free from controversy about some aspects of its expertise and every institution or organization is challenged *in toto* by somebody—the Flat Earth Society has no time for modern astronomical societies or university departments of astronomy. None the less, the existence of a general consensus within the various families or groupings of scientific experts and between the different groupings, about such matters as the certification of expertise, is an impressive background fact against which the numerous debates, frictions, and fundamental disagreements need to be seen. Even where there is great disagreement about what is to be believed on some subject-matter there can, and even must, be extensive agreement about who is worth listening to on the topic. Mistakes will of course be made: there is always the prospect of that romantic figure who is wrongly ignored because he is ahead of his time or otherwise unfashionable, but we, and the law, are interested in general reliability, not infallibility.

So we have a way to answer our first question, but what about our second? How can the court know that some field is a genuine area of science. We should distinguish several questions here. One is the question of bogus science, another is that of nascent science, another is that of applied science, another again is what we might call neo-science. Largely because of the massively impressive achievements, both abstract and applied, of the discipline now called 'physics', and associated disciplines, over the past three centuries or so, the application of the terms 'science' and 'scientist' have honorific significance. The physical sciences have, understandably, been thought to provide a model for any knowledge or rational belief worthy of the name. One consequence of this has been a philosophical and scientific interest in the 'demarcation' of this model of science from other ways of thinking and apparently understanding the world. It has been hoped that it might be determined what is distinctive of this scientific outlook or method so as to mark it off from such other cognitive phenomena as metaphysics, religion, ethics, and magic—to name just a few candidates for segregation. The name of Karl Popper is rightly associated with the most rigorous and ambitious attempt to bring off this feat but it is fair to say that his criterion of falsifiability no longer carries the conviction amongst philosophers or scientists that once it did. It is now generally conceded that Popper's picture of the physical sciences was inadequate but it is not clear what should replace it. It is generally agreed that not only was Popper's image, of the scientist as someone propounding bold conjectures and then seeking desperately to refute them, false psychologically and historically, but the logic of theory-rejection that he proposed was, for much of science, too simple and atomistic. A good deal of work in the physical sciences proceeds more holistically, in the sense that whole chunks of theory confront 'the tribunal of experience' at any time, rather than isolated propositions or hypotheses, and hence the falsifiability or rejectability of propositions which belong to a web of theory is no straightforward matter.

One does not have to be an extreme holist, like Quine for example, to see the force of this difficulty. It accounts for the fact that perfectly respectable theories in physics can survive, and indeed flourish, in spite of their being subject to 'falsifications' or conflicts with experience. These are treated as anomalies to be explained, it is hoped, in the simplest case by experimental error or in more complex cases by some, as yet unimagined, flaw, inadequacy, or incompleteness in a part of the theory. The most the theory may require is modest modification. It *may*, of course, need total overhaul or rejection, but that is not established by the mere falsification of some prediction licensed by it. Just what does establish that is a difficult matter into which we shall not venture, except to note that we need not assume it to be just one logical feature, nor even that, in the end, it is wholly a matter of logic. It is enough for now to realize the improbability of a simple criterion of openness to falsifiability doing the job of demarcating science from non-science.

I have spent some time on this issue of falsification and falsifiability for the reason that many have thought that a rather straightforward application of the test of falsifiability could settle the question of scientific status decisively. Popper thought that Marxist historical theory and Freudian psychology, both of which claimed 'scientific' status, could be rapidly consigned to exterior darkness in this way—though he had other arguments against these constructions as well. It is true that Marxists are unlikely to be called as expert witnesses in Western courts but psychiatrists commonly are. What was importantly true, both of the falsifiability test and the Viennese logical positivists' verifiability criterion (which, unlike Popper's criterion, was supposed to demarcate not only the scientific but the meaningful), was the insight that there is an historically and epistemologically important sense of the term 'science' in which scientific theories must be respectful of and accountable to experience. In this sense, careful observation and, where possible, experiment play an important role in science.[9] Part of what Popper and other 'demarcators' were anxious to do was to show that such subject-matters as phrenology, witchcraft, and astrology were too disrespectful of experience, too unconcerned with careful observation and experiment, to be classed with the sciences, even though they had pretensions to be so categorized.

Without agreeing with the exact demarcation proposals of the Popperians or positivists we can, on behalf of the courts, follow them so far as to acknowledge the powerful claims of the physical sciences and those classificatory sciences related to them, such as botany and geography. Such studies not only emphasize accountability to experience at some point but also place a great premium on reasoning and theory. It is the ramified theorizing that must be responsive to experience; this is what

---

[9] The problem child for this account is, of course, mathematics, which seems entitled to the honorific label of a science though it is not accountable to experience in any obvious way. Popper's attempt at demarcation can be found in *Logic of Scientific Discovery* (London, 1959). Significant criticisms of his theory can be found in Thomas Kuhn, *The Structure of Scientific Revolutions* (Chicago, 1970).

contrasts the scientist with the empiric. The latter is responsive to experience but instead of ramified theory he has rules of thumb and rough
generalizations. The bogus scientist, by contrast, is usually little concerned
with the test of experience, no matter how subtle, nor with the elaboration of theory beyond a primitive level. This seems to me to be true of
astrology, biological creationism, phrenology, and other pseudo-sciences,
but advocates of the scientific status of such activities may well be found to
deny this. Here we are concerned with how the courts should treat the
problem of the bogus scientific expert and my suggestion is not that the
courts should conduct, *ab initio*, a philosophical inquiry into the degree of
empirical relevance and theoretical sophistication possessed by the putative
expert's area, but rather that the court should once more have recourse to
the bodies of experts mentioned earlier and that, in doing so, they should
pay particular attention to the degree of consensus among expert bodies to
the proposition that some putative area of expertise *is* bogus. If such
institutions as universities refuse to acknowledge expertise in certain areas
and refuse to have certain 'subjects' taught, on the grounds that they are
fraudulent, then this provides a presumption against the genuineness of
those areas as scientific expertise for the court's purposes.

I do not say that should be the end of the matter, only that is provides a
sound starting-point. I am not urging any sort of relativism about truth or
scientific authenticity. It is perfectly possible for the academies to get it
wrong, as they notoriously have from time to time in the past. As Ivan
Illich[10] and others have pointed out in their attacks upon schooling, and
more generally upon the institutionalization of learning, there are many
problems created by the existence of educational bodies and scholarly
associations, not the least of which are inbuilt tendencies towards intellectual conservatism and towards the monopolization of social control
over knowledge conceived of as a kind of commodity. These tendencies
certainly exist and have their dangers, but the critique of the de-schoolers,
and intellectual anarchists like Paul Feyerabend,[11] does not really discredit
the point being made here. If there is such a thing as knowledge or
reasonable belief (which in a sense Feyerabend denies but the courts must
assume) then the development of specialized thinking must involve communities of thinkers, traditions of thinking, and a certain amount of
protecting, nourishing, and furthering of the tradition by those thinkers.[12]
Within such a framework there will of course be room not only for
criticism of particular verdicts, received opinions, or prevailing doctrine,
but also of the existing institutional forms that the discipline happens to

---

[10] Ivan Illich, *Deschooling Society* (Harmondsworth, 1971).
[11] Paul Feyerabend, *Against Method* (London, 1975).
[12] I am not arguing for the necessity of specialization in the sense of hermetically sealed
areas of investigation, expertise in one of which precludes one from skill in another. If there is
such a necessity it arises from a particular phase in the history of inquiry.

take. So my claim is relatively modest: the courts should give initial credence to the verdicts of such bodies as universities on the issue of bogus science, though they should be prepared to hear argument about the matter if it can be produced. Where the putatively bogus science is directly in conflict with the claims of an established science, the argument should primarily address the issues of experience and theory mentioned earlier. This is something that a court can undertake without having the particular scientific expertise itself, or at least without having a full measure of it. Here it is worth remarking that we should not exaggerate the distance the expert occupies from at least some of the officials of the court. Judges and lawyers used to a particular line of investigation will develop by experience a good deal of understanding of relevant expertise—workers' compensation lawyers with certain areas of medicine, commerical lawyers with economics, and so on.

Nascent science presents different problems again. There are branches of learning and study which have both a concern for, and a certain development of, theory and also a proper sense of empirical constraints, but have not yet developed the sort of confidence about method nor the solidity of agreed results that seem to be characteristic of such mature sciences as physics. In speaking thus of the contrast between mature sciences and nascent sciences I am engaging in a certain amount of simplification and idealization. A more detailed inquiry than ours needs to be would have to distinguish between the different parts, areas, and levels of mature science, for the sorts of confidence and agreement obtaining differ very much in both degree and significance within such sciences as physics. We should be more cautious and reserved in our thinking about even the most prestigious of the sciences and this is a point to which I shall return. None the less, the idealization clearly has a point for our inquiry when we think of the contrast between mechanics and psychology or between biology before and after Darwin. It has been common for many years to explain the contrast between the intellectual depth and explanatory power of physics and the relative superficiality and unimpressiveness of so many of the human and social sciences by invoking the idea of the immaturity or infancy of the latter. It is a real question whether this explanation can be regarded as satisfactory when these disciplines have endured so long in a state of supposed infancy and when there are other explanations for their lack of comparability to such studies as physics? None the less, many of them have gained the acceptance of academic and scholarly institutions, and they certainly aspire to some affinity with the acknowledged sciences, so it may be best to treat them as nascent sciences.

An interesting example of a nascent science is given by Kenny, who is himself a modest practitioner of it, namely, stylometry—the statistical study of features of literary style, such as choice of vocabulary, length and syntactic construction of sentences, etc. Kenny argues plausibly that stylometry is not a pseudo-science but, what I am calling, a nascent science. Evidence from stylometric experts has been accepted in the English courts (though not, I think, in American or Australian) and seems to have been decisive in at least one case in securing an acquittal. None the less, Kenny argues that this discipline is still too insecure to be a proper subject of expert evidence in court.[13] Whether or not he is right about stylometry his position here reflects a view about the admissibility of expert evidence to which courts in the United States, and to some extent elsewhere, are increasingly congenial. This is the requirement that an expert's skills pertain to a genuine area of expertise and the requirement has been developed precisely because of worries about nascent science and, to a lesser extent, bogus science. (The Australian case *R. v. Gilmore* is an interesting one in this connection since the trial judge rejected and the appeal judge accepted the standing of an expert witness on voice analysis. Both accepted the expert area requirement but differed on whether it had been satisfied.)[14] The requirement seems to me a good one, and indeed virtually dictated by the idea of a skill, though it should not be confused with various proposals for satisfying it and especially not with the Frye test which we shall discuss later. But we must ask: how is a court to settle such a question? Kenny has a proposal here. He suggests taking the matter out of the hands of the courts by setting up a register of sciences, admission to which should be determined by acknowledged experts in existing sciences whose discipline is near at hand to the subject claiming scientific status. If such a committee of experts determined that a discipline was still only a nascent science it would not be possible for its findings to be admitted in the courts.[15]

It will be clear from what I have already said that I am sympathetic to communities of scholarly experts having some say in the legal determination of various matters to do with expertise, but Kenny's proposal gives rather too much authority to them. It may be a good idea to set up a register having something of the character Kenny suggests but the question of admissibility should not be decided solely by presence or absence on the register. Imagine a case in which the Registration Committee decides narrowly, by a vote of 8 to 7, that discipline *A* is not yet a mature science. Suppose the findings of some reputable practitioners of *A* were unanimous on some proposition, *p*, being probably true. The truth of *p* is relevant to the innocence of Smith who faces a very serious charge. There is substantial evidence for not-*p* before the court but there is some independent evidence for *p* also. It is at least arguable that the findings of the reputable *A* practitioners should also be before the court, together with the verdict of

[13] See A. Kenny, 'The Expert in Court', in his *The Ivory Tower: Essays in Philosophy and Public Policy* (Oxford, 1985).
[14] Law Reform Commission (LRC *Evidence*, vii. 177), 39–62, esp. pp. 48 and 50.
[15] Kenny, 'Expert', 61–2.

the Registration Committee, the margin of the vote, and the reasons pro and con. More generally, the fact that a registration committee might have to defend its reasoning in open court should act as a brake upon the tendencies towards conformism and arrogance to which such a body may be subject. It is true, as Kenny argues, that there are advantages in having the status of a study discussed at leisure by experts who know about it from close at hand, rather than decided in haste in court, but these advantages could be made available to a court if it were able to consider the verdict of the experts and the reasoning behind it before deciding what weight, if any, should be given to expert opinion from the study in question. The reasoning behind the committee's decision may be more or less intelligible to the court but the benefits of making it available seem to me to outweigh the difficulties.

Technological or applied science involves the application of the theoretical knowledge of physics, chemistry, astronomy, or biology, as the case may be, to certain practical ends, such as the making of machines to serve human purposes, the curing and prevention of disease, and so on. In such matters there is a good deal of solid knowledge but also many areas of ignorance and room for much of the skill characteristic of the empiric, since experience of actual, often recalcitrant, practice provides essential modifications to knowledge which is often abstracted and idealized. It is important to recognize this because a great deal of the expert evidence produced in court comes from applied scientists such as engineers and doctors. There are complex and interesting reasons why one should expect considerable conflict amongst such experts and why it should be hard to resolve. The best discussion of expert evidence in the applied sciences that I know of is by George Smith. Smith is a philosopher with a background in engineering. A highly regarded expert on metal fatigue, amongst other matters, he has himself given expert evidence on engineering matters in court and has written a fascinating and instructive article on expert evidence. Smith cites several reasons for the clashes of expert opinions in technological fields.[16]

One reason he gives is the way in which quite different practices for achieving similar ends can exist in different businesses or fields. All of these practices may 'work' and it may be a difficult and delicate matter of judgement which ones work better than which. Moreover, within any given practice, some procedure may be essential to the success of that practice which would none the less be a disaster if operated within some other practice with the same or similar ends. Given past success, practitioners are liable to place great emphasis upon agreement about existing

---

[16] George Smith, 'Expert Testimony', unpubl. paper. I am grateful to Professor Smith of the Philosophy Dept. of Tufts Univ., Medford, Mass., for permission to quote from this paper.

procedures within a practice, and where two companies, for instance, operate different practices with different crucial procedures, then experts familiar with one can easily be emphatic, even dogmatic, in their rejection of the other. There are parallels here with sporting skill. Anyone who has ever had lessons from coaches with different backgrounds in cricket or golf or tennis will recognize the problem. Relatedly, it is a common experience that changing some element of a player's style to conform more to a textbook may prove disastrous because of the integrated nature of his existing 'practice'.

Smith cites the difference in approach to designing jet engine components by the major companies Pratt & Witney Aircraft and General Electric:

What one company considers a standard design approach for a given component, the other company often considers a little risky. In one sense, that judgement is invariably sound, for if almost all of a company's experience is with one approach, there is risk in trying something else, even though the other company is using it successfully. A design has so many subtle details, and each of them presents opportunities for error.[17]

Indeed, conflicts between established practices can turn on commitments to different areas or levels of perfectly acceptable theory, as well as different practical orientations. Smith instances a case in which a conflict arose between experts from two quite different backgrounds in turbo-machinery. Apparently, within the field of turbomachinery there is a split between engineers trained in aerospace applications, especially jet engines, and engineers trained in stationary industrial applications. The former use sophisticated analytical methods exploiting computers and test individual components and subcomponents in the laboratory, whereas the latter use simpler analytical methods and rely predominantly upon field tests of the overall equipment. The case involved a chemical firm which had purchased turbomachinery components designed by engineers whose prior experience had been wholly with aerospace applications. After repeated equipment failure, the chemical firm sued to recover lost revenues and their lawyers hired experts in industrial turbomachinery who testified that the equipment lacked certain features they considered normal and that the design approaches were unacceptable and, in their view, comparatively risky. The designers replied that the disputed features were almost never found in aerospace turbomachinery and the design approaches were thoroughly established in aerospace applications. The jury was faced with the vexing problem of determining whether it was improper to rely upon principles and practices of aerospace turbomachinery design in industrial applications. Fortunately (for the jury) it transpired during the court's examina-

---

[17] Ibid. 28.

tion of the expert evidence that the designers had violated one of the cardinal principles of aerospace turbomachinery design itself.[18]

The fact that practices can be accepted by one lot of experts and rejected by another lot, who are apparently in the same scientific or technological game, shows that one must pay attention not merely to what are accepted practices and theories in technology or in the purer sciences but also to the question why they are accepted. This point is particularly important in view of the widespread endorsement, especially in the United States, of the so-called Frye test. This test proposes that expert conclusions should only be admissible where the opinion is 'sufficiently established to have gained general acceptance in the particular field to which it belongs'.[19] As Smith points out,[20] general acceptance of some proposition can indicate many things other than its being correct or very nearly so. It may mean only that the view is a good working hypothesis, in that it is generally believed that things will go well in the long run if research is built upon it. More circumspectly, it may be accepted as the most reasonable view to try to build upon to see if some progress can be made. Even more cautiously, it may indicate, in some cases, that acceptance of the proposition does not lead to unacceptable results. Experts themselves are not always as self-conscious as they should be about such matters and, where they are, they are not always forthcoming about it. In any case, the courts need to be aware of such possibilities and to probe for them in context. Uncritical reliance upon the Frye test could inhibit this necessary process. In this discussion of applied science I have been concerned with certain peculiar or particularly striking aspects of it, rather than with the question of how the courts might distinguish it from pure science. This is because the question of distinguishing it is not as important as with bogus or nascent science. There is no controversy about whether engineers, doctors, or veterinarians should be allowed to give expert evidence and there is equally little dispute, except perhaps for some borderline areas, about which are applied and which pure sciences (though that does not imply that the nature of either is fully understood).

Let us turn now to the category of neo-science, after which we should briefly take stock of our position and address one major reformist recommendation about the giving of expert evidence. Early on I introduced the scientific expert as someone who was to be contrasted with both the ordinary witness and the expert I called an empiric. As our discussion of the technological scientific expert suggested, there is no hard and fast line between the category of scientist and empiric but, more to the present point, the category of scientist is Janus-faced, since it includes both the practitioners of science in the modern honorific sense that Popper sought

---

[18] Ibid. 29.
[19] See *Frye* v. *United States*, 54 App. DC 46, 293F. 1013 (1923).
[20] G. Smith, 'Expert Testimony', 29.

valiantly, but I think unsuccessfully, to demarcate and quite other theoreticians who would not be thought of as scientists at all by contemporary
lights. I mean such thinkers as literary critics, art critics, philosophers, and
historians. Such people are practitioners of the humanities or the liberal
arts and they usually aspire to at least a modest level of ramified theory, a
methodology or family of methodologies, and a vocabulary, even a jargon,
special to their discipline. This, I think, distinguishes them from empirics
like ship-builders, property-valuers, and jewellers, and was what led to my
broad use of 'scientist' early in this chapter, though much of our later
discussion focused on the more narrow sense. Such studies are institutionalized in universities and similar places where they are housed in arts
faculties, or the like, and it is they I had in mind in coining the barbarism
'neo-science', though if various of the human and social sciences fail to
develop beyond their present state it may be best to move them from
nascent to 'neo' status.

Do the courts make use of experts in such studies and should they? I
think it clear that they do and I think they are probably right to do so. If,
for instance, the law allows as a defence against a charge of obscenity that
the book in question is a work of substantial literary merit, then the
opinions of literary critics must prima facie have relevance. Similarly,
if a court case involves complex moral and conceptual issues on which
philosophers have expended a great deal of time and study, then there is at
least an argument for allowing the court to have the benefit of their
opinions. Issues involving the best definition of death, in cases like that of
the unfortunate Karen Quinlan, or the best way to think of and respond to
certain animals, may well reasonably invoke the expertise of philosophers.
Peter Singer, the philosopher, friend, and guide of the animal world, has
indeed been called as an expert witness in a Japanese court on the question
of the status of dolphins. The issue concerned the annual slaughter of
dolphins by Japanese fishermen in a Japanese harbour.[21] It may be said
that a 'real' scientist like a psychologist or marine biologist or somesuch
should have been called to give the court the benefit of his empirical
findings about the animals. There can be no objection to calling such a
witness but this does not rule out recourse to a philosopher as well. In fact,
one of the problems with the human sciences is that they are so heavily
dependent on the kind of interpretation and conceptual adjudication that
is the stock in trade of philosophy. They seem, as we saw illustrated in
Chapter 15, to have a philosophical core in a way that is, at least, less
obvious in a discipline like physics (though I speak very diffidently here

---

[21] For those who, understandably, fear that courts will be intimidated by experts it is
worth noting that the judge in this case responded to Singer's high estimate of dolphin
intelligence by asking: 'If they are so intelligent why do they come back every year at the
same time to the same place to be killed?'

about the relation of physics and philosophy where clearly there are many points of contact and much debate about their significance).

It may be objected that although philosophical expertise and other neo-scientific skills can be relevant to the legal process, their relevance lies in the lawmaking aspect of it rather than the adjudicational. Certainly, the appropriate legal definition of death or the legal status of the human embryo are matters about which legislators might reasonably seek advice from philosophers, though on these, as on all other philosophical questions, they would be foolish to assume any uniformity of opinion amongst the philosophical community. But it is another matter again to parade the philosophers' opinions in court.

It is indeed another, and in some respects a more hazardous, matter. Philosophical input to the legislature process can be debated at (relative) leisure and opposing views canvassed and assessed by the public and, more particularly, by the lawmakers. In the United States, for instance, the Hastings Center has, after a great deal of discussion and argument amongst doctors, biologists, theologians, and philosophers (and others), drawn up guide-lines on the definition of death which have been accepted by numerous State legislatures. Law Reform Committees in Australia have consulted philosophers, psychologists, and sociologists on a range of issues, including proposals for privacy legislation. Making use of such opinion and advice in the rather more hothouse atmosphere of a court of law carries two different disadvantages. The first is one we have already discussed in connection with the paradigm sciences, namely the risk of the court, and particularly the jury, being more impressed by the expert evidence than it ought to be. For pure and applied sciences we argued that the risk was worth taking, though it was important for both experts and the courts to be aware of the variety and diversity of the sciences and the uncertainties and controversies to which even the most solid are prone. In the case of nascent science the problem is compounded by the desire that so many practitioners have to be treated as scientific in the most honorific sense. Combined with a simple-minded, somewhat positivistic view of science, this desire often leads them to exaggerate the solidity of their claims and to close ranks in the presence of outsiders, so that disagreement and dispute go unacknowledged before the lay person. We saw something of this phenomenon in discussing the psychological work on testimony in Chapter 15. With the neo-sciences, the same danger may exist to some extent, but it is generally much less of a problem since the humanities do not normally aspire to the prestige of the hard sciences. Certainly, critics of art and literature, historians, or philosophers are well aware of the precarious nature of many of their judgements and the room that exists for divergent opinions. Moreover, this is usually true of the way these studies are perceived by the public at large. It must none the less be conceded that any specialist with an axe to grind can be tempted to make out that his expert opinion is less contentious than is really the case, so the danger cannot be dismissed out of hand. It can, however, be considerably minimized not only by cultivation of the awareness mentioned above but also by the workings of the adversary process.

This last point provides a natural introduction to the second difficulty and to the reformist proposal I want to discuss. It also broadens the area of our discussion to take in the third of our assessment questions proposed earlier in the chapter, that of assessing the credibility of particular expert depositions. The difficulty is that the clash of experts in court, made more dramatic and sensational by the requirements of the adversary system, is 'disedifying' in that it brings the discipline represented by the experts into public contempt or disrepute. This disrepute is increased when the disputing experts can be seen as motivated by greed or, at any rate, by the desire not to let down the side which has paid, often handsomely, for their services. It is usually for this reason that the proposal is sometimes made to remove the giving of expert evidence, as much as possible, from the adversary context. Those who urge this difficulty and those who promote the proposed solution are not only concerned for the good name of the discipline but also for the way the 'disedification' will affect the court's capacity to assess the expert testimony. Kenny has put forward a recommendation urging that, just as in deciding fitness to plead and sentencing the court calls for psychiatric reports, so in the course of the trial as well the court, and not the parties, should call the expert witnesses. Kenny thinks the court should be obliged to appoint two experts on any given issue and if they are not in substantial agreement their evidence should be inadmissible. Where they are in agreement the evidence should be presented by only one of them who would be subject to cross-examination by either party. Kenny adds: 'This would remedy the evil of the disedifying court tournaments between experts, and prevent an aura of expertise being given to testimony which would be contraverted within the expert's own discipline.'[22]

Certainly, this is one direction in which the law might proceed but, on balance, I think it has more disadvantages than merits. Like Kenny's proposal about a register of sciences, it takes too restrictive an attitude to what should be before the courts and could eliminate 'disedifying court tournaments' at the cost of giving too much weight and credibility to the court-approved expert. His opinion is, after all, supported by only one other expert in the field and it may well be that the two experts approached by the court have the same opinion because they have made the same mistake, come from the same (disputable) tradition, or are grinding the same axe. It is true that their opinion will be open to cross-examination, and this is a vital protection, but its protective strength is

[22] Kenny, 'Expert', 62.

considerably diminished by the prohibition on the defence or prosecution's being able to call expert evidence to rebut the court-appointed expert. In short, what is needed is not more authentication of expertise behind the scenes but more open scepticism about it and more opportunity to test it in open court. In spite of the problems with the adversary system, it still probably provides the best way of exposing what may lie behind the agreement or disagreement amongst expert witnesses. Here I side with the American jurist, Judge David L. Bazelon, who in commenting, in part, on the alarming way in which psychiatrists in the USA have come to have a dominant role in determining verdicts, concludes:

For monitoring the performance of a profession there is no substitute, in the end, for the adversary process. This discussion has focused on psychiatry because decisions grounded on this discipline and on counsel from its practitioners are employed by the state to confine people against their will and to treat people in ways they do not ask for... Much of what I have said, however, applies equally well to the public surveillance of other highly specialized professions on which the operation of our complex civilization depends... Challenging the expert and digging into the facts behind his opinion is the lifeblood of our legal system, whether it is a psychiatrist characterizing a mental disturbance, a physicist testifying on the environmental impact of a nuclear power plant, or a Detroit engineer insisting on the impossibility of meeting legislated automobile exhaust emission standards...[23]

A point which Bazelon's examples may serve to bring out is the degree to which the expert is not only subject to the objective complexities and uncertainties of his subject area but also to the human frailties that enter into any giving of evidence on issues of moment. Commitments of ideology or world-view can distort the judgement of an expert as much as, and in some respects more than, that of a lay witness. The cult of science, discussed earlier, also may play a distorting role. It can not only have bad effects upon the non-scientific audience but also upon the scientific witness, who often feels that his appearance in court must not only sustain his own position within his science but the status of the science itself. This can produce overconfidence, self-deception, even dishonesty. The adversary system is probably the best tool we have for detecting these effects though, ironically, it is itself responsible for one common defect, namely, the expert's temptation to identify overmuch with the cause of his 'side'. I do not know how the law should deal with this temptation but it should not tip out the baby with the bathwater. The adversary system does not need downgrading or abolition, though it may very well need reform. As things stand, lawyers are given far too much licence for rhetorical trickery and bullying of witnesses. These practices are, or should be, far more disedifying than clashes between expert testimonies.

[23] D. L. Bazelon, 'Psychiatrists and the Adversary Process', *Scientific American*, 230/6 (June 1974), 23.

Other suggestions are sometimes made for removing or distancing experts from the difficulties of the adversary context. One is to set up a panel of experts for judging disputed points between experts and another is to set up institutes of forensic science quite independent of the police force, whose experts would then be less open to the charge of favouring the prosecution case than the present practitioners. The first of these ideas has been tried in the United States and one can imagine cases in which such a panel might solve an impasse which the court found beyond its capacities. None the less, the institutionalizing of such an arrangement is fraught with difficulties. The role of the court is essentially to judge between conflicting claims, to determine the weight to be attached to different and often conflicting evidence, and, in very concrete circumstances, to produce a just adjudication which should as far as possible be intelligible and explicable to the parties in the case. The panel proposal, as a permanent feature of court proceedings involving experts (as most proceedings do), would be in danger of defeating this role and substituting the technical verdicts of a sort of priesthood of remote scholars for the practical judgement of something like one's peers. This danger would be mitigated somewhat if the panel were subject to cross-examination and if the parties could call their own experts in rebuttal of the panel's findings, but this seems rather out of kilter with the spirit of the proposal and, in practice, such a panel would have a status that would inhibit the sort of contest and challenge which, with all its problems, provides a safeguard of the rights and values that we want the courts to protect and promote. The second idea concerning independent institutes of forensic science may well be sensible, though it could have practical drawbacks. There would have to be considerable thought given to ways of ensuring that its independence was not illusory. However, the idea need not run foul of the sort of objections raised to the first proposal.

We may draw two morals from the discussion of the difficulties and proposals related to conflicts between expert witnesses. The first concerns the issue from which the discussion arose, namely, whether neo-scientists should be allowed to give expert evidence. Where the court seems likely to benefit from their evidence it should certainly be heard, but it should always be treated with the caution its status requires. Often the importance of such testimony will reside not in the conclusions such an expert provides, many of which will be controversial, but in the insight his evidence gives into the ruling arguments in the field on the topic— arguments which the court can take into account. The second moral concerns the matter of assessing particular acknowledged experts (the third of our questions on p. 281). It will be apparent from the above discussion of difficulties and proposals that I give a central place to the adversary system (suitably purged of abuses), though its supplementation by the advice of expert panels seems, with proper protections, unobjectionable. More generally, the assessment of the expert should proceed in similar manner to the assessment of the lay witness. Inconsistency, over-confidence, vagueness, vested interest, prejudice, previous history of deceit or incompetence, clashing testimony, all have to be taken into account with expert as with lay witnesses. In either case, there are difficulties, imponderables, and risks, but in neither case is this a reason for abandoning the insights and values which the system embodies, however imperfectly.

It is an attachment to these insights and values which causes alarm at the prospect of trial by expert supplanting trial by the court and, more particularly, trial by jury. The judicial process has many, perhaps too many, technical aspects—the very existence of a legal profession ensures that there will be a certain amount of the esoteric and jargonic—but at heart its concerns are moral and pragmatic. The citizen looks for justice, whether in the form of protection or condemnation, and the courts exist to deliver a fair, impartial verdict which is independent of the ruling powers or the élites who wield indirect power. The jury system, with all its imperfections, is an embodiment of this idea and of the thought that you are more likely to find practical wisdom and sound moral instincts in a random selection of a dozen lay people than in any class of soi-disant moral experts.[24] Against this background, the role of witnesses in an inquiry is to provide data for the tribunal to use in coming to a conclusion on the substantive issue before it. This is not to say that the data must be somehow 'raw' or quite uninterpreted—such an ideal is illusory and probably undesirable even for simple cases of observation, as we have seen in earlier discussion, but it is ridiculous for expert testimony. None the less, the expert is providing data for further assessment and decision by the tribunal and it is, as we saw in discussing Thomas Reid's attempt to contrast judgement and testimony, no merely superficial consideration that this is so.

It is sometimes suggested that the point is simply one of narrow professionalism—too great a role for experts would put lawyers out of work—or that it is arises out of contingent and highly debatable features of our present legal arrangements, such as the adversary or the jury system. No doubt there is some truth in each of these allegations but in any imaginable system of adjudication a distinction between the roles of providing information for assessment, on the one hand, and the making of the assessment and the providing of the verdict, on the other, seems inevitable. Consequently, it will be no more than reasonable to expect courts of any kind to be scrupulous about restricting witnesses to their data-providing role. The specific form of the tribunal will dictate which

---

[24] The reader should recall our discussion in Ch. 3 of the difficult question of moral expertise.

other particular roles exist and hence what usurpations by witnesses are to be guarded against. The jury system, as we have argued, places a special premium upon a certain sort of lay assessment of the evidence provided by witnesses and there is an understandable reluctance to have the jury put under any pressure to abandon its freedom of judgement to an expert witness, hence the law's nervousness about the experts' opinions on the ultimate facts. Similar considerations apply to the law's concern that witnesses, especially expert witnesses, avoid advocacy. The adversary system is designed to provide the best method of sifting and testing the information and putative information provided by the witnesses, so that the judge or jury is in a better position to assess it than if it were provided without examination or cross-examination and without constructions favourable to the contesting parties put by their respective advocates. There is certainly plenty of room for debate about whether the adversary system succeeds in its aims but, given its purpose, there is good reason to prevent witnesses adopting the advocacy posture.

Much of the above is of course in the realm of the ideal. Many things, irrelevant to the pure model, come to play an undesirable part in the real legal world: money, position, hysteria, political pressure, to name a few. Yet the ideal is a regulative one and embodies our hopes for the system. We try to guard against the abuses by such things as an educated, independent, and tenured judiciary, codes of legal ethics, and, more pertinent for our present interests, rules and practices designed to keep the expert from exerting too great an influence over proceedings. I will conclude by discussing two of these which are, I think, related. The first, which we have already discussed in part, is that of the prohibition on expert testimony to the ultimate issue and the second is that on expert testimony to the facts of ordinary human nature.

The considerations about the point of court proceedings and the moral-pragmatic dimension to them provide a possible rationale for the ultimate issue rule, but there have been reformist voices raised against it recently. Mostly, these voices insist on the alleged impracticality of the rule. The Australian Law Reform Commission's interim report on the law of evidence is characteristic. They point out the practical difficulties as follows:

Uncertainty is created by the gap between legal theory and practice. Many examples exist of evidence on ultimate issues being admitted. It is common for medical witnesses to be asked whether in their opinion the accused at the relevant time and place knew the nature and quality of his act and whether it was wrong where the ultimate issue is an insanity defence. Evidence has also been accepted on the materiality of the representation in an application for insurance, the issue in a marine case of proper seamanship or the issue of negligence in malpractice actions against professional men. In criminal cases a medical witness may properly be asked whether the deceased died from natural or unnatural causes, whether or not wounds were self-inflicted, whether the bride in the bath died from epilepsy or drowning.[25]

Partly because of these problems, attempts have been made by judges to clarify the rule by insisting that its real basis is that a witness must not give an answer 'which involves the application of a legal standard'[26] and which is therefore a mixture of law and fact[27] and hence a matter for the court itself. Though happier with this reformulation the Commission's report thinks generally that there is little harm in expert (or other) witnesses deposing in legal or quasi-legal terminology (e.g. negligence, fraud, responsibility) and recommends the abolition of the rule in any form, a recommendation which has also been made by a number of similar reform bodies throughout the world.[28]

Clearly there are difficulties with the rule but the Commission's criticisms of it, especially in its clarified form, seem to me rather feeble. The basic issue is what sort of effect on the court's capacity to exercise its legitimate role (sketched above) is the expert's freedom to testify to the ultimate issue likely to have. This is a difficult question to answer but the report seems unduly sanguine about the probity, self-knowledge, and persuasive effect of the expert witness. The authors say:

Its rationale is erroneously based upon the assumption that the function of the tribunal of fact will be usurped should testimony be given which touches directly upon the issues to be decided. It is on occasion argued, particularly if the testimony is that of an eminent expert, that the mind of the tribunal will be so overborne by evidence on an ultimate issue that a fair and properly considered decision will not be reached. The witness will effectively take over the function of the tribunal of fact. Such an argument misconceives both the function of witnesses and that of judges and juries. It is the witness' task to present his evidence and that of the tribunal of fact to evaluate it and treat it with the weight that it deserves. Even the most eminent and persuasive of experts cannot and does not step outside this framework and arrogate to himself an arbitral role.[29]

This quotation begins by misrepresenting the argument for the rule as if it is posited on certainties ('will be usurped', 'will be overborne') when it is really concerned with risks and tendencies. It then proceeds to treat ideal roles as though they are invariably realized in practice, whereas supporters of the rule would claim that, since they tend not to be, there is good reason to keep a rule which emphasizes the difference in role and puts some brake upon the expert. In practice, the brake may not be very powerful since

[25] Law Reform Commission Report, ii, s. 105, pp. 178–9.
[26] Justice Glass in *R.* v. *Palmer* (1981) 1 NSWLR 209, 214.
[27] Justice Bliss used the mixture formula in *Grismore* v. *Consolidated Products Company*, 232 Iowa 238, 5 NW (2d) 646, 663 (1942).
[28] See Law Reform Commission Report, i, para. 743, p. 415 n. 65.
[29] Law Reform Commission Report, i, para. 359, pp. 196–7.

skilled lawyers can get an expert witness to offer something very like an opinion on the ultimate issue but in circumlocutory, non-legal language. None the less, even the necessity to engage in such circumlocution may tend to drive the point home to the jury and provide some inhibitions on the experts themselves. The real question still remains whether the vastly increased role of experts in the law poses a threat to the proper exercise of the court's arbitral role. One can concede the important, even essential, role of the expert witness and yet worry about this question and answer 'yes' to it. The authors of the report are generally rather optimistic about experts—especially psychologists whom they cite extensively, though, to be fair, they also cite at least one philosopher—whereas others are less keen on the contributions they make.

This issue is particularly acute in the case of psychiatrists whose contributions to criminal proceedings can be crucial, are often addressed to the (or an) ultimate issue, and emerge from a theoretical background of controversial intellectual standing which gives rise to more than usual divergences of opinion among its practitioners. Indeed, in the case of psychiatrists, one may well argue that the fact that they are so frequently given as examples where the ultimate issue rule must be broken speaks not against the rule but against the absurdities and dangers of the legislative changes which have given their evidence such prominence. Kenny and Bazelon, in different ways, highlight the problems created by the various legal contortions attempting to accommodate modern psychiatry and the legal concept of responsibility. As Kenny points out,[30] the trial of John Hinkley, who attempted to kill President Reagan in 1982, intensified the drive for changes to the law on insanity and diminished responsibility. There was no dispute that Hinkley had attempted to kill the President but there was considerable dispute amongst psychiatrists about his mental condition and he was eventually acquitted, on grounds of insanity, though committed to a secure mental hospital. Defence psychiatrists testified that Hinkley was suffering from 'process schizophrenia' which prosecution psychiatrists denied. In the end, as he said himself, 'I was found not guilty by reason of insanity because I shot the President and three other people in order to impress a girl.' Clearly Hinkley's motivation was an odd one but equally clearly he would probably not have been acquitted on the plea of insanity if the court had been applying the undiluted standards of the M'Naghten Rules.[31] These lay down that for an insanity plea to succeed it must be established that the accused 'was labouring under such a defect of reason, from disease of the mind, as not to know the nature and quality of the act he was doing, or, if he did know it, that he did not know he was doing what was wrong'. The generally sensible import of these words has

---

[30] Kenny, 'Expert' 39.
[31] There are indeed problems with the M'Naghten Rules but I agree with Kenny that at least they raise the right questions.

been so eroded by gobbledegook about 'mental responsibility', 'irresistible impulse', and the like, that psychiatrists are now frequently in the position of being asked in effect the value question: 'Should this person go to jail?' rather than the difficult but relatively factual question: 'Did the person's mental state at the time enable him to understand what he was doing and that it was wrong to do it?' It is true that the psychiatrists do not entirely usurp the court's role at present because the judge and jury must still decide between the competing psychiatrists.[32] It is, however, very difficult for them to do this in the case of psychiatric testimony since it is so hard to extract the evidential basis for these experts' conclusions on the ultimate issue. In summary, then, I would say that the objections to the ultimate issue rule, especially in its clarified form, are not persuasive and the rule should be retained as providing something of a check upon the dominating tendencies of expert evidence.

Another restriction upon expert evidence which is sometimes criticized is the bar to expert testimony on ordinary human nature which itself seems to be an application of the rule that there can be no expert evidence on matters of common knowledge. Clearly, if something is a matter of common knowledge, there can be no expert evidence needed to establish it. There can, however, be room for doubt about whether something *is* a matter of common *knowledge* or even *known* at all. Equally clearly, however, the status of some proposition as an item of common knowledge is not something that waits upon proof from scientific or other expert findings. The most such experts can provide is a challenge to selected items within the corpus of presumed common knowledge (or, to give it another traditional name, common sense). The philosophical justification of the above claims about common knowledge needs a more thorough presentation that I can give it here, though it rests in part upon the way the

---

[32] It is a delicious irony, noted by *Newsweek* at the time, that Hinkley's lawyers can rely upon the prosecution's psychiatrists if they want to get him released from the hospital, whereas the state can urge the evidence of the defence psychiatrists to keep him in. Cf. Kenny, 'Expert', 40–1. A further problem concerns the considerable disarray within psychology and psychiatry about the status of the disciplines and their value for forensic purposes. Faust and Ziskin, for instance, argue that psychologists and psychiatrists are worthless as expert witnesses, and their employment as such is therefore dangerous for the legal process. In particular, they argue that psychiatry has failed to establish reliable classifications, that neither it nor psychology provides its practitioners with real expertise for the questions characteristically requiring answers in the courts, and both studies at present have inherently unstable methodologies and theories. Other psychologists object to these claims, but even one of the objectors (Matarazzo, see below) has conceded that 'clinical psychology is still an art based on some scientific background'. This suggests that it may have been better to class psychology (or at least those branches of it relevant to the law) with the neo-sciences rather than the nascent sciences, but in either case a certain degree of caution in its use is clearly called for. See David Faust and Jay Ziskin, 'The Expert Witness in Psychology and Psychiatry', *Science*, 240 (1988), 31–5. See also subsequent correspondence in *Science*, 241 (1988), 1143–4, between Raymond D. Fowler and Joseph D. Matarazzo on the one hand and Faust and Ziskin.

sciences themselves rely upon common knowledge, and some of the development it could be given was indicated in our discussion of psychological work on testimony in Chapter 15. That most of us know, and need to know for mere survival, a good deal about ordinary human nature and normal human reactions and behaviour seems clear, but it can hardly be denied that there is also room to be surprised.

Whether such surprises can be provided by some class of experts on human nature is another matter. In Chapter 15 we looked at the efforts of empirical psychologists to tell us about normal human capacities of memory, perception, and recognition and saw the difficulties experts had in steering between the Scylla of painful confirmation of the obvious and the Charybdis of exciting revelations that turn out to be fatally ambiguous, empirically suspect, or conceptually flawed. Where these pitfalls are successfully negotiated we tend to get conclusions which can provide some useful input to policy makers rather than directly to the courts. For instance, the psychological work on identification has had a salutary effect in heightening the already existing awareness of the difficulties involved in identifying suspects, especially where they were seen in bad viewing conditions or a long time ago. This may well provide useful background information to judges and also lead to policy improvements in such areas as the rules for conducting police identification parades, but its use in the courts as evidence is likely to be much less helpful, partly because there is so little understanding of any mechanisms involved in the gross regularities observed and statistics recorded. This fact means that the application of such findings to particular testimonies in court is hazardous, even where one can be confident in the value of the findings. Other findings about human nature from specialist fields such as psychiatry, sociology, or anthropology are so impregnated with moral and other value judgements, with philosophy and ideology, as to make their presentation to the court a substitution for the court's own necessary incursion into these fields. Psychiatry essentially involves judgements and theories about what is good for people, about moral responsibility and determinism, about guilt and punishment. Many sociologists and anthropologists (and socio-biologists for that matter) are committed to theories of the nature of morality and of man—some of them demonstrably silly and possibly harmful. In making this last remark I have in mind what Bernard Williams had called the anthropologist's heresy, the moral theory of cultural relativism, possibly the silliest and most confused account of the nature of morality that has ever been seriously propounded. It is a striking instance of the way in which studies like anthropology and sociology inevitably involve moral judgement and theory, but the point would remain even had it been a better theory. When one considers the tendency that experts have, even in disciplines much less value-oriented than these (such as forensic medicine),[33] to take a stand on the moral and social issues involved in the case and to let that stand influence their evidence, one can only view with dismay any suggestion that evidence from the human and social sciences be admissible as to human nature.

[33] I take it that it is 'common knowledge' at least amongst lawyers that this happens. It would be invidious, and possibly libellous, to name names, but I would recommend that sceptics read John Bryson's excellent book *Evil Angels* (Harmondsworth, 1986) on the death of Azaria Chamberlain and the trial of her mother, Lindy. More recently, the dreadful fate of the Birmingham Six is highly relevant.

Bibliography

ACHINSTEIN, PETER, 'Concepts of Evidence', *Mind*, 87 (1978), 22–45.

—— *The Nature of Explanation* (Oxford, 1983).

ALLPORT, GORDON, and POSTMAN, LEO, *The Psychology of Rumour* (New York, 1965).

ANSCOMBE, G. E. M., 'Hume and Julius Caesar', in *The Collected Philosophical Papers of G. E. M. Anscombe*, i. *From Parmenides to Wittgenstein* (Oxford, 1981), 86–92.

—— 'Authority in Morals', in *The Collected Philosophical Papers of G. E. M. Anscombe*, iii. *'Ethics, Religion and Politics* (Oxford, 1981), 43–50.

—— 'The Intentionality of Sensation: A Grammatical Feature', in *The Collected Philosophical Papers of G. E. M. Anscombe*, ii. *Metaphysics and the Philosophy of Mind* (Oxford, 1981), 3–26.

APPEL, KENNETH, HAKEN, WOLFGANG, and KOCK, JOHN, 'Every Planar Map is Four Colourable', *Illinois Journal of Mathematics*, 21/84 (Sept. 1977), 429–567.

AQUINAS, THOMAS, *Commentary on Boethius's De Trinitate* (Toronto, 1958).

—— *Summa Theologiae*, xxxi. *Faith*, ed. T. C. O'Brien (London, 1974).

ARISTOTLE, *Ethics* (Harmondsworth, 1976).

AUGUSTINE, *De Trinitate, De Magistro, De Utilitate Credendi, Retractiones*, all in *The Works of Aurelius Augustinus*, ed. Marcus Dodds (Edinburgh, 1871–6).

—— *Letters*, in *Fathers of the Church*, xx, ed. and trans. by Sr. M. I. Bogan (Washington, DC, 1953).

AUSTIN, J. L., *How to Do Things with Words* (Oxford, 1962).

AYER, A. J., *Language, Truth and Logic* (London, 1974).

—— 'Comments', in G. H. von Wright (ed.), *Problems in the Theory of Knowledge* (The Hague, 1972), 12–16.

BINET, A., *La Suggestibilité* (Paris, 1900).

BLACKBURN, SIMON, *Spreading the Word* (Oxford, 1984).

BLOCH, MARC, *The Historian's Craft* (Manchester, 1954).

BRADLEY, F. H., 'The Presuppositions of Critical History', in *Collected Essays* (Oxford, 1969), 1–76.

BUCKHOUT, ROBERT, 'Eyewitness Testimony', *Scientific American*, 231/6 (Dec. 1974), 23–31.

BURNYEAT, M. F., 'Aristotle on Understanding Knowledge', in E. Berti (ed.), *Aristotle on Science: The Posterior Analytics* (Atti dell'VIII Symposium Aristotelicum; Padua and New York, 1981).

—— 'Socrates and the Jury: Paradoxes in Plato's Distinction between Knowledge and True Belief', *Proceedings of the Aristotelian Society*, supp. vol. 54 (1980), 173–91.

—— 'Wittgenstein and Augustine *De Magistro*', *Proceedings of the Aristotelian*

Society, supp. vol. 61 (1987), 1–24.

BYRNE, EDMUND F., *Probability and Opinion* (The Hague, 1968).

CAMPBELL, GEORGE, *A Dissertation on Miracles*, ed. Lewis White Beck (New York, 1983; originally publ. 1762).

CARR, E. H., *What is History?* (Harmondsworth, 1964).

CHISHOLM, RODERICK, *Theory of Knowledge* (Englewood Cliffs, NJ, 1966).

—— *Theory of Knowledge*, 2nd edn. (Englewood Cliffs, NJ, 1977).

CLIFFORD, BRIAN R., 'A Critique of Eyewitness Research', in M. M. Gruenberg, P. E. Morris, and R. N. Sykes (eds.), *Practical Aspects of Memory* (London, 1978).

CLIFFORD, W. K., 'Ethics of Belief', in *Lectures and Essays*, ii (London, 1879), 177–211.

COADY, C. A. J., 'Testimony and Observation', *American Philosophical Quarterly*, 10 (1973), 149–55.

—— 'Collingwood and Historical Testimony', *Philosophy*, 50 (1975), 409–24.

—— 'Mathematical Knowledge and Reliable Testimony', *Mind*, 90 (1981), 542–56.

—— 'The Senses of Martians', *Philosophical Review*, 83/1 (1974), 107–25.

COHEN, L. J., *The Probable and the Provable* (Oxford, 1977).

COLLINGWOOD, R. G., *The Idea of History* (Oxford, 1970).

CONDILLAC, ÉTIENNE BONNOT DE, *A Treatise on the Sensations*, in *Philosophical Writings of Etienne Bonnot, Abbé de Condillac*, trans. Franklin Philip (Hillsdale, NJ, 1982).

CRAIG, JOHN, *Mathematical Principles of Christian Theology*, in *History and Theory*, Beiheft 4 (1964; originally publ. 1699).

CROSS, RUPERT, *Evidence*, 3rd edn. (London, 1967).

—— and JONES, A., *An Introduction to Criminal Law*, 4th edn. (London, 1959).

DAVIDSON, DONALD, *Essays on Actions and Events* (Oxford, 1980).

—— *Inquiries into Truth and Interpretation* (Oxford, 1984).

DESCARTES, RENÉ, *Discourse on Method*, in *The Philosophical Writings of Descartes*, ed. John Cottingham, Robert Stoothoff, and Dugald Murdoch (Cambridge, 1988).

DRETSKE, FRED, 'A Cognitive Cul-de-Sac', *Mind*, 91 (Jan. 1982), 109–11.

—— 'Conclusive Reasons', *Australasian Journal of Philosophy*, 49 (1971), 1–22.

EGETH, H. E., and McCLOSKEY, M., 'Expert Testimony about Eyewitness Behaviour: Is it Safe and Effective?', in Gary L. Wells and Elizabeth F. Loftus (eds.), *Eyewitness Testimony: Psychological Perspectives* (Cambridge, 1984), 283–303.

EGGLESTON, RICHARD, *Evidence, Proof and Probability* (London, 1983).

EVANS, GARETH, *Varieties of Reference* (Oxford, 1982).

FEYERABEND, PAUL, *Against Method* (London, 1975).

FRICKER, ELIZABETH, 'The Epistemology of Testimony', *Proceedings of the Aristotelian Society*, supp. vol. 61 (1987), 57–83.

GREGORY, R. L., *Eye and Brain* (London, 1966).

—— and WALLACE, J. G., 'Recovery from Early Blindness: A Case Study', in *Experimental Psychology Society Monograph No. 2* (Cambridge, 1963).

HACKING, IAN, *The Emergence of Probability* (Cambridge, 1975).

HARDWIG, JOHN, 'Epistemic Dependence', *The Journal of Philosophy*, 82/7 (1985), 335–49.

HARMAN, GILBERT, *Thought* (Princeton, NJ, 1973).

HINTIKKA, JAAKKO, *Knowledge and Belief* (Ithaca, NY, 1962).

HOBBES, THOMAS, *Leviathan*, ed. Michael Oakeshott (New York, 1962).

HUME, DAVID, *A Treatise of Human Nature*, ed. L. A. Selby-Bigge (Oxford, 1967).

—— *An Enquiry Concerning Human Understanding*, in *Hume's Enquiries*, ed. L. A. Selby-Bigge (Oxford, 1966).

ILLICH, IVAN, *Deschooling Society* (Harmondsworth, 1971).

JACKSON, FRANK, *Perception* (Cambridge, 1977).

JAMES, WILLIAM, 'The Will to Believe', in *The Will to Believe and Other Essays* (New York, 1898), 1–32.

KENNY, A., 'The Expert in Court', in *The Ivory Tower: Essays in Philosophy and Public Policy* (Oxford, 1985), 39–62.

KUHN, THOMAS, *The Structure of Scientific Revolutions* (Chicago, 1970).

LAPLACE, PIERRE, MARQUIS DE, *A Philosophical Essay on Probabilities*, trans. F. W. Truscott and F. E. Emory (New York, 1951).

LEHRER, K., and SMITH, J. C., 'Reid on Testimony and Perception', *Canadian Journal of Philosophy*, supp. vol. 11 (1985).

LINDSAY, R. C. L., WELLS, G. L., and RUMPEL, C., 'Can People Detect Eyewitness Identification Accuracy within and across Situations?', *Journal of Applied Psychology*, 66 (1981), 79–89.

LLOYD-BOSTOCK, S. H. A., and CLIFFORD, B. R. (eds.), *Evaluating Witness Evidence* (Chichester, 1983).

LOCKE, JOHN, *An Essay on the Human Understanding*, ed. John W. Yolton (London, 1961).

McGINN, COLIN, 'Charity, Interpretation and Belief', *The Journal of Philosophy*, 74 (1977), 520–35.

MACKIE, J. L., 'The Possibility of Innate Knowledge', *Proceedings of the Aristotelian Society*, 70 (1969–70), 245–57.

MARSHALL, JAMES, *Law and Psychology in Conflict* (New York, 1966).

MATHEWS, GWYNNETH, *Plato's Epistemology* (London, 1972).

MILGRAM, STANLEY, *Obedience to Authority* (London, 1974).

MORAVCSIK, J. M. E., 'Understanding and Knowledge in Plato's Philosophy', *Neue Hefte für Philosophie* (1978).

MÜNSTERBERG, HUGO, *On the Witness Stand: Essays on Psychology and Crime* (New York, 1908).

NOZICK, ROBERT, *Philosophical Explanations* (Oxford, 1981).

PASSMORE, JOHN, 'The Objectivity of History', *Philosophy*, 33/125 (Apr. 1958), 91–111.

PEIRCE, CHARLES SAUNDERS, 'The Doctrine of Chances', in *Collected Papers of Charles Saunders Peirce*, ii, ed. C. Hartshorne and P. Weiss (Cambridge, Mass., 1960), 389–414.

—— 'Answers to Questions Concerning My Belief in God', in *Collected Papers of Charles Saunders Peirce*, ii, ed. C. Hartshorne and P. Weiss (Cambridge, Mass., 1960), 340–55.

—— 'The Century's Great Men in Science', in *Selected Writings: Values in a Universe of Chance*, ed. P. P. Wiener (New York, 1966), 264–74.

—— 'Letters to Samuel P. Langley and "Hume on Miracles and Laws of Nature"' in *Selected Writings: Values in a Universe of Chance*, ed. P. P. Wiener (New

York, 1966), 275–321.

POPPER, SIR KARL, *The Logic of Scientific Discovery* (London, 1959).

—— *Conjectures and Refutations* (London, 1963).

—— *Objective Knowledge* (Oxford, 1972).

PRICE, H. H., *Belief* (London, 1969).

PUTNAM, HILARY, 'The Meaning of "Meaning" ', in *Philosophical Papers*, ii. *Mind, Language and Reality* (Cambridge, 1975), 215–71.

—— 'What is Mathematical Truth?', in *Philosophical Papers*, i. *Mathematics, Matter and Method*, 2nd edn. (Cambridge, 1979), 60–78.

QUINE, W. V., 'Epistemology Naturalised', in *Ontological Relativity and Other Essays* (New York, 1969), 69–90.

—— and ULLIAN, J. S., *The Web of Belief* (New York, 1970).

QUINTON, ANTHONY, 'Authority and Autonomy in Knowledge', *Proceedings of the Philosophy of Education Society of Great Britain*, supp. issue, 5/2 (1971).

REID, THOMAS, *Inquiry into the Human Mind*, ed. Timothy Duggan (Chicago, 1970).

—— *Philosophical Works*, with notes etc. by Sir William Hamilton and introduction by Harry M. Bracken (Hildesheim, 1967). This contains, *inter alia*, 'Essay on the Active Powers', 'Inquiry Into the Human Mind', and 'Essays on the Intellectual Powers of Man'.

RUSSELL, BERTRAND, *The Analysis of Matter* (London, 1927).

—— *An Outline of Philosophy* (London, 1927).

—— *Religion and Science* (Oxford, 1935).

—— *Human Knowledge: Its Scope and Limits* (New York, 1948).

—— *Logic and Knowledge*, ed. R. C. Marsh (London, 1956).

SAUNDERS, DAVID M., VIDMAR, NEIL, and HEWITT, ERIN C., 'Eyewitness Testimony and the Discrediting Effect', in Sally M. A. Lloyd-Bostock and Brian R. Clifford (eds.), *Evaluating Witness Evidence* (Chichester, 1983), 57–78.

SCHMITT, FREDERICK F., 'Justification, Sociality, and Autonomy', *Synthese*, 73 (1987), 43–85.

SCOTT, J. F., *A History of Mathematics* (London, 1958).

SEARLE, JOHN R., *Expression and Meaning* (Cambridge, 1979).

—— *Speech Acts* (Cambridge, 1969).

—— and VANDERVEKEN, DANIEL, *Foundations of Illocutionary Logic* (Cambridge, 1985).

SHOEMAKER, SYDNEY, *Self-Knowledge and Self-Identity* (Ithaca, NY, 1963).

SINGER, PETER, 'Moral Experts', *Analysis*, 32 (1971–2), 115–17.

STRAWSON, P. F., 'Intention and Convention in Speech Acts', *Philosophical Review*, 72 (1964), 439–60.

—— 'Austin and Locutionary Meaning', in Isaiah Berlin (ed.), *Essays on J. L. Austin* (Oxford, 1973), 46–68.

STROUD, BARRY, 'The Significance of Naturalized Epistemology', in *Midwest Studies in Philosophy*, 6 (1981): Peter A. French, T. C. Uehling, jun., and Howard K. Wettstein (eds.), *The Foundations of Analytic Philosophy* (Minneapolis, 1981), 455–71.

TRANKELL, ARNE, *Reliability of Evidence* (Stockholm, 1972).

TYMOCZKO, THOMAS, 'The Four-Colour Problem and its Philosophical Significance', *The Journal of Philosophy*, 76/2 (Feb. 1979), 57–83.

VANSINNA, J., *Oral Tradition: A Study in Historical Methodology* (Harmondsworth, 1973).

VERMAZEN, BRUCE, 'General Beliefs and the Principle of Charity', *Philosophical Studies*, 42 (1982), 111–18.

—— 'The Intelligibility of Massive Error', *Philosophical Quarterly*, 33 (1983), 69–74.

WAELHENS, ALPHONSE, 'Ambiguïté de la notion de témoinage', *Archiva di filosofia* (Padua Special Issue: 'La Testimonianza', 1972), 467–76.

WELBOURNE, MICHAEL, *The Community of Knowledge* (Aberdeen, 1986).

—— 'The Transmission of Knowledge', *Philosophical Quarterly*, 29 (1979), 1–9.

WELLS, G. L., LINDSAY, R. C., and FERGUSON, T. J., 'Accuracy, Confidence and Juror Perceptions in Eyewitness Identification', *Journal of Applied Psychology*, 64 (1979), 440–8.

—— and LOFTUS, ELIZABETH F., *Eyewitness Testimony: Psychological Perspectives* (Cambridge, 1984).

WHATELY, RICHARD, *Historic Doubts Relative to Napoleon Bonaparte* (1st publ. 1819 anonymously).

WIGGINS, DAVID, 'Truth, Invention and the Meaning of Life', *Proceedings of the British Academy*, 61 (1976), 331–78.

WIGMORE, J. H., *A Treatise on the Anglo-American System of Evidence in Trials at Common Law*, vii, 3rd edn. (Boston, 1940).

WILLIAMS, BERNARD A. O., 'Knowledge and Reasons', in G. H. von Wright (ed.), *Problems in the Theory of Knowledge* (The Hague, 1972), 1–11.

WILLIAMS, GLANVILLE, *The Proof of Guilt*, 3rd edn. (London, 1963).

WITTGENSTEIN, LUDWIG, *Philosophical Investigations* (Oxford, 1953).

—— *Remarks on the Foundations of Mathematics* (Oxford, 1964).

Index